FOR MOST CONSPICUOUS BRAVERY

FOR MOST CONSPICUOUS BRAVERY

A BIOGRAPHY OF MAJOR-GENERAL
GEORGE R. PEARKES, V.C., THROUGH TWO WORLD WARS

Reginald H. Roy

UNIVERSITY OF BRITISH COLUMBIA PRESS

VANCOUVER

FOR MOST CONSPICUOUS BRAVERY

A Biography of Major-General
George R. Pearkes, V.C., through Two World Wars

©The University of British Columbia 1977

Canadian Cataloguing in Publication Data
Roy, Reginald H., 1922-
   For most conspicuous bravery

   ISBN 0-7748-0068-2

1. Pearkes, George Randolph, 1888-
2. Canada. Army—Biography. 3. Statesmen—Canada—Biography.
I. Title. FC616.P42R69   971.06'42'0924   C77-002091-7   F1034.2

International Standard Book Number: 0-7748-0068-2

Printed in Canada

This book has been published with the help of a grant from the Humanities Research Council of Canada, using funds provided by the Canada Council, and other grants from The Royal Canadian Legion, Dominion Command and Pacific Command; the University of Victoria; The Leon and Thea Koerner Foundation; Mr. and Mrs. Lancelot deS. Duke; Mr. R. H. B. Ker; Mr. H. A. Wallace; and other contributors.

To My Mother

Contents

Photographic Credits

Plates 7, 8, 9, 10, 11, and 12 are from the Provincial Archives of British Columbia, Victoria, B.C. The Public Archives of Canada provided plates 21, 23, 24, and 29. Plate 26 appears courtesy of the Macdonald-Cartier Library, Kingston, and plates 31, 33, and 34 were supplied by the Victoria *Daily Colonist*.

Maps and Illustrations

Preface

I first met George Pearkes shortly after I started lecturing in Canadian history at the University of Victoria in 1959. As an academic and as a reserve infantry officer, I came into increasing contact with him at various functions both in Victoria and Vancouver. He was, without a doubt, one of the most widely known men in British Columbia and one of the most respected. As a soldier, statesman, and lieutenant-governor he had crowded into his life a wealth of experience both on the national and provincial scene. I felt, as an historian, that his biography should be written. Although I approached him a number of times on the subject, I was always put off as he protested that there really was not much to tell. With the help of Cmdr. Gar Dixon, Pearkes's private secretary at Government House, I finally persuaded him to co-operate with me in writing this book. In the years that followed I could not have wished for a more patient and helpful person.

At the outset it became apparent that I would have to rely a great deal on the tape-recorded interviews I had with him, Mrs. Pearkes, and a large number of persons across Canada who knew him well under a variety of circumstances over the past half century. He kept no diary as such, he habitually destroyed his correspondence, and his total "personal archives" would be about one foot of shelf space. Most of this, incidentally, comprised newspaper clippings kept by his wife, Blytha, several folders of photographs, and a few notebooks he kept while he was Minister of Defence, which dealt primarily with appointments. One of my main tasks, therefore, was to double and triple check, to the extent I could, the information he was able to give me on the eighty-five, one-to-two hour interviews I had with him. This I have endeavoured to do.

The account of Pearkes's activities during the Second World War is not as complete as it might be, and doubtless further light will be shed by future historians on certain circumstances. The full story of why Pearkes was not given the command of the 1st Canadian Corps is not available to me, but I see no reason to hold up the publication of this book until it is. After interviewing Pearkes and other senior officers who were overseas with him at the time, I can only intimate several likely reasons. I would have liked to have had further information on the so-called "general's revolt" and on the conscription crisis of 1944. Nevertheless, I was given access to Pearkes's personal file, and, together with personal interviews, letters in the Ralston Papers, and other material, some fresh light has been thrown on these events as well as on Pearkes's decision to retire.

Naturally, when dealing with Pearkes as a cabinet minister, I am aware of the limitations placed on the researcher attempting to get a clear picture of what went on behind the scenes where, owing to the closeness of the events, full access to all the pertinent material is restricted. Some of the topics I deal with—NORAD, the Avro Arrow, or the Bomarc-B, for example—deserve a book in themselves, a book written preferably by someone who has not only a post-graduate degree in history but in science as well. My main purpose has been to try to show how Pearkes looked at these problems and how, from where he stood, the decisions were made affecting policy in a period of rapid scientific and technological change. Once again interviews with a number of cabinet ministers and senior military officers and civil servants have helped me with the chapters on Pearkes as Minister of National Defence, and I am in debt to them. In time, when papers which are now classified become available to the public, more light will be thrown on some of the events I have described, but in two decades many of those who have participated in those events will no longer be available for questioning. To have access to both would be a joy to any historian; under the circumstances I must rest content with the sources I have been able to reach since I first started my research in the late 1960's.

During the course of preparing this book I have received several grants from the Social Sciences Research Committee and the Committee on Leave, Travel and Grants, both of the University of Victoria. Without their financial assistance this book could not have been written. The number of people who have contributed to the book by permitting me to interview them, by sending me military maps, or by reading and criticizing chapters are too numerous to mention individually. I have benefited from their advice and criticism, and I can only hope they will accept this acknowledgement as a token of my warmest thanks.

Finally, I must say a special word to Mrs. M. E. Adamson, who served as my secretary during most of the years when this book was being researched and written. If there was a medal for secretaries for patience, devotion to duty, and all-round excellence, surely she should be awarded it.

R. H. Roy

1

Prelude

The scene in Euston Station that evening in May 1906 was a familiar one as crowds of British emigrants surged about saying goodbye to their friends and relatives. The train which would take them to Liverpool had come gliding alongside the platform, its smoke intensifying the haze which filled the station. Behind the gates men, women, and children added their voices to the ever increasing volume of noise as departure time grew near. Here and there groups sang "Land of Hope and Glory" or the music hall ditty "I'll be a Long Time Away," reminiscent of the time a few years earlier when troops were going off to the Boer War. It was a noisy, happy, nostalgic moment, when excitement at the prospect of a new life in Canada was mixed with the emotion welling up in many at the thought of leaving England.

Among the emigrants bound for Canada was a tall, young, brown-haired Englishman named George Randolph Pearkes. How he came to be among them is a simple story; what was to happen to him and the country that became his over the next sixty years is a fascinating one.

By 1887 when Queen Victoria celebrated her golden jubilee surrounded by her colonial ministers, the British Empire had outposts on every continent and a quarter of the mercator map of the world was coloured red. Far more exciting than the internal problems of home rule for Ireland, free trade, or labour were the discoveries and battles on the edges of the far-flung Empire.

Though critics of Imperialism remained, for the average Englishman it had attained respectability in the last decades of the nineteenth century. Some saw economic gains to be made for themselves or for Britain; others viewed the imposition of British law and government and the bringing of the Christian religion as a benefit to the newly subject peoples. But for nearly all pride in the Empire grew with its size, and the popular imagination was captured by the pacification of India, the Maori Wars, the acquisition of African colonies, and the achievement of control over Egypt and the Suez Canal. Popular opinion was whipped to jingoistic frenzy by such events as the failure to relieve the siege of Khartoum and the death of General Gordon and by the defeats of the British army at the hands of the Boers in the Transvaal. Politicians and the popular press alike fed the enthusiasms generated in the people by imperial events and played on their emotions.

Into this milieu, where passionate patriotism and determined duty were staples of middle class principles, George Pearkes was born on 26 February 1888, the son of a prosperous businessman, a partner in the family department store in Watford, Hertfordshire. With his younger brother, Edward, and his sister, Hilda, he enjoyed the comfortable childhood of his class. Superintended by governesses and trained first at a "dame school," in these early years George, like countless others, collected tin soldiers in immaculate battle array and thrilled to the stories of G. A. Henty, the poems of Rudyard Kipling, and the heroic adventures in the *Boys' Own Annual*.

In 1896 when he was eight, George was sent to Berkhamsted School, some fifteen miles from Watford, where he was to spend the next ten years. Berkhamsted was typical both in its curriculum and its routines. Hard work, discipline, team spirit, and fair play were instilled in the boys, and the effect on Pearkes was great. Later he said "My public school days influenced my whole life more than anything else I can think of." He felt that subordinating his own ambitions to the interests of the team was later to bring out "the sense of duty in the war to your battalion, to your men and even when one goes to Parliament to your constituency."

For a young man of his background either the army or the church seemed a promising career. Though the Boer War had been far from glorious, the reports of the campaigns still called to the teenage George Pearkes's spirit of adventure, and his successes in the school cadet corps with its ceremony and drills had made a strong impression on him. Whatever his hopes for entering Sandhurst and accepting a commission might have been, however, they were dashed by financial reverses which made it impossible for his father to provide the supplementary income necessary for an officer in the British Army. No more could he hope for the university education which would allow him to enter holy orders.

Emigration, therefore, was held out to him as a possible means by which he could gain enough materially to allow him to return to England self-sufficient in a few years. It was not entirely by chance that George Pearkes chose Canada over the other colonies and dominions. The headmaster of

Plate 1. George R. Pearkes, aged 17, at Minstead, New Forest, Hampshire, England.

Plate 2. The house built on the Pearkes homestead a few miles from Dovercourt, west of the Clearwater River in 1912. It replaced the crude cabin George and his brother Ted had built.

Plate 3. George Pearkes (standing centre) with other members of the Dominion Land Survey crew working in northern Alberta in the summer of 1912.

Plate 4. Constable Pearkes, R.N.W.M.P., at Whitehorse, Yukon Territory.

the school, Dr. Thomas C. Fry, had bought a farm near Red Deer, Alberta, a number of years earlier, with the intention of operating it as a practical agricultural school where Berkhamsted boys could train before going into farming on their own. As a student Pearkes had heard his efforts praised by Lord Strathcona, and he decided to follow the course advised by both Fry and his father. Pearkes left Berkhamsted during the Easter holidays of 1906, his formal education at an end. He travelled south to say goodbye to his mother and then went to London to see his father, who had arranged for him to sail for Quebec from Liverpool on the S. S. *Hungarian.* What lay before him he did not know, but whatever he might accomplish, he would have to do it by his own efforts.

2

Homesteading

The voyage to Canada was uneventful. As the S. S. *Hungarian* sailed up
the broad waters of the St. Lawrence George Pearkes and his friend Love
began to appreciate the tremendous size of Canada. On the evening of
23‑24 May the ship anchored below the cliffs of Quebec which, with its
lights ablaze in the darkness, seemed like a welcoming beacon. On the following day they boarded a tourist-class coach on the Canadian Pacific,
and four days later, at Calgary, they caught their first sight of the foothills
of the Rocky Mountains.

Due north, about midway between Calgary and Edmonton, is Red Deer.
Near this town of some 2,500 people Dr. Fry had bought the two sections
of land which comprised Berkhamsted Farm. Alberta had been a province
for about one year. Its population of less than 400,000 was steadily being
increased by immigrants from Great Britain and elsewhere. Although in
comparison to England the country appeared almost as empty as it was
expansive, an ever increasing amount of land was being put to the plough
as newcomers arrived to take up homesteads under the fairly generous
terms given by the federal government. Before he could do so himself,
George Pearkes had to learn something of farming, and though he found
Berkhamsted Farm something less than he expected, it provided an anchor
or a base of operations for him.

A Berkhamsted boy who arrived at the School Farm about a year before
Pearkes described it as follows:

> We are situated in a large plain, which is surrounded on the north,
> south, and east by ranges of low bush-covered hills, while eighty miles
> to the west we can just see the snowy peaks of the Rockies. A great

part of the land is clear of scrub, but a good deal of it is covered with short brush. Here and there are to be seen clumps of trees—wild and cultivated—which serve to break up the monotony of the prairie. All round us, as far as the eye can reach, are the houses or shacks of the settlers. Nearly the whole district is settled up, and as the owners increase in wealth we can see the shacks being replaced by wooden houses, generally of two stories.

The house, which is situated nearly in the centre of the section, is on a slight rise, and commands a good view of the country. It is a large two-storied building, and comprises a kitchen, a dining-room, a drawing-room, a wash-room, a hall, two pantries, a bath-room, a box-room . . . and five bedrooms, one of which is divided into six cubicles. On the south and west sides runs a verandah. About forty yards to the north are the horse stables; and the barns, pig-pens, and numerous other out-buildings are to the east, about two hundred yards away.[1]

The farm operations were quite different from what Pearkes anticipated. He had thought he would be riding all day long on a large herd of beef cattle, learning to rope, brand, and so forth. Instead, he found his first job was hoeing turnips. The only regular riding he did was later when he purchased a pony and was sent to round up the cows from the pasture. The cows were far from being first-class stock and did not receive the attention which even an amateur such as Pearkes felt they should have.

The terms under which the young men worked were simple. Each was paid on a graduating scale according to the estimated value of his work. He would be paid, when competent, about fifteen dollars plus his bed and board and might earn as much as twenty-five dollars a month by the time he completed his two years' residence. With the arrival of Pearkes and Love there were six boys, and only two of them, the Gurney brothers, were sons of farmers. Living in the main house with them were the manager, foreman, cook, and housekeeper. Dr. Fry's first manager had left, and filling the position temporarily was one of the first Berkhamstedians to come to the farm when it was established some three years previously. Alfred Pointer was hardworking and conscientious, but he had neither the experience nor the training to instruct others. Fortunately, he had a good foreman, a Swede, who imparted little theory but much practice in the form of chores. The manager also relied on the housekeeper, Miss Sophia Robinson. She was a large, strong woman who came from an Ontario farm and knew more about farm operations than Pointer. He used to consult her frequently and her advice was generally sound. Thus between the English manager, the Swedish foreman, and the Ontario farmwoman the farm progressed but was not yet flourishing.

Since most of the farm had been brought under cultivation by the time Pearkes arrived, there was plenty of work to do. The day started with the young men rising about 5:30 and feeding the horses and milking the cows. The day usually ended with the same chore. Aside from the cows there were over one hundred head of cattle to look after, about fifty pigs, and a good number of hens. The main crops were fall wheat, oats, barley, and hay, and, of course, the work varied with the season. The haying and ploughing appealed to Pearkes since it meant working with horses, as did seeding and thrashing. Driving the team in winter across the snowy trails to cut trees was hard but pleasant work, even though hours of backbreaking sawing followed. Collecting eggs, feeding the pigs, splitting wood, fencing, separating the cream, repairing harness, cutting brush, cleaning the stables, harvesting, and a hundred and one other chores were tiring but not too difficult. There might be an hour or so to read a farm paper or one of the British journals, write a letter home, listen to the gramophone, or perhaps play a game of cards. By 9:00 most of the young men were in bed.

The hard work on the farm left little time for amusement during the week, but everyone took advantage of such opportunities as were available. There was some duck shooting to be done in season, and in the fall the prairie chicken offered some sport. Occasionally someone would kill a coyote. The fall was also the time for local fairs, and harvest dances or "box socials" were sometimes held under the auspices of the church in nearby Springfield or at the home of a farmer. One of the local farmers whom Pearkes got to know quite well was L. F. Page, a Berkhamstedian who lived with his mother about two miles away. There was some swimming and skating on nearby sloughs, but perhaps the main source of amusement was in Red Deer itself. Depending on tastes and finances one could have dinner at a restaurant, beer at the hotel, or meet friends at Gaetz's Drug Store for an ice cream soda. There was also a theatre, and, depending on the day and the weather, the local brass band might render a concert in the park.

George Pearkes stayed at the "Baby Farm," as the local residents called it, for two years. It was a wholesome, healthy outdoors life and he liked farming. However, to gain more experience and to increase his pay, George decided to move on and accepted the offer of a nearby farmer, George Root, to work for thirty-five dollars a month.

Root was an American who had settled in Alberta some years previously. He had one large farm at Wetaskiwin and another near Red Deer. The latter was a well-run stock farm for purebred horses and cattle. Pearkes admired his Percheron horses, and his shorthorn cattle were shown at most local agricultural fairs. Buyers came from all parts of the province to bid $125 to $150 for them. Root's offer had much to commend it. Not only were the wages good, but the opportunity to work on a well-run farm with first-class stock also meant better experience. Mr. Eversole, the farm manager, ran Root's Red Deer farm with the help of his brother and one other farmhand. They were a most congenial group, and Pearkes would still be no more than a few miles from his brother Ted, who had joined him at the School Farm, and his friends the Pages.

Life on the Root farm was close to what Pearkes had imagined he might be doing when he came to Canada. He was working entirely with animals, and few things pleased him more. Moreover, these were well-kept sleek beasts, and the work animals were kept in fenced pastures and well-tended barns. One of the jobs Pearkes enjoyed was displaying them either at the fairs or to purchasers who visited the farm.

Feeding, watering, and caring for the animals kept Pearkes and the others busy. In winter hay had to be hauled from Root's other farm five miles west of Red Deer. Pearkes usually went with Eversole's brother, each driving a team. Returning through the town, the sleighs loaded with hay, the Percherons demonstrated their strength with the ease with which they pulled their load. The journey was made almost every day during the winter, no matter what the weather. Sometimes the trail would be so rough that a sleigh would tip over. Reloading bales of hay in mid-winter helped to build up muscle and work up an appetite. Having to handle a ton of it three times in one trip, however, was a bit too much.

While he was with Root Pearkes first brushed against Canadian politics. Root was a Conservative, and in the 1908 federal election he ran in the local riding. Pearkes was interested and enthusiastic. On numerous occasions when the election campaign was underway, he drove Root to nearby towns and villages, listening to the give and take of the political meetings. Root lost the election, but presumably he made one convert who, many years later, would be on the platform himself with greater success.

Shortly after his defeat, Root decided to go into semi-retirement on his farm at Wetaskiwin and as a result reduced his activities on his Red Deer farm. At this time his farm manager, Mr. Eversole, moved to the Berkhamsted Farm to manage it, and Pearkes went with him. Pearkes, however, had been thinking of striking out on his own to take up a homestead. He had saved as much of his wages as he could to make the down payment on a 160 acre homestead. In addition to the small down payment, and as a curb to speculation, the candidate had to cultivate thirty acres of land in three years and live on the homestead for not less than six months in the year. When these basic conditions had been met, the farm was considered to be "proved up" and became the property of the homesteader.

While at the School Farm, Pearkes received a letter from an English family homesteading in the Dovercourt area near Rocky Mountain House. The Baileys had four sons who had gone to Berkhamsted, and aware of George's ambition, Mr. Bailey had written about some available land near their own farm close to the Clearwater River. Pearkes decided to visit the family and examine the area himself. There was homestead land in the area both to the west and east, each with attractions and liabilities. To the east was the open, flat prairie country which lacked wood for building a house, barn, or fences but which was easier to cultivate. To the west was the rolling foothill country where trees were more plentiful but where there was less cleared ground. The decision was based on other factors as well; certainly a limited amount of capital could not be ignored.

In straight line distances it is about fifty miles from Red Deer to Rocky Mountain House, but in 1909 there was no road or railroad. To get there Pearkes would have to ride; so early one morning, mounted on a big bronco, he set out on the longest ride he was ever to make in his life. He crossed the Red Deer River, struck south to Marketville, and met the Innisfail Trail which ran west to Raven, at that time no more than a combined post office, store, and roadhouse. From Raven the trail went north through Stauffer and passed close to the Baileys, about ten miles south of Rocky Mountain House. By the time Pearkes arrived at the end of the day he had ridden seventy miles, a remarkable feat for both man and horse. It was a lonely ride, with the wilderness broken now and then by an occasional farm house or tiny hamlet. At the same time it indicated the extent to which George had become accustomed to life on the farming frontier and his youthful self-confidence.

After a day's rest at the Baileys, he looked over prospective homestead sites. He decided on a quarter-section a few miles from Dovercourt west of the Clearwater. There was a good spring on the section, and the river would provide water for the animals as well as be a source of fish. There was not much open land except around the sloughs, but the poplar and willow scrub was comparatively light, and trees to construct a log house were available. The section seemed attractive, so George returned to Red Deer, once more making the trip in one day. In due course he registered his claim at the land office, paid his ten-dollar fee, and undertook the conditions of homesteading.

In the next few weeks Pearkes was busy preparing for his new venture. He bought a team of horses, a cow, two pigs, a few chickens, a tent, stove, provisions, some tools, and various other necessary items. With his supplies in the wagon, the hens clucking in their coop, and the cow trailing along behind, Pearkes once more set out along the Innisfail Trail, only this time the journey took three or four days. When he arrived he set up a tent on a rise close to the river and, with the optimism of youth, began his career as a homesteader. Some of his first problems he later described:

The first thing that one had to do—well, the horses were there, the cow was there, but there was nothing to keep them in. They could wander through the bush anywhere. Eventually I got a couple more cows—I think the most I had . . . was four—and the trouble was that they did wander through the bush. And while you could hobble the horses, you couldn't very well hobble a cow. You put a bell on it. But I know each morning I wasted many hours walking through the bush trying to find the blessed cows until I got a little bit of fencing done. The fencing meant cutting tamarack posts, hauling them to where you wanted to build your fence and then either putting barbed wire around them or cutting poplar poles and nailing them onto the posts . . . .

The land had to be cleared of brush and had to be cut out with an axe. Then you had to get the stumps out and then you had to plow it. Well, I got very, very little plowing done that first year, if any. There was no revenue and the cash that I had was quickly used up. I was very poor in those days. I had nothing. I had to cook my own meals. [They] consisted mostly of porridge and rice . . . . The nearest store was at Stauffer some twelve miles away . . . . I had taken what I thought would be enough to carry me for several months. So one lived on a little bit of bacon, porridge and occasionally, for a treat, put some raisins into the rice and bannock . . . .

I had thought that it would be possible to cut hay around the edges of the sloughs as many farmers did. It was poor hay, but it kept the horses alive. The first summer was very wet and you couldn't get near any slough to cut hay. I did get just a very little of the upland hay which was in places where I had tried to clear off a little bit. It was a wild hay . . . but it wasn't good enough to carry all the stock through. So quite early in the game I had to get rid of the two pigs . . . . They had grown to marketable size and I was able to sell them.

Then, with winter coming along, I had to have some sort of shack to live in. It was made from a few logs, very small ones, because I hadn't the time to go and get good logs. They were chinked with moss . . . which stopped the wind coming through.[2]

This rough cabin was devoid of comforts. Barrels or boxes served as chairs, and a table constructed with a few boards was about the only other piece of furniture. There was no bed, and indeed no wooden floor, so for many months, including the first winter, George slept on a bundle of fir branches wrapped in the few blankets he possessed with his coat on top. A small tin stove kept him warm as long as it was fed with logs, but usually after midnight, when the trees were cracking with the frost outside and the embers were turning grey in the stove, the water inside the shack would begin to freeze which meant cracking the layer of ice in the bucket before he could wash up in the morning.

That first summer and winter were rough. He was no cook, and eating porridge and bannock made him relish all the more the occasional dinner invitations from the Baileys. Once he attempted to make bread. "The baking of bread," he said later,

> was a new experience and I didn't feel that I could spend the whole day kneading the dough and watching it rise. So, having well kneaded the dough and it being a very hot day, I put it on the roof of my shack to rise. The sun was hot and I went away and continued cutting brush. The bread rose at first but then a thunderstorm came up. Before I could get back to the pan of dough, naturally it fell flat.[3]

Food was never wasted, no matter how it was cooked. The two pigs, which used to follow Pearkes about like cats, ate any scraps from his table, and when he was working they would be on the lookout for any edible roots.

The constant, hard, and exhausting work of clearing land coupled with the loneliness of the homestead was relieved somewhat in the following year when Ted left the School Farm to take up an adjoining homestead. Rough as it was, George's cabin represented a home. Ted had none, so they decided to build a larger log cabin on Ted's section where both could share domestic duties. Together they constructed a much better house with larger logs. The cabin had two rooms on the main floor, while above was an attic reached by a ladder which served as sleeping quarters. The sloping roof held sods rather than shingles, but it kept the rain out. Moreover, the cabin had windows with glass panes and a decent door. The furniture was still basic, but at least George no longer slept with only a few fir boughs separating him from the bare ground.

The greatest single problem faced by the brothers was the lack of income. Neither had indicated to their parents the conditions under which they were living nor their financial stringency. By this time their parents had separated, and neither had any desire to add to their mother's problems by asking for help. With no money coming in, George had to seek work wherever he could find it to provide food for himself and his animals. Later, when Ted joined him, they agreed that George, older and stronger, would go out to work while Ted tended the stock. Ted had brought only a riding horse with him, whereas George had a team which could be used for freighting when the prospects offered.

The practice of working on the homestead part of the year and working at whatever job one could get elsewhere was common. If there was a family homesteading, it was easier since a father and one son might work constantly earning money, while another son and the homesteader's wife continued to improve the homestead. Initially, when he was alone, George could pick up a few days' work locally. During the first winter, he recalled,

For a few days I remember digging coal at Rocky Mountain House out of the bank of the river. There were some negroes . . . who were sort of contractors to get it, and I worked for them. They were quite decent and paid me a proper wage—not the same as one man that I did quite a bit of hauling for when they were building the railway to Nordegg. Times were really tough. There was no revenue coming in except [from the sale of] butter and a few eggs—very few eggs because we ate most of them. The butter was . . . made with a churn and . . . it wasn't good butter at all. It wouldn't have passed any standards now, but the store at Stauffer accepted that in exchange for goods. What they did with it I don't know. Then, in order to pay the bills for food and flour and that sort of thing from Stauffer, I used to take the team and go into Innisfail and bring back a load of goods for the store. There was nothing at Stauffer except just a store [run by a Swiss family].[4]

Fortunately for George, it was at this time that a railway line reached the building stage. The crews and construction camps needed supplies, and men and teams were needed to freight them. Whenever he could, he freighted, sometimes working with another man in winter, since not infrequently two teams were required to haul a loaded sleigh up a steep hill. When at the camp, the freighters were expected to pay for their bed and board as well as for the keep of their horses. The construction camp bunkhouses were grim affairs and unique for a young man unaccustomed to them. However, George was quite capable of taking care of himself. Although he had the pleasant manner of a well-bred young Englishman, he was tough.

George's second year as a homesteader brought changes which made his life more comfortable but otherwise no easier. In 1910 his mother and his sister Hilda decided to come to Canada. Both George and Ted had written optimistically about the homestead. George still had hopes of carving out a good farm and felt that he might be as successful one day as his former employer, Mr. Root. In England his mother, who had not the faintest idea of pioneer life in Canada, probably thought of her sons' combined 320 acres in terms of the farms she was familiar with.

The journey from Innisfail to the homestead must have been a terrible experience for Mrs. Pearkes. The women were happy at the family reunion, but the glow of expectation must have dimmed with every jolt as the wagon bounced along the trail. When they arrived at the log cabin which, to George, was such an improvement, one can only imagine what Mrs. Pearkes thought. Since there was no bedroom, the boys could only help her up the ladder to the loft which they had partitioned with a blanket, the women sleeping on one side and George and Ted on the other. There was no chest of drawers for their clothes. Some nails on the walls served the boys and, for a while, had to serve Mrs. Pearkes and Hilda as well. Of course there was neither running water nor electricity, and bathroom and toilet facilities were as rustic as the cabin. To the seventeen-year-old Hilda, fresh from Cheltenham College for Young Ladies, it was all very much an adventure—exciting, different, and at first, perhaps, tinged with romance. For Mrs. Pearkes, after the initial pleasure of seeing her sons, the situation was anything but an adventure. The longer she remained, the more dissatisfied and pessimistic she became. The farmers and homesteaders in the area, with the exception of the Baileys and one or two others, were not the type of people she had mixed with in England, and unlike George and Ted, she did not take readily to the easy informality of the agricultural frontier. The great loneliness of the country affected her more than Hilda. Mrs. Pearkes had a modest amount of capital, and as it was obvious that the cabin, built for two bachelors, was most unsuitable, she hired Ernest Ross and his brother to build a larger, more comfortable log house on George's homestead. She had also brought over some of the family linen, silver, and various small items which added a certain grace to the limited pieces of necessary furniture she purchased. With Hilda, she took on the domestic chores of cooking, washing, sewing, and cleaning which her sons had undertaken in the past two years with indifferent success.

These homey comforts were welcomed by George, but the addition of his mother and Hilda meant also additional responsibilities. Such limited crops as he got in were consumed by the stock, so that although he was keeping abreast of the summer and fall demands of the animals, he was unable to harvest a sufficient surplus to see them over to the spring. As a result he still had to go out for long periods of work to provide basic necessities. During the second winter he was able to do more freighting, and, as usual, he also worked at any job available. There was little money in freighting, however. As he said later:

> They paid only a low amount for the goods hauled by the pound, and that always went to pay the bills which were owing for the food, and not very much was left. There were times when I'd gone to Innisfail and just slept by the roadside while going in [because] I couldn't afford to go to a roadhouse. There were times when I walked in to Innisfail because I was going out looking for a job and wasn't going to take the horses. I went and worked with a threshing gang and made money at

that. I remember walking through . . . Marketville. It was dark at night and I saw a light and went to a farmhouse. There was an Icelandic family there and never have people been kinder than those people were to me. They took me in and gave me meals and they let me sleep in the house. Occasionally I have slept in barns and slept by the roadside because it was a tough time. But I liked it and in the Spring, when the leaves were coming out, I can remember . . . riding over to the Baileys, singing happily, almost thinking I was going out hunting.[5]

Although work on the homestead was almost unremitting, occasionally there were times when one could take a day off. The Pearkes family became acquainted with their neighbours—the Baileys, the Sinclairs, the Hankinsons, and others—during the course of their first year. Many were English immigrants who, for one reason or another, had come to Canada and were meeting with some measure of success in their new environment. Others were Canadians from Ontario and Quebec, who brought a greater familiarity with Canadian ways and carried on a social life somewhat similar to what they had known in the East. The vastness of the area, the distance between the farms, and the lack of community services all made for a casual and spontaneous social life. Visits were infrequent but lengthy. The local school was more than a centre of learning, for here too would be planned the picnics and box socials. At the dances held in the autumn and winter, there was a certain amount of drinking behind the barn and sometimes a fistfight for good measure. It was not unusual to travel fifteen miles by horse and buggy to a dance attended by young and old, with families bringing a hamper for supper. The music would be supplied by local talent. Music also entered into home entertainment as well. The Pearkeses visited the Baileys often, and they frequently had singsongs on Sunday evenings when neighbours would gather there. George liked music but had no ear for it. He could not sing a solo as others could, yet everyone was supposed to contribute to the entertainment. As a result he learned by heart a number of Kipling's poems—"Gunga Din," "England is a Garden," "The Flag of England," among others—and so earned a round of applause. Generally speaking, the time spent on social affairs was limited. For the most part George and his brother could enjoy only sports such as riding or hunting, while Mrs. Pearkes restricted herself to local visits and looking after her sons.

In the late spring of 1911 George was away from home for the longest period he had ever been since he started to homestead. He had heard that men were being hired in Edmonton to go north with dominion land survey crews. It sounded alluring and a far better paid job than freighting, so he went to Edmonton. Fortunately, the crew was short an axeman, and after months of clearing his homestead, George qualified easily. Almost immediately the party set out for the area north of Fort McMurray (now Waterways) on the Athabasca River.

The trip lasted over six months, and it gave George a fascinating glimpse of Canadian frontier life which even then was beginning to disappear. The railway ran north for only a short distance, and once at the end of steel, the party, led by Albert Tremblay, D.L.S., transferred their instruments, equipment, and personal gear into wagons which carried them to Athabasca Landing. When they arrived, there were scenes of great activity: the terminus of the railway was under construction, loads of freight were arriving at all hours, and on the shores of the Athabasca River flat-bottomed scows were being built for the Hudson's Bay brigade.

On one of these shallow scows the survey crew journeyed some three hundred miles down river to Fort McMurray. This craft could carry a surprising load. Steered with a long oar by an experienced riverman, it travelled easily with the river current with the occasional help from oars to speed it along the quiet stretches. There was no cover except for the pieces of canvas carried by the survey crew. The men on this job, however, were hardy individuals, accustomed to outdoor life and quick to lend a hand with the oars when necessary. Accompanying Tremblay's party was a small flotilla of other scows transporting freight to the northern outposts or carrying passengers ranging from constables of the Royal North West Mounted Police to missionaries. Among the latter was the Right Reverend Dr. I. O. Stringer, bishop of the Yukon. A few years earlier he had been caught by a sudden freeze-up on one of the arctic rivers. His party had had to abandon their boats and make a grinding trek through the wilderness before they came upon an Indian village. On this trip Pearkes met others who had faced the rigours of the north, including the men from the Mounted Police, and his admiration for them steadily increased.

For the most part it was a delightful way to travel. Here and there were chunks of ice left over from the breakup, and not until the last third of the voyage, roughly between Grand Rapids and Fort McMurray, were there any serious rapids. Most spectacular was Grand Rapids itself. An island split the current, and loaded scows shot the upper part of the rapids to the head of the island. There they were unloaded and their freight carried by a narrow-gauge, hand-operated tramway to the lower end. The empty scows were then hauled back upstream and shot through the channel on the right of the island. As they neared the end of the island the men on land threw a cask into the water. Attached to it was a line which the crew of the scow caught up and pulled to reach a heavy rope knotted to it. Once they had secured the rope, the men on the island pulled the scow in, reloaded, and prepared to continue their journey. Another portage had to be made at the Big Cascade, and when they shot Pelican Rapids, the scow hit a rock, and it was only after three hours work, hip-deep in water, that it was freed.

Shooting the rapids, however, occurred infrequently and added excitement to an otherwise placid journey. Sitting in the scow George saw sights which he had read about only a few years earlier in school. There were a variety of animals—lynx, bear, moose—in fact, the crew captured a baby moose which was near exhaustion and made a pet of it. The size of the land, with the forests spreading to the horizon, was impressive. So, too, was the sight of a huge column of flame which had been burning for years —caused by a natural gas vent.

Fort McMurray was the southern terminus of a riverboat which ran down the Athabasca to Great Slave Lake and on into the Slave River. For the surveying crew, however, it was the end of the journey. Here they unloaded, gathered together a pack train of ponies, and prepared to take their supplies into the bush where they established their first camp. They also encountered the mosquitoes, black flies, and bulldog flies which pestered and irritated them throughout the summer. Pearkes later described his job:

> Once we established camp we started on the survey work. There were two instrument men running the lines giving the direction and the elevation so as to run the survey. The axeman had to go out in front. First of all you had a rodman who went out, which frequently wasn't very far because there was fairly dense bush there, and he would get the line from the instrument man. Then the axeman would have to cut that line . . . and then it was all measured by chain . . . . a reconnaissance had to be made on either side of the line to report the type of ground . . . . And so this work went on with establishing camps . . . for three or four days. Then having cut the line a certain distance, the camp would be moved to another suitable place . . . .
>
> I thoroughly enjoyed it. It wasn't too hard work . . . . After a while, through the kindness of the assistant surveyor . . . Charlie Lindsay, who brushed me up on my logarithm tables, I was taking an instrument and helping out . . . . The mathematics one had learned at school made it comparatively easy.[6]

The survey party worked steadily into the fall. It had been a long and expensive trip to Fort McMurray, and evidently it was decided to work as far into the winter as possible before returning to Edmonton. There was little recreation available. Time was passed playing poker or chequers or yarning around the campfire in the evening, with the tales getting taller as the fire grew lower. Axes were sharpened to a razor's edge for the next day, and even on Sunday there was little to do except wash and mend clothes or fish in a stream if there was one handy. The one bright spot for George, aside from his liking the out-of-doors work, was that he was saving money. Forty-five dollars and board might not be a handsome salary, but since there was neither the need nor the opportunity to spend it, he was able to save everything he earned.

It was not until December that Mr. Tremblay and his survey crew returned to Fort McMurray and prepared to make their way back to Athabasca Landing. By this time, of course, the weather had turned very cold, snow was everywhere, and the river had frozen solid. The only way to get out was by pack train, walking along the path on the river shore made by Indians who hauled the scows upstream. By the time the party reached Fort McMurray, trappers and Indians from farther north were beginning to come in with their furs to the Hudson's Bay Company post. One of the delightful sights Pearkes remembers was the dog teams, their harness gaily decorated with ribbons, pulling their sleighs up the one and only street of the post.

The trip south was not easy. It was bitterly cold with the temperature ranging far below zero. Sometimes the crew camped without tents, sleeping on fir boughs underneath the trees with someone always awake to keep the large fire going during the night. They stopped only when it was necessary to eat or sleep. Towards the end of the second week food was rationed, and if one had suddenly come across the weary, bearded group, slogging steadily through the snowy wilderness, one might have taken them for a tiny detachment of the Grand Army retreating from Moscow. For young Pearkes, however, it was a marvellous adventure. He had fallen in love with the north, and he had plans to return. The snow, the cold, the isolation, and the vast sweep of the country offered themselves as challenges rather than obstacles.

While Pearkes was away in the north, there had been few changes on the homestead. By this time George had proved up his homestead, and the 160 acres now belonged to him. However, he had plenty of time to think about his future, and when he returned he talked the matter over with his family. It was obvious that he was not going to make either fame or fortune in the Canadian West by farming. His mother and sister, although they had not complained, were not enthusiastic about homesteading nor even about the future once the farm was developed. George's brother Ted, who was developing his own homestead, found the life of a prairie farmer quite different from what he had expected. Mrs. Pearkes and Hilda talked about the excellent climate and opportunities in British Columbia, which they had heard about from a cousin visiting Vancouver. Ted was to remain in Alberta to prove up his homestead until he received clear title, and George, now twenty-four, decided to join the Royal North West Mounted Police.

3

Constable Pearkes—R.N.W.M.P.

After coming to Alberta, Pearkes often met men of the Royal North West Mounted Police. Formed in 1873 on a paramilitary basis, the "Mounties" had gained an international reputation for their ability to bring and preserve law and order in Western and Northwestern Canada and the Yukon. Their reputation was well deserved, and the tales of their exploits provided the content of numerous adventure stories which, then as now, thrilled schoolboys in Great Britain and in Canada. Pearkes had read about these men before he met them, and meeting them did not tarnish their image. With the survey party in northern Alberta he became well acquainted with several constables. His own brief experience in the bush, together with the limited headway he was making on the homestead, led him to enquire about conditions in the force from the R.N.W.M.P. superintendent at Athabasca Landing. He had proved up his homestead, he was single and had no dependents, and the adventurous life the scarlet-coated force seemed to offer was irresistible. It might not be a military force, but it was the next thing to it. Having tried to carry out his father's wishes by wresting a living from the soil, he wanted now to try his own first choice and serve in uniform. His health and education were excellent, and he had no difficulty getting the necessary letters attesting to his character. Having secured these, he left for Regina, the headquarters of the Royal North West Mounted Police, in February 1913.

He made the trip in the luxury of a railway coach. After roughing it in the Athabasca country for so many months, it was a delight to travel in comfort—to sleep between white sheets and to eat decent meals while watching the frozen scenery slide by. Pearkes had not enjoyed such luxury since he came west, and with several hundred dollars in pay fattening his wallet, he was prepared to enjoy a brief fling before entering into a life which was noted for hardship and challenge.

The police barracks and headquarters in Regina were fairly large. Located on ample grounds several miles from the city, the buildings were utilitarian and functional. Pearkes, who was sworn in as a recruit constable on 13 February, was shown first to the recruits' barracks. Nearby were the stables and riding school, and the horses seemed as well treated as the recruits. They were lovely looking animals—sleek, well groomed and well fed. A short distance away were two older houses for the non-commissioned officers (termed the "Rabbit Warren" and "Rat Pit" by their occupants), and rounding out the headquarters were the mess hall, church, and assorted buildings for administrative purposes.

Pearkes found himself with a group of recruits whose backgrounds were varied but who quickly absorbed the force's discipline and *esprit de corps*. Many were young Englishmen like himself, joining for adventure and excitement. Most were good horsemen, and some had served a short period in the British cavalry. Few, if any, had any outside income, and the sixty cents a day pay of a constable would never have induced any to join for the salary. Those who could not take the rigid discipline or whose character and temperament were unsuited to the demands of the force quickly found themselves seeking employment elsewhere. For the majority who remained, the life was quite active. In wintertime reveille was at 6:30, and half an hour later the daily routine began with stable parade. As Pearkes recalled later:

> This would consist of going out feeding and grooming your horse, looking after your saddlery, and cleaning out the stables . . . . The horses were fed according to the amount which the veterinarian ordered . . . . The parades were always in charge of an officer and a good deal of emphasis was laid on the grooming and keeping the horses in first class condition . . . . Then, after stables, breakfast, and then there would be a certain amount of drill, a good deal of riding in the riding school which I thoroughly enjoyed, and after lunch, there was a limited number of lectures on what a policeman should do and on law and that sort of thing.[1]

There was some musketry training, and firing with the carbine and the revolver provided a break from routine, for Pearkes and the other recruits were not permitted outside of barracks in civilian clothes, and, further, even on Sunday there was a compulsory church parade in full dress or review order. This meant, after stable parade, a hectic rush to polish buttons, burnish spurs, shine the Sam Browne equipment, and bring a glow to the brown leather boots which would satisfy the gimlet eye of the inspecting

Plate 5. "Rough-riding corporal" Pearkes breaking in a mount for military duties during training with the Second Canadian Mounted Rifles at the Willows Camp, Victoria, B.C.

Plate 6. The Canadian Mounted Rifles trained as cavalry, but they fought as infantry overseas. In open country a soldier's mount could be used to provide cover.

Plate 7. The bar of the Kaiserhof (Blanshard) Hotel, Victoria, B.C., where the "*Lusitania* Riot" broke out on 8 May 1915.

Plate 8. Troops departing from Victoria, B.C., en route for overseas, 1915.

N.C.O. Men such as Regimental Sgt. Maj. Probie and Sgt. Maj. Griffiths were well known to Pearkes and to hundreds of recruits who had preceded him. Whether they were instructing in drill, riding, or police work, something of their character and pride rubbed off on the newcomers who, in turn, looked upon giving their very best to their work as a matter of simple duty.

Six weeks after he began in Regina a call came for volunteers to go to the Yukon on detachment duty. Pearkes and seven others were chosen, and in April they boarded a train for Vancouver where they were to catch a ship north. The trip through the mountains of British Columbia captivated Pearkes. The mountains, covered with snow, provided a magnificent spectacle, and when the train came down into the Fraser River Delta, the lush greenery and early flowers of the coastal area were a pleasant change from the prairies. Vancouver, a bustling city of a little over 100,000, was beginning to feel something of its potential power as a great seaport, and along the waterfront Pearkes and his comrades could see ships of all sizes and national register taking on cargo or transferring goods onto the docks. Although he had only a brief time in the city, Pearkes managed to see his mother and sister. He found they were planning to move to Victoria, a place which had been described to them as being "a little bit of Old England" and far more congenial to them than Vancouver.

The trip north along the inland passage was most attractive. From the totem poles at Alert Bay to the forest-covered mountains sweeping down to the shore, the sights were enough to keep most of the passengers on deck at every opportunity until they reached Skagway. There the small detachment stayed overnight. The proprietor of the hotel, Mrs. Pullen, was a remarkable character who had been there for a long time. She was there when Skagway had been part of the territory in dispute between Canada and the United States during the gold rush. Skagway had earned an evil reputation during the heyday of "Soapy Smith" in the late nineties, but in 1913 it was peaceful and quiet compared to its earlier turbulent era. From Skagway the R.N.W.M.P. group took the Yukon Railway over the White Pass, going through Bennett and Carcross to Whitehorse. This narrow gauge railway wound its way slowly up the pass over the trail taken by the gold-seekers in 1898. At the summit was the boundary between Canada and the United States where there were big snowsheds through which the train went. At either end were the respective customs sheds. Once over the summit the train sped down to Bennett where everyone got out and had a tremendous meal. The next major stop was Whitehorse, farther up the Yukon River, where Pearkes and another constable got off, while the others continued on to Dawson City. Whitehorse, located right on the river and surrounded by hills, was exactly the sort of frontier town Pearkes thought it would be. "This was in the early summer," he said later, "and my first impressions were that this was just what I was looking for."

The R.N.W.M.P. subdivision at Whitehorse had a fairly substantial barracks on the outskirts of town built during the gold rush when the town was one of the most important commercial centres of the territory. Inspector Acland, Staff Sgt. Head, Sgt. MacLaughlin, and about half a dozen constables comprised the force in town, while outside on detachment duty there were about the same number of men who were relieved in rotation on a yearly or half-yearly basis. Pearkes, as a very new and junior man, found himself on fatigue duties for the first few weeks, but then he was attached to the town station where he worked under the eye of an old hand, Sgt. MacLaughlin. There was little crime in Whitehorse, and Pearkes found most of his work consisted of patrolling a rather large Indian village making sure there were no disreputable whites hanging around peddling whiskey. Weekends tended to be much busier, for with miners coming into town there were bound to be arrests for brawling and drunkenness. It was good experience for a young constable, and, of course, he absorbed much of what his seniors told him about other police problems which ranged from the tragic to the humorous. He also had an opportunity to meet some of the outstanding men in the force whose exploits had made them famous beyond the boundaries of Canada. These were men who were accustomed to travelling in frigid weather tracking down criminals or perhaps carrying out missions of mercy and enduring incredible hardships.

In the early summer Pearkes was posted on detachment duty to Summit on the border of the Yukon and Alaska. When the snow began to melt, it was customary to send a mountie to assist the customs and immigration official. In the snowshed at the top of the pass there was a two-room shed where Pearkes had his office in the front and his quarters in the rear. Nearby was a section house for employees of the railway. The section boss was a Scandinavian, and arrangements had been made for the constable on duty to have his meals with him. One of Pearkes's duties was to see that no undesirable characters came into the territory, and there were photographs of wanted men which he checked daily. However, as he related later,

> I also had instructions to see that prostitutes didn't come in. Now that was quite a problem, because prostitutes didn't walk over the Pass and while the train was waiting at the summit, I used to board it because the passengers had to go through customs at the time. I'd walk through the coaches. There weren't many women travelling at that time and whenever there were any, I glared at them. I never had the

nerve to ask them whether they were a prostitute or not, so I don't know how many I let through![2]

Everyone had to check in at the border where the constable recorded names, noted weapons, and found out if the arrivals had sufficient money or provisions to maintain them or perhaps jobs to go to. Not infrequently men would try to avoid the R.N.W.M.P. post. Pearkes made it a habit to catch a ride in the train from the border to Bennett, about sixteen miles away. He would ride in the cab with the engineer, and if he spotted anyone walking whom he did not recognize, he would have the engineer let him off. The train would continue on while the travellers' papers were checked. It meant a long walk back, but he had always been fond of walking and running so it was good exercise. It was also an example of performing one's duty conscientiously without supervision as the force expected.[3]

Pearkes's time at the summit of White Pass was a summer duty, and most of his tour of duty was spent at Carcross, about midway between the summit and Whitehorse. This hamlet, originally called Cariboo Crossing, was on a narrow strip of land between two lakes. It was a well-known portage during the gold rush, and in 1913 it was a major transportation point for Atlin in British Columbia. There was a fair amount of mining in the vicinity and a considerable number of Indians in the area. In Carcross was the Chooutla Indian Mission School, an Anglican church, a small collection of buildings, and a little wooden shack which housed the one-man detachment of the R.N.W.M.P.

In this small community of about fifty white families, Pearkes soon became well known and established warm relationships. A young woman living in the town remembers him well. She wrote later:

This young man had the unmistakable stamp of one destined to be a leader. He was tall and handsome, very slim, an excellent horseman, and afraid of nothing. He cut quite a figure in that red coat, ruddy complexion and flashing smile. His courtesy and unmistakable breeding made him unusually popular with the townsfolk who were not normally impressed with the R.N.W.M.P.[4]

One of Pearkes's main duties at Carcross was patrolling the surrounding area which involved travelling by horse, canoe, or dogsled, depending on the season. Usually he could stay overnight at a mine or a trapper's hut, for his area was sufficiently compact and populated that there was no need to go out for days or weeks. Patrols were carried out for a variety of reasons, but primarily it was to "show the flag" in the remote areas and to keep a general eye on the area for which he was responsible. He might perform a number of duties on such patrols. If a trapper living in a remote log house had not been heard of for several months Pearkes would visit him to ensure that everything was well. While there he might write a few letters for him if the man was illiterate, as was not uncommon. Since the nearest lawyer was in Whitehorse, Pearkes might be questioned regarding legal matters and might help draft a will. Sometimes he had to search for missing persons, now and then act as a bank for a quantity of gold for a few days, and always there were the periodic visits to mines and farmhouses where he would ask if there were any complaints. Generally there were few, but there was always a welcome for a mountie, with a warm meal and a shakedown bed in the cabin before he had to push on.

By 1914 Pearkes was giving serious thoughts to his future. He enjoyed being in the R.N.W.M.P. and liked the Yukon, However, he was now in his mid-twenties and realized that he should improve his position. He began taking a correspondence course in law which would help him whether he stayed in the force or left it to go to a law school after his three-year term of service was completed. As far as he could see, the future as a constable was not too bright. The force was small and their duties were confined mainly to part of Western Canada, the Yukon, and the Northwest Territories. In the Yukon, for example, there were approximately forty all ranks, and the opportunities for promotion were limited. Moreover, there were many who were senior to Pearkes, and among them were men whose accomplishments had placed them well up the list.

Pearkes was in Carcross in June 1914 when news came through about the assassination of the heir of the Austro-Hungarian Empire in Sarajevo. The first person to hear of major events was the telegraph operator at the railway station, and he acted as a major source of information for the entire community as events in Europe began to take an ominous shape. Those who received the Whitehorse newspaper and who were interested in European affairs knew that the Balkans had long been a powder keg where Pan-Slavism and nationalism had posed a serious threat to the empire of Austria-Hungary. To add to an already unstable situation, an aggressive Germany had started to increase its navy to a point where Great Britain felt it to be a dangerous threat to the Royal Navy. For some years before 1914 two strong blocs—the Triple Alliance and the Triple Entente—faced each other against a background of mounting armaments and deep-seated fear and suspicion. The assassination of Archduke Francis Ferdinand provided the spark which was to set Europe aflame. Within a month diplomacy had been replaced with mobilization, and in the first week of August Great Britain was at war with Germany.

As the crisis deepened, the telegraph office became a focal point for the small community at Carcross, and among those who used to congregate in the railway office was Constable Pearkes.[5] When war was declared Pearkes immediately applied for permission to purchase his discharge. However, a great many other members of the force also wanted release. Those who were reservists in the British Army, and there were about a dozen in the Yukon division, were able to get their discharges and leave immediately. This sudden depletion made it all the more difficult for men such as Pearkes to get theirs, and thus he waited impatiently, following the retreat from Mons on a school map of France as news came in of the fighting retreat of the British Army. When he was posted back to White-horse, Pearkes made further enquiries about his discharge, but again without any luck. Finally he hit upon an idea to get his release. The R.N.W.M.P. would not let him go to join the army, but Section 1039 of the Rules and Regulations permitted a constable to purchase his discharge under other conditions. On 26 December, quoting this section, Pearkes again wrote. "The reasons for requesting this discharge," he stated, "are that an opportunity, whereby he may materially better his position, has presented itself and that property owned by Constable Pearkes in Alberta, requires his immediate personal attention."[6]

It took a little over six weeks for permission to be granted, but on 19 February Pearkes received his discharge. His homestead, of course, was furthest from his mind. Locally, Joe Boyle was raising and equipping a detachment of machine-gunners. Pearkes, although tempted, thought it might be some time before it was sent overseas, and there was a general feeling among many young men in Canada that the war would be over before the end of the year. Ever since the Crimean War wars had been short, and this, in part, accounted for the long queues at Canadian recruiting offices during the early months of the conflict. Pearkes felt that, with his cadet training in England and his experience in the R.N.W.M.P., he might be able to obtain a commission in a British regiment. He decided, therefore, to leave immediately for Vancouver and get back to Great Britain in the shortest possible time.

Before he left, his friends both from the force and the town held a dance in his honour at the Whitehorse Club and a purse was collected to help defray the cost of his journey.[7] It was a moving send-off and a testament to his popularity. The next day he took the train to Skagway en route to Vancouver.

4

On Active Service

When Great Britain declared war against Germany in August 1914, a wave of patriotism swept over the British Empire. In Canada the call to the colours was overwhelming. There were few militia regiments which could not promise the Minister of Militia a full complement of officers and men keen to volunteer for service overseas. They were eager to get into the fray since the popular belief was that Germany and Austria-Hungary would soon be defeated. In the early months of the war, it was common to see men queued up to enlist in their local regiment. The recruiting officers could select the best of those who offered their services and not infrequently had a waiting list of men to fill any vacancy. Every battalion wanted to be sent to France at the earliest possible moment, and at war's outbreak the Minister of Militia, Colonel the Honourable Sam Hughes, received a flood of telegrams and letters from commanding officers pleading that their particular unit should be selected to go over with the First Contingent. Rather than follow the mobilization plan which had been drawn up by his staff, Hughes decided to form a group of numbered battalions which would be brought up to establishment by selecting drafts of men from the militia units. Initially, therefore, the battalions of the First Contingent of the Canadian Expeditionary Force contained men from all parts of Canada. Later many of the numbered battalions were composed of men recruited primarily from one locality or district.

The 2nd Canadian Mounted Rifles was a case in point. It was raised as a cavalry unit in 1908 in the Okanagan, and by 1912 several cavalry squadrons from the area were grouped together to form the 30th Regiment, British Columbia Horse. It quickly made a very good name for itself. Both officers and men were accustomed to riding; there was among them a good sprinkling of former British cavalry veterans, and the enthusiasm of the Okanagan townsmen, ranchers, and farmers soon brought the unit to a high state of efficiency. When the war broke out, Lt.-Col. J. C. L. Bott had offered the regiment for overseas service, but, as the primary need was for infantry, he was turned down. Early in October 1914 the unit was still in the Okanagan, the First Contingent had gone overseas, and the men waited with growing impatience. Later in the month, German and Turkish warships bombarded Russian Black Sea ports. On 5 November Great Britain declared war on the Ottoman Empire, and the following day Lt.-Col. Bott was offered the command of a battalion of mounted rifles, one of four authorized initially for the Second Contingent. The new Canadian Expeditionary Force regiment, the 2nd Canadian Mounted Rifles, was to be composed of 544 all ranks. Headquarters and two squadrons were to come from the Okanagan cavalry regiment, while a third squadron would be formed from the Victoria Independent Squadron of Horse.[1] Late in November the 2nd C.M.R. assembled at the Willows Exhibition Ground in Victoria to train and await the call to go overseas. Here on 2 March 1915 the unit accepted a new recruit, No. 107473, Trooper G. R. Pearkes.

When Pearkes had arrived in Vancouver at the end of February he immediately made enquiries about local regiments and the possibility of enlisting. He was directed to Hastings Park, which had been turned into a military encampment, but soon found that none of the units were going overseas immediately. Moreover, there were no vacancies as the battalions were up to strength. Someone suggested that he might try the 2nd C.M.R.'s, since it was rumoured that they might be going to Egypt soon to help defend Suez. The chance of joining a cavalry unit, together with the opportunity to visit his mother and sister, made him decide to take the C.P.R. steamer to Victoria immediately. When he arrived, he took the tramcar to the Willows, presented himself to the adjutant, and found to his delight that there were one or two vacancies. A medical doctor found the new recruit in excellent physical shape. Pearkes then swore the oath of allegiance, and after filling out the usual forms and gathering his uniform and equipment, he found himself in Major M. V. Allen's "B" Squadron with Lt. A. V. Evans as his troop commander.

Although he had no idea that for the next thirty years he would be in the army, George Pearkes knew he was in his element. His comrades were a congenial lot. Many, like himself, were Britons who had been attracted to Canada and had taken up farming in the Okanagan. A large number were first generation Canadians who held Great Britain in as high esteem as their native land, even though they had never set foot on British soil. The squadron from Victoria, commanded by Maj. Walter Bapty, was similar in makeup. The rough khaki uniform of the Mounted Rifles was not dissimilar from what he had worn in the Mounted Police. The tunic, riding breeches, puttees, and leather bandolier[2] looked very smart both on parade and off, and indeed there was somewhat less brass to polish and leather to shine than he had been accustomed to.

Within his troop, and later his squadron, Pearkes soon began to make friends. Trooper R. Meadows, the Ibbertson brothers, Troopers E. C. Warren, Douglas, Manning, Griffin, Joyce, and others became his particular friends, and as time went on he widened his acquaintance and began to get a reputation as a particularly good horseman and rider. He had had his share of falls from bucking broncos while he was at Berkhamsted Farm, but with experience over the years he had learned how to handle some of the more unruly beasts. The additional training he had had with the R.N.W.M.P. made him exceptionally good at managing them. As a result, six weeks after he joined the regiment, he was promoted to lance corporal and became his squadron's "Rough Riding Corporal." Under the overall direction of Sergeant MacDonald the three rough riding corporals —L/Cpls. R. Shuttleworth, D. Wright and G. Pearkes—had their hands full training and schooling the half-broken range horses which had been gathered up from as far east as Alberta.

During their stay at the Willows the unit, except for the officers, lived under canvas. The horses had stables, and in one of the large, barn-like exhibition buildings an indoor equitation school had been established. Elsewhere on the former fair grounds was a parade square, while at nearby Willows Beach a jumping course was in frequent use. Further along the waterfront, at Clover Point, the squadrons spent considerable time at the rifle range. Although it was a mounted unit, the lessons of the Boer War had sunk in deeply. The 2nd C.M.R. was to be primarily men who could shoot as well as the infantry but with the additional mobility of cavalry. Swords and lances were used only at military gymkhanas. Thus the rifle bucket replaced the sword scabbard, and the Vickers machine gun section was capable of doing more damage than the entire regiment armed with lances.

Training was comparatively limited and in a sense unrealistic. Most of the men still thought they would go to the Middle East and fight in Palestine, Egypt, or somewhere on the rim of the Turkish Empire. In France the war seemed to be reaching a stalemate with trench warfare sapping mobility. In Victoria, however, the unit went on long marches, both on foot and on horse, and periodically engaged in manoeuvres between the Willows and Royal Oak. Mounted and dismounted action, the popping of blank cartridges, the overnight bivouacs as far away as Sooke, and the usual round of lectures, stable duty, picquets, and the rest of it rounded off the daily routine.

Most evenings the men were allowed to go out until 10:00, and as the 2nd C.M.R.'s was a popular unit, invitations were numerous. Sometimes concerts were put on especially for the soldiers, and usually they were permitted into the theatres and the cinemas at reduced rates. Since "C" Squadron was raised in Victoria, there was an especially close link between the city and the unit. With his mother and sister living on Oxford Street Pearkes could always be sure of a warm welcome, a dinner which was a delightful change from army rations, and a chance to relax and chat with both women. Sometimes he would bring his friends home for dinner, and later, somewhat to their surprise, he would suggest they walk back to camp rather than take the streetcar.

During the late spring of 1915 the calm of Victoria was shattered by an incident involving the 2nd C.M.R.'s. Lt. J. Dunsmuir, a popular young officer in the unit, resigned his commission early in April to go overseas and enlist in a British regiment. He travelled on the ill-fated *Lusitania*, which was sunk on 7 May. On the following day, Saturday, the Victoria newspapers carried headlines describing the incident and listed Dunsmuir as one of the victims of the disaster. That evening, when many of the 2nd C.M.R.'s were in town, several were in the bar of the Blanshard, formerly the Kaiserhof, Hotel. Some insulting remarks were passed, and the combination of anger at the sinking of the *Lusitania*, the apparently unpatriotic remarks of German-Canadians working in the hotel, and, undoubtedly, the drinking which had been going on resulted in the bar of the hotel being wrecked. A small crowd went from there to the former premises of the "Deutscher Verein," the local German club on Government Street, and thoroughly destroyed it. By this time the crowd had grown much larger, and an unruly civilian element, excited at what had occurred, began to demolish several wholesale and retail stores with German names, and much greater damage was done to the Blanshard Hotel until "the place looked as if a cyclone had hit it."[3] Pearkes had observed some of the crowd. He had not seen the crowd grow to several hundreds, however, and it was not until a squadron of the 2nd C.M.R.'s was called out—Pearkes included—to quell the disturbance that he and most of his comrades realized that the situation was quite out of hand. A squadron of mounted rifles, together with a company of infantry,[4] marching into the business section of Victoria had a calming effect. The crowds melted into the darkness and soldiers were placed to guard stores where looting had been in progress. Pearkes was on sentry duty at the local brewery, but there were no disturbances.

Some three weeks later the 2nd C.M.R. received instructions to go overseas. Immediately before their departure, however, Bott paraded the battalion to inform them that there was little likelihood they would be required as a mounted unit and asked if they would volunteer as infantry. Almost the entire unit accepted the condition, and on 4 June the regiment marched through the city to the docks. "We pretty nearly had to fight our way through the crowds," Pearkes related later. On board the C.P.R. ship, soldiers crowded the decks and swarmed up the rigging, singing and cheering as the ship eased away from the dock.

The train trip from Vancouver to Camp Hughes, near Brandon, Manitoba, went smoothly. On the various coaches signs such as "Berlin or Bust" or "Here Comes the 2nd C.M.R." indicated some oversight in security measures, but the movement of hundreds of men is difficult to keep secret. When the train stopped briefly at Salmon Arm, for example, it seemed as if all the people in the Okanagan Valley were there, laden with fruit, cake, and other edibles which they pressed on the soldiers. At Camp Hughes the unit joined the 1st C.M.R. from Winnipeg and the 3rd C.M.R. from Medicine Hat. Here the three units met for the first time, the brigade headquarters staff was assembled, and within forty-eight hours word came for the 1st Canadian Mounted Rifles Brigade to entrain for Montreal. The unit boarded the R.M.S. *Megantic*, and on 12 June began the voyage to the United Kingdom. It was nine years since Pearkes had arrived in Canada as an eighteen-year-old youth. He had seen more of Canada than most Canadians and had worked as hard under difficult conditions as anyone. He was not returning home with a fat purse as he had once hoped. On the other hand, he was in the army, which was what he had wanted to do even before he left England.

The ten-day trip on the *Megantic* was uncomfortable. Troops were crowded on board, mealtimes were brief with many sittings, the hammocks were awkward, and entertainment was almost non-existent. On the upper decks were large details of men armed with rifles, ready to pot away at any enemy submarine, but primarily there to spot any subs the ship could outrun. Near Ireland an escort of destroyers came up to the ship amid the cheers of the troops. This was their first sight of British destroyers in the war zone, and they gave everyone a greater sense of participation in the conflict. A short time later the distant outline of the coast of Britain could be distinguished, and finally, to the great comfort of those who had been seasick, the *Megantic* eased into Plymouth Sound and up to the harbour at Devonport.

For Pearkes it was a special homecoming. "As far as I can remember," he recalled later,

> there was a feeling of "this is my home, my native land" and I was thrilled at the opportunity of coming and fighting for England. [I felt] that I had come back to fight for the Crown and for England. I can't say that I ever thought much at that time about fighting for Canada or fighting for democracy—we were fighting for England. "Your King and Country Need You" posters were everywhere. The men of the colonies were coming home to fight. This was my reaction.[5]

It was the reaction of many, if not most, of the battalion as well. Most of the men were of British origin, and they had been brought up in the late Victorian and Edwardian eras when church, school, and society in English-speaking Canada had basked in the reflected glory of the British Empire.[6] Recruiting posters in Canada were very similar to those in England except for the names of the regiments, and even their titles were similar. Canadian military uniforms, weapons, organization, training, and administration were all based on the British model. Canadian divisions were commanded initially by British officers on the divisional staffs. There was a deep attachment in Canada to the British monarch, and it was generally realized that Britain's strength was Canada's.

No man enjoyed the train journey across southern England to Shorncliffe more than Pearkes. He was home again, and much as he had enjoyed the foothills of the Rockies and the wilderness of the Yukon, the sight of the English countryside brought on a wave of nostalgia. At Shorncliffe, the 2nd C.M.R. was marched to Caesar's Hill South, a section of the large area dotted with the tent lines of various Canadian regiments. Here the unit was to train until it would be ordered to France, but before serious work began, a week's disembarkation leave was given to all ranks. For Pearkes it meant the opportunity to see his relatives in London and Watford, to wander through the grounds at Berkhamsted, and to renew old friendships.

The training at Shorncliffe was neither all cavalry nor all infantry but a mixture. Their horses and saddlery were not taken overseas, and while in camp the 2nd C.M.R. had frustrating experiences. Some weeks after their arrival horses were brought in but no saddlery. The squadrons had been taken on numerous route marches on foot, but with the horses they could travel much further afield, even bareback. A short time later the horses were taken away, and then several hundred saddles arrived. The men were set to work cleaning and polishing the leather in happy anticipation that there soon would be horses to put the saddles on. Horses and saddles did get together for only a short time, then both were taken from the unit leaving them with only their spurs and "cavalry style" puttees[7] as distinguishing marks.

Not long after the horses were withdrawn, Pearkes was sent on special duty for a few weeks at the main Shorncliffe camp as an instructor. At that time all the senior infantry officers were mounted, and many of the officers coming from the city needed practice in equitation. Owing to his experience and education, Pearkes was sent to teach them some of the finer points of horsemanship. Since the school provided the mounts and he was an instructor, he not only did not have to attend to stables when the bugle went, but he could also sew on a spur over his chevrons and anticipate a pay raise to the $1.10 per diem of a corporal.

The training the unit received at Caesar's Camp was fairly basic and instruction was comparatively simple. There were numerous route marches through the Kentish countryside to make the men physically fit, and the miles went by all the easier when the troops sang popular marching songs. Great emphasis was placed on musketry as well. The Ross rifle was an excellent target rifle under camp conditions where the weapon could be kept clean and the rate of fire moderate. The combination of rapid fire and dirt in trench warfare, however, made the rifle jam and the bolt would not open. It took months to convince the Minister of Militia, Colonel Sam Hughes, that the British Lee-Enfield was a much better rifle for trench warfare. Fortunately for the 2nd C.M.R., they were able to turn in their rifles to have the chambers reamed out before they went to France.[8]

Aside from marching and musketry, there were lectures on such things as sanitation, map reading, and organization. There was also instruction in gas warfare, an ugly innovation introduced to the Western Front by the Germans in April 1915. All the men were issued with gas masks, primitive hoods which completely covered the head with two round "windows" for the eyes and a nose clip. These awkward contraptions were to be improved upon steadily during the course of the war, but considering the fate of those who had first suffered the effects of chlorine gas in France, everyone was anxious to learn about them.

Pearkes was especially interested in the training with bombs. Trench warfare had become stabilized during the winter of 1914-15, and in many parts the front line trenches were very close. The supply of Mills grenades at this time was very limited, so the troops were taught to improvise with homemade bombs which they termed "Tickler's Artillery." The container for the bomb was usually a tin can which, when emptied of Tickler's plum-and-apple jam, was especially suitable. One or two one-ounce gun-cotton primers would be placed in the centre of the can, and around them would be packed any bits of metal available, the contents being tamped tight with clay. A detonator would be inserted in the primer, and a few strands of wire were wound about the can to help hold the contents together. Into the primer would be stuck a short length of fuse, timed to explode five seconds or less after it was lit. There was quite a trick to throwing it, and Pearkes became expert. He describes the method in these words:

> You held the tin can in the flat of your hand and you bowled it at a target, the theory being that if you threw it, which meant a bent elbow, you would not be able to keep up a sustained throwing for a long time. It was easier to bowl it with a stiff elbow. Now that was all right for a cricketer but for the average Canadian—well, he wasn't accustomed to bowling, so it took quite some time before our men got accustomed to

bowling the ball. You had to have it in the flat of your hand so that, when you released it, it rotated in the air rather than spinning over and over. . . . If it span there was a great fear that the detonator would fall out.

You judged the time [of the fuse burning] so that it would explode the moment it hit the ground or the enemy's trench, which after all was only throwing distance away . . . . At Shorncliffe we were not so concerned with using live bombs. We were using dummy bombs . . . filled with clay. You had a target to aim at . . . and there were competitions as to who could get the most into that target area. You had to get the idea of height so you threw either from a trench or behind a screen which represented the trench parapet.[9]

With this general type of training, together with a good portion of foot and arms drill, Pearkes and his comrades were considered ready for France. There were no manoeuvres on a brigade scale and few, if any, on a battalion level. Since trench warfare had set in and advances were considered in hundreds of yards rather than in miles, probably the authorities felt large-scale manoeuvres unnecessary. Although the men were physically fit, they were by no means hardened. There was very little training in laying out barbed wire, for it was felt to be a job for the engineers. More important, there was hardly any instruction in getting through it, and it was only later that sufficient wire cutters were issued to each platoon. Although there were lectures on patrolling, there was insufficient practice in it, particularly at night. The same held true for planning and carrying out raids. There was ample bayonet practice, but aside from his personal weapons, little thought was given to training the soldier to use and fire other weapons. Machine guns, for example, were considered weapons for experts.

Generally, the battalion was trained for the defensive rather than the offensive. The men would be able to give a very good account of themselves in holding a trench but would require further instruction before they could take an enemy position. Early in September, word went around that the brigade was to be part of Maj.-Gen. Turner's 2nd Division, and the orders came quickly enough. The regiment sailed for France on 22 September.

The trip to Boulogne took only a few hours, and then the units marched to a transit camp. On the following day the 2nd C.M.R. made its first acquaintance with French troop railway cars carrying the notice: "Eight Horses or Forty Men." From the dirt it was assumed that the last occupants had been horses, but dirty, crowded, and uncomfortable as they were, the men's morale was high. They were on the way to the front.

That evening the unit reached Bailleul, a town of several thousands which had only been battered slightly in the first months of the war.

Pearkes was among those billetted in a convent. In the next few days they had an opportunity to look over the town. Bailleul was popular with the Belgian and French soldiers as well as the British. To Pearkes, the Belgian and French soldiers seemed poorly turned out. The Belgians had a dark brown uniform, and the French wore pale blue overcoats and black puttees. Their officers, in contrast, were smartly dressed. He was also struck by the civilians. The only young men were obviously casualties, men who had lost an arm or a leg. Women and older men looked after the business of the town, whether it was serving rather weak beer in the estaminets or trying to work the farms in the neighbourhood.

A few days after their arrival, the 2nd C.M.R. was moved to the Ploegsteert area where it was to get its first taste of warfare by relieving a dismounted regiment of the Canadian Cavalry Brigade, at this time operating under the command of the 1st Division as infantry.[10] To initiate the new battalion, a number of 2nd C.M.R. officers and N.C.O.'s went into the line to learn the routine of the trenches. Among those selected was Cpl. Pearkes, and he remembered it vividly many years later.

> One's first impression was that of a thrill. You were there in the front line, nobody between you and the enemy . . . . Bullets whined over your head, shells occasionally went back and forth—it was a quiet front . . . . At the early dawn of a September morn with a certain amount of mist about, it was eerie. During the night there had been some Very lights going up. There was a sort of strangeness to it all which, at the same time, keyed one up and I was excited. . . .
>
> I think the main thing which we learned was the routine of the trenches—the stand-to at dawn and in the evening, the need for most of the men to be alert all night. One or two men in each bay would be watching as sentries . . . . Work had to be done in the way of draining the trenches, repairing boardwalks, filling sand bags, repairing where the parapet or parados had been hit by a shell . . . .
>
> Units in the line had to report each day the number of enemy shells that landed in their area. This gave the staff information about any build-up of enemy artillery on the front. There was always the possibility of a raid and there was always a certain amount of patrolling out in No-Man's-Land . . . . There was always the thought of enemy deserters coming over . . . and then we were on the lookout for our own patrols when they went out.[11]

The thrill Pearkes felt in his initial visit to the front line came as a result of the nearness of the enemy, but as the months wore on what was new and exciting became old and routine. Since he was to live in this military atmosphere until 1918, however, it might be well to examine more carefully the organization and operation of the 2nd C.M.R. at the front, for although there were changes in location and method, some generalizations hold true for the entire period.

Trench warfare had been imposed on both sides during the fall of 1914, and by the winter of 1914-15 mobile warfare had ended. From the English Channel to the border of Switzerland two trench systems scarred Belgium and France. Between them, at distances varying from a few yards to a hundred or more was No-Man's-Land, a shell-pocked killing ground strewn with the debris of war. In front of each trench, hung on wooden stakes or iron rods, was barbed wire. It varied in depth from one or two strands to ten or twenty feet, and in height from three to five feet. Subjected to the weather and the pounding of artillery and mortar shells as well as small arms fire, it frequently needed replacement in part or in whole. It was the last physical barrier to coming to grips with the enemy, and it could impose a disastrous delay on the attackers.

The trenches themselves varied according to terrain, the water level, the degree of observation enjoyed by the enemy, and other factors. Generally speaking, they were dug to a depth which would permit a soldier to walk along them upright without exposing his head. Where possible they were wide enough to permit soldiers to pass one another. Sandbags formed a parapet and parados in front of and behind the trench. Ideally the trenches were revetted with corrugated iron, brush-work, or other items to prevent the walls from crumbling under the impact of enemy fire or rainy weather. Sandbagged trench walls were common, but much depended on the material available and enemy activity. Whatever revetment was used, constant work was needed to keep them in repair. On the enemy side of the trench, in the firing bays which the trenches connected, was the firing step. This was several feet wide and permitted the soldier to fire over the parapet during an attack or to observe No-Man's-Land when the front was quiet. Snipers prevented any but the foolhardy from exposing his head in daytime. Observation might be done from a slit between sandbags, a crude trench periscope, or perhaps some camouflaged position which permitted an enfilade view.

Each bay contained several men and was only a few yards from the next one. It was in essence an enlarged section of the trench. Here, dug into the sides of the walls, were what were usually called "funk holes." Here the soldier received his rations, slept, wrote home, cursed the war, cleared the lice from the seams of his tunic, cleaned his weapon, washed and shaved, performed "sentry-go" or "stand-to," played cards, joked with his comrades, and often fought desperately for his life. As the area was usually open to the weather, he used his ingenuity to keep comfortable. An iron bucket, punched with holes and containing a small supply of coke, was his hearth, stove, and kitchen. His ability to construct small but useful items from jam tins, wire, a few boards, a shell casing, and the bits and pieces of material available was truly remarkable. Hanging from the trench walls would be his equipment, trench tools, signal wire, and a variety of items ranging from an empty shell case which was struck to warn of a gas attack to boxes containing extra ammunition. His rifle and bayonet were always within arm's reach, and his gas mask was rarely much farther away.

Usually an infantry battalion had two companies in the front line trench and two more in the support trench situated a short distance from the front line and connected to it by communication trenches. Behind the support trench would be battalion headquarters. Here one would find the commanding officer, his adjutant, and a small headquarters staff consisting of runners, signallers, and one or two clerks. Well behind the front were the unit's cooks, quartermaster stores, and regimental aid post where duties did not require them to be at the front. In this area, often termed the "transport" or "horse" lines, rations would be made up on a company basis and taken to a designated spot where company carriers would pick them up. Usually each platoon would have a sandbag filled with bread and jam, cheese and bully-beef, or perhaps the cooks might be able to send up a dixie filled with hot stew. With the rations would come extra ammunition, the rum issue, mail, and perhaps a few reinforcements.

There was a marked difference between night and daytime activity in the trenches. Generally, once the sun went down, there would be a great deal to do. It was under the cover of darkness that patrols slipped into No-Man's-Land. Some were ambush patrols, some were fighting patrols, some listening patrols—there were many types, and their size and equipment depended on their purpose. Night was also the time to repair the barbed wire, to dig trenches, and in general to carry out work that, if observed by the enemy, would result in either shell or machine-gun fire. The movement of troops, the relief of companies, the activities of the work parties, and so on came to a halt with daylight. This was a time to get some sleep or rest. It was a time, too, when there might be visits by staff officers. These did not occur too often, and when they came they were often referred to as "birds of ill omen," for their visits frequently preceded an attack, either by the Canadians or the enemy.

Fortunately, the 2nd C.M.R. was not involved in the battle of Loos which raged between 25 September and 4 November, exacting over a quarter of a million French and British casualties for a gain of some two or three miles. During this period the battalion was in and out of the front near Messines, taking complete responsibility for a section of the front line for the first time. It was a quiet sector, but the trenches were in very poor shape. After a gruelling march past Dickibusch along a road ankle-deep in mud, the unit entered the line described by the regimental historian in these words:

> The sector . . . was flat, with the water close to the surface. As a result, the defences were built chiefly above ground, with very shallow trenches dug down; the shelters also, such as they were, consisting generally of a sheet of corrugated iron and a layer of sandbags for headcover . . . and these, though furnishing a certain amount of shelter from the weather, gave but little protection from the lightest kind of shelling.[12]

This was only the beginning of the men's experience with the sodden Flanders winter. Trenches filled with water and roads were ground into muddy tracks. Unremitting work was required to keep the front-line defences in decent condition.

It was not until the early part of December, when the unit was still on the Messines front, that Pearkes had his first taste of close action. The battalion had taken over a stretch of muddy trenches on the left of the road leading to Messines on 28 November. Almost every day the enemy's artillery battered the trenches. Countermeasures by the artillery supporting the Canadians were limited owing to a scarcity of shells, so the Mounted Rifles did their best to strafe the Germans with rifle and machine-gun fire. This evidently had some effect, for by 3 December a roadblock some 150 yards distant had been reinforced with sandbags. This news brought an order for the roadblock to be destroyed that night. There was no time for those in the two attacking parties, including Pearkes, to reconnoitre, but the attempt had to be made. Just before dawn one group reached a wire entanglement close to the enemy position, and the Germans began to lob "potato masher" grenades at them. The loss of the element of surprise, the explosions, and the difficulty in gathering up the two sections to assault the barrier made the officers in charge of the fighting patrol decide to return. Pearkes and the other bombers hurled their bombs in the general direction of the barrier before they retired. "Perhaps if we had been more seasoned troops," Pearkes later reflected, "and had had more opportunity of preparing an attack on it we'd have done better." Although personally reluctant to be ordered back without having come to grips with the enemy, he realized the folly of an assault under existing conditions. The mud-caked patrol which slipped back into their own trenches bringing two wounded men with them may not have achieved their objective, but they had more than made up for it in the experience they gained.

Later in the month the regiment was informed it would be converted to infantry and have four companies rather than three squadrons. In Pearkes's company, someone suggested that the changeover should be fittingly marked. When relieved from the front line, therefore, the company sergeant major paraded the men to an empty field and there the troopers took off their spurs and buried them in the ground. It was treated as a joke, of course, but everyone there carried out the "parade" with suitable decorum.

Infantry battalions had a bombing platoon at this time, and Lt. M. V. McGuire was ordered to form such a platoon within the enlarged battalion. Pearkes had had some experience, and the excitement of the job made him welcome the opportunity to join McGuire's new subunit. He was sent to take a course at the Second Army Bombing School near Casselles, and although the course lasted only a few weeks, his proficiency resulted in Pearkes being retained at the school as an instructor for several months.

Here Pearkes received excellent instruction in trench warfare. At the school he came in contact with British, Canadian, French, and Belgian officers and N.C.O.'s from a great variety of regiments whose experience stretched back to the retreat from Mons. Although Pearkes had become an expert with bombs and taught the officers all he knew about them, he learned a great deal about offensive fighting. There were lectures, with maps and models, of some of the early trench raids by officers who had taken part in them, and heavy emphasis was placed on prior organization and reconnaissance, the supply of bombs, and accuracy. A sort of carpenter's apron was made for the bomber. The plan or drill for carrying out a bombing mission is best described by Pearkes himself:

> The organization was a . . . combination of bayonet men proceeding around the various bays and traverses of the trench . . . to be attacked. Two bayonet men preceded the first thrower [who] was protected from a sudden rush or counter-attack by the enemy coming down the trench. The practice was to throw a couple of bombs into the two bays in front of you and as soon as they exploded the bayonet men rushed forward followed by the first thrower and one or two . . . men carrying sand bags with bombs. As soon as he threw his bombs, the bayonet men went down the trench and reported it clear. Then the thrower moved up . . . and repeated the process. When he got tired or his supply of bombs was expended, then another . . . [second] thrower would come up and relieve him . . . . There were spare bayonet men if a bayonet man . . . had to be replaced. There was also a commander of the squad who directed the thrower . . . rather like an artillery observer. The second half of the squad was responsible for dealing

with any deep dugouts . . . and with any prisoners which were taken . . . .

In a small bombing raid you would have perhaps three bombing squads—one to go to the right, one to the left and one to go up any communication trench and establish a block. You could figure more or less that if you put two bombs into two bays ahead of you and perhaps one into the traverse, that you would be using up perhaps eight bombs before you could make any advance at all . . . . The supply of bombs went pretty quickly at any distance . . . one or two hundred yards of trench was about as far as you could go.[13]

The "battle drill" which emerged from the school was both systematic and sound. Pearkes was to put what he learned to good use in the near future.

During January and February, 1916, the 2nd C.M.R.'s were reorganized as an infantry battalion, receiving an additional two hundred men to bring them up to strength. It had been in and out of the trenches near Bailleul,[14] and shortly before it went into the Ypres salient, Pearkes was posted back to the unit to be a sergeant in Lt. McGuire's bombing squad. When the battalion went into the salient, it entered one of the most sensitive and active sectors of the Western Front. The Mounted Rifles took up positions on either side of the Menin road near Hooge, and the bombing squad found itself charged with the duty of holding a series of trench posts including the remains of the Hooge stables.

Bombing and counterbombing attacks during the night climaxed on the evening of 24–25 March. The Canadians were at a considerable disadvantage, for not only were the Germans higher, but they had also erected a high wire fence. In Pearkes's section only one man, Pte. Percy Smith, was strong enough to hurl bombs over the fence. All others hit it and bounced away. Smith's ability annoyed the enemy and they decided on a night attack. One German bomb landed right inside the Canadian post and Pte. F. H. Vaughan, shouted a warning, seized it, but it exploded while he was throwing it out. The others were saved from serious injury, but Vaughan died. The next day another raid was beaten back, but in the mêlée a German grenade exploded close to Pearkes, who received eight small pieces of shrapnel in his left arm and four more in his head. He was evacuated to No. 1 Canadian General Hospital at Etaples, but within a week he was discharged. The unit was about to be relieved, and while they were moving through Ypres a German shell fell among a group of officers and men killing some and severely wounding others. Among the latter was Lt. McGuire, the bombing officer. Thus, when Pearkes returned he had sole command of the bombers. As a sergeant he was well liked and respected by his men, and his ability to lead them in battle had been noted by Lt.-Col. Bott. His background and education qualified him for a commission, and late in April the commanding officer brought him before the brigade and then the divisional commander recommending that he be made a temporary lieutenant. Both senior officers, after interviewing him, agreed that he should be commissioned "in the field," and as there was no one better qualified to command the battalion bombers, Temporary Lieutenant Pearkes was appointed in McGuire's place.[15]

During the next few weeks the battalion served in the front line at Sanctuary Wood and Hooge. Although there were no major attacks, the snipers and bombers were kept busy, for the trenches, at times, were very close. To increase the range of the "jam tin" or Mills grenades, several ingenious contraptions had been devised. One was the "Gamage Catapult," which resembled a large sling-shot. The bombers would put a grenade instead of a stone in the pad. Another, rather heavier, device, resembled a medieval catapult and threw the grenade up in a great looping arch when the tension on the throwing arm was released. More accurate were several types of rifle grenades, which had the additional advantage of being simple, light, and easily adaptable.

The toughest fighting was when the enemy raided the Canadian trenches. Pearkes was in the midst of repelling one of these frequent raids when he was wounded once more. The first sign of the enemy presence was the loud explosion of bursting "potato bomb" grenades. The riflemen brought their fire on them, and Pearkes was quickly on the scene leading his bombers. Once again a German bomb exploded near him. This time a jagged piece of the wooden handle struck him so hard close to his eye that it entered his temple, sticking out like a horn. He was stunned and almost blinded with blood. The enemy was beaten back, and once more Pearkes was evacuated to a hospital, this time to Boulogne. Here the doctors wanted to evacuate him to England, but Pearkes protested that the wound was not that bad, lied somewhat about the discomfort it was causing him, and persuaded the medical staff that he should be allowed to remain in France. He was anxious, as usual, to return to his comrades at the front. His recent command of the bombers was another factor. He felt his duty was with them, "the best bunch of boys I have ever run across,"[16] and whereas most soldiers would have welcomed a "Blighty,"[17] Pearkes looked upon it as an irritating event.

In one way, however, it was fortunate he was hospitalized for the next two weeks, for during that time the 8th Brigade suffered severe casualties in and about Mount Sorrel. On 5 June, the day before Pearkes returned, the entire brigade paraded with only seven hundred all ranks. The 2nd Canadian Mounted Rifles had lost 50 per cent of its fighting strength, and Pearkes returned to a battalion composed of large numbers of reinforcements. For the next several weeks, therefore, great emphasis was placed on training, interspersed with sports. The competition he and his men gave to the rifle companies made it obvious that he was physically in fine shape and as aggressive on the sports field as he was in battle.

As a sergeant Pearkes had been restricted to carrying out the orders of his superior. As a bombing officer responsible directly to Lt.-Col. Bott, he was given more leeway in decisions and arrangements. When the battalion went back into the line in July near Sanctuary Wood, No-Man's-Land consisted of shell-splintered stumps and trees, shell holes, mounds of grass-covered debris, and the usual clutter of the battlefield. The smell of death was everywhere, and daily bodies, both German and Canadian, were un-covered as new trenches were built to replace the battered lines caused by the earlier fighting. On this front all units were more aggressive, deter-mined to dominate No-Man's-Land by day and by night. Pearkes took a number of patrols out between the lines, crawling on his stomach most of the time, listening for the enemy and ready for them should they be en-countered.

On 25 July he and his sergeant, C. K. Douglas, located an enemy listen-ing post in an old communication trench running out from the German lines. About twenty-five yards from their front they had blocked the trench with sandbags, and during the night Germans would crawl out and occupy it, ready to bring fire on any Canadian patrols. This presented a challenge, and Pearkes decided to take it up. Observation indicated that the post was unoccupied in daylight, so he decided to go out during the day, pack an explosive charge under the sandbagged barrier, and then go out again at night and blow it up. Moreover, Pearkes "thought it would be rather a joke, not having any other explosives, if we blew the German [post] up with German explosives."[18] They opened a cache of captured enemy gre-nades, extracted the explosive, and packed it into an ammunition box. The two men deposited this deadly parcel on a daylight patrol. That night, when they inserted the detonator and fuse, the fuse was found defective. This was as exasperating as it was dangerous. The next night, therefore, they went out again. The Germans were on the other side of the sandbags, and, as Pearkes said later, "we had no right to get away with it." As Pearkes stealthily inserted the detonator into the explosive almost under the rifle barrels of the German sentries, Sgt. Douglas crouched a few yards behind him, a revolver in either hand. If they were discovered, they planned to leap into the enemy post, revolvers blazing. Pearkes slowly backed away, paying out the fuse, until he and Douglas reached the cover of a shell hole. Within a few minutes the entire listening post was blown sky-high. The Germans soon began to bombard the Canadian trench oppo-site their post's location. Pearkes and Douglas, expecting this action, remained in No-Man's-Land until things had quietened down, then crawled back. They were pleased with themselves, but not terribly popular with the men in "C" company working on repairs to their parapet. Both men were recommended for decorations for this audacious piece of work, but none was granted.[19]

Two days later the battalion was relieved and went into support at Ypres. This old medieval city was well within reach of the enemy's artillery, and shelling occurred daily. Battalion headquarters, to which Pearkes was attached, had billets in the casernes of the old wall which gave good protection, but the companies located in the old Belgian cavalry barracks were less fortunate. Parts of the city, such as the major road crossing nicknamed "Hellfire Corner," were more dangerous than the front line under normal circumstances, but at least being in support one could enjoy briefly the rough comforts found away from the trenches.

In mid-August Pearkes left the 2nd Canadian Mounted Rifles on his appointment as brigade bombing officer to the 8th Canadian Infantry Brigade. Here he was responsible to Brig. Gen. J. H. Elmsley for the training of all the bombers in the brigade. Pearkes was not one to use his new status to remain behind the front line. While there was fighting to be done, he felt it his duty to be in the thick of it with his bombers, but the better the bombers were trained, the more casualties they would inflict and the fewer they would suffer.

He was with brigade headquarters only a few weeks when he was at the front again. The Battle of the Somme raged during July and August. By the end of August, when the Canadians were ordered to relieve the 1st Anzac Corps near Pozières, British and French casualties had mounted to over a quarter of a million. What had been planned as a major attack to crack the German line had changed to a bloody battering when the enemy attacked the French at Verdun. To relieve the pressure on the French and to inflict heavy losses on the Germans, Sir Douglas Haig, the British Commander-in-Chief, had poured in division after division. Tens of thousands of shells beat down trees and houses and churned up the earth. Although some gains had been made, the Germans had established behind their original front a series of strong lines with deep tunnels, reinforced dugouts reaching thirty to forty feet underground, and wide belts of barbed wire. Camouflaged machine-gun nests, many strengthened with concrete, took their toll of the waves of men who stormed their trenches. Despite the losses and limited gains, Haig decided to renew the attack in mid-September and called upon the Canadian Corps to take over a section of the front north of Pozieres where the enemy was defending Courcelette and Thiepval.

The 8th Canadian Infantry Brigade was the first to enter the line on the 3rd Division's front. The brigade's task was to protect the left flank of the neighbouring 2nd Division when it attacked Courcelette. Southwest of

Courcelette the 8th Brigade was to seize a line of German trenches which had as its anchor Moquet Farm. On 14 September, three days after the 8th Brigade had taken over their section of the front line, orders for the attack were received from Maj.-Gen. Lipsett. The bombers in all the battalions were to have their work cut out for them, for the network of German trenches which the two assaulting battalions were to seize meant that the bombing platoons would be active in every phase of the operation.

Pearkes had the overall responsibility for supplies of bombs, for helping the battalion commanders with reinforcements, and, in general, for assisting the unit bombers. With about twenty bombers under his own command, he was located in a chalk pit some three hundred yards from the farm which formed part of the front line of the 1st C.M.R.

Early on the morning of the fifteenth the attack went in behind a barrage of shells. On the right the German trenches were seized, but on the left the 1st C.M.R. could reach no further than Moquet Farm. This pushed the Canadian front forward, but at the same time exposed the brigade's left flank to severe enfilade fire. Later in the day a renewed attack on the right gained further ground, while on the left the 2nd C.M.R. came forward to relieve the 1st around Moquet Farm. So far, except on the left, the attack had gone well. Casualties were heavy, and during the day, as Pearkes led his group to the advanced positions, he lost a number of men as they raced over the open ground where communication trenches had not yet been dug. It was literally a case of running for one's life over a stretch of two hundred yards, loaded with a case of Mills bombs, reminiscent in a sense of the field manoeuvres he had had with the cadet corps at school. The grim realities of the shell and machine-gun fire, however, made him and those around him concentrate on the one job he had in mind—get the bombs up, for every one was needed to help beat back the enemy counterattacks.

During the evening of 15–16 September the two forward battalions were subjected to heavy artillery fire as they worked to dig trenches. On the left the 2nd C.M.R.'s under the command of Maj. W. W. Foster, pushed out saps to encircle Moquet Farm and established posts within bombing range. The farm by this time was little more than mounds of debris, but it had been prepared as a strongpoint weeks beforehand. Deep dugouts with tunnels leading to them had been dug, and a network of tunnels and trenches enabled the enemy to take shelter during the Canadian barrage and then emerge with rifles and machine guns to cut down the advancing infantry. This fortified rabbit warren, which could be reinforced from the north through tunnels and trenches leading back to Zollern Redoubt, stuck out into the 8th Brigade's lines, and on the sixteenth the 2nd C.M.R.'s were ordered to eliminate it.

On the evening of the sixteenth Pearkes was forward with Foster, and as the 2nd C.M.R. worked their way forward by bombing and sapping on either flank, Pearkes was asked to reconnoitre behind the farm. Taking a patrol of three bombers with him, he left the forward sap on the right and crawled out into No-Man's-Land. Fortunately, although he found one German trench which could connect the two "horns" of the 2nd C.M.R. front, there were no enemy in it. The patrol crossed behind the front and contacted the battalion's left flank, and Pearkes was able to show the working parties where to dig to encircle the strongpoint.

Meanwhile, the 2nd C.M.R. companies had entered the area of the farm itself and, using bombs and bayonets, had cleared the enemy's trenches. By this time, slightly after midnight, the relieving battalion from the Dorset Regiment was coming into the line. The Canadians had had numerous casualties; there was confusion as the men tried to orient themselves in the new area, everyone who could worked furiously to connect the trenches, since they knew they would be targets for enemy fire at dawn; and as a consequence Foster did not have the men to probe through the tunnels into the dugouts under the farm. The enemy still occupied the positions, however, and when Pearkes reported to Foster he told him he had seen flares and heard shots at the entrance to one of the tunnels.[20]

Since the commander of the relieving British battalion was reluctant to accept a takeover of trenches which encircled an underground nest of Germans, Foster asked Pearkes to deal with them. Pearkes gathered up a dozen bombers, a good supply of Mills bombs, and several boxes of large Stokes mortar bombs and returned. By working over the debris methodically they located the tunnel entrances. Shouts down the tunnel for the enemy to surrender brought few results, and several Mills bombs hurled into the dark openings had little effect. Pearkes then threw several of the larger mortar bombs into the openings, bringing down the entrance and sealing it off. Working from the north Pearkes and his party sealed every opening, eliminating the last enemy position on the brigade front. It was almost dawn by the time he reported back to Maj. Foster, but the job was completed, the Dorsets secure in the trenches immediately north of the farm. If anyone deserved a double rum ration that morning it was Pearkes.

5

For Most Conspicuous Bravery

The gains made on the 8th Brigade front had been won at considerable cost. During the few days of fighting an estimated 860 casualties, both dead and wounded, had been suffered by the four battalions.[1] The 5th Canadian Mounted Rifles, which had born the brunt of the attack, suffered heavy losses among the officers. When the brigade went into support on the seventeenth its commanding officer, Lt.-Col. D. C. Draper, reported to Brig. Gen. Elmsley that he needed replacements for eleven officers. It was perhaps at this time that Elmsley recommended Pearkes to take command of a company. As brigade bombing officer he was known to both, and his leadership qualities were unquestionable. In any event Draper agreed to try him in an acting capacity, and on 27 September Pearkes found himself in command of "C" Company, 5th C.M.R.

The "Fighting Fifth" came from the Eastern Townships of Quebec and were a rather different group from the 2nd C.M.R. Initially Pearkes found the new unit a bit strange. A good proportion of the men were French-Canadian, while most of the remainder were of United Empire Loyalist stock. Draper ("Daddy Draper" as he was nicknamed), a gentleman farmer from Brome County in the Eastern Townships, combined a commanding personality with a no-nonsense approach to his job. Pearkes was the only officer from Western Canada to come to the unit, and possibly had the brigade not been in the midst of the Somme fighting, there might have been some jealousy about his assuming command of a company. As it was the brigade was soon to be recommitted to the attack, and the 5th C.M.R. was to be more than proud of the young officer from Western Canada.

On 18 September, when the 1st Division relieved the 3rd, all of the Canadian Mounted Rifles battalions needed a rest period to make up their losses in men and equipment. Most of the companies were down to half strength, and all were weary from constant fighting, lack of sleep, and the strain of battle. For the next twelve days, therefore, they were out of the line but not beyond the reach of the enemy's heavy guns. Moreover, even in "rest" the men were called upon for working parties to repair trenches, roads, wire entanglements, and so forth during the night, and there was a steady dribble of casualties.

The battle of the Somme, however, was by no means over nor was the Canadians' part in it. On the twenty-fifth the British Fourth Army, after a thirty-hour bombardment, launched a major attack and gained two thousand yards. This made it necessary to bring up the front of the army reserves in the Thiepval-Courcelette area. The British Second Corps was ordered to clear the enemy from the east of the Pozières ridge, while on the right the Canadian Corps was to push forward along an area stretching from Moquet Farm to a position north of Courcelette. Initially the Canadian attack was to be launched by the 1st and 2nd Divisions against a triple line of enemy trenches. The first and nearest was Zollern Graben, the second was Hessian Trench, and the third strong line, just over the crest, was Regina Trench. These trench systems, fortified by strong redoubts, had been prepared by the enemy weeks previously. On the outskirts of each system were one or more belts of heavy barbed wire entanglements, ten to fifteen feet wide, and sometimes strengthened by concertina wire. The trenches themselves were deep, and some of the German trenches the Canadians now occupied had dugouts reaching forty, fifty, and more feet underground. Even in front of Courcelette there was strong evidence of the enemy's confidence in his ability to retain his position, for on the fifteenth, when the 5th C.M.R. captured their objective, they found the German trenches "well stocked with food, wines, liqueurs, cigars and cigarettes, and large quantities of bombs, rifles and . . . ammunition."[2] The low, rolling hills and comparatively dry weather left the trench walls firm and strong. The lines to be assaulted, therefore, were considered formidable obstacles, a conservative estimate as it turned out.

On 26 September eight hundred guns and howitzers roared out to announce the Canadian offensive. The defenders ran into their dugouts or went forward of their own lines to take up positions in shell holes to await the assaulting Canadians. During the day the 1st and 2nd Divisions were engaged in some of the heaviest fighting they had encountered, but stubborn enemy resistance and counterattacks prevented complete success. On the following day the corps commander ordered them to continue the attack. During the night, on the right sector, the enemy withdrew to Regina Trench, but on the left, where the 1st Division occupied most of Hessian Trench, the German 8th Division not only continued its counterattacks but succeeded in retaking several hundred yards. After forty-eight hours of continuous struggle, much of it in hand-to-hand combat, and suffering from very heavy casualties, the battalions were exhausted, especially those in the 1st Canadian Division. It was time for their relief, and the 8th Canadian Infantry Brigade was ordered to move up.

In the 5th C.M.R. preparations to return to the front had been issued even before the attack. The battalion was in Bouzincourt, about two miles southwest of Thiepval, when the opening barrage had started, and on the twenty-seventh the 5th C.M.R. moved close to their old positions near Courcelette. Two days later the battalion was ordered to move into the front line ready to attack Regina Trench on 1 October. During the evening of the thirtieth, therefore, the companies began to "dribble up" to the sections of the Hessian and Zollern Trenches to relieve the 1st C.M.R. On its left, the 4th C.M.R. was relieving the 2nd C.M.R., while on the right, the 28th Battalion, reduced in strength to about 120 effectives, held grimly to their line of trenches.

The capture of Regina Trench was to be the opening phase in a general push to the north which General Haig had ordered as a continuation of the Somme battle. For the Canadians it was to start what came to be called the Battle for Ancre Heights. The immediate objective of the 5th C.M.R. was Regina Trench, and the method of attack was typical of the difficulties of siege warfare as commonly practised on the Western Front.

The section of the trench to be captured by the 5th C.M.R. was about six hundred yards long and was bisected by the Grandcourt Road. It lay over a low ridge of ground, and in order to see how far the thick barbed wire in front of the trenches had been cut, patrols were sent out on the night of 30 September–1 October. Zero time for the attack was 3:15 P.M. From 3:15 to 3:16 P.M., the artillery was to put an intensive shrapnel barrage one hundred yards in advance of the objective. It would then lift, and for the next three minutes, while the Canadians were advancing over No-Man's-Land, the barrage would fall directly on the German trenches. From 3:19 to 3:22 P.M. the barrage would move one hundred yards further on to play havoc among the enemy's support trenches, after which, for another six minutes, the barrage would fall two hundred yards behind Regina Trench to hammer his reserve positions. For the next half hour, while the field artillery kept up a curtain of fire three hundred yards behind the enemy's trench, the heavy artillery was to engage the roads leading up to Regina Trench as well as Grandcourt Trench which ran approximately parallel to it some one thousand yards further back. Prior to zero hour, the howitzers and heavier artillery were to attempt to cut the wire in front of Regina Trench as well as pound the trench itself and other enemy defensive points.

Within the battalion, the attack would be made by "B" Company on the right and "A" on the left. They would have about 250 yards to reach their objective and would advance in waves or small columns at the discretion

WESTERN FRONT, 1914 - 1918

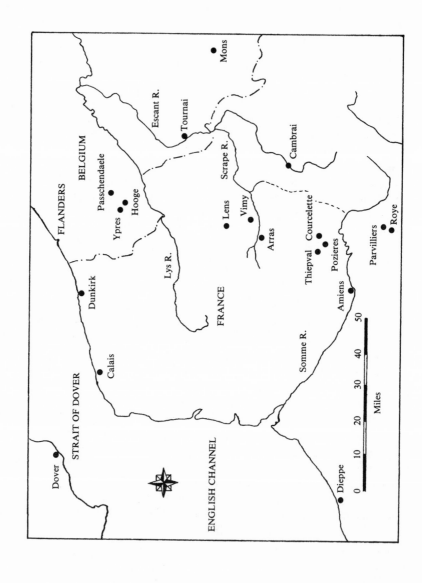

of their company commanders.³ "C" Company, commanded by Lt. Pearkes, would occupy the forward trenches once the two assaulting companies had gone over the top, and "D" Company, close by, was to await orders. Since Pearkes had the most experience among the officers of "C" and "D" Companies, he was put in charge of both—a heavy responsibility since he would have to act on his own judgment as reports came directly to him from the attack before being sent back to Lt.-Col. Draper.

During the morning of 1 October, as the shells from the 4.5″ howitzers and 60-pounder guns whooshed overhead, reports filtered back from the scouts that much of the wire remained uncut.⁴ Early in the afternoon the enemy's guns, which had been active, began to fire in the area where "D" Company (commanded by Lt. Chauvin) was waiting to attack. Within a few minutes the company sergeant-major, most of the N.C.O.'s and the bombing section attached to the company had been wiped out. Pearkes immediately sent a platoon forward from his own company to go into the attack with "D". Shortly after this, at precisely 3:15 P.M., the shrapnel barrage was laid down, and a minute later, all along the brigade front, the Canadians scrambled over the top to the attack.

On the left "A" Company got to within one hundred yards of Regina Trench before the enemy opened up with intense rifle and machine-gun fire, causing heavy casualties. The men pressed forward, and by the time they reached the trench the Germans were fleeing to the rear and were being cut down by Canadian fire. Both officers with this company were casualties, but under the direction of the N.C.O.'s work was started at once to repair the trench. On the right "B" Company was less successful. Only a few reached Regina Trench owing to long belts of uncut wire. Their casualties were also heavy, and those who remained retired to their original positions, reinforced by a platoon from "D" Company. On the left of the battalion, the 4th C.M.R. were experiencing the same tough fighting. One of their companies had been almost wiped out and another, stopped by wire, had great difficulty. Some of the men reached the trench and stayed fighting to retain it to the last man.

During the remainder of the afternoon the fighting on the 4th C.M.R. front began to resemble a mêlée as the men fought tenaciously to beat off enemy counterattacks coming overland as well as enemy bombers trying to roll up the flanks which were still insecure. A captured enemy machine gun helped to beat off some of the attacks. There was a constant call for more bombs and more ammunition, and another platoon of "D" Company was sent up to help secure the section of Regina Trench still held by the 5th C.M.R.

By 5:20 P.M. Pearkes, who was located about mid-way between Zollern and Hessian Trenches, reported back to Draper. "A" Company still hung on to about one hundred yards of Regina Trench and had blocks at either end, but their casualties were mounting as the remainder of "D" Company was sent through the shellfire to help them. On the right "B" Company was in Hessian Trench where it ran close to Regina Trench. Here, too, the casualties were heavy, so a party of fifteen men, including batmen and pioneers, was sent forward to help them. For some time the artillery's light and heavy guns and howitzers had been maintaining a heavy defensive barrage behind Regina Trench, but with both flanks open, the Germans were closing in from either side.

By 6:30 Draper welcomed two platoons from the 2nd C.M.R. and immediately put them under Pearkes's command. Pearkes kept them with him temporarily as a last reserve. Every man was committed to battle, was carrying ammunition and supplies forward, or was digging a communication trench to connect with Regina Trench. Later in the evening, a company from the 1st C.M.R. was sent to Draper, and this group he also sent forward to Pearkes, with an order to use them in a counterattack. Draper's message was brief and to the point. Pearkes was to form a strong fighting patrol from the 5th C.M.R. and company bombers and bomb down Regina Trench some five hundred yards to the original battalion boundary on the right. As the trench was captured, the company of 1st C.M.R. now available would be used to occupy and hold it. Pearkes himself was to have charge of the operation.

At 10:30 P.M. two platoons went forward to Regina Trench with Pearkes, who had visited the front during the daylight. Once in the area, and working under all the difficulties imposed by darkness and the confusion of battle, Pearkes gathered together a group of bombers and two flanking patrols of eight riflemen. Rather than work along the narrow confines of the trench, Pearkes decided to proceed along the top, just outside the parapet. He was in the open and exposed, but darkness gave some cover except for flares. His idea was that the bombers, with himself in the lead, could quickly run up on the parapet, look over to see if any Germans were in the trench, and if so quickly nip back and toss several grenades into their midst. While that part of the trench was being dealt with, another group of bombers with a section of bayonetmen on the other side of the trench would leapfrog forward and take on the next bay. The method was risky, but it worked.

For the next eight hours, even though he was wounded in the leg during the course of the action, Pearkes was in the middle of the fight, leading his men on, encouraging those who lagged, bringing reinforcements up when needed, helping to repel counterattacks, and stirring his exhausted men to further efforts. The group had won 150 yards of trench when it encountered a strong enemy force which drove the bombers back. Under Pearkes's direction, however, the flanking parties and 1st C.M.R. platoons "rushed overland into the trench and beat the enemy back with their bayonets, accounting for quite a number of them."[5] Once again Pearkes reorganized the bombers and led them forward another 500 yards before large numbers of Germans counterattacked and pushed the Canadians back some 200 yards. Here they were held. By this time it was 2:00 A.M., and with the remainder of the 1st C.M.R. platoons now available, Pearkes reorganized his men and again pushed along the trench.[6]

By about 4 A.M. some six hundred yards of Regina Trench was in the hands of the Canadian Mounted Rifles. Pearkes had cleared the trench up to the original right-hand objective and placed a block in the trench, since the trench beyond, the objective of the 24th Battalion, was still held by the enemy. Eighteen unwounded German prisoners had been captured, and many more had been killed or wounded. There were heavy casualties among the Canadians as well, and Pearkes set out to obtain reinforcements. He rounded up ten men from Hessian Trench, ordered the last remaining platoons from the 2nd C.M.R. forward and ordered up about two dozen men from the 8th Trench Mortar Battery with as much bombs and ammunition as they could carry. Before these reinforcements arrived, Pearkes wrote,

> the Germans commenced another counterattack on REGINA trench . . . . Our men hung on . . . until two of our machine-guns had been put out of action and the supply of bombs exhausted. At 7 A.M. the position became untenable and our men retired in good order, bringing the majority of wounded out. The reinforcements arrived a few minutes too late to retain the trench which had been so stubbornly held. I took immediate steps to hold HESSIAN trench and by 8:35 A.M. the situation was again normal.[7]

During the remainder of the day Pearkes, one of the few surviving officers, remained at the front. During the afternoon a furious bombardment began on the right and started to spread towards the 5th C.M.R. lines, so Pearkes asked for a heavy barrage on Regina Trench on his front. Only a small enemy attack was made, and this was beaten back before the battalion was relieved that evening by the Royal Canadian Regiment.

After thirty-four hours of continuous fighting the 5th C.M.R. was bone weary. Their losses had been heavy with 4 officers and 46 other ranks killed and 6 officers and 168 other ranks wounded, or almost half the strength of the battalion in the line. Among the walking wounded was Pearkes, who went to the Casualty Clearing Station only when the unit was relieved. Rarely had a new company commander holding a subaltern's rank[8] had such responsibility thrust on him, and never did Pearkes's qualities of leadership shine more brightly than in that confused mêlée at Regina Trench.

Although the 5th C.M.R. was not committed to another attack in the Somme area, other brigades in the Canadian Corps launched another major attack against Regina Trench on 8 October. The results were the same. By mid-October, therefore, with the weather turning cold and wet, most of the exhausted, shrunken battalions were withdrawn and moved north to a quieter sector in the Arras-Lens district. The Battle of the Somme had some weeks to go before General Haig called a halt. Before this was done the 4th Canadian Infantry Division captured Regina Trench. In the fighting since June the British suffered about 400,000 casualties.[9] Of this number 24,000 were Canadian. In the winter months which followed, the Canadian Corps, although holding down part of the front, was to rest and recuperate.

In the area around Vimy, between Lens and Arras, Pearkes got to know the officers and men in his new regiment, and they, him. He had established his reputation as a courageous and determined officer in the Somme. As a former "ranker" himself he had an appreciation and sympathy for the men under him, yet at the same time he demanded that his N.C.O.'s and men should be as thoroughly trained for battle as possible. One N.C.O. in his company wrote later the following impression of him at this time:

> As a commander and leader of men he proved to me he had no fear whatsoever and I would follow him anywhere. I was one of the first men in our company to go on patrol in no-man's-land with him, and got to the enemy's front-line barbed wire and we could hear the Germans talking. I felt safe with him.
>
> He was also a generous officer by giving money as prizes in sports and to Section N.C.Os. for the best warfare training while out for a rest. He has offered to carry a man's pack while the man rode his horse on a route march from one town to another . . . . This was the kind of an officer he was.[10]

Now that he was responsible for four platoons rather than one, Maj. Pearkes had more administrative work to do, and he found himself attending more conferences at battalion headquarters with Lt.-Col. Draper. Pearkes learned much from him and from Capt. Rhoades, the adjutant, who had been a former regimental sergeant major in the Royal Canadian Dragoons.

If Pearkes had a considerable amount to learn, he also had much to teach. Owing to the heavy casualties at the Somme, almost half of the

Plate 9. Shorncliffe Camp, Kent, where Pearkes and the other members of his unit trained between their arrival in June 1915 and their departure for France a few months later.

Plate 10. Loos, France, 1917. Constant shelling and close-fought battles destroyed the villages, farms, and fields of northern France.

Plate 11. Preparing to go over the top during The Battle of The Somme, 1916.

Plate 12. No-Man's-Land, The Somme, 1916.

officers and men in his company were new to the unit. Trench routine usually meant six days duty in the front line, six in support, and six in reserve. In this area of the front the Canadians were frequently very close to the German lines—sometimes as close as fifty yards. No-Man's-Land was dotted with huge, water-filled craters, and as the winter weather set in, patrolling between the lines was an unenviable job. As a company commander Pearkes did not go on patrols as extensively as he did when he was a bombing officer, but he would sometimes take out a small group to check unusual activity or to examine some new enemy fortification.

The trenches required constant attention to repair the damage caused not so much by enemy artillery fire as by the elements. The winter of 1916–17 was wet and cold, with thin sheets of ice forming over the water in the shell holes and at the bottom of the trenches. Trench-foot was a common complaint, and in late January and early February, when snow covered the battlefield, Pearkes did what he could to alleviate the sufferings of his men. When in reserve, some of the more fortunate ones managed to get a short leave to Great Britain, and in mid-November Pearkes, who had been in France for over a year, was given a furlough during which he was able to get himself properly kitted as an officer, see his father and uncles in London, and have a few days to enjoy the luxury of good meals and hot baths.

Towards the end of March 1917, the weather began to break, and with spring would come the beginning of another campaign season. At this time the 5th C.M.R. was up to full strength of over one thousand all ranks, and while in rest near Mont St. Eloi there was a considerable amount of retraining owing to the reorganization taking place within the infantry platoons. The platoon was made into a self-contained tactical unit consisting of a small headquarters with light machine-gun, bombing, rifle, and rifle grenade sections. This gave the platoon more firepower, and at the same time a drill was established for the clearing of trenches, one based on the experience accumulated during the past year. It was a busy time for Pearkes, but he was enthusiastic about the new set-up. Within the division there were competitions on the new "battle drill" on an intercompany, interbattalion, and interbrigade level. One platoon in Pearkes's company placed second in the entire division. Pearkes, whose experiences at Moquet Farm and Regina Trench made him in demand as a lecturer at various brigade and divisional schools, was also gaining a reputation as a first-class training officer whose enthusiasm kindled the spark of competition in his company and raised the morale of his men.

At this time preparations were underway for an attack on Vimy Ridge as part of a major Allied offensive by the British in the north and the French in the south in the hope of a breakthrough. The Germans, however, had been planning to shorten their front, and since September 1916, they had been working on the Hindenberg Line, to which they retired in March 1917. They could now release thirteen divisions from the front. There was no change at Vimy, however, and indeed the ridge, "tactically one of the most important features on the entire Western Front," remained a keystone in the German defence system.[11] For the offensive which was to open in April, the Canadian Corps had been allotted the task of capturing the ridge.

On 5 April the 5th C.M.R. received their operation orders for the morning of the ninth. The 1st, 2nd, and 4th C.M.R. were to go into the attack while the 5th C.M.R. would be in immediate support. "All ranks are calmly confident," wrote the 5th C.M.R. war diarist on Easter Sunday, and, he added prophetically, "tomorrow will make history."[12]

During the night of 8-9 April the rifle companies of the 5th C.M.R. began to move forward. It was a moment which those who were there would never forget. "Looking over the communication trench," Pearkes said later,

> you could see row after row of troops moving up . . . some in other communication trenches, some in the open. It was a tremendous sight in the half dark. When a shell burst or when a Very light went up you could see best. The tremendous number of troops moving up has always stuck in my mind.[13]

By 2 A.M. "C" Company was busy picking up materials from supply dumps. Half an hour later Pearkes led his company into Goodman tunnel, one of several long, commodious tunnels leading towards the front line which were now filled with men awaiting the attack at dawn. Outside the weather was becoming colder, until around 5 A.M. the wind began to blow a freezing combination of sleet and snow towards the enemy lines. Zero hour was at 5:30 A.M., at which time the hundreds of guns along the corps front heralded the attack. The war diarist wrote at this time:

> The intense artillery bombardment was one continuous roar. The ground trembles and there is mingled with the roar of the guns the swishing and screeching of the shell-filled air. 60 guns are covering our own advance, forming a "rolling barrage." Smoke and debris, thrown up by the bursting shells, give the appearance of a solid wall.[14]

The success of the Canadian attack which followed this wall of steel was a tribute to the courage, training, and determination of all ranks in the Canadian Corps. The casualties were not light, and even those battalions in the supporting role such as the 5th C.M.R. suffered from enemy artillery fire and determined pockets of enemy resistance.[15] During the day the battalion's companies first took over the former front line of the brigade, and 5th C.M.R. carrying parties brought supplies to the other units in the brigade as the latter pushed the enemy over the crest and down into the Douai plains beyond.

For the next five months the 5th C.M.R. remained in the area between Lens and Arras. Here brigades and divisions of the Canadian Corps were engaged in a number of battles, but there were no offensives calling for the full strength of the corps. For the 8th Brigade, the summer of 1917 was one of routine trench warfare.

When the battalion went into rest, it usually had billets on the other side of Vimy Ridge, an area generally free from enemy artillery fire. For Maj. Pearkes it was a period which he used to good advantage, both to know his officers and men better and to improve his own military knowledge. When he had enlisted he had been very conscious of the danger to Great Britain, and if he had been asked at that time why he joined up, probably he would have replied automatically "to fight for King and Empire." During his two years with the 2nd and 5th Canadian Mounted Rifles, however, this attitude began to change as he himself became more "Canadianized." A little more than a month after Vimy Ridge he was to write his mother:

> It always seems to me that I'm not fighting for King and Country but just for the company, which seems to be everything to me these days. I hate to be away from them and I don't worry the least about leave. The boys are great and I have many of the firmest friends among the rank and file.[16]

Pearkes, or "Pearksy" as he was nicknamed by the men in his company, was apparently as well liked by his men. They knew that he would never ask them to do something he would not do himself. He exuded confidence, and his cheerful presence in the line or in the attack raised morale. Whether in or out of the line Pearkes did all he could for his men. If the billets were poor or the rations cold, they knew that Pearkes was trying to improve them. If a furlough was due, Pearkes would see the adjutant on the man's behalf. If a man had no money, Pearkes would try to get an advance. Pearkes's nature was such that he felt the duties and responsibilities of his rank more than the privileges which went with it. Out of the line Pearkes continued to keep in excellent physical shape by running several miles every morning, and occasionally he had the opportunity to ride. He encouraged sports competitions within his company and in the battalion and frequently dipped into his own slender funds to buy trophies or put up money prizes. Financially, however, he still had to live very much within his four dollar a day army income, and his commission meant he had to buy an officer's uniform, Sam Browne belt, and other equipment. Liberal as he was within the company, he also sent what he could to help his mother and sister in Saanich. They had recently bought a small farm and were entering the dairy business, and George knew that, with most of his mother's capital put out on the farm and cows, any contributions of his would be welcome.[17]

Whatever his problems, Pearkes kept them to himself. If he knew fear, and he did, he put his trust in God, for he was sure that duty had a prior claim. He hated the suffering of war, yet even at this time he was giving some thought to making the military his career. As a field officer he still had much to learn, and he was learning it in a hard school. His personal experience was invaluable, but he noted the staff work which went into the training of the entire corps. Similarly, he was learning the administrative routine of a battalion and how to handle companies in actual battle.

During the months while the Canadian Corps was holding the line between Lens and Arras there had been severe fighting on other parts of the Western Front. During April and May the French had suffered such huge losses for such limited gains that mutinous behaviour was growing in their divisions. The combined British-French blow against the German forces was soon reduced to attacks of attrition, and as the French capabilities dwindled, Sir Douglas Haig felt it all the more necessary to keep the enemy engaged in the north. His intention was to clear the Belgian coast by thrusting out from the Ypres salient and in a series of successive, but limited, attacks to wear down the German forces. During the first four weeks of battle the British suffered 68,000 casualties. Despite these losses, poor weather, limited gains, lukewarm support for his strategy, and warnings from senior French officers that his route would be "a duck's march through the inundations," Haig persisted during the fall of 1917. By mid-October the British lines were within half a mile of the village of Passchendaele. This village stood on a slight ridge, and Lt.-Gen. Sir Arthur W. Currie was ordered to bring his corps to complete its capture on 13 October.

When the Canadians moved into the new area late in October, they found themselves close to positions which the 1st Division had held early in 1915, but those who had been there now saw an unrecognizable waste. About half the area in front of Passchendaele was covered with water or deep mud. Vast preparations had to be made behind the lines to build roads and wooden "duckboard" paths which would allow guns to be moved into position and ammunition to be supplied to them. Currie, determined to support his infantry with all the guns he could muster, did what he could to repair or replace those field pieces which had sunk to their axles or which were out of action because they could not be moved in the morass of mud. He had hoped to put back the timing for the three waves of attacks going in, but owing to prior arrangements of the flanking corps, the first Canadian attack was timed for 26 October.

The Canadian attack was on a two-division front. In the centre a stream, the Ravebeek, had been churned into an almost impassable swamp. On the left was the 3rd Division, and on the left of this division (bordering the 63rd [R.N.] Division), the 8th Brigade made the initial assault with the 4th Canadian Mounted Rifles. It rained on the twenty-sixth, and owing to the deep mud, the strength of the enemy's defences, and the inability of the 63rd Division to maintain pace, the 8th Brigade was unable to reach its objective. Indeed, it was not until two days later that the 3rd Division's attacking battalions were in a position for a renewed assault. In this phase the 5th C.M.R. was to take over from the 4th C.M.R., and Maj. Pearkes's company was assigned the doubtful honour of being the leading company on the extreme left of the corps' front.

As they headed into the Passchendaele area, Pearkes related that their "big impression . . . was the appalling state of the ground. Everywhere there were deep shell holes filled with water."[18] Mud was everywhere, and plank roads had to be built to carry even the lightest wheeled traffic over the sodden ground. Nearer the front, where the ground had been churned to a semi-liquid state by shelling, wooden duckboards had been laid to permit the men to walk overland. Another feature in the debris laden area was the numerous circular, concrete machine-gun posts, the pillboxes, destroyed in whole or in part by artillery fire during the British attacks earlier in the autumn. Their five-foot thick walls protected a platoon of men, and only a direct hit could demolish them. A few had been taken intact, and these were being used as headquarters and casualty clearing stations closer to the front.

On the twenty-seventh, when the 5th C.M.R. moved up to what had been the starting line of the attack on the previous day, the companies took over in trenches which were little more than the linking up of a series of shell holes. In front of battalion headquarters, located in a former pillbox called Kron Prinz Farm, there were no trenches and no shelter. It was difficult to identify locations, but ahead the long, low ridge was the ultimate objective, while here and there rubble indicated the sites of formerly prosperous farms. Ahead, and slightly to the right, a group of stumps and battered tree trunks in a slight depression identified Woodland Plantation. The state of the ground made it very difficult to locate even the German pillboxes which normally stood several feet above ground.

On the morning of the twenty-ninth Lt.-Col. Draper outlined the plan of attack. On the 8th Brigade front, the 5th C.M.R., with the 2nd C.M.R. in support, would attack at first light with "C" Company (Major Pearkes) on the left and "A" Company (Major Duggan) on the right. The second wave, consisting of "D" and "B" Companies, were to follow. Since the area around Woodland Plantation was so deeply mired, "C" Company was to go left and "A" Company right of the swamp. On "C" Company's left was the corps boundary, so that Pearkes would have a British battalion, the Artists Rifles, advancing on his left flank. The distance to be covered was approximately one thousand yards, with the ground improving only slightly as one reached Vapour Farm, some two hundred yards from the objective. The attack, timed for 5:50 A.M., would commence with a barrage, which would lift every eight minutes and advance one hundred yards, a very slow rate but one timed to the estimated advance of the men over the muddy wastes. At an intermediate point there would be a thirty-minute pause to allow the attackers to reorganize their platoons, fill in the gaps caused by casualties, and permit the supporting companies to close up for the final assault.

The night before the attack a bright moon shone over the battlefield, and enemy bombers, which had struck at the battalion several nights previously, could be heard droning overhead. Pearkes spent much of the night with his company, speaking to his men and explaining the problems to be overcome the next day. Owing to the terrain the advance was to be made by men advancing in sections in file rather than in a straight line. Pearkes also saw that his men had a hot meal and their rum ration, for once the attack was underway they would have to rely on iron rations until relieved. Pearkes himself received a visit from a couple of British officers from the Artists Rifles and learned that this was the first attack they had ever been in. The company commander asked, among other things, what a barrage appeared to be like. "They were nice young men," Pearkes said, "but they were quite inexperienced, and it was not very reassuring to know that on one's left there were . . . [green] troops who would be playing an important part in looking after our flank."

At 5:20 A.M. on 30 October the 25 officers and 565 other ranks of the 5th C.M.R. were assembled in position for the attack. Consistent and fairly heavy shelling on both sides had continued during the night and early morning so that even before the attack the 5th C.M.R. had suffered numerous casualties, including the commander of "D" Company. As zero hour approached it was barely light. It was cold and windy with a promise of rain when, at 5:50 A.M. the intense artillery and machine-gun barrage opened up. Within minutes, just as the Canadian companies were clambering out of what shelters they had, the German guns replied with their own heavy barrage. Pearkes remembers the moment vividly:

As I stepped out into the open . . . there was a good deal of illumina-
tion at the time what with flares and rockets going up, both German
and our own. Although it was hardly daylight . . . you could still get
glimpses of men clambering out of the "trench." . . . We'd hardly got
out . . . when that counter barrage came down. At that time I was hit
in the thigh [by shrapnel] and was knocked down. I rather thought:
"Now I've got it!" There seemed to be a little uncertainty among the
men immediately alongside me, whether they should go on when I'd
been hit. For a moment I had visions of going back wounded and I
said to myself: "This can't be. I've got to go on for a while anyway,
wounded or not." So I clambered to my feet and I found a stiffness in
my left thigh but I was able to move forward and then the rest of the
company all came forward.[19]

The effect of the counterbattery fire on Pearkes's company would have
stopped many. As Pearkes stated:

They had had heavy casualties, there seemed to be appallingly few
going forward, and our principal concern during the first few minutes
of the attack was to adjust ourselves to the semi-darkness and how
best to navigate round the shell holes. The mud was a terrible handi-
cap to us. On the other hand, the mud saved many from the enemy's
artillery fire because the shells buried themselves in the mud . . .
[which] deadened the effect of the explosion and the spread of fragments from the shell.

There was a good deal of machine-gun fire; there was the overhead
fire from our own [supporting] machine guns . . . and there was also a
lot of enfilade [enemy] machine-gun fire. We started, it seemed just a
little group of men working forward through the mud holes. We
found that the barrage ran away from us; we couldn't begin to keep
up with it [even though] it was moving at the rate of a hundred yards
every eight minutes . . . . It was the sheer difficulty of moving through
that morass . . . . I was carrying a rifle and I remember turning around
and helping men who were not wounded but who had got stuck in
shell holes. I'm certain that there were men who, . . . wounded, fell
into the shell holes and were drowned. If you got in [to a big shell
hole] you just couldn't climb out by yourself . . . because the sides all
kept oozing down if you reached out to help yourself.[20]

As the day slowly became lighter, Pearkes and his men could see "A"

Company swinging off to the right as they struggled ahead, avoiding the impassable terrain around Woodland Plantation. Of greater concern, however, was the increasing amount of enemy machine-gun fire coming from their left flank. It was soon apparent that the British unit had not kept pace, and indeed it was later found that this battalion, struck by the force of the enemy's counterbarrage, suffered so many casualties at the outset that they failed to make any advance at all. Thus with every yard "C" Company advanced, it exposed itself to more enemy fire from some half dozen pillboxes which the British were to have attacked, and consequently the casualties it suffered rose proportionately.

Shortly after 6:30 A.M. Major Pearkes had reached the intermediate objective. The pause gave the platoons behind time to catch up, and at the same time the two supporting companies began to move forward. Off to the right "A" Company was engaged in hand-to-hand fighting[21] and out of touch with "C" Company, and in the next few minutes it lost three of its four officers. In front of "C" Company, the halting of the barrage had given the enemy in front a break, permitting them to retire to the east towards Source Farm and Vapour Farm where they were able to continue to fire against the advancing Canadians.

"C" Company had not encountered many of the Bavarian troops defending the ridge. Those who were met were quickly overcome and sent back as prisoners, frequently helping Canadian wounded to return.[22] While the machine-gun fire on the left flank was causing the most trouble,[23] there was also fire from Source Farm, Vapour Farm, and Vine Cottage, which lay on the ridge. Source Farm was just on the other side of the boundary and had been an objective of the Artists Rifles. Pearkes ordered Lt. Otty to take some of his platoon and see if he could take out this troublesome nest when the advance continued. Otty was successful, but he was killed soon after.

When the protective barrage lifted and began to advance, it seemed a little thinner, perhaps as a result of some of the guns being knocked out or sinking out of line despite the platforms which had been built for them. Although his left flank was completely unprotected, Pearkes continued to advance, and the closer the men came to their objectives, the more enemy fire they encountered. "All the way across the marsh," one of "C" Company's sergeants wrote later, "I could see the bullets hitting in the ponds of water in every shellhole. The guns were firing at us but [the shells] buried in the mud before exploding so unless a direct hit did not affect us, although I remember that my steel helmet kept jumping up and down on my head and would have blown off if not for the chinstrap."[24] By the time "C" Company closed in on its objective at Vapour Farm, it had been reduced to about three dozen, but even with his company reduced to platoon strength Pearkes was able to clear out the enemy. On the left Lt. Otty with a handful of men was in possession of Source Farm, but the two companies coming up to assist them were suffering heavy casualties from the machine-gun posts on the open left flank. On the right "A" Company's ranks had been so badly depleted that as they emerged beyond the Plantation they were unable to take out Vine Cottage. The few men who managed to reach the front eased to the left to join with Pearkes. When they arrived he had about fifty men to hold about four hundred yards of front.

With both flanks "in the air," Pearkes sought means of sending a report back to Draper. There were so few men that none could be sent back. One of his runners had been assigned to take two carrier pigeons in a basket. On the outside of the basket were two capsules containing small message forms. To make sure the capsules would not get lost or wet in the mud, the runner put them in his pocket. Unfortunately, he was killed on the way up, but a stretcher bearer saw the basket and passed it on to a soldier who carried it up to Vapour Farm. In the drizzling rain Pearkes wrote a brief message on his field service pocketbook and ripped out the page which was almost large enough to cover the pigeon. Someone took out a length of fibre from a sandbag and tied the message to the pigeon's leg. The bird was hurled into the air with the folded piece of paper dangling beneath it like a kite's tail. It was about the only humorous incident of the day, but as the bird flapped upward and circled about the mud-covered survivors in the manure-strewn rubble of the farm, Pearkes could not help but laugh. It must have been a patriotic bird, for the message did get back, although the second bird, apparently, was a casualty.

Shortly after seizing Source Farm and Vapour Farm, Pearkes attempted to take Vine Cottage as well. It was the objective of "A" Company with "B" Company in support, but owing to the limited advances made on their right flank by the 49th Battalion and their heavy casualties, not only were the men unable to take it but also few managed to infiltrate beyond Woodland Plantation to join their comrades on the left. Enemy fire, especially sniper fire, made life extremely uncomfortable for Pearkes and his men, and with both flanks wide open, his position was becoming precarious. Behind him "D" Company was strung out along the bullet-swept ground. A few had managed to reach Lt. Otty at Source Farm, but many had been killed or wounded, and one platoon was cut off. The Artists Rifles, hammered by artillery and machine-gun fire, had advanced less than two hundred yards, while Pearkes and his men were almost half a mile beyond.

As the remnants of "C" Company and their comrades were attempting to dig in about the farm houses, one or two German planes strafed them. Pte. A. Molyneux, Pearkes's batman, started to fire at it with his rifle when he was hit. Before he fainted, he related, "I saw 'G. R.' He was still on his feet going up these would-be trenches and looking around to see if [any enemy] was there. I could see blood on him. I could see where his pants were torn but he was still going."[25] The planes were an annoyance; of greater moment was a shout from Sergeant Rutherford calling his attention to a strong enemy force coming over the crest of the ridge only a few hundred yards away. During this attack Lt. Otty was killed, and the few men from the unit attempting to take Vine Cottage were overcome. As Pearkes stated later:

> We saw the Germans quite clearly coming forward. Practically none of them actually reached our shell holes. We had enough riflemen and we had, I think, two Lewis guns at the time. They were effective in discouraging the Germans from pushing their attacks home with the bayonet. We accounted for a great many of them.[26]

By the time this attack was beaten back, it was close to 12:00. With both flanks still open, the assault and supporting companies had lost over half their strength. Great difficulty was being experienced in evacuating the wounded. At the Advanced Dressing Station the medical officer, Dr. Ireland, and most of his assistants were killed. A replacement medical officer was soon so severely wounded that he died also. Two companies of the 2nd C.M.R. had been ordered by the brigade commander to help the 5th C.M.R., and both were committed by Lt.-Col. Draper. "A" Company of the 2nd C.M.R., ordered to reinforce Pearkes and establish some sort of defensive flank, had taken a severe pounding from the enemy's fire from the moment it started forward. The company commander was wounded, and despite every effort only six or eight men actually reached him. At 1:45 P.M. Pearkes managed to get the following message back to advanced headquarters:

> Germans are digging in on top of ridge about 200 yards away. Are in force. I have 8 2nd C.M.R. and 12 5th C.M.R., all very much exhausted. Ammunition running short. Do not think we can hold out much longer without being relieved. Both flanks still in the air.[27]

Pearkes had no idea at the time whether the messages he sent back with the walking wounded were getting through. Fortunately, from advanced battalion headquarters Maj. W. Rhoades, the second-in-command, could see something of what was going on, and although it was an hour before the above message reached him, he had seen the enemy massing for another counterattack on Pearkes's position and had asked the artillery to place a barrage near Vanity Farm where they were gathering. Pearkes himself recalls the situation as follows:

We couldn't go on any further, we had no men . . . . You could see back [but] at this time nobody else seemed to be coming up and it was doubtful whether they could through the machine-gun fire. It looked as though we would have to stay there practically without reinforcements until dark. The enemy were on the ridge and it looked a pretty hopeless position. We were short of ammunition because we used up practically every round we had carried. We had taken all the ammunition from any casualties who were there but what else could we do. To have gone back and given up everything we had gained that morning didn't seem very sensible as, if we had started to drift back there would have been more casualties.[28]

Wounded though he was, Pearkes kept a good control of his men, encouraging them by his presence as he crawled from one shell hole to another and, whenever the Germans showed themselves, adding to the defensive fire of his group by using his own rifle. It was most unlikely that the enemy knew how weak the Canadians were and, especially, how little ammunition they had. Their counterattacks during the afternoon were beaten back by a combination of courageous leadership and determination to hold. There were times, too, when Pearkes was very depressed, and none more so than in the afternoon when he looked back over the morass to see "A" Company of the 2nd C.M.R. trying to get forward to help him. Almost one hundred men made the attempt, but Pearkes could see them being struck down. He needed them and their ammunition desperately, but only Lt. Mavor and nine men reached him, and Mavor's hand was smashed by shrapnel so he was sent back. With each hour Pearkes's original party suffered casualties, and the small number of men from the supporting companies who dribbled up to the farms helped to maintain his strength. What he had won—and no group in the entire division had penetrated to the depth his men had—he was determined to hold.[29]

As the afternoon wore on, the morale of Pearkes's men began to rise. Exhausted, low on ammunition, hungry, plastered with mud, their members reduced to a mere handful, but with the enemy still kept two hundred yards away, they knew that dusk and then darkness might give them the reinforcements they needed. The same thought was in the mind of Maj. Rhoades. The four companies of the 5th C.M.R. had been committed as well as two companies of the 2nd C.M.R. "C" and "D" Companies of the latter unit had come up to the starting line during the afternoon, and as dusk began to fall, he ordered them to try to get forward and relieve the 5th C.M.R. They were also to report on the situation on either flank, bring in any men lost or wounded, and contact any small groups of men in defensive pockets on either flank.

In the gathering darkness the British Columbia companies under the command of Maj. L. W. Miller set out. On the right they found the 49th Battalion had not been able to get further than four hundred yards beyond their start line. On the left the Artists Rifles advanced about one hundred yards. The thrust to the right of the Woodland Plantation had become bogged down, and although a few men had managed to filter forward, the right flank was open. When the leading platoons managed to reach Vapour and Source Farms, frequently wading knee-deep in mud, they were greeted with joy. It took time to round up the men from the 5th C.M.R. from their shell holes, collect the wounded, and start them back through the black night. There were only about thirty-five men to return, and Pearkes waited until the last group was on its way before turning over the area to the two hundred men who came up to relieve them.

It was a grim task getting back. There were few who were not wounded. For Pearkes, bone weary after almost two days without sleep, his leg stiff and numb from his wound, and sad at the loss of so many good men, there was a sense of a duty done despite tremendous odds. As he said later: "We had got on when nobody else had got on; we had survived . . . [and] we were all thankful.[30]

When he hobbled into battalion headquarters late that night to report to Lt.-Col. Draper, the adjutant, Lt. H. F. C. Cocks, noted that his trouser leg was caked with blood. No message which Pearkes had sent back mentioned that he had been wounded, so Draper ordered him to report to the Casualty Clearing Station immediately. A stretcher-bearer helped him, but it was a painful walk over the slippery boardwalks. When he arrived there was still no rest until the wound was probed—a process Pearkes found almost as aggravating as reaching the Passchendaele Ridge.

When Lt.-Col. Draper gathered together an account of what happened during that long day when a small handful of men under Pearkes's leadership accomplished the impossible, he recommended a number of the survivors for awards. Chief among these was the Victoria Cross for Maj. Pearkes, whose citation reads:

> For most conspicuous bravery and skilful handling of the troops under his command during the capture and consolidation of considerably more than the objectives allotted to him, in an attack.
>
> Just prior to the advance Major Pearkes was wounded in the thigh.

Regardless of his wound, he continued to lead his men with the utmost gallantry, despite many obstacles.

At a particular stage of the attack his further advance was threatened by a strong point which was an objective of the battalion on his left, but which they had not succeeded in capturing. Quickly appreciating the situation, he captured and held this point, thus enabling his further advance to be successfully pushed forward.

It was entirely due to his determination and fearless personality that he was able to maintain his objective with the small number of men at his command against repeated enemy counter attacks, both his flanks being unprotected for a considerable depth meanwhile.

His appreciation of the situation throughout and the reports rendered by him were invaluable to his Commanding Officer in making dispositions of troops to hold the position captured.

He showed throughout a supreme contempt of danger and wonderful powers of control and leading.

(Nr. PASSCHENDAELE, FRANCE. 30/31 10-17.)[31]

Sometime later, while still at the Casualty Clearing Station, Pearkes wrote his mother. He did not describe the battle, but nothing could repress his admiration for his men. "As for this battalion," he wrote, "its equal can't be found. Our men cannot be beaten and they are the bravest, most loyal chaps I have ever been with."[32] The feeling was reciprocal. Many years later one of the men under his command wrote: "I . . . would have followed him through Hell if I had to."[33] At Passchendaele the men of the 5th and 2nd C.M.R. did just that.

6

Commanding Officer

By the time Pearkes was allowed to return to his battalion in mid-November 1917, the third Battle of Ypres had ground to a halt. There were no happier troops on the Western Front than the Canadians when they were relieved from the mud of Passchendaele and told they were to go to the Lens-Vimy front. The 5th Canadian Mounted Rifles had been visited by Lt.-Gen. Currie on the seventh, and he warmly congratulated them on the success of their attack. The divisional commander added his praise a few days later. It was not until the following week that Pearkes returned—without taking any furlough, as usual. He disliked being an invalid, and fortunately his wound was a clean one, the piece of shell having gone right through the fleshy part of his thigh without any complications. The fragment, however, had driven part of his clothing into the wound, and it was both painful and undignified to have to lie on his stomach while a nurse probed for the small wads of cloth. His general good health made recovery quick, and he rejoined his comrades in the Wieltje area close to Ypres.

He was with the 5th C.M.R. for only a few days when Lt.-Col. Draper called him into his orderly room. There were few officers in the unit whom Draper would less like to lose than Pearkes, but there was an opportunity for promotion from acting to temporary major and possibly for command of another battalion should Pearkes wish the appointment. Pearkes had been recommended to the post of senior major in the 116th (Ontario County) Battalion by the divisional commander, and the decision was his.

It was not an easy one to make. He had been with the 5th C.M.R. for almost a year and a half, a little longer than he had been with the 2nd C.M.R. On the other hand, there was his own military future to think about, and despite the misery and danger of warfare, he could not think of returning to homesteading or the Mounted Police. As he wrote his mother a short time later:

I believe this work suits me because I don't have to worry about money matters. I never could take any interest in them and I knew I should never make a success of things until I found some work to do in which money did not count . . . . I'm not looking forward to civil life again. The Army will be the place for me.[1]

Professionally, therefore, a transfer would be wise, and Pearkes was advised to report for duty at the end of November. Before he left, Lt.-Col. Draper paraded the entire 5th Canadian Mounted Rifles, thanked Pearkes for his service, and congratulated him on his promotion.

The 116th Battalion traced its history back to the Fenian Raids in 1866 when it was formed as the 34th Ontario County Regiment.[2] It was not until October 1915 that the unit was ordered to recruit a battalion for overseas service. Because it was among the last raised for overseas, it had an unusually high number among the battalions of the Canadian Corps and as such was nick-named the "Umpty Umps" by older units. The 116th embarked for Great Britain in the summer of 1916, and there was considerable apprehension that it, as with other units late in arriving, would be broken up to reinforce those battalions already in the field. The commanding officer, Lt.-Col. S. S. Sharpe, had been a Conservative member of Parliament since 1908 and managed to bring the unit intact to France in February 1917.

The 116th Battalion became part of the 9th Brigade[3] owing both to Sharpe's influence and to the reinforcement situation in Canada. The 60th Battalion from Quebec suffered many casualties and found it very difficult to raise reinforcements from its "home" area. Although it was popular in the brigade, it was withdrawn and its place taken by the 116th. Something of the feeling engendered by this change was discovered by the "Umpty Umps" in the summer of 1917 when one of their companies

came across a memorial to the 60th Battalion erected by some of their men close to the village of Vimy. The memorial was in the shape of a cross with the inscription: "In memory of the 60th Battalion. 1915—Raised by Patriotism. 1917—Killed by Politics."[4]

During 1917 the 116th Battalion was introduced to trench warfare, although up to Passchendaele, where it provided working parties, it did not experience hard action. Nevertheless at Hill 70 and later in the Vimy area the 116th had shown up quite well, particularly when it put on a big raid near Avion.

When Pearkes presented himself to Lt.-Col. Sharpe, he met a gruff, well-built man who was pleased to have such an experienced officer replace his former second-in-command. Sharpe was again a candidate for his former riding and doubtless mentioned that voting would take place the following day. Sharpe had personally recruited the battalion, and most of the "originals" were from his riding. Many of the replacements for casualties came from Toronto and Hamilton, and Pearkes found some antipathy between the two groups. Morale was good, but not as high as Pearkes thought it might be. Sharpe was a bit inclined to favouritism, and although courageous he lacked the leadership qualities and organizing ability which could weld together the factions which had begun to emerge towards the end of 1917. Pearkes learned all he could from Sharpe before the latter left towards the end of the month to attend a senior officers' staff course in Great Britain. The command of the 116th was given to Pearkes on 7 January 1918, at which time he was made acting lieutenant-colonel.[5]

Pearkes made a considerable impact on the unit from the outset. The battalion orderly room sergeant at the time wrote later:

> I found him to be a soft spoken, well-mannered gentleman who was held in the highest esteem by all his officers and other ranks. His officers he took for granted; the comfort and welfare of his other ranks was his chief concern. He was a strict disciplinarian . . . . He never displayed anger by voice or action, but if you looked closely you could read it in his eyes.[6]

One of his junior subalterns wrote:

> He made a wonderful impression on me, a young Lieutenant. He was . . . tall, slim, handsome and keen. Later on when I came to know him better under action conditions, I concluded that he was the bravest man I ever knew.[7]

Another remembered him as inspiring "confidence which seemed to be felt by the whole regiment," and knowing the reputation of the new major, all ranks "could not but feel that we had a 'leader' second to none."[8] Both officers and men remarked about his concern for the private soldier. "He was always interested in the comfort of his men and their training," wrote one of them later,[9] and although Pearkes was strict, "the troops admired him from the first day he took command because they soon realized they

Plate 13. Lt.-Col. G. R. Pearkes (right) accompanying Field Marshal Earl Haig on his visit to Winnipeg in the summer of 1925.

Plate 14. Pearkes with No. 14 Troop, Calgary, which he formed in the spring of 1921, at their camp near Cochrane, Alberta.

Plate 15. George and Blytha Pearkes at the time of their engagement in 1924.

Plate 16. Brig.-Gen. G. R. Pearkes, D.O.C., M.D. 13, with Maj. Hugh Young at Medicine Hat, Alberta, 1938.

Plate 17. Brig.-Gen. G. R. Pearkes with Lt.-Gov. J. C. Bowen of Alberta reviewing a militia cavalry regiment at Sarcee Camp, 1939. Canadian forces were ill-equipped and unprepared to wage a modern war.

would always get a fair hearing." "He would never ask anyone to do any-thing or go anywhere that he himself would not be willing to carry out," wrote another,[10] expressing a sentiment which was voiced by others in the 2nd and 5th C.M.R.'s.

For the next several months the 116th Battalion was engaged in routine trench warfare. The weather was generally miserable, the trenches frequently ankle- or knee-deep in mud, and the enemy fairly lively. Although he could no longer take out any patrols, Pearkes believed that No-Man's-Land for the enemy stopped at their own barbed wire, and aggressive patrolling became a strong and standing feature of the 116th Battalion.

The active defence policy pursued all along the front was a reflection of major events elsewhere. In Russia the October Revolution of 1917 had brought the Bolsheviks into power, and in December the Treaty of Brest-Litovsk permitted the Germans to transfer thousands of men from the Eastern Front to the west. By mid-February the enemy had 178 divisions in France and Belgium, ready to launch a major offensive against the Allies before the Americans arrived in large numbers. Late in March, backed by twenty-five hundred guns, the Germans attacked with 32 divisions and drove a deep wedge between the British and French forces. Within a week the bulge was twenty-five miles deep and fifty miles wide at the base. A further ten days' constant attacking had deepened the bulge another thirteen miles, and the crisis seemed to be reaching a disaster.

The German attack was south of the area held by the Canadian Corps, but its effect was felt everywhere. As more British divisions were withdrawn to help stem the German onslaught, the Canadians were ordered to extend their front so that by 27 March the 116th Battalion had all four companies in the front with little in support or reserve.[11] Fortunately, the unit's strength had been increased from about 650 to 1,000 all ranks.

At this time, both in and out of the trenches, Pearkes worked hard to weld the unit into a hard-hitting group. Some three hundred new officers and men had to be fitted into the companies, and this involved considerable reorganization. Every company commander was impressed with the need for constant patrols, and everyone became quite good at it. On 1 April, for example, the brigade commander told Pearkes that both corps and army wanted information about the German forces opposite the brigade front. Pearkes called his company commanders together and laid plans for a raid that night. An enemy fighting patrol was encountered in No-Man's-Land, and, in a desperate hand-to-hand struggle, two prisoners were nabbed and hustled back to the Canadian front line. This was the first time any identification of enemy formations opposite the Canadians had been received by the intelligence officer for a long period. Both the brigade and divisional commanders sent congratulations to the unit. "All ranks in the Battalion felt quite elated," wrote the war diarist,[12] and

Pearkes, who always felt any losses "very keenly,"[13] was especially pleased that the raiding party suffered only two lightly wounded casualties.

Out of the line, and especially after the German push had been halted, Pearkes trained his battalion hard. During May and early June, special emphasis was given to training in mobile warfare. Battalion, brigade, and even divisional manoeuvres were refreshing to men accustomed to trench warfare, and Pearkes knew that his men must master the "new" techniques for the coming offensive. "It's a very grave responsibility having the lives of over a thousand men dependent on one's action," he wrote, and he was so busy that he did not have time to visit his brother Edward, who had transferred to the 2nd Canadian Mounted Rifles.[14] "During these continual manoeuvres," wrote one of his officers later, "for weeks and weeks, day after day, Lt.-Col. Pearkes seemed to be everywhere, watching every detail in the arduous training for fighting that was so different from the old trench warfare."[15]

Ordinarily there were few times when the battalion had entertainment. It was a treat to see the division's "Dumbells" concert, and very occasionally there would be a cinema show. Pearkes also stressed sports whenever the opportunity offered. Frequently he would offer a barrel of beer to the company which won the interbattalion football match, a game with fifty men on each side and four balls in play. He once organized a five-mile cross-country race.

> There were a number of entries. I forgot who won but I do remember who came in second. It was Lt.-Col. Pearkes—I saw him finish quite fresh. That shows what a real sport he was . . . [and] that certainly didn't do him any harm in the eyes and the minds of his men. He was quite a bit older than most of the men in the race.[16]

Late in July 1918, some ten days after the French had started their successful counterattacks on the Marne, the Canadian Corps was withdrawn from the front. Plans had been made for the British Fourth Army and the French First Army to launch an offensive east of Amiens. The Canadians were to move south to join the Australian Corps and the British III Corps on the Fourth Army Front. The plan called for the Canadians to concentrate behind the Australian lines without revealing their identity. Then, at the last possible moment, they would take up a sector of the front between the Australians and the British preparatory to going into the attack.

It was important that the Canadians' move should be secret, for the Germans regarded them as an élite corps. The movement of all battalions, whether by foot, truck, or railways, was made under the cover of darkness.

Pearkes was unable to tell his officers where the 116th Battalion was going because he himself did not know. Each day the unit received its marching orders for that day alone, and as the route was purposefully circuitous, it was not until the unit began to near Amiens that many guessed they were being concentrated for an attack. As they neared the city, the men began to notice the large dumps of ammunition and supplies. Near Hebecourt they passed a large number of tanks, and the intention behind the printed order—"Keep Your Mouth Shut"—which was pasted in every man's pay-book began to make sense.[17] By the evening of 5-6 August the battalion rested in the Bois de Bovés, some six miles southeast of Amiens, and here Pearkes was able to tell his company commanders that the battalion would be going into action soon.[18]

The attack, planned for 8 August, was to be on a very large scale. On the right the French First Army would attack with seven divisions on an eight-mile front. On the left the British Fourth Army was to attack with eight divisions. Together the armies were to be supported by almost three thousand guns. There was to be no preliminary bombardment, but at 4:20 A.M. a rolling barrage would commence which, with the assistance of the tanks, would both cut the enemy's barbed wire and reduce his defences. The tanks were to be parcelled out so that each battalion would have at least three, and provision had been made for other tanks to bring forward ammunition to the leading companies. Heavy aircraft would help conceal the noise made by the battalions and tanks coming into position on the night of 7-8 August. The area to be attacked was open country, dotted with woods and rolling hills. A major feature of the German defence system, aside from its scattered trenches and defence posts, were the many concealed machine guns.

The 9th Brigade was to be on the extreme right of the corps, with the 116th Battalion in the centre. The time permitted for a reconnaissance was extremely limited. Pearkes and Lt. K. Wood, his scout officer, managed to get near the front line on the evening of 6-7 August, and it was heartening to know that, although the Australians realized they were to be relieved from the sector, they had no idea by whom. The Australian officer was very helpful in suggesting the best positions for a forming-up place, but even at that, the frontage for the attack was so narrow that one company's assembly area had to be placed forward of the Australian front line.

When issued with his maps and given his objective, Pearkes realized that the initial attack presented considerable difficulties. The front line was in a valley through which ran a small river. Ahead were two hills, separated by a gully. On the right was the road to Roye, a tree-lined highway which, roughly, formed the boundary of the battalion's line of attack. The other boundary angled off to the left. On the map, therefore, the start line looked like the base of a funnel with the boundaries widening as the unit advanced eastward towards the Bade Trench system (the first objective) and on to Hamon Wood (the final objective), some five thousand yards away. To make things more difficult, the configuration of the ground forced the leading companies to advance through Hourges directly south, then wheel hard left to follow the barrage and advance to the east. Here is where the hard and constant training in mobile warfare would prove its worth. For the first time, all along the front, the Canadians would not go into the assault in long waves, but rather in sections in line or in arrowhead formations. In the final briefing Pearkes stressed the need for close control.[19]

On the evening of 6–7 August, the battalion moved forward to take up positions in Gentelles Wood. The concentration of men in the area was tremendous, and the congestion was in proportion. One officer wrote later:

> There were trucks of all kinds hauling all sizes of artillery shells and dropping them at appointed places marked out for them. There were tanks being led by a man with a lantern so that they would not get into pitfalls . . . . Heavy guns were being hauled into position and covered up with camouflage. There was shouting and yelling by everybody trying to find room to go forward and get to their positions before dawn.[20]

On the night of 7–8 August the 116th Battalion was ready to go. Last minute instructions were issued, a generous rum ration given to those who wanted it, scouts who had been close as possible to the front rejoined the unit to guide the companies in to their forming-up place, and Pearkes led his men forward in single file towards the Australian lines. Near Hourges the men had to cross the River Luce and climb up a slippery bank. It was time for the leading companies to pass on, so Pearkes remained on the bank, helping many of the heavily-laden soldiers up the bank, grasping their hands and wishing them well. He would be going into the attack with them, and there was no need for him to remain where he was. But the incident was typical of him.

At twenty minutes after four the ground trembled as hundreds of guns opened up the barrage. After it had hammered the German trenches and begun to lift, "A" Company rose up and began the complicated manoeuvre to the south and then to the east across the valley and up the hill towards the Bade Trench system. Behind it the other companies were on the move, some hearing Pearkes's runner, a bugler in the band, sounding the regimental call and then the advance. Behind "A" came "C" Company which would be further to the left, coming around the base of the first hill and driving for the enemy's positions north of Hamon Wood. "D" Company, once out of the "funnel," was to follow "A", pass through the Bade Trenches, and attack the enemy in the wood from the right. Next came Pearkes with his battalion headquarters, and behind this group the reserve company, "B", ready to mop up the final objective. Lumbering behind would be the tanks, ready to help clear out the machine-gun nests.

For the first hour it was difficult to know what was going on. A dense fog made it difficult to see anything in the early dawn, and when the enemy's counterbarrage came crashing down, the dust and smoke made visibility even more restricted. Fortunately, the road marking the right boundary was lined with tall poplars, and this helped the companies gain the right direction.[21] "A" Company, the first off the mark, got into the fight early when it attacked the German front line. It suffered severe casualties, including all the officers. About halfway up the hill where the Bade Trench system dominated the crest, this company ran into numerous machine-gun nests. The poor visibility favoured the attackers until they emerged from the mist. "The dash of the men," wrote the unit chronicler of this battle, "was most marked, their training in open warfare showing a marvellous difference from the old staid method of following the barrage shoulder to shoulder at the high port."[22] Many enemy posts were cut off and surrendered. When "C" and "D" Companies were coming forward, they encountered the first of a stream of prisoners.

"C" Company, meanwhile, was making good progress working around the base of the hill towards the hamlet of Demuin, after which it was to swing right into a re-entrant and take out the enemy in Hamon Wood from the rear. This wood offered a perfect location for enemy artillery. Tucked behind a hill two miles from the front, screened by trees, it was thought to harbour artillery positions whose strength was not known. "D" Company was fighting its way forward close to "A" Company, determined like the others to gain its objectives in this first major attack the unit had experienced. It, too, overcame numerous enemy machine-gun posts and was inflicting more casualties than it received.

Because of "A" Company's losses the Bade Trench system on top of the hill was still intact. Pearkes amalgamated the remnants of "A" Company with his headquarters and ordered Lewis machine-gunners to cover their assault up the slope. On the left, further ahead, was Capt. Baird and his "D" Company. As Pearkes related later:

We could see the darn machine-gunners in Bade Trench. . . . Baird was leading his men more or less in a frontal attack and he was hit.

Then his men went in and bayonetted the machine-gunners. They were gallant Germans; they were fighting to the last and they didn't surrender until the soldiers were right on top of them.

In the meantime the enemy was still in parts of Bade Trench. There was a little dip in the ground to the right . . . . I took what men I could get . . . and we went up this hollow where we were more or less immune from enemy fire and we came in on the rest of Bade Trench from the right flank. I remember seeing the tanks over on the right and signalling them to come over and help.[23]

In a final assault the composite company overcame all resistance and rooted the Germans out of their trenches. By 6:15 A.M. Pearkes had his headquarters firmly established in the Bade Trenches, more German prisoners were en route to the rear, and the men in "A" and "D" Companies were mounting captured enemy machine guns on the parados facing down the slope towards Hamon Wood.

At this point the battalion front had widened to well over one thousand yards and control was not easy. Pearkes's second-in-command was making sure the left flank was secure with the 58th Battalion in the village of Demuin. When he heard it was, Pearkes ordered "C" and part of "D" Companies to press forward. "A" Company was almost exhausted, so "B" Company was ordered forward, and it amalgamated with Pearkes's headquarters, part of "D" Company, and a few men from "A". All over the hill the enemy was being overcome. Artillery observers were directing their guns on enemy strongpoints located on the hills beyond.

The stage was now set for the final assault. Pearkes had the remnants of "A" provide covering fire for "D" and "B" Companies on the right, while "C" surged ahead from the left, taking the enemy on the flank and in the rear. Their advance had been rapid, and the men were eager and in high spirits when they attacked the wood itself, with Pearkes going in with them. As the battalion report stated later:

The enemy artillery [in Hamon Wood] had evidently been reached before they had realized their danger; some of the gunners fought to the finish, firing with open sights, on the advancing infantry until surrounded. A few rounds of rapid fire from the East side, together with the bold dash of infantry straight to the guns was sufficient to prove to the enemy the futility of further resistance. Consequently a record capture of enemy guns was made, and the survivors of the artillery group, which were numerous (they had taken refuge in the deep dugouts at hand) came streaming forth and marched to the rear, led by artillery officers.[24]

With Hamon Wood cleared, Pearkes had some of the platoons establish outposts up the hill east of the wood to clear out some enemy posts firing down on the 116th. He knew the 7th Brigade was close behind, and he wanted his front clear of the enemy so that the follow-up battalion could push on through his area at 8:30. This gave him about an hour to consolidate his position while the barrage remained stationary directly in front of his outposts. A number of the 116th managed to reverse a couple of the enemy's guns and got an 8-inch and 5.9 howitzer in action against positions well beyond the German lines. Others chalked the number "116" on the backs of prisoners before they were sent back to make sure that the "Umpty Umps" would get "credit" for them. They may have been the junior battalion in the brigade and in the division, and they may not have had the experience of those units which had been in action much longer, but in this attack their performance had been first-rate.

When the battle swept beyond Hamon Wood and the 116th were able to take account of their action, the scope of their victory was outstanding. About forty machine guns were captured, and as they had broken right into the German artillery lines, the men had also captured sixteen enemy guns. The unit lost 32 killed and 158 wounded or missing, but it had captured 450 prisoners alone. "No battalion could have done better," their commanding officer said later, "and few did as well."[25] Pearkes, of course, was elated with the accomplishments of his battalion, as were his brigade and divisional commanders. For his "masterly" handling of the 116th Battalion as well as his "splendid and fearless example" of leadership in the midst of the action, he was awarded the Distinguished Service Order.[26]

The general success gained by the Canadians on their front was shared in many respects by the British, Australians, and French. By the end of the day the Germans had been thrown back as far as eight miles by the Canadians, up to seven by the Australians, five by the French, and two by the British. It was a shattering blow to the Germans, so much so that Ludendorff was to term it "the black day of the German army." It was the beginning of the end. There were to be another hundred days of warfare, however, and much hard fighting before the enemy sued for peace. Nevertheless, the prospect of another winter of trench warfare was fading. The use of the tanks combined with the infantry gave solid promise of a return to mobile warfare lost in the autumn of 1914, and the roar of aircraft overhead pointed the way to the philosophers of warfare of yet another element which might be used to gain flexibility.

The battle continued for another ten days. For the first two days everyone was exhilarated with the pace and speed of mobile warfare. Everybody seemed to be on the move as the enemy was pushed back to the old 1916 front lines. For a brief period there was a feeling of being in open country away from the muddy trenches and belts of barbed wire and all that it implied. This lasted only a short time, however, as the Germans rushed reserves up to plug the gap and made full use of the old 1916 trench system to slow the Allied advance.

Three days later Pearkes was ordered to bring his battalion into the line once again, this time near Parvillers, some ten miles east of Hamon Wood. On the march forward the unit passed hundreds of horses, killed when the cavalry brigade had attacked on the afternoon of the eighth. At one point, too, they encountered a group of tanks put out of action by a German gun in a concealed position until it had been destroyed at point-blank range by another tank. Near Le Quesnoy the 116th took over a section of the old 1916 front-line trenches from a British regiment on 11 August, and on the following day, in conjunction with the Princess Patricia's on the left and the 52nd Battalion[27] on the right, was engaged in several sharp actions. At one point several companies of the 52nd and 116th caught a column of German reinforcements marching towards Damery and caused them heavy casualties. By the fifteenth, after several days of close action which included some hand-to-hand fighting, the 116th was relieved from the front. A short time later it was en route to Arras.

The move of the Canadian Corps from Amiens to Arras was instigated by Lt.-Gen. Sir Arthur Currie. With the element of surprise now lost and with the enemy thickening their defences daily, he proposed that the corps should be withdrawn and used to launch a surprise attack east of Arras. On their new front the Canadians were faced with formidable enemy entrenchments. As it was necessary to keep hitting the enemy hard first in one area and then the other, there was little time given for rest or reconnaissance. Thus, almost immediately after arriving in their new position near Harbarcq, the 116th Battalion was ordered up to take its part in the assault.

For Pearkes it was a frustrating time. He had expected, as usual, to lead his men into battle, but he had been ordered by Brig. Gen. D. M. Ormond to let his second-in-command, Maj. Sutherland, take charge. Ormond was following a policy in force for some months, whereby officers commanding battalions and companies were periodically left out of battle to allow those under them to gain experience. It was a new experience for Pearkes to remain back of the lines when the guns were thundering at the front.

The 116th Battalion was committed to the attack early on the morning of 27 August, and for the next two days it was engaged in bitter fighting.

The first line of the enemy's trenches were captured and lost three times before the men finally pushed on to their objective. During this action Maj. Sutherland was cut down by German machine-gun fire, and Maj. Pratt, the next senior major, assumed command. Before the unit was withdrawn early on the twenty-ninth, it had advanced two miles beyond its original starting place, but so constant was the fighting that it had suffered some three hundred casualties. In his report of the action two days later, Pearkes had great praise for his men:

Throughout the whole operation the officers and N.C.O.'s showed great devotion to duty and an indomitable spirit to push forward. The difficulty of attacking a well organized system of enemy defences was considerably increased owing to the fact that there had been no opportunity for anyone to reconnoitre the assembly positions or view the ground over which we attacked; the supply of aerial photographs was very limited, and the time which could be devoted to explaining to the rank and file even the merest outline of the plan of attack was almost negligible; the fatigued condition of the men who were exhausted on the 2nd day, due to the heavy fighting and the severe strain that the Battalion had undergone since the first of the month.[28]

Much of Lt.-Col. Pearkes's concern for his men comes out in this report, as does his desire that his companies should have all available support and intelligence prior to the attack. The 116th had lost more men in this two-day battle than in any similar period. He was happy to have the men back under his control, and with them he mourned the deaths of fifty of their comrades.

For a week the battalion was in reserve, but on 4 September it went into the line again. The corps had pushed so deeply into the German defences that the 3rd Canadian Division's front lay twelve miles beyond the line where it had started its offensive ten days earlier. The 116th Battalion was located in the area of a small village, Ecourt-St. Quentin, which had been damaged only slightly, and as usual Pearkes had the companies establishing posts close to the Canal du Nord and Sensée River. On this tour of duty Pearkes himself went out on several patrols. Naturally there was no need for the colonel of the regiment to undertake a task generally given to a subaltern, and Pearkes later admitted that he should not have. However, he had been left out on the first phase of the attack, the battalion's front was unscarred by barbed wire or trenches, there was good cover, and he wanted to take a look for himself. After two or three scouting expeditions of this nature, he knew the area as well as any man in the battalion. It was a quiet front, for the moment, but only a mile or two to the south the Canadians were soon to attack across the canal in a major thrust to Cambrai.

After a week's tour at the front, the 116th were relieved by the 2nd Canadian Mounted Rifles. The 116th were given billets at Guemappe, a small village behind the lines but, as was usually the case, within reach of the German artillery. On 17 September about a dozen or more shells exploded close to the battalion just as one of the companies was lining up for a meal. Pearkes was at battalion headquarters and, hearing the explosion, went over to see if any of his men had been harmed. He had just reached the company when another flurry of shells landed. Four were killed and seventeen were wounded. Among the latter was Pearkes, who was hit in the arm and the side by shell fragments. The blast knocked him out, and he regained consciousness in the ambulance. The pain was intense, and the drive over the cobblestone roads was an agony.

So serious were Pearkes's wounds that those who helped to put him in the ambulance thought that his chances of survival were slim, for part of his intestines were exposed and had to be held in. When he was given a preliminary examination at No. 1 Canadian Clearing Station, somewhat the same opinion prevailed. When his blood-soaked tunic and shirt were removed, it was obvious that quick and expert surgery was needed. Fortunately, Dr. J. Charles, who had been the chief surgeon at the Ipswich Hospital, was on staff. In a nearby tent was Pte. William Carmichael of the 42nd Battalion, who had a badly sprained ankle. "About midnight," he related,

> an orderly came over . . . where I was lying on a stretcher and took me over to the operation section. The nurse told me about Lieut.-Col. Pearkes and that I had the type of blood required. I said, go ahead, I am full blooded. The nurse made a slit at my right elbow and drew two tumblers full of blood, then gave me a good shot of brandy. I was then put to bed in a ward filled with wounded soldiers minus arms and legs. It looked like a slaughter house.[29]

For the next several hours Dr. Charles worked steadily on Pearkes. The muscles of his left arm were torn, but it was comparatively simple to attend to. The dangerous and complicated task was to repair the damage done to the internal organs. The angle of the shell fragment's penetration through the side and out the upper section of the stomach called upon all of the doctor's skill, but no vital organ had been hit.

For two weeks Pearkes's life hung in the balance. Within the regiment "it seemed hopeless to expect that he could survive."[30] His father, still living in London, was given special permission to come to France[31] and stayed with him as long as he could. Maj.-Gen. L. J. Lipsett, the commander of the 3rd Canadian Infantry Division, who had recommended Pearkes for his colonelcy, sent his aide-de-camp to enquire about him, and Brig. Gen. Ormond visited him several times while he was still unconscious.[32] Four times he had been wounded but this, the fifth time, looked as if it might be the last. In the second week, however, when an officer came to see him, Pearkes opened his eyes and managed a weak grin. He was going to make it. The word of his recovery soon spread, and no one was happier to hear it than his mother and sister in Victoria. "It was just like him," a friend wrote to her from England, "to go to the assistance of others who were hurt by those shells and so get wounded himself, yet that gives you a fresh cause for pride—his unselfish care for his men."[33] Mrs. Pearkes thought she might be able to go to England to be with her son, but the daily news of his continual improvement made this unnecessary.

Nevertheless, it was a month before the doctors considered Pearkes sufficiently fit to be moved, and another two weeks before he could be sent to England. By 2 November he was well enough to be transferred to the I.O.D.E. Hospital in London. In the hospitals in London he met a number of his friends and soon joined the group of Canadian officers who used to rendezvous at the Savoy Hotel bar at noon. His father owned and managed a residential hotel in the city and gave a special welcome to officers in his son's battalion. Periodically a group of them would gather there for dinner and catch up on the news from the unit. Every officer coming to London was pumped for information, and the more he heard, the more Pearkes wanted to get back. When the doctors suggested that he should return to Canada, he refused.

On 11 November Pearkes had been invited to lunch by his uncles, the Reverends W. A. and F. Pearkes, at their club in Piccadilly. He heard the booming of the guns and the church bells ringing announcing the end of the war, and en route he saw the Londoners pour out of their shops and offices into the streets. It was the beginning of a tremendous and spontaneous celebration which was going to continue far into the night. Nearing Piccadilly his taxi driver said he could never get through the crowd, now thronging the streets and sidewalks. A pound note helped to change his mind. Near the Strand a uniformed woman spotted Pearkes and called out: "Look, here's a Canadian V.C.!", and with that her group jumped into the taxi with others riding on top, shouting, waving flags, and waving to the crowds. It was a rather flustered young man who finally reached the Conservative Club where his uncles were waiting for him. After a rest back at the hospital, Pearkes went out again that evening to dinner. At the restaurant everybody was having a whale of a time. I remember someone sending over a magnum of champagne for us to have. Then I was called upon to make a speech . . . . I'm sure we were all feeling pretty good . . . . I don't know how I got back that night. I remember being out in Regent St., and all the young people were dancing round and round. There was no traffic moving at all; Regent St. and Oxford Circus were all just packed with milling, cheering crowds. They were joining hands and forming circles, but they always made way for any man who was in hospital uniform.[34]

It was a glorious, memorable day, and if there was any one place Pearkes might rather have wished to be other than the heart of Empire, it would be with his regiment in France.

In the two months after Pearkes was wounded, the 116th Battalion took part in several major actions, starting with the attack on Cambrai and ending with the capture of Mons. Before the hour when hostilities came to an end, the battalion was ordered to march beyond the city along the road to Brussels. At 11:00 they stopped at Casteau, the spot where the British cavalry patrols first encountered the Germans on 22 August 1914.[35] The battalion was still in this general area when it heard that Lt.-Col. Pearkes was to reassume command, and they arranged a greeting for him on 25 November. When Pearkes came on the parade ground to take over command, an order rang out, and a thousand rifles came to the "present." After this formal salute, someone called for three cheers for the colonel, and the air-splitting roar of welcome which followed attested the delight of all ranks that Pearkes was back with them.

The next three months were fairly routine. For many it was difficult to believe that the war was over. Now that the moment actually had come, their one thought was to return to Canada and pick up the threads of civilian life. Pearkes was well aware of this attitude, and he realized that everything must be done to make the transition as smooth as possible. Thus, while discipline became less stringent, it never became lax, and mixed with the routine parades were generous periods of sports, entertainment, tours of nearby points of interest, lectures on rehabilitation, and educational courses for those interested in vocational or academic training. Moreover, Pearkes made sure that his officers did not abuse the privilege of their rank by spending a great deal of their time away from their men on leave to Brussels or London, leaving the burden of their responsibilities to the sergeants and other N.C.O.'s.

For Pearkes himself it was also a time of decision. In weeks he would be thirty-one. His health was good, despite his five wounds. He was unattached, and had no thought of returning to farming, and indeed he was to sell his homestead to a neighbour, Ralph Sinclair, in 1919. Pearkes had enjoyed his service with the Mounted Police, but he had left it with the rank of constable and he was now a lieutenant-colonel. The more he considered a career in the army, the more it appealed to him. In mid-December he wrote his mother a letter to explain his reason for returning to his battalion as well as his thoughts on the future:

No doubt you think that I am cruel and selfish not to have returned home . . . after this last wound. I admit I had the chance last November and for many reasons I should have liked then to have returned. But I do not consider that my work has yet finished. The war is over . . . but we have yet to win the great victory of Peace. This can only be obtained by the very best influence being brought on all the men; law and order has got to be maintained; we cannot allow for one moment discontent and undisciplined action to creep into our midst. German agents are doing their best by underhand means to tempt our men and I honestly believe that now is the time when strong and popular officers will be required to keep our army straight. So far the men of my battalion seem very happy and content, and orders are obeyed as cheerfully now as they were last August when we started our push. May it remain thus to the very end. Then, too, was the selfish reason —I wanted to be with my own men, I want to bring them back to Canada, then again I also want to see this part of the old world for I may never have another chance.

As for what I'll do after . . . well if there's half a chance I'll remain in the army. It's the one life that really appeals. Of course I should prefer the Canadian, if possible; if not, why it must be the English.[36]

Shortly afterwards a notice was sent around enquiring about officers who wished to serve in the permanent force after returning to Canada. Pearkes put his name down, since not only did he wish to serve in the Canadian army, but he also felt he would be better off financially than in the British forces. He thought, too, that the postwar Canadian army would be larger than formerly, and although it might not offer the variety of service abroad one could expect in the imperial forces, there might be some opportunities to serve beyond the borders of Canada. Several weeks later Maj.-Gen. F. O. W. Loomis, now commanding the 3rd Canadian Infantry Division,[37] visited Pearkes. He told him that five vacancies had been set aside for Canadian officers at the British staff college at Camberley. The selection was based on the war record of the officers, and the corps commander offered Pearkes one of the vacancies should he want to take it. It was an excellent opportunity. All of Pearkes's experience had been gained in the field. He had never held a staff appointment, nor did he have staff training. However, the road to promotion lay through the staff college, and if he hoped to make the army his career, everything pointed to his acceptance of the offer. Pearkes made his formal application on 1 March, about two weeks before the battalion embarked for Canada. It was a decision which, in later life, he was never to regret. The sword which his officers presented to him in England was more than symbolic of the life he had chosen.

7

On Staff in Western Canada

When Pearkes arrived in Canada with his regiment late in March 1919, he knew that there would be little time before he had to return to Great Britain. It might have been more convenient to remain there, but he had not seen his mother or sister for four years, and his men wanted him to lead them in the victory parade through Oshawa. There Pearkes said farewell to his officers, and in due course the 116th Battalion handed over its colours and battle honours to the local militia regiment.[1] Its accomplishments would not be forgotten, nor indeed would the leadership and valour of its last commanding officer. His oil portrait was to hang in the Officers' Mess of the Ontario Regiment as a permanent tribute to his service, and he, in turn, later presented a sword given to him by the officers of the 116th Battalion when they had their last mess dinner at Bramshott, England.

After the Oshawa celebrations, Pearkes had a few days in Toronto with his mother before going to Ottawa to receive his travel warrant and last instructions. It was the first time he had been in the nation's capital, but there was little time for sightseeing. At the Chateau Laurier he was greeted by the former Minister of Defence, Sir Sam Hughes, who introduced himself and chatted for a few moments. Hughes was the first politician of national repute Pearkes had ever met, and the idea that one day he would hold the same ministerial post never entered his mind.

Early in April Pearkes reported at Camberley as one of five Canadian officers who were to take the staff course. Lt.-Col. H. E. Boak and Maj. L. C. Goodeve were artillery officers, while the others, Lt.-Col. K. M. Perry and Lt.-Col. R. O. Alexander served with the infantry. Although most of the students were British, there was a good representation from other parts of the Empire, especially Australia and New Zealand. Among the latter Pearkes became friendly with Lt.-Col. B. C. Freyberg, V.C.,[2] who in his spare time at Camberley was training hard to swim the English Channel. A number of his other classmates were to hold high office. Lt.-Col. A. F. Brooke, for example, was to become the Chief of the Imperial General Staff and a field marshal. Maj. J. S. S. P. Viscount Gort, V.C., with whom Pearkes corresponded for many years, also became a field marshal as did one of his instructors, Brig. Gen. J. G. Dill. Another classmate, Maj. P. C. S. Hobart, became a well-known proponent of armoured warfare.

There was some tendency at first for the Canadians and other dominion officers to stick together, and indeed they sometimes jokingly referred to themselves as the "coloured troops." Lt.-Col. G. J. Giffard, who had served in East Africa during the war, considered himself part of this group, as did one or two others. However, this did not last long. A number of students and instructors, for example, Brooke and Brig. Gen. G. J. Farmer, had served with the Canadian Corps, and certainly the reputation of the Anzacs and Canadians had achieved was such that few British officers regarded them as inferiors. Pearkes felt perfectly at home from the day he arrived, and soon he and other "coloured troops" were being invited to spend the weekend at the homes of their British classmates. The contacts made during this nine-month course were to be most useful over the next two decades. For the Canadian officers particularly, correspondence with friends at Camberley was a means of keeping abreast of British military thinking and of finding out what was going on "behind the scenes."[3]

Pearkes thoroughly enjoyed the course. There he was exposed to ideas on tactics other than infantry and to strategy other than that practised in France and Flanders. The major campaigns of the Great War were part of the curriculum, and there were few campaigns in which some classmate had not taken part. Here, too, was an opportunity to learn the theoretical side of logistics, staff organization, and military administration. The standard of lectures given was high, and major political and military figures were invited to talk on problems they faced in times of crisis and how they attempted to solve them.

The students were required to lecture as well. Pearkes selected "Infantry Battalion tactics"[4] as his major topic, partly because it was his own specialty and partly because many of the student officers were either from other arms of the service or had not had the opportunity to see the infantry in combat. Pearkes traced the change in infantry tactics from the massed attacks in 1914 through the "attack by waves" in 1915–17 to the style developed late in 1917 and in 1918 whereby the attack was by sections. On another occasion Pearkes took part in a debate with Lt.-Col. F. S. G. Piggott on the renewal of the Anglo-Japanese Treaty. Piggott had been a military attaché in Japan and took the position favouring renewal. Pearkes argued against it but lost. He may have had some satisfaction later when the diplomats decided on non-renewal.

Although there was much to learn in the classroom and the library, the student officers frequently went out into the country on "TEWT's" (Tactical Exercises Without Troops), sometimes riding bicycles and at other times horses. Pearkes was pleased that the training exercises were for mobile rather than trench warfare. There was considerable discussion about the role of cavalry as compared to the tank, an argument which was to continue in British, American, and Canadian military journals for many years. The fact that one of the instructors had been a cavalry officer in Palestine, one of the few areas where mounted regiments had proved very useful in the field, tended to dampen the argument for tanks which, in 1919, were still in their pioneer stage. More hope was given for the future of armoured cars. There were no prophets who foresaw "blitzkrieg" tactics, although one of the student officers, Maj. P. C. S. Hobart, was to become the commander of the first permanent tank brigade in the British Army. In 1919, however, even the continued existence of the Tank Corps was in doubt, and one distinguished general publicly gave his opinion that the tank was "a freak," brought into use by exceptional circumstances.[5] The tremendous development in the internal combustion engine in the 1920's and the subsequent development and improvement of the tank were to win converts to the Royal Tank Corps in the next decade, but in 1919 Pearkes probably expressed the view of many of his classmates when he said "I don't really think we appreciated the value of the tank [at that time]. It came later."[6]

It was not all work at the staff college. There was ample time for sports, but Pearkes, still feeling the effects of his wound, had to take it easy so went with the cricket team keeping score rather than playing. Riding, however, was something else, and drag hunts were arranged one or two afternoons a week. London and Watford, where most of his relatives lived, were only an hour away by train, and in a variety of ways there was much to enjoy in the brief vacation during the summer or on the occasional free weekend.

Late in 1919 Pearkes received word that, on his return to Canada, he was to be stationed in Calgary and be appointed to the Princess Patricia's Canadian Light Infantry, one of the three infantry regiments in the Permanent Active Militia.[7] In January 1920, after a rough voyage on the S.S. *Royal George*, Pearkes once more arrived back in Canada and took the train to the same general area where he had first come fourteen years previously.

Calgary was the headquarters for Military District XIII, which comprised the entire province of Alberta. Commanding the district was Brig. Gen. A. H. Bell, who had had a distinguished career during the war. He was a first-rate officer, and "nobody could have been kinder or more helpful to a young Staff Officer."[8] Pearkes was to be G.S.O.II to Bell at Calgary, and during the next few years a strong bond of friendship grew between them. For a short time he lived in the Ranchmen's Club, where he first met R. B. Bennett, a wealthy lawyer and businessman who later became Prime Minister. Living at the club, however, was a strain on Pearkes's financial resources, so he rented a small apartment not far from the armoury.

Pearkes found the new military scene interesting but rather frustrating. The headquarters staff under General Bell was small. Aside from Bell's second-in command, Lt.-Col. D. Spry, a service corps officer, an engineer officer, a paymaster, cadet officer, an administration officer, and, sometimes, a musketry officer pretty well completed the staff. A squadron of Lord Strathcona's Horse was quartered in part of the armoury, and it was understrength. The squadron officers had a room as a mess, and occasionally held a formal dinner to which they would invite headquarters staff officers. The popular place to go was the combined mess, belonging to the local militia officers, which was furnished by the Military Institute. The latter was a flourishing group, made up of serving or veteran officers, both permanent and non-permanent, who had served in the Canadian or other forces of the Empire. The Institute, which Pearkes joined almost immediately, carried on an active programme which included a series of lectures given by officers in the area talking on wartime experiences.

The main task faced by the staff officers of the district was to revive and reorganize the Non-Permanent Active Militia. After four years of war, there were few veterans who were interested in volunteering to serve in the militia. No group was more aware of the horrors of war, and none more anxious to put military life behind them. Moreover, victory had come to the Allies. The German, Austro-Hungarian, and Ottoman empires lay in ruins. The Russian Empire, recently convulsed by the Bolshevik revolution, had so many internal problems that its former great power status was seriously weakened. With the Allies so recently triumphant, why worry about defence?

This general postwar apathy towards all things military was matched by the Canadian government and reflected in the Department of National Defence. There was a tremendous war debt to be paid, and far more attention was given to re-establishing the veterans than to the future of the armed forces. A definite defence policy did not exist. It was felt that if another war broke out, Canada would probably do what she had done before, that is, contribute an expeditionary force raised from the militia regiments and volunteers. This policy emerged in the early 1920's as staff officers in Ottawa attempted the difficult task of merging the traditions and battle honours gained by units in the Canadian Corps with the prewar militia regiments which, in 1919, existed more in theory than in fact. The job facing district staff officers such as Pearkes, therefore, was to re-organize and train the militia regiments in their areas, despite public indifference, meagre finances, and few training facilities.

During 1920 and 1921 the existing militia units were little more than veterans' clubs. When the militia unit received authority to reorganize and a commanding officer was appointed, it was necessary to try and attract the best and most experienced officers to serve in it and then to gain recruits. In both phases they turned to the permanent officers for guidance, and Pearkes and his colleagues did all they could to help.

Pearkes realized that although it might not be too difficult to get officers and senior non-commissioned officers, it would be hard to get young men to serve in the ranks. He felt that one of the best ways to attract the latter was through athletics. Pearkes organized boxing tournaments as well as indoor basketball and even baseball games in the armouries. The idea was to show the participants that militia service could combine many of the athletic and social activities young men enjoyed with the opportunity to play a modest but honourable role in the defence of the nation. As the months and years went by, more young men slowly filled the ranks, as much for the comradeship as anything else. With recruiting for the permanent force very restricted, any young man interested in army life found the militia units the only outlet for military service. Others might be attracted by the uniform, by a desire to play in the band, by family association with the regiment, or by a dozen other reasons. Pearkes, who was elected president of the Military Athletic Club, was pleased to see the gradual emergence of the militia units in Calgary, Edmonton, and elsewhere.

From a very early period Pearkes did what he could to arouse and retain interest in military affairs among senior militia officers. Periodically, on Saturday afternoons, he would collect a half a dozen of them and take them on a tactical exercise in the hills beyond Calgary. In this way he attempted to pass on what he had learned at Camberley. In the winter of 1921–22, he gave the first militia staff course in the district since the war ended. The preparation of lectures took up much of Pearkes's time, for this was one of his main training duties as G.S.O.II. Lectures were given one night a week, and indoor exercises and examinations were all part of the job. The lectures were not restricted to Calgary, nor indeed were Pearkes's efforts. Edmonton, Red Deer, Lethbridge, and Medicine Hat were other major centres where regiments were recruited. Aside from six infantry units, there were four cavalry regiments, not counting the headquarters and "B" Squadron of the Lord Strathcona's Horse. In addition, there were artillery, engineers, signals, machine-guns, ordnance, medical, and other units.

Pearkes had no desire to restrict himself to his army interests, and he was encouraged by the District Officer Commanding. "Very wisely, I think," he said later,

> General Bell said to his staff officers: "Don't lose touch with the civilian life." He joined the Rotary Club and I joined the Kiwanis Club. I was quite interested and a regular attendant at the Kiwanis meetings. I found that very useful in later life. I think it's one thing I always tried to impress upon permanent officers—that they shouldn't live a little, cloistered life. There's too much tendency for them to go into a mess and stay and mix only with their own people . . . . I always maintained it's not the regular soldier you're going to lead in battle, it's the civilian soldier and you've got to understand [them].[9]

Of the various non-military activities in which Pearkes was engaged, none interested him more than the boy scouts. A school friend first interested him in the movement, and the way he organized and led the boys is best told by some of the former members of his troop. One of these was Fred Auger, at that time a young boy whose father, seriously wounded in the war, had recently died. Pearkes's apartment was only a short distance from the Augers' home. In the spring of 1921 Auger and some boys were playing baseball in the street, and, as he related later,

> Pearkes came along the street. He was certainly a handsome guy . . . and a real figure of a man too in his . . . uniform and its [red stiff capband, etc.] . . . riding breeches and highly polished riding boots. He was a sparse figure—no spare weight on him—really a very handsome man. Well, he was just a passer-by as far as we were concerned, but he stopped and . . . started talking to us . . . . He said: "Do you fellows have any Boy Scouts around here?" We didn't. "Would you be interested in starting a Boy Scout troop?" Well, we would, so he invited us to come over to his apartment [later] and bring along any boys who would be interested. So, we rounded up half a dozen or a dozen boys in the neighbourhood and we came over to talk to him about it. This was the origin of what became the 14th Troop of Boy Scouts of Calgary.
>
> No man ever put his heart into a project for the benefit of young people more than Pearkes did. In no time we had this troop built up to . . . about 35 boys, and that was the limit. From then on, as long as that troop remained in existence, we always had a waiting list.[10]

Organizing and running the troop took almost all of Pearkes's spare time. Sports, of course, played a large role in their activities. In winter Pearkes organized a scout hockey team and a scout soccer league in spring. Hiking was another activity the boys liked. Pearkes sometimes took them out for a winter camp, and one of the best moves he made was to establish a summer camp in a forest reserve not far from Banff. It was an excellent location in a mountain meadow on the banks of the fast running Kananaskis River. Close by was a good swimming hole. Pearkes had obtained permission from the Alberta Department of Forests, and the Calgary Kiwanis Club gave some financial support. Then he contacted the Canadian Pacific Railway and arranged to have it provide a colonial coach to take his troop and their gear to Seebe, the nearest stop. The scouts had a marvellous time,[11] and Pearkes thoroughly enjoyed himself, teaching the boys how to rough it in the bush somewhat as he had done when he was home-steading. Very soon the camp, which came to be called Camp Pearkes, was being used by the other troops in Calgary. Fishing, swimming, hiking, mountain climbing, games, woodcraft, nature study—all played their part in making it an ideal location which hundreds of boys were to remember fondly many years later.[12]

Pearkes's salary, then $2,500 a year, did not permit him to contribute heavily to the financial needs of the troop, but his contacts in the army and with local clubs, together with his ability to influence others to help instruct the boys, made the troop's activities the envy of other scouts in the district. Army musketry instructors taught his troop how to shoot with small-bore rifles in the basement range of the Mewata Armoury, and the boys won numerous Canadian and one British Empire trophy. Pearkes got some former officers of the 8th Field Ambulance to teach his scouts first aid, and as a result No. 14 Troop won the provincial and dominion titles in first aid and mine rescue work. The troop had a drum and bugle band, taught by an army bandmaster sergeant who was happy to contribute his talents. An army engineering officer was persuaded to teach the troop how to construct simple bridges using material found in the forests. When not roaming in the countryside,

they learned rope spinning and other cowboy arts from Guy Weadick, went to fire-fighting classes in city firehalls with Chief Cappy Smart and his lieutenants, sold apples for Kiwanis on "apple day," collected old clothes for the Salvation Army, held "bean feeds" in the Congregational Church basement, listened to tales of big game hunting in Africa, pioneer days in Alberta, exploration in the Arctic—all told by men who had taken part in the events they talked about and who were glad to accept Pearkes's invitation to speak to his boys.[13]

During the weekend camps, as well as the annual summer camp, Pearkes arranged a steady round of events to enhance their normal scout work.

> They learned Alberta history from the lips of one of the men who made it—Ven. Archdeacon Timms whose services they used to attend in his little church on the Sarcee Reserve.
> Their troop "yell" was in the Cree language. Their troop emblem was an old Indian trail sign.
> They were among the few white people ever to watch parts of the Sarcee "Beaver Dance" which is held only once in twenty-five years. They listened in reverend awe as old Paul Amos sat at their campfire and told them tales and legends of the Indian tribes—and awed the Stony Tribesmen in return by swimming en masse across the Kananaskis River at a point where the Indians usually detoured three miles if they wanted to get to the other side.[14]

One of the outstanding events arranged by the Calgary Boy Scouts was the jamboree prepared for the visit of Lord Baden-Powell, founder and head of the boy scout movement, in the early spring of 1923. By this time Pearkes had accepted the additional task of assistant district commissioner. Every troop was involved in the jamboree, and each tried to outdo the other. Pearkes decided that the Chief Scout would expect to see some horsemanship, and as a result he interested members of the Lord Strathcona's Horse in teaching his troop how to ride. While one section was being taught by cavalrymen, Pearkes contacted some of the veteran cowboys he had known to teach them how to pack a horse. The Victoria Arena was packed when Baden-Powell attended the jamboree, and, as a reporter wrote,

> a picked team from No. 14 Troop staged such a dashing display of bareback acrobatics and trick riding [that] the Chief Scout made speeches about it for months afterwards.
> At the same time another section of the 14th . . . drew roaring applause from pioneers in the audience with a display of pack train and trail riding technique that included loading half a dozen pack ponies and cinching the loads with the famed "diamond hitch" in what old-timers said must have been record time.[15]

Later, Pearkes received a telegram from Baden-Powell expressing his delight, and the following year he invited the troop to England to put on the same display at the Wembley Exhibition.[16]

Pearkes's interest in and success with the boy scouts was known far beyond Calgary. Early in 1923 Dr. Robertson, the chief commissioner of the Boy Scouts Association in Canada, approached the Chief of Staff, Maj.-Gen. J. H. MacBrien, suggesting that the association would be happy to pay Pearkes's salary for six months of the year if the army would permit him to use that time to train other scoutmasters.[17] Had he wanted the job Pearkes could have had it, but he had looked upon scouting primarily as a hobby rather than a career, and he felt the latter might suffer if he tried to serve two masters. He was to retain his interest in the boy scout movement for the next half century, and when in time he became the distinguished visitor to scout camps and gatherings, he was to surprise the boys with his knowledge and the scoutmasters with his appreciation of their problems.

Pearkes was also keenly interested in the veterans' organizations which were forming in the postwar years and attended many of their meetings. There were numerous organizations—the Army and Navy Veterans, the Great War Veterans Association, not to mention the various regimental associations which grew up after 1920. Many officers would have little to do with the larger organizations, but Pearkes, as he explained later,

> didn't take that attitude. I had been with the men, I'd been a private soldier . . . . I thought very, very highly of the men who had served with me, served under me, and I felt that one should try to influence [the veterans] by mingling with them rather than shunning them. So I did go . . . to meetings of the G.W.V.A. and Army and Navy Veterans and so forth.[18]

This interest in and concern for the veterans remained with Pearkes both during his service and later his political life.

Sports, of course, continued to interest Pearkes, even though he could not yet take part in playing some of the more demanding games. He accepted the position of president of the Calgary and District Soccer League and learned a great deal as a result—not of the game, but primarily how to conduct a meeting, for there were a number of Scotsmen among the rival clubs who knew the rules of procedure, and Pearkes had to be on his toes when the meetings warmed up.

During his years in Calgary, Pearkes had one brief period on duty outside the military district. Late in 1921 Baron Byng of Vimy came to Canada as the new Governor General, and in the summer of 1922 Pearkes was appointed his honorary aide-de-camp when Byng made his first tour of Alberta. In December Pearkes was asked to go to Ottawa as an A.D.C. to the Governor General owing to a temporary shortage on His Excellency's staff. Here for the first time he met Maj. Georges P. Vanier, who was acting in the same capacity. It was an interesting time for Pearkes. Many of the things he had to do were routine—checking invitation lists, accompanying Baron or Lady Byng on official visits, visiting the military messes and embassies on New Year's Day with Byng's calling card and attempting to keep sober in the process, and all the time learning and absorbing the procedures and protocol at Government House which were to be very useful later. He liked the Governor General and used to accompany him to hockey games. Every afternoon, too, Byng would go for a walk, taking one of his A.D.C.'s with him. "He would discuss innumerable things," Pearkes said later.

> He [Byng] was very anxious at that time that the returned soldier should fit into the life of the country and take a lead. He felt that the politicians of those days were mainly old men and he hoped that there would be a group of young men either form a special party or else take an active interest in politics. And he rather looked to Bill Herridge who became Ambassador to the United States. . . . He thought that he was one of the leading people. And then there were one or two French Canadians who had done well in the war . . . ; he thought they had a lot to contribute to the future of Canada.[19]

In all it was a happy month for Pearkes. Living in Rideau Hall was far more pleasant than in his Calgary bachelor apartment, and, of course, the social life, if somewhat rigorous, was a pleasant change. There were lots of parties, an opportunity to make new friends, and since he was a bachelor, there was no shortage of invitations to homes.

If there was one thing a permanent force officer could rely upon, it was that he would be transferred frequently. Shortly after Lord Baden-Powell visited Calgary, Pearkes was informed he had been selected to replace Col. A. H. Borden, then G.S.O. I at Winnipeg, who was going to command Military District No. II. For Pearkes the move was a promotion, although not a change in rank, which brought with it an increase in pay and additional and different responsibilities. Thus, although he disliked leaving his friends in Calgary, his troop of scouts, and the warm associations he had made, the new position in Winnipeg meant a step forward.

Winnipeg was a thriving city in 1923, and it had a larger complement of troops than Calgary. Here there was a squadron of the Lord Strath-cona's Horse, a battery of the Royal Canadian Horse Artillery, head-quarters and two companies of the Princess Patricia's Canadian Light Infantry, and smaller ancillary units of the permanent force. It was the largest city Pearkes had lived in since he came to Canada, and it contained the largest number of regular and militia forces. Maj.-Gen. H. D. B. Ketchen commanded Military District X. He had served with the Strath-conas during the South African War and later had commanded a brigade in France. A practical man, Pearkes found him very congenial to work with and shared his keen interest in veterans and the militia. With the larger concentration of troops, Pearkes also was able to widen his circle of friends both among the officers at Fort Osborne barracks and among the several militia regiments in Winnipeg.

Pearkes's major task in his new job was the training of the troops in the district, but he also had charge of preparing plans for internal and external defence. In 1923 there was no immediate problem respecting internal dis-orders. Four years had passed since the Winnipeg General Strike had resulted in a call for assistance by the civil powers. During the tense days when the strike was in progress, the local armed forces had played a con-siderable role in maintaining law and order. The memory of those days had not altogether faded, and although there was no expectation of a similar situation arising, it was the duty of the staff to prepare plans against any emergency, no matter how remote.

In the same context were plans against external aggression, only the possibility was even more remote. Pearkes had probably never considered even the possibility of an attack from the United States, but shortly after his arrival in Winnipeg he was made aware of Defence Scheme No. 1, a two hundred-page document which was the official strategic doctrine for Canada for the first ten years after the end of the war. This document was prepared by Col. J. Sutherland Brown, the Director of Military Operations and Intelligence at Ottawa from 1920 to 1927. In this document Brown examined the various dangers whereby Canada might be called upon to mobilize her forces in her own or the Empire's defence. It seems obvious that he reached his conclusions with little reference to political or economic reality. The scheme was a most secret document, and it is possible that even the minister did not know of its existence.

Of the various potential dangers envisaged by Colonel Brown, the most direct and immediate would be an attack by the United States on the British Empire. Since the bulk of Canada's population lay close to the American border, it would be imperative for Canadian forces to gain space by offensive action which, Brown felt, would keep the United States off balance until Canada could be reinforced from other parts of the Empire. If the United States attacked, he surmised that the main objectives would be the larger cities in Ontario and Quebec, with smaller columns aimed at Winnipeg and Vancouver. To counter these strokes Canadian forces should be prepared, in general, to remain on the defensive in the east but to go on the offensive in the west.

When Col. Brown asked the various district commanders to review the scheme late in 1923, Maj.-Gen. Ketchen revealed its contents to Pearkes. Pearkes thought war with the United States was a "remote possibility . . . . Nobody considered it was very likely," he added, "but soldiers had to be prepared for all eventualities and, as Winnipeg was a strategic centre . . . we spent some time discussing what action should be taken."[20] At that time the people in Winnipeg were interested in the construction of a railway to Fort Churchill. While they supported it from an economic standpoint, the staff officers favoured it as a route which would transport troops and supplies from Hudson Bay. Colonel Brown's suggestion that routes to and even beyond the border should be reconnoitered was carried out as an exercise more than anything else. In 1924 Pearkes and two others on the staff made a trip by car from Port Arthur to Duluth and then on to Grand Forks, "noting the topographical features, the ridges, roads and that sort of thing . . . . We did look into the armoury at Duluth," Pearkes added, "and were shown over that and we saw the tanks that they had there."[21] A full report was made of the trip and eventually sent on to Col. Brown. For Pearkes and his fellow staff officers, the entire journey was looked upon as a rare opportunity to visit the United States with the government paying the expenses, combined with an exercise in reconnaissance which had more flavour to it than the usual exercise of "redland" against "blueland." The welcome given the visiting American polo team playing the team fielded by the Lord Strathcona's Horse, however, typified the feeling of the Canadian forces towards the Americans rather than the occasional "recce" over the border.

By the mid-1920's, Canada's militia regiments were beginning to thrive. Memories of the war were softening; and the postwar apathy and antimilitary feeling were no longer rampant. The Chanak incident of 1922 brought some resurgence of interest in the militia, and as the years went by a new generation began to enlist in local battalions and batteries. Pearkes found plenty of work to do not only during the day but frequently in the evenings as well. Each militia regiment trained at least once and usually twice a week at the local armoury. During the autumn and winter, militia training was in full swing, and since the militia was entirely volunteer, there was a slow but steady turnover in personnel, which meant a continuous process of teaching the military arts to all ranks. Among the officers and N.C.O.'s the turnover might be less, but those who stayed a long time with their unit could expect promotion, which meant new responsibilities and required greater knowledge.

One of the main tasks of the permanent force was to teach them, usually through Royal or Provisional Schools of Instruction. In the former case a selected number of militia officers and N.C.O.'s would come to the permanent force barracks for a period of four or six weeks. Here they would receive intensive instruction and ultimately write an examination qualifying them for promotion. But it was impossible for all of those in the militia seeking to improve their knowledge to attend. Aside from the limited accommodation at the barracks and the restricted amount permitted for allowances, many volunteers could not get such a lengthy absence from their occupation. To overcome this problem, Provisional Schools were established at local armouries. A permanent force officer or N.C.O. would be sent to a locality for a number of weeks, and there, several nights a week, he would instruct specialist groups in anything from wireless telegraphy to small arms.

Pearkes had overall charge of this training and ran several militia staff courses as well, usually one in Winnipeg and one in Brandon. The arrangements and preparations for these took up a great deal of time, and when they were in progress the schools, classes, and courses had to be visited all over the province. During the winter and early spring, he had to plan the training for the summer. Usually it would start with "C" Battery, R.C.H.A., going to Camp Hughes, and it would be followed by other artillery units from the militia. Next would come the cavalry regiments—the Fort Garry Horse, the 12th Manitoba Dragoons, the Manitoba Horse, the Manitoba Mounted Rifles, and other units from Saskatchewan. The timing of these regiments coming to camp was important. Many of the militia cavalrymen were young farmers with their own horses, and it was preferable that they arrive after haying but before harvesting. They enjoyed the cavalry training and perhaps especially the mounted races and sports.

After the cavalry other troops would come into camp for their seven to twelve days of training. For regiments which had companies or squadrons scattered about in several towns, it was the one time in the year when the unit could get together. It was a period when the commanding officer wanted to give his men as much practical experience as possible, and thus field manoeuvres, range practice, route marches, and so on were carried out during the day while the evenings were left free for sports, band concerts, and interbattalion visits.

After the militia had completed their training at Camp Hughes and, later, Camp Shilo, the practical portion of the Militia Staff Course was held at Sarcee Camp outside Calgary. All the staff officers in Western Canada together with the Director of Military Training from Ottawa attended. Each staff officer formed a syndicate with about five militia officers, and these groups, mounted on horses provided by the Lord Strathcona's Horse,[22] would spend the fortnight riding about the countryside working on tactical exercises without troops under the guidance of the staff officer. The scheme and exercise were prepared by officers at the Royal Military College and in many ways were based on the system at Camberley. After this course was over and before the autumn training began, most of those in the permanent force went on leave.

For Pearkes this furlough usually included a brief trip to Victoria to visit his mother and sister. In the summer of 1924 Mrs. Pearkes and Hilda were living on Mills Road and managing a fairly large dairy farm at Sidney, some fourteen miles from Victoria. The demanding work brought only a modest income, and for years George had sent them such additional amounts as he could from his own pay. They had appreciated this, and it is unlikely that they knew how few financial reserves he had. Pearkes had been generous to a fault during the war, and, as a result, when it was over and he decided to remain in the army, he had found it a financial strain to buy the various uniforms as well as the civilian clothing which an officer and a gentleman was expected to possess. The government allowance for living out of barracks never equalled the actual expenses, there were mess bills to be paid, a social status to maintain—in brief, if he was not strapped for money, he certainly had no surplus.

During the early 1920's most of Pearkes's holidays were taken up with the scouts, and even in 1923, when he left Calgary, he had promised to return and spend at least a week of his furlough in camp with them. As a rule a week seemed to be all the time he could spare for his visit to Sidney. The countryside was pleasant, the climate marvellous, and the rural social life not unlike that in England. He met some people his own age and younger through his sister, but social life was limited owing to the demands on Hilda's time both by the farm and her mother, who, possibly because of her separation from her husband, tended to dominate her children. Moreover, ever since he had gone to Berkhamsted School, Pearkes had had remarkably little to do with women and his long association with men had made him shy with them. "I've never been much of a ladies man,"23 he admitted later, and although he had met and escorted a number of women to a variety of functions, he had never become seriously interested in them. In the summer of 1924, however, Pearkes's attitude underwent a radical change. He fell in love. When attending the small Anglican chapel at Patricia Bay, his attention to the service was diverted partly by a group of naval cadets visiting Holy Trinity Church but more particularly by a pretty, vivacious girl sitting in a nearby pew. Pearkes found her extremely attractive, and after the service, he was delighted to find that his mother and sister greeted the girl's parents as old friends. He was introduced to Blytha Copeman and wasted no time in arranging to meet her again. Ordinarily he would have found it "necessary" to return to his job, but this time he found he had almost another week before his leave was up.

Every day he managed to see Blytha—at tennis parties, dances, teas, picnics, or at some other gathering where the young men and women in the Saanich area met during the summer. Each time they met Pearkes became more convinced that he had found the girl he wanted to marry.

The more frequently they met, the more Pearkes learned about Blytha. Her parents, born in Norfolk, England, had come to Canada in 1900. Mr. Copeman took up cattle ranching in the Bow River Valley near Cochrane, Alberta—not far from where Pearkes used to take his scouts for their summer camp. Blytha was born at the ranch, but in 1906, when she was four, her parents sold the ranch and moved to Vancouver. As a young girl she could remember gangs of men clearing huge trees from the Kitsilano area. Two years later her father decided to move to Sidney on the northern tip of the Saanich Peninsula. Here he engaged in a profitable real estate business, an enterprise he continued when he moved into town where it was easier for Blytha and her brother to attend school. In 1914, when her parents decided to move back to England, she left St. Margaret's School in Victoria and spent the next four years attending girls' public schools in Britain. Prior to returning to Canada in the spring of 1918, Blytha was a part-time student at Cheltenham College where Hilda Pearkes had been educated.

For the next several years the Copemans lived in northern Saanich where Mr. Copeman resumed his real estate business. It was a small, rural community containing a fair number of retired and semi-retired British families, most of them carrying on the style of life they had been accustomed to in England. In their educational and social background, their religion, their sense of values, and in many other ways Blytha and George were well matched. To Blytha, Pearkes was a handsome man, rather quiet but full of vim and vigour with a buoyancy of spirits which helped to gap the difference in their ages. "We just clicked," she said later.[24]

For a man who had a reputation for being shy, Pearkes was a tenacious suitor once he had made up his mind. Within nine days of meeting Blytha he asked her to be his wife, and she agreed. When they broke the news to her parents, her mother was astonished and her father did not know what to say. It all seemed rather sudden, but after the initial surprise the Copemans were delighted. This was not the reaction in the Pearkeses' household, for evidently Mrs. Pearkes thought in terms of losing a son rather than gaining a daughter. Pearkes hoped this attitude would change in time,[25] but he was so delighted with his own good fortune that he took little heed of it. Moreover, as a husband-to-be, he had more to consider than his mother's cool attitude. They had decided to get married in August 1925, which would give him time to gather together furniture and various household necessities and make arrangements for an apartment. Meanwhile, from Winnipeg he wrote Blytha every day. The months dragged by interminably, but finally the militia staff course was over. Pearkes and his best man, George Paton, a Winnipeg militia officer, arrived in Victoria on the morning steamship from Vancouver. Two days later, on 26 August, Blytha and George Pearkes were married at St. Paul's Garrison Church at Esquimalt. Later that day they left for their honeymoon at Banff. Romance may have come late in Pearkes's life, but it was to last a long, long time.

8

Soldiering in the Twenties

Any misgivings Blytha Pearkes might have had about living in a completely different milieu were dissipated with the passing months. It was September 1925 when the Pearkeses arrived in Winnipeg. Captain Colquhoun of the Princess Patricia's had made arrangements for them to use his quarters at the Fort Osborne Barracks. The officers' wives welcomed Blytha as an old friend, and she was to find that being married to an army officer was like joining a large family. The total number of officers and men in the permanent force was so small that the family feeling was exceptionally strong. She was a naturally cheerful and gregarious person and fitted easily into the various social functions. It was convenient to be able to entertain civilian friends in the mess, especially in the early months when, having rented a flat in the Cornwall Apartments, they were busy getting their furniture together. The flat was in a lovely location overlooking the Assiniboine River across from the legislative buildings, but it was almost five miles away from the barracks. Just prior to his marriage Pearkes had bought a Durant coupe, and as Blytha was a good driver, she was never at a loss for transportation. On most days the groom would bring a horse for the major, and he would ride to work, taking the back streets to avoid the automobile traffic, or sometimes he would walk the distance.

In these early years of his marriage Pearkes began to appreciate how frequently he was away from home. Occasionally, on one of his frequent trips throughout the province, he would take Blytha with him, most often by car. These trips together helped to make up for the loneliness of those days when they would be apart. For Pearkes marriage, as he wrote a friend, "was the only life. It's all great fun," he continued, "especially getting a home together. Living in a place of one's own is entirely different to living in barracks or in a camp."[1]

Pearkes also found it pleasant to be able to come home and talk about his work, the people he met, and the various day-to-day events. In the mess one could not discuss politics, but in his own home he could relate to Blytha how Gen. Ketchen managed to manoeuvre around politicians. One trip with Ketchen to Kenora in particular amused him.

> The officer commanding the unit in Kenora . . . later became Secretary to the Minister of Labour in the Liberal government at the time, so we were strongly in favour of the Liberals in Kenora. Coming back we got on the same train as Mr. Bracken, Premier of the province and leader of the Farmer's Party, so we at once swung very much in favour of the Farmer's Party. We changed at Winnipeg and got into the train going to Portage la Prairie where we had an inspection to carry out that night of the local unit there. It was commanded by Major Taylor, head of the Conservative party in the Manitoba legislature for a time, so we switched politics again.[2]

The militia units in Manitoba were gaining strength, and if they still had Great War equipment and uniforms, at least there seemed little danger abroad. Certainly it would have to be an exceptional danger before Prime Minister Mackenzie King would even consider committing troops abroad. As head of the Liberal party he was concerned primarily with healing the wounds caused by the conscription crisis of 1917, and he was determined that he would never get himself in a position destructive of political unity.

In the late 1920's there was no threatening cloud on the horizon. The militia estimates could be and were cut to the bone, and only the volunteer work put in by the militia kept some semblance of a military potential extant in Canada. The annual parades by the units on Armistice Day at Portage and Main in Winnipeg, the field days in May near the barracks, and frequently the extra time put in by the militia on weekends or perhaps in preparing for a tattoo were "at no expense to the public." If it was sometimes discouraging work, there was also a sense of achievement. It was an accomplishment even to have a moderately trained militia, and permanent force officers such as Pearkes were well aware of the sacrifices made by the men.

Early in 1928 Pearkes was advised that he was being transferred in April to Headquarters, Military District XI at Esquimalt. Few postings could have pleased him more. The district headquarters was only a few miles from where Blytha's parents lived in Victoria, and Blytha was expecting a child in the spring. A month before they were due to move, Blytha gave birth to a girl, whom they named Priscilla Edith. Their joy over the birth of their daughter soon turned to concern, however, for before leaving the hospital the baby picked up an infection which resulted in large boils. Her condition became so serious that there was some doubt if she would survive. Priscilla, or "Pep" as she was nicknamed, passed the crisis but the poison she had in her system never left her. Her health was never robust, and over the years she was to pass through a succession of illnesses which steadily drained her strength.

In M.D. XI, Pearkes replaced Maj. L. C. Goodeve, who had been a fellow student at Camberley, as the senior staff officer. The District Officer Commanding was Brig. Gen. A. G. L. McNaughton, whom Pearkes had met briefly when, as Director of Military Training in Ottawa, he had come west to oversee the militia staff course at Sarcee. McNaughton was probably the most interesting of the three D.O.C.'s under whom Pearkes had served. As an artillery officer in the Great War he had gained fame for his brilliant staff work, especially in the field of counterbattery fire. He took a great interest in world affairs, and his mind ranged far beyond military matters. He was interested in almost all aspects of science, and on the frequent trips he took with Pearkes he talked about the development of the Columbia River basin, the St. Lawrence Seaway, and other projects which seemed visionary in 1928. Whenever the opportunity offered, he took a delight in visiting sites which demonstrated some aspect of engineering accomplishment, whether it be a dam on the Bridge River, the cable station at Bamfield, or the power station at Jordan River.

These visits were side trips to the numerous journeys made on military affairs. Although the majority of military units were located in the greater Vancouver and Victoria areas, others were scattered among the interior valleys. On one trip the two men had to examine land belonging to the Department of National Defence in the Cariboo area, land which had been acquired years earlier in exchange for Stanley Park in Vancouver. Located near Risky Creek, it had good potential as an artillery range, and it would be less expensive than sending British Columbian artillerymen to Sarcee. It was hard to reach with horse-drawn transport, however, and until the field artillery became more mechanized, it would have to be held by the Crown for some years to come.

One of the major tasks facing McNaughton and his G.S.O.I was the siting and location of coastal battery positions. This took a great deal of time, but there were few men in Canada better qualified than the D.O.C. to determine the best sites for guns to defend Esquimalt, Victoria, Vancouver, and the inland water passage between Vancouver Island and the mainland. By this time Defence Scheme No. 1 had almost been forgotten, and the only possible external threat, it seemed to Pearkes and McNaughton, might come from Japan. Pearkes had read Homer Lea's *The Valour of Ignorance*, written before the Great War. In this volume the author discussed the total unpreparedness of the United States to withstand a determined attack on its coast by the naval and military forces of Japan. Although Lea dealt solely with the United States, his imaginative account of Japanese troops fighting their way through passes in the mountains south of the border could have been applied to Canada. Once again it was a remote possibility, but it was the task of the staff officer to be prepared for the unexpected as well as the obvious. Certainly McNaughton felt the same way, and it was largely owing to his influence that the only infantry unit on Vancouver Island, the Canadian Scottish Regiment, was given permission in the following year to recruit a second battalion.[3] When he left at the end of the year to take up his new appointment in Ottawa, his last words to Pearkes were: "Remember, George, keep your eyes on the Pacific. You can't trust those Japanese."[4]

Shortly before he left, McNaughton wrote a confidential report on his G.S.O. I. Since he returned to Canada Pearkes had received a succession of favourable annual reports commenting on his ability, energy, and professionalism. McNaughton's report contained the same high praise. "He has discharged his . . . duties to my complete satisfaction," he wrote in December 1928, "and has taken a deep interest in and has been most helpful with the broader defence problems which have been engaging my attention."[5] Earlier, in August, he had occasion also to praise Pearkes and another staff officer, Maj. K. Stuart, for the preparation and exposition of an attack scheme illustrating the role of a division in the attack. Mc-Naughton considered their presentation "an outstanding piece of work and shows that both these officers have a thorough knowledge of their subject."[6] This is probably the first time one future Minister of National Defence ever wrote a confidential report on another.[7]

McNaughton was followed as District Officer Commanding by Brig. Gen. J. Sutherland Brown, the author of Defence Scheme No. 1. His attitude towards the United States had mellowed only slightly, and when Pearkes showed him around the actual and potential gun positions on the coast, Pearkes got the strong impression that he would have wished their range would reach the American coast. Aside from this, "Buster" Brown was a popular officer. He was more interested in the militia than Mc-Naughton and had a better understanding of their role. McNaughton tended to expect too much from these volunteers, and when inspecting a militia regiment he would be extremely thorough, sometimes keeping the battalion engaged after midnight. His intention may have been sound, but the volunteers would have put in a full day's work before coming to the armoury.

To get men to come out two evenings a week for militia training demanded high qualities of leadership and constant attention to a nice balance between hard work and sports and social activities. The pay was minimal, and in most cases it was turned over to the regimental fund to help purchase uniforms or even to pay part of the rent for the drill hall. Officers had to pay for their own uniforms. If a regiment was to flourish, it had to have a strong esprit de corps, and the remarkable thing about the officers, N.C.O.'s, and men in the militia was their willingness to serve under frustrating conditions.

Brown appreciated the difficulties under which the militia laboured, and he devoted the greater part of his time to training the various corps. Since the end of the war, the militia regiments in British Columbia had lacked a central training camp. Through the efforts of Brown and Pearkes the Mission Hill Camp on the outskirts of Vernon was first used for this purpose in the summer of 1929. By opening up the camp and improving the facilities at the one central site, it was possible for the regiments to get to know each other. Except for the artillery, who had to go to Sarcee Camp, it also provided an opportunity for the different arms of the service— cavalry, maching-gunners, infantry, and so forth—to observe each other's role in practice and added variety to the training.

Perhaps Pearkes's major contribution to training in this era was his idea of a combined operations exercise. During his course at Camberley, Pearkes's interest in military campaigns other than those on the Western Front had been stimulated. He read widely in the field of military history, and during the 1920's he had contributed several articles on military affairs to service journals. He had read particularly a number of books on Gallipoli and was impressed with the difficulties inherent in landing a force of men on a hostile shore and in recapturing an area on the coast seized by enemy troops. Up to that time no troops in British Columbia ever practised an assault combining the naval and military forces in the area as well as the few aircraft available for reconnaissance. Brig. Gen. Brown was enthusiastic about the idea and told Pearkes to prepare the exercise as summer training for the infantry units in Vancouver and Victoria. Pearkes had secured the co-operation of the naval authorities in Esquimalt and was promised assistance from the captain of a Royal Navy cruiser visiting the area.

It was the sort of thing Pearkes enjoyed doing, and his enthusiasm was catching. The exercise was new and exciting. In mid-June 1929 Pearkes met with the officers of the 23rd Infantry Brigade[8] in Vancouver and outlined the plan. He also gave a lecture on the loading and unloading of troops into ships and boats. On the twenty-fourth he had drawn up the detailed administrative and operational orders and distributed them to the units in Vancouver and Victoria. Early on the twenty-ninth, the companies of the Canadian Scottish Regiment embarked on a destroyer and two minesweepers and set out for Maple Bay, near Duncan, where they were to make an assault landing to clear out the "enemy" holding the area. The "enemy" consisted primarily of the Vancouver militia units, which had come over on the British cruiser, as well as a detachment of the Royal Marines. On entering Sansum Narrows the small flotilla from Esquimalt slowed to half speed while each company of the Scottish assembled at boat stations for a briefing. As the naval craft drew close to the shore, boats were manned and lowered. A pinnace towed the boats as close to the beach as possible, but the last few hundred yards were covered by sailors using oars. As the Scottish stormed up the beach, the "enemy" held their fire until the last moment when the entire coastline resounded to the sound of blank rounds. An umpire declared the beaches won, and the defenders, somewhat chagrined, could only wait their turn on the following day when the roles would be reversed. That evening all ranks, including the District Officer Commanding and Pearkes, camped in the open. Here again Pearkes added a touch of realism as well as saving time which the militiamen could use to devote to training.

Exercises in combined operations were carried out for the next two years. The troops enjoyed the change, and the staff officers learned many lessons from planning and observing the exercises. For two of the regiments involved—the Seaforths and the Canadian Scottish—the training was almost prophetic, for the former was to assault the beaches of Sicily and the latter the beaches of Normandy. The advantages held by the defenders against men landing from ships were obvious even in these simple exercises, and even though wartime experience would produce better assault craft and assault techniques which would include air cover, the same experience would improve the measures available for defence. Pearkes did not forget the lessons he learned in preparing and observing combined operations exercises in the 1929–31 period. They were later to shape his opinion when the raid on Dieppe was proposed.

An outstanding feature of British Columbia is its mountainous terrain. It had been commonplace for military staff officers, charged with the task of considering theoretical or potential dangers to Canada, to consider the various mountain ranges running through British Columbia as almost insuperable barriers to any enemy forces attempting to push inland from the coast. If an attack had come, the passes were to be defended. However, Pearkes found that there never had been any training carried out in mountain warfare and that little thought had been given to how such a defence might be undertaken. There were no units in the district which had any special equipment designed for mountain warfare. Moreover, neither the staff officers on the coast nor the militia officers in the interior seemed to know how mountain warfare was conducted. Pearkes, at least, could read up on it. Later, he found that there were several retired British army officers in the Okanagan district who had served on the North West Frontier of India. It was impossible to train the units in mountain warfare, but

Pearkes did arrange several "staff rides" for senior officers in the foothill country north of Vernon. These officers, divided into groups or "syndicates," rode over the area and were exercised in various military problems posed by the influence of high ground, mountain passes, and restrictive valleys. It was a very useful exercise, and one so obviously needed that it is surprising it had not been done before.

Since the greater part of British Columbia's population, and thus most of the militia units, was concentrated in the southwestern part of the province, Pearkes spent less time away from home than was necessary in either Calgary or Winnipeg. Pep's recurrent illness was a matter of periodic concern, and she required almost constant care. Although their daughter's condition reduced the Pearkeses' social life, it did not dampen it completely. Most of Blytha's friends lived in the Victoria-Saanich area, and at their house on Fort Street George and Blytha made their guests welcome. In Victoria social life tended to be both leisurely and somewhat more formal. House parties were popular, and there was a considerable amount of social activity at Work Point Barracks, not only within the small group of permanent force officers stationed there, but also among civilians who participated in a variety of social functions based on the officers' mess. Another centre of social life was at the infantry and artillery messes at the Bay Street Armoury. The Empress Hotel, of course, provided the main centre for civilian functions. Formal or fancy dress balls at that venerable institution were major affairs for young and old. Greater informality and usually more fun could be found at the periodic weekend dances held at the Yacht Club or the Tennis Club.

In 1929, Canada, and it seemed the entire world, had never seen such boom times. There were numerous stories of small-time speculators reaping immense rewards by smart investment. Bank clearances were increasing every month, and there was a sense of heady optimism among leaders in finance and business that made tens of thousands of men "take a fling" in the stock market. Wages and prices continued their upward spiral, and the Pearkeses found the prices advancing much quicker than their income. Their house at the corner of Fort and Belmont cost forty-five dollars a month, even though George rented it from his father-in-law. The price of food and clothing was climbing steadily, and they still had major household appliances to buy. Thus, although he was not hard up, George had no spare cash to invest. As the coming months were to show, it was well he did not.

Late in the summer of 1929 Pearkes was informed that he was being appointed G.S.O. I at the Royal Military College at Kingston. It meant duties and responsibilities of a higher nature than those at the headquarters of a military district. It also meant an opportunity to live in Eastern Canada. Moreover, Kingston was in the centre of the area where much of

Canada's early history had been created. This, together with the excellent library available at R.M.C., was to stimulate further Pearkes's interest in Canadian military history, and in time he was to publish articles based on his own research.

The Pearkeses had scarcely unpacked when they were off on a longer trip—by sea to England. Largely at the instigation of the Prince of Wales, the British Empire Service League had made arrangements to have a reunion of winners of the Victoria Cross in London on the eleventh anniversary of the armistice. The Department of National Defence decided that Pearkes should have charge of the Canadian contingent when it assembled in London. It was a smooth trip over on the S. S. *Duchess of York*, enhanced by an invitation to tea to the Canadian V.C. winners on board by the British Prime Minister, Ramsay MacDonald, who was returning home on the same ship.

The reunion was an outstanding success. Of 467 living V.C. winners, 321 attended the ceremonies in London, and of these 31 came from Canada. The arrangements made by the B.E.S.L. were excellent, and two especially were outstanding. The first was the V.C. dinner held in the Royal Gallery of the House of Lords and presided over by the Prince of Wales. Passing under an archway over which hung a huge replica of the Victoria Cross emblazoned with Earl Haig poppies, the men took their seats amid the semi-medieval splendor of the gallery while the string band of the Grenadier Guards played well-known songs of the 1914–18 period. Military rank and social standing counted for nothing in this assembly; seats were chosen by ballot. Young or old, rich or poor, "the wearing of a little Maltese Cross of bronze placed all the guests possessing the decoration on equal footing,"[9] and that is probably how they would have preferred it.[10] Of the four men who responded to the Prince of Wales's speech to "the most democratic and at the same time most exclusive of all orders of chivalry," two were Canadians. Lt.-Col. W. A. ("Billy") Bishop spoke for the air force, while Pearkes spoke for all overseas V.C.'s attending. His speech, reported in *The Times* the following day, described his own feelings about the decoration. "Holders of the cross," he said,

realized the Cross was never gained without the sacrifice of gallant lives. No matter whether it was won during some desperate assault or during some grim defence, the loss of gallant and faithful comrades went with the deed. It was natural, therefore, that they should think of those less fortunate than themselves, and it was with humble thankfulness for the miracle of their existence today that they joined in commending to the nation the cause of ex-Servicemen.

We are simply the lucky ones.... There aren't enough V.C.s to go round, and the man who gets one is lucky, for there are tens of thousands as gallant as he.

Possibly the second outstanding occasion of the reunion was the service at the cenotaph in Whitehall on Armistice Day. This time representative contingents from famous British regiments marched through London to the cheers of the crowd, but at the end of the procession, when the body of over three hundred Victoria Cross winners swung into view, the cheering became a continuous roar of welcome. It was a most moving ceremony, one Pearkes was never to forget.

There were other functions to attend in the few days to spare before returning to Canada. Blytha was able to meet a few of her husband's relatives, but not his father who had died the previous year. Pearkes did manage to get in one day's hunting in the New Forest where he had hunted as a boy, and there was a pleasant lunch with Lord Byng, who retained a keen interest in Canadian affairs. The visit was over all too soon, however, and when they returned to Kingston to take up quarters at Barriefield House, winter had set in.

Barriefield House,[11] the Pearkeses' residence for the next four years, was a large, three-storey, stone house with very thick walls built a century earlier. Little had been done to improve the house for decades. Located on a hill close to Barriefield, it commanded a sweeping view of the college, the Rideau Canal, Kingston itself, and Lake Ontario. Their remoteness from Kingston, however, made it difficult to secure help, though Blytha was expected to entertain frequently. George enjoyed the gardens, developing what was to become one of his favourite hobbies next to riding. Fortunately R.M.C. had a good stable of horses, and he rode on Saturday afternoons. With Capt. Basil Price, an exchange officer from the British Army, and others, Pearkes formed the "Barriefield Hunt Club." The club was essentially a mounted paper chase, and as the cadets noted at the time, "is at all times kindly disposed towards the fox, the hare or any stag that may stray into its country."[12]

Although he was deputy commandant at the college and had his office on the campus, Pearkes was not involved with the daily routine of instruction. A small military and civilian staff looked after the training of the cadets, although Pearkes sometimes gave them lectures in military history. His old friend from Victoria, Maj. L. C. Goodeve, was on staff lecturing on tactics, others instructed on drill, artillery, law, administration, English, and a variety of other topics. On the parade square Capt. R. F. L. ("Rod") Keller was in charge of drill and physical training. Keller later commanded a division in the Second World War,[13] while a number of the cadets who did well at the college while Pearkes was there were to be tapped by him for appointments on his own staff.

The major responsibility attached to Pearkes's new appointment was to prepare and administer the militia staff course for all of Canada. This course was divided into two parts, the theoretical, which was carried out during the winter, and the practical, which came in the late summer. Each year, in the various military districts, a number of militia officers would apply to take the theoretical portion of the course which would be under the overall supervision of one of the district staff officers. This officer, in turn, would be supplied by the G.S.O. I of R.M.C. with a précis[14] of the course. The preparation of the précis, and the instructions covering it, took a great deal of time.

After taking the course and doing as much outside reading on the various topics as they could, the militia officers would be given a fairly rigorous examination, set by Pearkes. The greatest difficulty after the exam was to select the very best from the different districts. As the thirties wore on the Depression cast a deepening shadow over the country, the militia estimates were cut, and fewer officers were permitted to take the summer or practical portion of the course. Thus many potential militia staff officers who not only had the ability but who had also sacrificed time and money to take the course had to be eliminated.

Well before the results were known, Pearkes drew up the two weeks of tactical exercises which constituted the practical portion of the course. Pearkes worked diligently to make these exercises as varied as possible, with the overall intent that the officers should get training in the advance, attack, consolidation, and withdrawal phases of the theoretical battle. Officers from Eastern Canada who had gained entry to this final phase of their training usually gathered at Lennoxville or Kingston. As soon as these officers had completed their course, Pearkes immediately set out to oversee the training of officers from Western Canada who took the same course at Sarcee Camp.

If such training were to be beneficial to the students, it had to be conducted with as much realism as possible. Ideally it would have been much better to conduct a tactical exercise with troops, especially in training officers who might be expected to fill positions on brigade and divisional staffs. But at this time, if the department had given permission to gather at Sarcee one brigade of permanent force troops, it would have meant collecting almost every single officer and soldier in the entire force from the Atlantic to the Pacific. This, of course, was out of the question, and consequently the students had to imagine battalions of infantry and batteries of artillery manoeuvring over the ground. Accompanying each syndicate would be an experienced officer such as Pearkes, pointing out errors of judgment when they occurred and posing problems for the students to solve if the enemy forces countered their tactics or threatened a weak point in their defences. Fortunately for Pearkes and other senior Canadian officers, there continued through the years a warm liaison with the British army, and reports of British staff exercises helped keep the Canadians up-to-date. With their imperial commitments and consequently larger forces, the British were able to conduct exercises with troops, an advantage which the Canadians were not to have until the outbreak of war.

It was partly owing to the difficulties under which the Canadians laboured that Pearkes was given an additional task. For some time a few senior Canadian permanent force officers had been attending the staff college at Camberley. Promotion usually depended on an officer receiving a favourable report in the course. The major difficulty facing those wishing to write the entrance examination was obtaining the time and facilities to prepare for them, and there were only one or two institutions in Canada which had decent military libraries. As a result, Pearkes was instructed to prepare a "Staff College Preparatory Course" which would be conducted at Kingston.

To assist him, Pearkes had a British staff officer attached to R.M.C. on an exchange basis. For the first year this officer was Maj. George Roupell, V.C., and they worked closely together. Roupell found his immediate superior a likeable, modest, and hospitable man, who was rarely fussed or bothered despite the pressures which might be put upon him. "He never courted publicity nor popularity," Roupell continued, "but his friendly, unassuming and cheerful character made him popular throughout the whole College and it was a great pleasure to work with him."[15] During Pearkes's last year at R.M.C. his G.S.O. II was another British army officer of Canadian birth, Maj. C. A. P. Murison. Rarely had he worked for an officer who had such outstanding enthusiasm for his profession as Pearkes. "I can best illustrate this," he wrote later, "by an anecdote."

> On my arrival at Kingston to take up my appointment, my first contact naturally enough was with the British service officer from whom I was taking over. Among the many questions I asked him about the job was . . . "What is the boss like?" This was the reply: "George is a wonderful chap to work with. The only trouble is, I think he must have been bitten by a mad soldier when he was a baby!"[16]

Although only about half a dozen army and air force officers took this course each year, their later success was remarkable. Captains C. R. S. Stein, H. W. Foster, R. F. L. Keller, and C. Vokes all became divisional commanders during the war. Captains E. G. Weeks and W. H. S. Macklin became adjutant generals. Flight-Lieutenants K. M. Guthrie and A. H. Hull both became air vice-marshals, while F/Lt. C. R. Slemon became an air marshal. There were others who reached general's rank as well.

Pearkes's interest in his profession was reflected not only in his own reading and researches at R.M.C. but also in the lively discussions he encouraged among the officers. It was one thing to be competent in military affairs as they existed, but what of the future? Automobiles, and thus armoured cars, were improving each year, and so too were the power, range, and carrying capacity of aircraft. There was no money available to permit Canadian officers to experiment with these new machines to any significant extent, but at least one could read about what other armed forces were doing and talk about their potential role. Pearkes describes something of this as follows:

> We used to get a couple of Air Force staff officers on the Staff College Preparatory Course, and we always arranged to get some outside lecturer to come and speak on the Air Force, mainly from the point of view of army co-operation and reconnaissance. We didn't discuss very much the major bombing role of aircraft. . . . There was a good deal of discussion about the co-operation between armoured cars and cavalry. . . . Tanks were being considered at that time . . . much as they had been employed during the First World War. Somewhere about this time there was an armoured exercise in England . . . . The exercises were not very successful; at least they were probably very successful in that they showed many of the weaknesses of the thinking of that day. It was decided after that there was not going to be an armoured division for a while and that they [tanks] would be used more in co-operation [with the infantry]. . . . We were considering movement a lot—movement by motor vehicles and [using] motorized artillery.[17]

Although officers speculated on the role of tanks and armoured vehicles, in the early 1930's there were none available to the Canadian forces. The information they received about their use came primarily from British sources, and owing to a combination of poor manufacture, disinterest among senior army commanders, and lack of funds, it was not until the latter part of the decade that the British military authorities began to consider seriously the potential of an armoured force. In Canada there was a long argument between the proponents of tanks and those advocating the retention of cavalry. Pearkes had been an avid horseman all his life, but he had seen what barbed wire and machine guns could do to attacking infantry, and the cavalryman offered an even larger target. Some officers felt that since Canada could not afford to purchase tanks, there should be a study of the potential use of "motor guerillas."[18] Others, Pearkes among them, were keenly interested in knowing more about a motorized army, one that not only had tanks but also whose infantry, artillery, and other corps could be moved on wheels.

The co-operation between the army and the air force was another facet of military operations which interested Pearkes. He had had his first flight when he and Col. Godson-Godson had visited the R.C.A.F. base at Victoria Beach near Winnipeg. Pearkes had visited the station to get a better idea how the aircraft might benefit the militia forces should the need arise. While he was there, G. R. Howsam took Pearkes on his first flight in a British Vickers Viking seaplane.[19] He was delighted with the experience. Moreover, it gave him a better idea of the abilities and limitations of aircraft at an early stage in his career and made it easier for him later to appreciate the point of view of the air force when army-air co-operation exercises were discussed. Owing to the financial crisis, most military aircraft in Canada were employed on non-military duties, and though staff officers might theorize about their potential, there was no way of putting their theories into practice.

The four years Pearkes spent at R.M.C. were busy but rather routine. R.M.C. tended to resemble a closed shop, and as he was not an ex-cadet himself, Pearkes sometimes felt a bit out of it. There were only about two hundred cadets attending the college, and of this number only a small percentage intended to join the permanent force. At this period, the cadets paid a modest fee to attend the college, but they were under no compulsion to serve in the armed forces, and indeed even in the summer, after a few days in camp at Petawawa, they were free. Some of the keener ones might attend a summer camp with a militia unit in their home town, but generally speaking they received most of their military training, as well as their academic instruction, while they were attending R.M.C., and the emphasis was on the latter.

Pearkes would have liked to have spent more time with the cadets, but his duties kept him involved with militia training. When the commandant, Brig. Gen. W. H. P. Elkins, was away, he assumed his duties, but these were primarily supervisory over the institution. Periodically he might accompany the college hockey team when it went to West Point to challenge the cadets there. Aside from occasional lectures, probably the most pleasant meetings Pearkes had with the students were on Sunday afternoons during the winter sessions when a dozen or more would be invited to come to Barriefield House for tea. To put them at their ease, Blytha would engage them in the preparations for tea, and the cadets' natural reserve at the home of a senior officer broke down as they toasted buns in front of the old fireplace or played with Pep. One of these visitors, a cadet from British Columbia, remembers these visits well.

> On Sundays all the professors' homes were open to cadets. The custom was . . . not to have too many call at any one house on a particular Sunday. This was easier said than done, for some families were very popular and friendly, as the Pearkes were, and attracted cadets to their homes.
>
> There was a small general store across the road from the Pearkes' house. . . . Whenever I would walk up the hill from the college to this retreat I would keep a weather eye out for Mrs. Pearkes who often was out walking with the baby. She was always a pleasure to chat with, even for a moment or two, to a home-sick lad from B.C. who missed family life.[20]

Should the conversation swing to political personalities Pearkes could tell the cadets a bit about Bennett, whom he knew in Calgary, or J. S. Woodsworth, who stood at the other end of the political spectrum in the House of Commons. Although he had always voted Conservative, Pearkes had been impressed with Woodsworth since striking up an acquaintance with him some years previously on a long train journey. Then as later, he was sympathetic to the plight of the working man. Depending on the year, there might be some talk about the serious events taking place in China where Japan, using the Mukden Incident, had begun to employ its military power in Manchuria.

With a roomful of cadets, conversation can flow in a dozen directions. But it is likely, in the early 1930's, that at some point one of the cadets might bring up Canada's defence policy. In such a case, Pearkes probably would have given much the same opinion he gave George R. Howsam. In 1930 Howsam was attending the R.A.F. Staff College, and he was warned he would be giving his class a talk on Canada's policy on defence. He immediately wrote Pearkes, who had been instrumental in convincing him years earlier that he should consider the air force as a permanent career and who had urged him to try for the staff college. Pearkes had replied to his urgent request for suggestions with a ten-page précis containing contemporary doctrine and his own opinions. Armed forces in Canada are necessary, he wrote, for the following reasons

a. Direct defence of Canada.

b. To form [an] expeditionary force to help other parts of the British Empire.
c. To fulfil treaty obligations incurred by membership in the League of Nations.
d. To maintain [the] neutrality of Canada in the event of war between the U.S.A. and any other power.
e. As protection against internal disorders and aid to the civil power.[21]

Pearkes stressed Canada's geographic advantages respecting attack from overseas. He felt an attack from the United States was "most unlikely," and indeed "is not considered as a possibility by either the Canadian or British governments.... I think you would agree with me," he added, "that it would take years to work up public sentiment either in Canada or the U.S.A. before war could be entertained by the bulk of the nation." If Canada's direct defence was the sole problem, Pearkes felt that votes for defence purposes would be very limited.

With respect to organizing a force to assist either the League of Nations or the British Empire, Pearkes felt that the time factor was an essential consideration. "The sooner a C.E.F. [Canadian Expeditionary Force] could appear in the theatre [of war], the greater would be the assistance rendered." This should be the main consideration for the organization of Canada's land forces. He added:

Our peace time organization should be such that it could expand *rapidly* into a corps of two divisions to be followed shortly by two more divisions. Our present organization does not fulfil this requirement (in my opinion). We have (again in my opinion) far too many units of the N.P.A.M.—e.g., some 130 infantry battalions. [We should] Reduce the number of units—increase the efficiency of those retained and increase the number of P.F. [Permanent Force units]. You would then reduce the time factor.

With respect to the role of the Royal Canadian Navy, Pearkes suggested that it could be defined as "to protect our coastline and the harbours so that convoys can assemble in Canadian waters in safety." After describing the main sea lanes to be protected, Pearkes added that "it appears that mine sweeping and submarine chasing are the chief roles of the Canadian Navy" and suggested that he would personally like to see an additional four destroyers on each coast.

His views regarding the need for forces to maintain Canadian neutrality are most interesting, especially in view of later events:

Force must be available to prevent any hostile power using any of our harbours, or harbours that might be developed upon islands off our coasts, as Advanced Bases. If we are not able to do this, then the U.S.A., for her own protection, might have to occupy parts of Canada. Take for example the Queen Charlotte Islands. If we cannot prevent a trans-Pacific power at war with the U.S.A. from using these as a base, you may feel certain that U.S. troops will occupy them whether we like it or not.

Pearkes felt that, what with the municipal and provincial police, as well as the R.C.M.P., the permanent force could supply sufficient additional force to cope with any internal disorders "short of revolution or civil war." Whether he would have still held this opinion once the Depression had settled deeper into Canada is doubtful. Aware of the financial difficulties faced by the government, he stated that he did not think "it would be in the best interests to increase by any considerable amount the votes [of money] now applied to National Defence." Any additional money should be spent on aircraft and anti-aircraft defences, the reorganization of the land forces, and small naval craft. He admitted that "of course as soldiers we would all like more money to spend," and certainly the need of the armed forces of Canada to modernize was obvious. He felt, however, that basically Canada's policy was sound, and although Canada might contribute more to imperial defence, like Sir John A. Macdonald and later Ministers of Militia, he believed that one should include Canada's contributions to the continent's communication and transportation network when considering her part in imperial defence.

From Barriefield George and Blytha had made numerous long motor trips all over the area, and as Pearkes's interest in Canadian military history grew, he was able to appeciate all the more the visits to the old battlefields and drives paralleling the routes taken by the British and American forces a century or more ago. They would miss the life at R.M.C. too—the June Balls, the visits by the cadets, and their numerous new friends. However, four years was the normal tenure of a G.S.O. I at the college, and in July 1933 Pearkes was informed of his new appointment.

Perhaps owing to his previous lengthy experience commanding an infantry battalion during the war, Pearkes was given a senior staff position. This experience also exempted him from attending a course at the Senior Officers School in England, but his superiors in Ottawa decided he should attend it in the autumn of 1933. Evidently it was felt that attending the course would be an excellent refresher, enabling Pearkes to familiarize himself with the most up-to-date British military thought and training methods. During the 1920's and 1930's it was a rare opportunity for any permanent force officer to get permission to study abroad except for the few who would be taking the course at the staff college at Camberley or, later, at Quetta in India. Had there been a staff college in Canada, even this opportunity probably would have been cancelled. There was still the tremendous gap in the training of senior Canadian officers owing to lack of funds to permit any large-scale manoeuvres in the field. In Britain, at least, one might get the opportunity to observe such manoeuvres or to talk with officers who had been involved in them.

When Pearkes sailed for England in the autumn of 1933, he took his family with him. There were now two children to care for. A son John had been born in 1931, and Blytha might have been in a very awkward position in the isolated house had an emergency arisen. She was delighted to make the trip and soon found a place to live close to Sheerness where the school was located.

Most of the sixty to seventy officers attending the school were majors or lieutenant-colonels in the British army who were being groomed to take command of a battalion. The training was demanding but interesting. It covered a variety of fields, but Pearkes was primarily interested in the tactical exercises which were carried out up to the brigade level. Moreover, he enjoyed the method of instruction, whereby one worked as part of a syndicate but, when the solution to a problem was asked, the questioning and probing of the answer was carried out as if the officers were part of a university seminar. It was a refreshing change in army teaching methods which Pearkes was to encourage among similar groups of Canadian militia officers.

Part of the value of such a course was not only the new information but also the officers one met and the old acquaintances renewed. Pearkes found that the commandant was an old friend from his Camberley Staff College days, W. G. Lindsell. Another friend from the same class was Maj. A. H. Hopwood who, after serving in China and Bermuda, was an instructor. Maj. R. H. Dewing was there also. He had been the attached British staff officer at R.M.C., and Pearkes had met him in the course of normal training. F. A. M. Browning, a classmate of Pearkes at the school, was second-in-command of the 1st Battalion Grenadier Guards. The very epitome of a Guards' officer he was, in Pearkes's opinion, "one of the most brilliant of the students." On one free weekend Browning invited the Pearkeses to his home where they met his wife, Daphne du Maurier. Later George accompanied him on a tour of inspection of the various posts guarded by the Grenadiers when his battalion was on duty. On visits to London, Woolwich, and elsewhere, George also had the opportunity to renew acquaintanceships from his staff college days. He never missed the opportunity to ask questions about the much wider experience his friends had had both in Britain and abroad. Periodically the students of the Senior

Officers School would be taken by bus to visit some of the army establishments in Southern England, and this, too, helped Pearkes gain an idea of some of the experimental work being carried out by the British Army. Fortunately there was about a week's gap between the time the course ended and the sailing of the ship for Canada, so Pearkes was able to accept an invitation from Browning to help him run a series of indoor and outdoor exercises for his battalion. The course was devised for the officers and N.C.O.'s of the Grenadiers, and Pearkes was unofficially attached to the unit, lived in their quarters, and thoroughly enjoyed the whole experience. The work he was called upon to do was based, primarily, on what had been taught at the Senior Officers School, so for both the regimental course enabled them to put into practice some of the theory they had learned.

When Pearkes returned to Canada early in 1934 he half expected to be given some task to complete in which time was of the essence. When he had applied for leave to visit Europe, he had been ordered to return as soon as possible. On his arrival, however, he found there was only the same routine to be followed. His disappointment was tempered shortly thereafter by a glowing report[22] from the Senior Officers School and, within a matter of weeks, his appointment to a senior staff position at Ottawa. In March 1934 he was to assume the responsibilities of the Director of Military Training and Staff Duties. Once more he would come under his former district commander, A. G. L. McNaughton, now Chief of the General Staff. For the next five years Pearkes, in Ottawa and later in Calgary, was to occupy a front row seat in Canada's small military hierarchy and was to observe the spectacle of Canada's frustratingly slow realization of the growing danger in Europe.

9

Preparations for War

In the day and a half journey to Ottawa from Halifax, Pearkes noticed the idle men, the stilled factories, the women and children wearing clothing which five or six years before they would have donated to the poor. In February 1934, Canada was still caught in an economic and financial slough which had slowed almost every aspect of national life. It was also having a profound effect on every department of the government, and, as Pearkes was to find, those in charge of the nation's defence were engaged in a struggle merely to keep the armed forces in existence.

It was not until he reported in to Ottawa that Pearkes was told definitely about his next appointment. He had hoped it would be the command of the Princess Patricia's Canadian Light Infantry. He had belonged to the regiment since he had become a permanent force officer after the war, but although he wore its uniform and knew most of its officers, he had never served in a regimental capacity. However, his superiors had another task in mind. The Director of Military Training and Staff Duties, Col. H. E. Boak, was due to be promoted to command a district in the near future. Pearkes was told he was to understudy and then succeed Boak. In a sense it was disappointing, but the new job carried greater responsibilities than a regimental command and with it would come promotion to the rank of temporary colonel.[1] Climbing the rungs of success in the Canadian permanent force in the interwar years was a slow process. Senior openings were limited, and at that temporary and acting ranks were employed very widely. Nevertheless, for Pearkes the future looked promising, and by the time he had Blytha and the children settled into their new house in the Sandy Hill district, he found his new job becoming more and more interesting.

The Directorate of Military Training was located in the Wood Building on Laurier Avenue, a twenty-minute walk from Pearkes's home. Small as the building was, it housed most of the headquarters staff of the Department of National Defence. Owing to the smallness of the forces Pearkes found that he knew most of the army people in other offices. The Adjutant-General was Brig. C. F. Constantine who had been commandant at R.M.C. when Pearkes had first arrived there. The Director and Assistant Director of Engineering Services were Col. E. J. C. Schmidlin and Maj. C. R. S. Stein, both of whom Pearkes knew well at R.M.C. Another recent posting from Kingston was Maj. R. J. Leach, whom Pearkes met as an officer serving there with the artillery. Col. D. W. B. Spry and Col. A. E. Snell[2] had both served at district headquarters in Calgary when Pearkes was there. In Victoria Pearkes had known Lt.-Col. D. S. Tamblyn, and he was now in charge of the Canadian Army Veterinary Corps. The very existence of his office said much of the lack of modernization of the forces. Another friend was Maj. G. R. Turner, who had been the district engineer officer in Winnipeg. An officer whom Pearkes had met only casually but whom he got to know and admire was Maj. E. L. M. Burns. He was with military intelligence and active in translating air photograph intelligence onto maps.[3] Close to Pearkes's office was the Director of Military Operations and Intelligence, Lt.-Col. H. D. G. Crerar. He and Pearkes were the same age, both were veterans, and they had first met some years earlier at military exercises in the west. They were to work closely on several projects and make a good team.

Down at the end of the hall was the office of the Chief of the General Staff, Maj.-Gen. A. G. L. McNaughton. He had held that position since 1929 and recently had his term of office extended to December 1936. As usual his interests were far-reaching, and, perhaps as a consequence, he was not able to give all of his time to the main function of his office. When Pearkes arrived in Ottawa, for example, McNaughton was deeply engaged with unemployment relief camps. Since 1932 McNaughton had been keenly aware of the large numbers of men whose morale was being sapped by unemployment and bleak prospects for the future. The municipalities and provincial governments were straining to care for the married unemployed, but McNaughton was especially concerned with the tens of thousands of unemployed single men. The social danger was considerable, and certainly these frustrated, embittered men presented a prime seedbed to communist agitators. The Chief of the General Staff, therefore, suggested to the government that, using army organizational, engineering, and other services, he would be able to establish camps where single, transient men would be able to find a bed, food, clothing, and medical treatment and be given work to restore their morale and self-esteem.[4] Late in 1932 Prime Minister R. B. Bennett and his cabinet accepted the scheme, and in the following year eight thousand or more men were at work in over two dozen relief camps scattered across the country. Pearkes, of course, had been aware of McNaughton's efforts before coming to Ottawa, but he had no idea of the extent to which defence headquarters officers were involved and how much of their time was taken up in unemployment relief affairs.

McNaughton had been in his present appointment only months before the onset of the Depression. In his first year he had managed to increase the modest budget allotted to the army. From 1930 onward there was a steady and understandable pressure to reduce expenditure on defence. The pressure became so great that McNaughton went so far as to suggest that the Royal Canadian Navy might be disbanded. The task of patrolling and defending Canadian coastal waters could be taken over by the air force, an arm of the service which McNaughton felt more indispensable than the navy. The attitude of the Chief of the Naval Staff towards this suggestion can be imagined, but it was only by the utmost effort that the navy was kept in being as a separate service.

Aside from the battle McNaughton was having with the navy, Pearkes found that relations between his chief and the Deputy Minister of Defence, L. R. LaFleche, were very strained. Pearkes describes the difficulties as follows:

I think the deputy minister felt that he was deputy to the minister, and that the Chief of the General Staff should submit all policy matters through the deputy minister . . . whereas the Chief of the General Staff felt that he had direct access to the minister. [He felt] all matters of policy should be presented . . . to the Minister and it was just the financial aspect of these which would concern the deputy. The deputy was responsible [only] for seeing that the programmes could be kept within the estimates which had been passed by the Department. Now you just cannot draw a hard and fast line between those two offices and the only way is to have complete cooperation. The deputy minister, while he doesn't advance policy, had to know all about the programmes that were being prepared. . . . He is in the House sitting at the table when the estimates are presented, not the Chief of the General Staff, and the deputy minister has to be able to answer all these questions. Well, unfortunately there was a great clash of personalities. La Fleche was a very able deputy. I always got on well with him as well as with McNaughton, but it was unfortunate that . . . McNaughton resented the deputy and really tried to keep [him] in the dark as to what was going on. It wasn't a very happy time.[5]

One of the few directorates not involved in the relief camp scheme was military training. Indirectly, however, McNaughton's interest in the camps did have an effect. "If I could get in to see him once a fortnight I'd be darned lucky," Pearkes said later.

> He [McNaughton] . . . was most enthusiastic about [the relief camp scheme]. It was his baby and he was reporting direct to the Prime Minister on these things. I think his interest was in the challenge of the job. There was the secondary thought that if he could show the army could do something, why then the army would be kept in existence.[6]

The precarious state of the armed forces was apparent everywhere. Shortly after Pearkes arrived in Ottawa, G/C G. M. Croil, the senior air officer, reported to McNaughton that "at the present time the R.C.A.F. is not in a position to put even one completely equipped service Flight into the field in the event of a national emergency."[7] In 1935 the situation had grown even worse. McNaughton wrote to Bennett outlining the sad state of the nation's defence:

> As regards reserves of equipment and ammunition, the matter is shortly disposed of. Except as regards rifles and rifle ammunition, partial stocks of which were inherited from the Great War—there are none.
>
> As regards equipment, the situation is almost equally serious, and to exemplify it I select a few items from the long lists of deficiencies on file at N.D.H.Q.:
> (1) There is not a single modern anti-aircraft gun of any sort in Canada.
> (2) The stocks of field gun ammunition on hand represent 90 minutes' fire at normal rates for the field guns inherited from the Great War and which are now obsolescent.
> (3) The coast defence armament is obsolete and, in some cases, defective . . . .
> (4) About the only article of which stocks are held is harness, and this is practically useless . . . .
> (5) There are only 25 aircraft of service type in Canada, all of which are obsolescent for training purposes . . . .
> (6) Not one service air bomb is held in Canada.[8]

Despite the extremely low ebb of the army's fortunes, Pearkes's enthusiasm and energy in his new position were not clouded by pessimism. If the resources were limited, it was up to him to make the very best use of them. Aside from Pearkes there were four other officers in the directorate: Maj. J. C. Murchie, recently posted from Victoria; Maj. G. A. McCarter, another artillery officer; Maj. J. K. Lawson, who was in the directorate when Pearkes arrived; and Maj. K. M. Holloway, of the Royal Canadian Regiment, whom Pearkes knew in Kingston when he was staff adjutant at R.M.C. Holloway was in charge of cadet training, while Lawson was responsible for weapon training.

Pearkes was responsible for the training policy of all militia, and he and his staff had to prepare estimates of expenditure for training. The training at R.M.C. as well as the administration and training at Petawawa also came directly under D.M.T., as did the various cadet corps scattered from one end of the country to the other. Schools, both Royal and Provisional, were authorized by the directorate through the district officers commanding. Pearkes and his staff, in conjunction with the adjutant-general's branch, arranged the moves of general staff officers as well as those going on various special appointments.

To keep abreast of military affairs in Great Britain, Pearkes had access to the liaison letters which were sent out monthly by the British Chief of the Imperial General Staff to the Chiefs of Staff in the Dominions. Pearkes was also in correspondence with various senior British officers he had met at the staff college and the Senior Officers School, and these private letters, supplemented by reading, enabled him to remain as up-to-date as he could in an era when there was an increasing amount of experimentation. Another source of information was the periodic secret "scales of attack" reports issued by the Committee of Imperial Defence. These reports, based on intelligence flowing into the War Office, estimated the size and scale of enemy attacks which might be made on various parts of the Empire and Commonwealth in case of hostilities. They were designed as guides as to what garrison would be necessary at the time of mobilization and what arms and equipment should be available to meet the contingency. "We accepted those scales of attack as being a considered opinion which we should take cognizance of and be guided by," Pearkes said later. The reliance on the British for information regarding both training and intelligence reflected in part both the inability of the department to send its officers abroad and the close relationship which continued to exist between the British and Canadian military forces. The warm bond between the War Office and the Department of National Defence, however, was not paralleled between the Foreign Office and the Department of External Affairs. The Prime Minister held the portfolio of Secretary of State for External Affairs, but the Undersecretary, Dr. O. D. Skelton, was opposed to any Canadian participation in any scheme of collective security. He was "very much an isolationist" and suspicious of British foreign policy. As a result, those in External Affairs "were not enthusiastic about the army at all."[9]

During the greater part of Pearkes's first year as Director of Military Training, the Conservatives were in power. Pearkes met Bennett occasionally, but he met his minister far more frequently. Pearkes had struck up an acquaintanceship with Lt.-Col. C. R. Scott, who was military secretary to the minister, the Honourable Grote Stirling. It was at Scott's house, over bridge games, that the Pearkeses got to know Stirling quite well. Pearkes found him a charming man, not very forceful but easy to talk to. As a serving officer he was especially careful not to use these social occasions to further his own views or enquire about matters which might embarrass the minister.

In 1935, however, it would be unusual if, at a bridge party at the Scotts, the conversation did not drift at times towards the series of interesting events which were occurring both at home and abroad. In Canada it was an election year, and after five years in office the Conservatives were being held accountable for the continuing depression. Early in October while the election campaign was in full swing, Italian troops invaded Ethiopia. For the next seven months the progress of the war was to be front page news. At the League of Nations it was initially proposed that economic and other sanctions should be brought to bear on the aggressor. The Canadian delegate to the League, lacking decisive instructions, spoke out strongly in favour of sanctions. Dr. Skelton did not favour such measures, but the Prime Minister, although in the midst of the election campaign, argued that this was the proper attitude to take. On 15 October, however, Mr. Bennett's government was overwhelmingly defeated, and when Mackenzie King assumed office four days later, he was much more sympathetic to the isolationist views of the Undersecretary.

In the League the debate over sanctions continued for two months while the Italian army cut deeper and deeper into Ethiopia. There was little doubt where the sympathy of most Canadians lay, but the government was cautious to the point of being noncommittal over what action it might take. Mr. King hated war and wished that the boundaries between European and other states were as peaceful as those between Canada and the United States, a condition he rarely failed to mention when he had the occasion to speak to European politicians. King's hatred of war was never reinforced by decisive measures, either diplomatic or military, to prepare the nation or inform its friends what Canada might do in the event war came. Apparently the greatest lesson the Prime Minister had learned from the last war was neither Canada's unpreparedness in 1914 nor the accomplishments achieved by the Canadian Corps by 1918. Rather it was the political crisis caused by conscription issue in 1917. During the 1920's Mackenzie King had rebuilt his party, a slow and painful process which he had no desire to repeat. He believed anything which might disturb the European scene should be avoided, whether it was sanctions against Italy or an expression of opinion by a Canadian diplomat which might be misinterpreted. His fears in this respect were almost pathological. During 1935 and 1936, for example, Vincent Massey, whom King had appointed as the Canadian High Commissioner in London, together with other high commissioners used to meet frequently with the Secretary of State for the Dominions to be briefed on the crises which were becoming more frequent in Europe. Occasionally Massey and others would meet informally with the Foreign Secretary as well. When King heard of these meetings he found them "very disturbing" and thought they might create "an erroneous impression in Canada." According to Massey, at the slightest suggestion that a Canadian might express a firm opinion, King "exhibited his usual fear that by some remote chance Canada might be committed to some course of action which her government alone should determine."[10]

Early in 1936 German troops marched into the Rhineland, violating both the Versailles Treaty and the Locarno Pact. Massey was told that the government had no desire to express a view one way or the other. "Such a course," he was informed, "would in our opinion only serve to provoke controversy from one end of Canada to the other. Our task in [the] interest alike of Empire and of Canada is to keep Canada united. We believe this can best be done by avoiding insofar as may be possible any premature statement."[11] Those who sought to have Canada's voice heard in the councils of Europe, or even in the anterooms, soon learned that the Liberal Prime Minister was exceptionally noncommittal. "It would be gratifying," Massey remarked later, "to be able to record that this episode was an unheroic exception to the usual attitude of the Canadian government in foreign affairs at this period. Unhappily it was all too typical. Never during these years did our position err on the side of boldness."[12]

The deterioration of the world situation could not be ignored at defence headquarters, and indeed it stimulated another reorganization of the militia as well as a revision in mobilization plans. Pearkes was deeply involved in both.

The postwar reorganization of the militia units had resulted in a vastly inflated and inefficient force which, theoretically, could be transformed into a wartime group of eleven infantry and four cavalry divisions. McNaughton had first proposed the reduction of this force in 1931 when, at the government's request, he examined the armed forces with a view to the contribution Canada could make in arms reduction to the World Disarmament Conference in 1932. He suggested that the militia should be reduced to six infantry and one cavalry division and that there should be a much better balance of supporting artillery, signals, and other units. In 1933 and continuing for the next three years, work went on steadily. In some ways it was almost as difficult to disband units as it had been to raise them in the early 1920's. However, many would not be required, and the limited amount of money available made it increasingly imperative that weak units should not drain money from vigorous ones. Many regiments, especially rural ones, had trouble finding officers who were both competent and financially able to carry out their duties. To be as fair as possible in the selection of units to be maintained, the committee in charge

> discussed [the problem] with the Conference of Defence Associations which was held every year. The Conference . . . [included] representatives from the infantry, artillery, cavalry, engineers . . . . We took them into consultation and, of course, the district officers commanding. We were able to make the changes with the least possible friction. Some units were amalgamated, some had their names changed, some had their role changed, and some were disbanded because they were inactive.[13]

With the reorganization, the militia became a much better balanced force. The number of artillery and engineer units was increased while the cavalry was reduced from 35 to 20 regiments, and of these 4 were made into armoured car regiments and 2 were mechanized. The postwar infantry and machine-gun regiments were reduced from 135 to 91, and 6 of the latter were redesignated as tank battalions. They were not given tanks, of course, but there were plans to establish an armoured fighting vehicle school in Canada which, eventually, was to find a home in Camp Borden.

In July 1936 when the Spanish Civil War broke out, a further impetus was given to a task in which Crerar and Pearkes had been engaged since they had assumed their directorships. Since 1932 "Defence Scheme No. 3" had been approved as the plan which would become operative should there be a major war in Europe involving participation by Canada. In 1935 a committee was formed under Crerar's chairmanship to re-examine the latest defence scheme and bring it up to date. With so much attention still being given to the relief camps, Crerar and Pearkes were the only two senior staff officers who had much time to devote to the planning.

In view of the noncommittal attitude of the government, far less stress was laid on the sending of a large expeditionary force overseas than had been the case in earlier years. Indeed during the late 1930's there was a growing popular belief that the next war would be short, owing to the increasing firepower and mechanization of armies and aircraft which was becoming more evident each year. Thus the plan[14] which Crerar and Pearkes worked on had as its basis the raising of two divisions with suitable ancillary troops which would be sent overseas to fight alongside other Empire formations.

The selection, composition, and mobilization of all the units comprising the divisions were considered from every angle. The majority of units would be from the N.P.A.M., but the permanent force regiments were to be included. They were understrength, and their ranks would have to be filled up rapidly in an emergency. At the same time it would not be prudent to send all the regular force officers and N.C.O.'s overseas in the first division to go, for these men would be needed to provide training cadres. The planners also had to take the geographic distribution of the units into consideration, so that in each division, as far as possible, there would be regiments from the various military districts across Canada.

It was also necessary to keep a close check on the units selected. Sometimes a weak commanding officer might replace a strong one, and as a consequence the strength and efficiency of the regiment would begin to deteriorate. In that case the regiment's position as a first choice to be mobilized with the overseas force would be changed and another put in its place. Somewhat the same held true for the selection of officers to fill vacancies on the staffs of brigade and divisional headquarters. There were not enough permanent force staff officers in Canada to fill all the appointments, especially as many would be required to serve at home. Thus militia officers who had done particularly well at militia staff courses were named, unknown to them, to serve should the need arise. Recommendations from district officers commanding were considered, and of course there were small but continual changes in the proposed lists owing to the individual's health, age, or other personal factors.

Pearkes enjoyed the challenge and the excitement in Ottawa. When McNaughton was replaced by Maj.-Gen. E. C. Ashton in the summer of 1935, Pearkes found the new Chief of the General Staff very easy to work with and far easier to see. As Director of Military Training, problems from all over Canada crossed his desk, and he was able to get the broadest view of the achievements and the difficulties relating to training. He was also able to travel more widely on military business, not only to inspect training camps during the summer, but also to lecture to groups of officers and military institutes in Quebec and Ontario. One officer who remembers his visits was Lt. D. C. Spry, at this time a subaltern in the Royal Canadian Regiment. "I particularly remember him," he related later

out at Connaught Ranges . . . for what used to be called the Junior Officers' Tactical Course. . . . As D. M. T. Pearkes used to come out almost every day because this was one of his babies and he was very keen on the course itself. . . .

I think one of the influences [Pearkes] brought in was the whole idea of what was then modern thought in mobile warfare. We studied General J. F. C. Fuller's writings in detail. . . . We were thinking and training in terms of mobile warfare even if we didn't have the equipment with which to do it. . . . I can remember one of his great hobby-horses was an expression which I think he got from General Fuller's writings—the defence of a moving area. Now this was a completely new concept, that an armoured force could move through hostile territory. . . . This was nothing but the modern stuff which we saw in the blitzkrieg in 1940.[15]

Capt. H. D. Graham, serving with the Hastings and Prince Edward Regiment, recalls Pearkes when he was taking the practical portion of the militia staff course at Connaught Ranges. There were several officers from the "Hasty P's" taking the course, and all were impressed that Pearkes knew so much about the history of their regiment even though it had only recently (1920) been reorganized from two others. Moreover, "he always seemed to know us whenever he met us and was friendly. We went away thinking that he was the kind of a fellow that you would want to go to war with if you had to."[16] Graham also remembers the training at the time which he describes in part:

There weren't any horses around because we had motor cars and we went out on our exercises without troops... in motor cars which belonged to students.... I remember on that occasion, too, the first occasion I ever rode in an airplane. We went up in a tri-motor Ford airplane from Rockcliffe Airport.... [It] carried about 15 or 16... and it wasn't just a joyride. We were told that there would be certain messages laid out by strips on the ground in certain areas and we were supposed to find them.... We could tell...that the feeling at Army Headquarters under the direction of Pearkes, as far as training was concerned, that aircraft and ground movement in a big way was going to be part of any new war.[17]

The scenes from the battlefronts in Ethiopia, China, and Spain in news-reels and in newspapers brought home to permanent force and militia officers all over Canada how little prepared their own units were. Despite the annual warnings by McNaughton and Ashton in the mid-thirties, little was done to bring about any improvement in Canada's armed forces. The staff officers at headquarters were well aware that the units were in a very poor state of training. For almost two decades the militia had been using equipment brought back from Europe in 1919. The average infantryman, when he went to summer camp, would be issued the same uniform, webbing, rifle, and bayonet the 1914-18 veterans had. Despite the tremendous advances made in wireless communication, the infantry battalion's signallers still practised with flags and heliographs or perhaps with field telephones manufactured in 1917 or 1918. The regiments in Canada converted to tank battalions in 1936 had no practice with tanks until after the outbreak of war. A few of their officers might see a Carden-Lloyd carrier at Camp Borden, but otherwise they would have to use their imagination by training with motor cars carrying flags of different colours to indicate which was a truck and which was a tank. Even these, of course, would be civilian cars.

Much of the training was accomplished through the sacrifice of the militiamen themselves. With finances so restricted, both the number of men in a regiment and the number of paid training days were strictly limited. If an infantry unit had 250 men available to go to camp, frequently permission to pay only 175 of them could be granted from Ottawa. The remaining 75 either went to camp voluntarily without pay or were paid from regimental funds. If any regiment or battery had not voluntarily and without pay put in at least double the training days allotted, it would have become inefficient. Pearkes and others in the permanent force often found their task frustrating in the extreme, but balancing this was a spirit of duty and sacrifice among the militia regiments which was rarely equalled in Canadian military history during the years of peace.

The change in government in 1935 had brought little change to Canada's defence posture. Ian Mackenzie replaced Stirling as Minister of National Defence and shocked the senior staff officers on his first day in office by calling them in and saying "I expect loyalty from you." Pearkes was more than shocked; he was indignant. "I remember going out [of the office] and talking about it . . . to some of the other directors who had been called in, and I said: 'Of course we're loyal. We're not concerned in politics, we give advice.' "[18] This initial impression of the new minister could only improve, as indeed it did. Mackenzie was more aggressive than Stirling and at the same time more "anxious to see that his particular friends got preference in numerous ways, both in connection with contracts and in connection with appointments."[19] In the House of Commons, which Pearkes attended if possible when defence debates were underway, Mackenzie was a fluent speaker and, on the hustings, a good orator. The strongest opponents in the House to defence spending belonged to the C.C.F., and for years Agnes Macphail proposed that no more than one dollar should be spent on cadet training, a course which she felt would stop inculcating militarism. The Conservatives would criticize how money might be spent or perhaps question priorities, but few questioned the need for defence. At a time when only the faintest cracks were appearing in the leaden economic depression, however, it was not easy to ask for even $20 million.

Late in 1936 Pearkes was told by Maj.-Gen. Ashton that he had been selected to attend the Imperial Defence College in London. The Pearkeses spent Christmas of 1936 at sea[20] and after a rather rough voyage arrived in England at the beginning of 1937. Fortunately, they had managed to arrange through friends to rent a house at Chislehurst, Kent, for three months, and later they were able to obtain another for the remainder of the year at Claygate, near Esher. Both locations were within easy reach of London. Every day George would catch the train to Waterloo Station. From there it was a pleasant walk to Buckingham Gate where the Imperial Defence College was located. By the end of the first lecture those attending could hear the faint sounds of a military band playing one of the royal regiments up to the palace to perform the Changing of the Guards cere-mony. It was always a stirring sight to see them march by, and work would be suspended until they had passed. London was taking on the appearance of a festival, for in mid-May King George VI and Queen Elizabeth were to be crowned in Westminster Abbey. But the pomp and splendour of the Guards parading in peacetime was a far cry from the military studies inside the college.

The purpose of the Imperial Defence College was to give officers who were likely to hold command during wartime a general view of the world situation. The number attending was only about two dozen. Most of them were British, but there were representatives from the larger Common-wealth countries,[21] together with two or three senior civil servants. The major theme was world strategy and the impact a future war might have on the Empire and Commonwealth. The students were grouped in small syndicates and given strategic problems to study and report on in depth. Pearkes describes it as follows:

We studied the possibility of certain wars and I remember very defi-nitely we considered a war with Japan and what might be the course of action taken. . . . One syndicate . . . represented the Japanese and . . . another the British. You might say a plan of campaign was con-sidered . . . [one] dealt very largely with the defence of Hong Kong. It was the considered opinion of everybody on the course that Hong Kong was indefensible. . . . We felt [it] would fall before [it] could get sufficient reinforcements. . . . We discussed the possibility of another European war. We spent considerable time preparing memoranda on these strategic problems, working as a syndicate and writing long memoranda and staff studies for recommendation to the govern-ment.[22]

There was an urgency given to the study of imperial defence in 1937 as political events in Europe and elsewhere began to boil. In Spain the civil war was raging and Madrid was being hammered by shellfire. Late in January Hitler repudiated the war guilt clause of the Versailles Treaty. Inside Ethiopia Mussolini's forces were still engaged in putting down native resistance, and in July Italians acclaimed Hitler's Nuremburg speech in which he stated that Japan, Italy, and Germany were linked to save Europe from chaotic madness. Beyond Germany and Poland, Russia was still in the throes of one of its bloodiest purges, and in June came word that another group of generals, sentenced to death for treason on the eleventh, were executed on the twelfth. During the summer the Japanese were strengthening their stranglehold on China. By the end of July they had captured Peking, and in the following month the United States declared a partial embargo on arms shipments to both China and Japan.

And so it went throughout the year. Shortly after the Japanese extended their blockade along the Chinese coast, Franco declared a blockade of the ports still held by the government forces. When Italy recognized the Japanese régime in Manchukuo, Japan did the same for Franco. Hitler, never far from the centre of the world stage, was engaged in a rapid arms buildup and preparing to consolidate the command of the German armed forces under his direct control. The instability of the world was increasing every month and with it the danger of war.

The Imperial Defence College had a first-rate library, and during the year prominent figures in politics, government, and the armed forces also came to lecture to them. Clement Attlee, for example, gave his views on current affairs from the point of view of the Labour Party, while Maurice Hankey, who for years was secretary of the Committee of Imperial Defence and Clerk of the Privy Council, gave them an invaluable insight into the decision-making process in the government. The students were also privy to a great deal of confidential and secret information. Periodically, too, the students would be taken on tours of major military and industrial sites. To be taken on a guided tour of the Port of London by an expert who could point out the complicated functions of that huge entrepôt deepened the understanding of those on the course. There was an added fillip when the students were taken on a battlefield tour in France. The purpose was to show the problems in the retreat from Mons, and as usual a senior officer who had been involved was on hand to point out the topographical and other features which helped determine the plan of the retreat. The group passed by Passchendaele, and Pearkes gave his colleagues an account of the Canadian attack in 1917. The peaceful countryside was in stark contrast to the area he remembered, but the main features were not too difficult to recognize.

Aside from their own researches, lectures, tours, and so forth, those at the college also learned much from each other, for the students themselves came from a variety of backgrounds and most were to attain distinction during the war. Lt.-Col. W. C. Holden, who lived near Pearkes at Claygate, had been G.S.O. II at the War Office and was to become Deputy Master-General of Ordnance in India in 1944. Another student was William J. Slim. Prior to coming to the I.D.C. he had been an instructor at the staff college at Camberley. He was to become Commander-in-Chief of the Allied Land Forces in Southeast Asia and later Chief of the Imperial General Staff. Cecil G. Hope Gill, a civilian with the Foreign Office, had been serving as a consul in various countries in the Near East and had been in Addis Ababa when the Italians attacked Ethiopia. Another civilian from the Foreign Office was John Balfour, who had served with British embassies in Budapest, Sofia, Belgrade, and Madrid. Lt.-Col. A. G. Cunningham was to be a divisional commander in East Africa during the opening phases of the war, while an Australian, Lt.-Col. S. F. Rowell, was to become Chief of the General Staff of the Australian Army after a distinguished career in the Far East. There were many others. The instructional staff was small, but here too the potential was great. Capt. W. G. Tennant, R.N., after serving in the major areas of the war at sea in 1939-45, retired with the rank of admiral. Representing the junior service was Charles F. A. Portal, who was to become a marshal of the Royal Air Force and Chief of the Air Staff during the war.

Although the work at the college was demanding, George and Blytha received invitations to attend some of the coronation year festivities. Among visitors from Canada were Maj.-Gen. Ashton and Col. "Harry" Crerar who were able to bring Pearkes up to date with military affairs in Ottawa. The highlight of all the events for George and Blytha was the coronation itself. Later they attended a garden party at Buckingham Palace, the Naval Review at Spithead, and other major events. Through the courtesy of Mrs. Vincent Massey, Blytha was presented at court. It was the only function which Blytha had to face by herself, but at the reception following the ceremony, the natural courtesy and warmth of Their Majesties put everyone at ease.

During August and September the Imperial Defence College closed down. Rather than take a vacation, Pearkes expressed a desire to see something of army manoeuvres and was offered the post as assistant chief umpire to Maj.-Gen. C.N.F. Broad,[23] who was chief umpire of the 1st Division. The interdivision exercises were to last almost a month. They were held in East Anglia between the 1st Division, commanded by Maj.-Gen. C. C. Armitage and the 2nd Division, commanded by Maj.-Gen. H. M. ("Jumbo") Wilson, whom Pearkes had met at Camberley. This was an opportunity which was not available to any senior officer in Canada, which did not have the troops, the equipment, or the finances to mount such large-scale manoeuvres. Moreover, although the divisions employed were infantry rather than armoured, they were fully equipped with the most modern weapons and vehicles. Maj.-Gen. Broad gave Pearkes a car and driver, a communications vehicle, and several despatch riders so he could keep Broad informed at divisional headquarters. Those weeks out in the field with the British formations taught him more about modern military tactics than all the tactical exercises without troops he had attended or conducted himself since 1919. The speed and distance covered by the divisions were remarkable. He had been told, by some of his cavalry friends, that all the "romance" had been taken out of army manoeuvres. However, his experiences that summer made him feel otherwise. "I got the same sort of thrill . . . out of motor vehicles starting up and going off into the darkness of the night," he said later.[24] The possibilities as well as the problems of divisional command impressed themselves on Pearkes's mind. Seeing the British regiments in the field also underscored the degree to which Canadian troops had fallen behind and the tremendous amount they had to learn—not only the men, but more especially the officers, who had few opportunities to train and exercise the troops on a large scale. Pearkes's experience by the end of the summer with large bodies of troops on manoeuvres was far greater than any other senior officer in the Canadian permanent or non-permanent militia.

The last three months at the Imperial Defence College went quickly, and Pearkes was becoming convinced that it would be a miracle if a European war did not break out soon. When he returned to Canada, he did so with a sense of mission. In the next two years Pearkes worked harder than he ever had to prepare for the war which he felt sure was coming.

On New Year's Day, 1938, the Pearkeses boarded the "Ocean Limited" at Halifax en route for Montreal and Ottawa. Pearkes had been told that on his return he was to be appointed District Officer Commanding of M.D. XIII. With this new command he was promoted to brigadier, and as the train sped through the snow-covered forests of Nova Scotia and New Brunswick, Pearkes was thinking more of the new responsibilities he was to have rather than celebrating the higher rank and the additional pay it brought. During the next few days, while Mrs. Pearkes made arrangements to have their stored furniture shipped to Calgary from Ottawa, Pearkes was busy at Defence Headquarters visiting various senior officers before continuing the journey westward.

When he arrived in Calgary on 10 January, he was met by Lt.-Col. C. V. Stockwell and Maj. G. R. Bradbrooke, both staff officers at district headquarters located in the then newly constructed post office building. They had reserved rooms at the Palliser Hotel until the Pearkeses could rent a house. A large number of their old friends had gathered to meet them, and, indeed, on the next day when he went to his office to meet his staff, "it seemed more like a home-coming rather than taking over a new appointment."[25]

Eventually George and Blytha selected a house on Riverdale Avenue on the banks of the Elbow River, and by the end of the month they had settled in. Nearby was a small private school run by a Mr. Miles Ellison who was happy to accept John in mid-term. John was for a while the centre of attention of other boys and quickly made friends. That he had two prize-winning bull terriers at home as well as a mother who seemed to have an inexhaustible supply of cookies made friendships warm up that much faster. Mrs. Pearkes, as the months went by, not only found herself engaged socially more than ever before, but she also shouldered her usual share of church work. At the Pro Cathedral they were delighted to find the Reverend H. R. Ragg, whom they knew in Winnipeg, was Dean. Blytha took charge of a group of girl guides as well. George, who still firmly believed that permanent force officers should not isolate themselves, rejoined the Ranchman's Club and the Kiwanis Club.

During the late winter and spring of 1938, Pearkes spent a great deal of time visiting his command, which covered all of Alberta. At Calgary the new Currie Barracks built on the southwest outskirts housed the Lord Strathcona's Horse commanded by Lt.-Col. Fred Harvey. The city itself supported several militia units—the 15th Alberta Light Horse, the Calgary Highlanders, the Calgary Regiment (Tank), and the 19th Field Brigade, R.C.A. In Edmonton there were the 19th Alberta Dragoons, the Edmonton Regiment, the Edmonton Fusiliers (M.G.), and some artillery batteries. There were other units at Lethbridge, Medicine Hat, Red Deer, Macleod, and Drumheller. Pearkes was especially interested in the quality of the officers and N.C.O.'s, for their energy and ability usually set the pattern for the rest of the unit. He took special note of units which he knew had been selected for inclusion in an overseas expeditionary force. The commanding officers did not know of this selection, but Pearkes made sure that their officers had first choice in course openings and in other ways.

Wherever he went Pearkes did all in his power to stimulate enthusiasm in the various regiments. He praised militiamen for their voluntary work and yet urged them to even greater effort. He spoke to the officers about the growing danger overseas and made even the most sceptical aware that their training and preparation might be tested sooner than they thought. He was able to give them some encouragement that the long period of neglect by the government was changing and that the recent additional funds[26] voted for defence would mean a longer period in summer camp and some items of new equipment.

As the senior military officer in the district Pearkes was often called upon to talk to groups and clubs where he stressed the need for preparedness and the co-operation of the business community with the militia. He used these efforts, also, to stimulate his audience to assist their local units any way they could. It was an era when militia units had to pull themselves up by their own boot straps. The increased expenditure on defence in the late 1930's did little more than save the militia from approaching disaster. Two decades of neglect were not to be made up overnight.

The summer camp in 1938, however, did reflect some modest improvements as a result of increased expenditures. As Pearkes related later:

> The average strength of units in camp was about 100. We endeavoured to get as much tactical training at the platoon and company level [as possible]. The men were young but with a few old hands soon settled down to camp routine and took a keen interest in the field work. Most of the men in the cavalry units owned their own horses, coming from various farms and ranches. Most of them were fairly good horsemen but it took time and patience to get men and horses accustomed to carrying a rifle while mounted. The Ld. S.H. (R.C.) were in camp at the same time and, by lending officers and N.C.Os. to help with the instruction, and by providing demonstration units, the Militia units made remarkable progress during the short time they were in camp.[27]

The slow improvement made by the militia during 1938, while welcome, brought little comfort to Pearkes and others who kept a keen eye on the deteriorating international scene. Hitler was putting increasing pressure on Austria, and in mid-March, after a series of political crises, German troops crossed the border as the first phase of the incorporation of Austria into the Third Reich. In Spain the forces of General Franco had advanced to within one hundred miles of Barcelona, while in China Japanese troops continued to wage war with China which, by this time, had caused well over one million military and civilian casualties. The protests of the Western powers over the indiscriminate bombing of Chinese cities by Japanese aircraft went unheeded, and the arrogance of the Japanese was matched only by the Germans as they began to persecute the Jewish population in their own country more openly.

In September came the crisis over the Sudeten Germans in Czechoslovakia. Day by day the newspapers reported the growing tension, until finally, Prime Minister Neville Chamberlain flew to Berchtesgaden to confer with Hitler. For two weeks Europe stood on the brink of war as the Czechs defied Hitler and put up a brave front while German divisions gathered along the border. At the end of the month, at Munich, Czechoslovakia was sacrificed for another year of peace. Canada, which under

Mackenzie King's leadership remained noncommittal and made little formal protest, looked on in shocked amazement. Those who had charge of the nation's defence said nothing, but at least more people were beginning to realize how unprepared the nation was and how closely war had brushed by.

The year 1939 started out with the drums of war beating louder and louder. The civil war in Spain was dragging to its wretched end when Germany again began to put pressure on its weaker neighbours. Czechoslovakia was occupied in March, and Lithuania, under threats from the dictator, yielded up the port of Memel. In April Italian troops invaded Albania, a few days after Great Britain announced her guarantees of support for Poland, Romania, and Greece. Ten days later Chamberlain's measure authorizing compulsory military training was approved by the House of Commons by a strong majority, and using this partly as an excuse, Hitler abrogated his Munich agreement with Chamberlain and his non-aggression pact with Poland.

In the midst of these crises King George and Queen Elizabeth made their formal visit to Canada. Their visit did much to stimulate interest in the militia. The militia provided the great majority of troops which lined the streets, provided guards of honour, and performed many other military duties attending the royal visit. Every regiment wanted to play its role in the royal welcome, and re-enlistments soared while new recruits were molded into shape. Their Majesties were to come through Calgary on their way to Vancouver and through Edmonton on their return to Eastern Canada. It was a busy time for Pearkes, but in this as in military affairs generally he found the premier, William Aberhart, most anxious to help. "Nobody could have cooperated more whole-heartedly with me than Aberhart and his government," Pearkes said later. Aberhart asked George and Blytha

to go up to Edmonton ahead of time [before Their Majesties' arrival] so as to tell the members of his cabinet how they would be received and how they would act when the King and Queen were there. We had rather an amusing time. We took the part of Their Majesties while Mr. Aberhart and his cabinet and their wives came and were presented to us and the wives curtsied. . . .

They had a tremendous reception in Edmonton and when they came to the banquet which Mr. Aberhart gave . . . the crowd [outside the hotel] almost got out of hand. . . . Aberhart gave a very excellent dinner. . . . I was sitting next to Her Majesty . . . and I remember her asking Mr. Aberhart to explain what Social Credit was. I don't know how successful he was in selling the idea.[28]

As the situation in Europe grew more ominous, Pearkes began to receive from Ottawa a number of up-to-date instructions to be acted upon immediately upon the receipt of a coded message. These instructions included not only the mobilization of military units and the guarding of certain vulnerable points from possible sabotage, but also action to be taken as well by certain civilian authorities. Here, too, Aberhart was helpful.

He [Aberhart] realized quite definitely the approaching danger and he was prepared to give the military every encouragement. I remember I had certain dealings with his Minister of Lands, Mr. Turner, at the time. We wanted some area for mobilization. We [also] wanted an internment camp because . . . the Mounted Police knew certain people who . . . had to be picked up in case they were spies. We had to have . . . before war was declared, a place we could put them in. I had made arrangements to take over a disused forestry camp at Kananaskis so the day the war was declared . . . we had a place prepared for them and they were interned at once. This was one of the preparations which we had to make secretly and Mr. Aberhart's government was so willing to make this camp available to us and keep quiet about it.[29]

In the summer of 1939 there were more militiamen training in camp than there had been for years. Their equipment was still of the Great War vintage. A militiaman who had trained in the summer of 1914 would have been very much at home. There were a few cars, but far more horses. Some of the weapons the old veteran knew had been refined and improved, but their range, rate of fire, and capability were similar. The drill, the route marches, the field tactics, and even many of the lectures on map reading, field hygiene, and administration had not changed very much. If he remained in camp for any length of time, however, he would have detected a number of changes. He would have heard lectures on chemical warfare, protection from aircraft attack, and methods of dealing with armoured cars and discussions on the best ways of constructing anti-tank obstacles. He would find the cavalrymen as adept at driving and repairing wheeled and tracked farm vehicles as they were at riding and grooming a horse. The camp had all the outward aspects of the type held a quarter of a century earlier, but the potential in it was what counted.

During the later part of the summer tension mounted in Europe. In the newspapers were pictures of men digging air raid shelters in the parks of London and others showing British children being fitted with respirators. Germany was demanding the Polish corridor, and in magazines, newsreels, and elsewhere there were pictures of massed German troops with modern arms, trained and eager to march in whatever direction Hitler pointed. Over the radio one could listen to Der Fuhrer's passionate speeches and be chilled at the roars of approval and applause which punctuated his denunciations of those countries he felt were encircling him. Late in August Pearkes made sure that, whenever he was away from his office, he could be reached by phone if the order to mobilize came from Ottawa.

When the warning did come that war was imminent, Pearkes was at Sarcee Camp. The militia staff course was ordered to terminate immediately, and both the directing staff and militia officers were to return at once to their stations and homes. He called the officers together and told them war would probably be declared in a few days. Then Pearkes returned to Calgary himself. Everything that could be done had been done. Neglect, apathy, financial restrictions, isolationism—all had contributed to Canada's unpreparedness for the war which now loomed ahead. As a veteran and as a professional soldier, Pearkes was well aware of the time it would take to bring the militia up to a decent standard of efficiency. What his own future would be he did not know, but he felt his background and experience would be taken into consideration when the selection was made of the divisional and brigade commanders. Meanwhile the units and brigades had to be raised, housed, uniformed, trained, equipped, and molded into shape. Within hours Pearkes was directing his staff to set in motion the plans which had been prepared in anticipation for this day.

10

Forging the Weapon

On 1 September 1939, Brig. Pearkes and his staff officers were up before dawn preparing to put into effect orders for mobilization when they came.[1] In the next few weeks activity was intense at the offices of District Headquarters. There were few of the demonstrations which marked the outbreak of war in August 1914. There were no flag-waving crowds or bands playing patriotic airs to inspire recruiting. Rather, volunteers came in to militia regiments and recruiting offices in a steady stream, so that even before Canada officially declared war on 10 September, Pearkes was able to report that recruiting was brisk although harvesting was still in progress.

One of the most immediate needs was to clothe, house, and equip the volunteers. In the first instance, *pro tem* arrangements were made in local armouries, but these had never been designed to accommodate large bodies of men. Constructing barracks for the men enlisting in Calgary and Edmonton was one of Pearkes's first concerns. As he related later:

> We had some considerable difficulty in finding housing for them. I started, really without authority, in building huts because I said they were not going to mobilize in the stables at the Exhibition Grounds. . . . I [called in] the contractors in Calgary and they promised to supply materials and do the work at minimum cost in the first instance. Eventually the Quartermaster General . . . came out and approved [of the action]. He told me afterwards he had some considerable difficulty selling it to the Treasury Board.[2]

The quartermaster stores of the militia regiments held only a very limited stock of uniforms, and even those who did receive one were not issued boots, socks, shirts, or other articles of clothing. Many of the men who entered the recruiting office wore all the clothing they possessed. Their need was greatest. When Pearkes mentioned this to his wife, she started a campaign to have women's clubs and organizations knit socks, sweaters, and scarves. The results of this appeal began to be felt in weeks as first dozens and then hundreds of knitted items were offered to men throughout the district.[3]

The lack of preparedness for war could be seen everywhere, particularly in the age of the equipment. Not only were the uniforms and webbing a carry-over from the Great War, but so too were the rifles, bayonets, Lewis machine guns, and signalling equipment. There were no mortars or Bren-gun carriers, and indeed hardly any Bren guns. The artillery lacked modern guns, and the service corps lacked transport. The engineers tried to train without tools, and staff clerks lacked stationery. Until barracks were constructed, most of the men lived at home and reported to the local armoury at eight in the morning and left at five in the afternoon. Even the training pamphlets were in short supply. Pearkes had a tremendous amount of work to do, and he was very conscious of the difference between the enthusiastic amateurs and the well-equipped, hard, and dedicated German forces which had swept through Poland by the end of the month and must now, surely, turn west towards France.

Although everyone expected that a Canadian division would be sent overseas, it was not until the last week in October that Pearkes received official notification that he would command the 2nd Brigade.[4] He had hoped for such a command, and he half expected he would be appointed. He was then fifty-one years old, in excellent health and one of the most thoroughly trained senior officers in the Canadian Permanent Force. He had passed with flying colours the Staff College, the Senior Officers School, and the Imperial Defence College. During the last twenty years, he had not had command of any of the three permanent force infantry regiments, even though these units had on strength only an average of 350 all ranks and these were usually scattered for most of the year on instructional duty. The last practical experience senior Canadian officers had had in training with or manoeuvring a body of men larger than a full strength battalion was during the Great War. Pearkes, by good fortune, had been involved with large-scale exercises with British troops during the summer of 1937 but even this was through his own initiative rather than any arrangements made by Canadian authorities. In 1939, therefore, he was as highly trained for his command as was possible in a neglected military force. For the first time he was to be given the men and, later, the arms and equipment to weld into a fighting formation.

Headquarters of the 2nd Canadian Infantry Brigade began to function in mid-November. It was to be comprised of western units—the Seaforth Highlanders of Canada located in Vancouver, the Edmonton Regiment, and the Princess Patricia's Canadian Light Infantry, which, as a permanent force unit, had companies in Victoria and Winnipeg. The Saskatoon Light Infantry, a machine-gun battalion, was attached temporarily to the brigade. These regiments had been recruiting up to war establishment and slowly collecting the necessary stores.

Collecting together his brigade staff was an immediate task, but as he had three weeks warning, most of his officers were on hand within a matter of days. The senior among his staff was his brigade major, R. F. L. Keller. Maj. A. C. Gostling of the Winnipeg Grenadiers was appointed staff captain. He was later to command the Queen's Own Cameron Highlanders of Canada. Capt. L. J. Perry, of the Royal Canadian Army Service Corps, was the only other veteran of the Great War besides Pearkes on the brigade staff, and his experience was to be very valuable in his role as supply officer. Pearkes remembered Lt. J. W. Proctor as a bright cadet at R.M.C., and when he wired asking for employment, Pearkes appointed him transport officer. Lt. D. K. Robertson of the Calgary Highlanders had struck Pearkes as an exceptionally keen officer, so he was selected as the brigade's intelligence officer.

Leaving Keller to collect the men who would be the cooks, orderlies, clerks, drivers, and other members of the brigade staff,[5] Pearkes set out to visit the units which made up his brigade. In Winnipeg he inspected two companies of the Patricias and met Maj.-Gen. A. G. L. McNaughton who was to command the division. A few days later, Pearkes accompanied McNaughton on his inspection of the Seaforths. On this occasion he wore the new battledress, which was very different from the smartly tailored tunic and breeches he usually wore, so that the Seaforths would see that their brigadier wore the same working dress as the men in the ranks.

On these tours there was a lot of work to do, not the least of which was to ensure that the officers in each unit were the best available and to weed out any who might be better relieved of the command of an overseas unit. In his own district he knew the units which were to be selected before war broke out so he had kept a sharp eye on them. The Patricias presented a quite different problem. This permanent force regiment contained so many highly qualified officers that a proportion of them had to be selected to remain in Canada to help train the militia units and to fill staff positions. Pearkes was also eager to see what he could of his battalions off the parade square. Recognizing the limited facilities available in the first months, he wanted to see what the commanding officers were improvising to whip their units into shape.

On 4 December Pearkes and his headquarters staff boarded the train for Halifax to prepare for embarkation. Pearkes had no time for leave, and indeed he had had less time to spend with Blytha and his son John in the past few months than at any time since he was married. They planned to remain in Calgary until his return, for neither he nor Blytha felt she should attempt to come overseas with him as many other officers' wives were planning to do.

Four days later Pearkes and his staff boarded the S. S. *Duchess of Bedford* at Halifax. Although the *Bedford* carried several thousand troops and had stringent blackout rules, the men were able to enjoy something of the delights of a prewar ocean voyage. But the destroyers and the battleship H.M.S. *Resolution*, which led the convoy out of the harbour on 10 December, were sobering reminders that the Atlantic was now a theatre of war. Part way across the convoy was joined by H.M.S. *Repulse* and H.M.S. *Furious*, the latter an aircraft carrier which, weather permitting, kept aircraft patrolling for enemy submarines.

A week after leaving Halifax the convoy entered the Clyde. When the workers in the shipyards lining the river banks realized the ships passing were carrying Canadian troops, they gave them a tremendous welcome. The men, excited at their first close look at Great Britain and the enthusiastic reception they were given, responded as warmly.[6] The following day the troops on board the *Duchess of Bedford* boarded trains for the south, and by the evening of the eighteenth they had all arrived in the Aldershot-Farnborough area.

The 2nd and 3rd Brigade headquarters messes were allotted quarters at the Bramshott Golf Club near Fleet on the outskirts of Aldershot. The 3rd Brigade was commanded by Brig. C. B. Price, an officer who had been in the militia from the time he returned from overseas in 1919 after serving with the 14th Battalion, C.E.F. Pearkes's mess was very much a family affair, and new members coming to replace those who left found it took a little while to be fully accepted by the group. The newcomer would be welcomed, of course, but apparently there was almost a period of probation to see if he fitted in with the staff, not only professionally but socially as well.

The first few months in the United Kingdom were frustrating in many ways. The barracks had not been completed, and not only was the slowness with which the builders proceeded irritating, but also, as Pearkes recalled,

according to the priority of the contract they were building the cricket pavilion on the playing fields. They couldn't get the contractor to switch from building the pavilion to completing the huts. [Nor] were we impressed by the speed . . . [of] the carpenters and labourers. . . . There didn't seem to be any drive; they seemed to be doing things in rather the leisurely English manner, always stopping for a cup of tea.[7]

More serious was the sickness which swept through the ranks when the remaining regiments arrived early in January. Britain was experiencing the coldest winter it had had for half a century, and the combination of rationed fuel, poorly insulated barracks, and the change in climate resulted in an epidemic of colds, influenza, and bronchial illness. The extent to which it affected the Seaforth Highlanders of Canada is fairly typical:

Within the regiment, one officer stated later that at one point ". . . one third of the battalion was recovering from 'flu, one third had it and one third was getting it. By the last week in January the outbreak was at its peak when 267 officers and men were hospitalized or sick in quarters."[8]

Early in January Maj.-Gen. McNaughton, his brigade commanders, and several of his staff officers visited the British Army in France. It was expected that the Canadian division would be going to the continent within a matter of months—probably late in the spring. Pearkes reported later:

I was attached to [Headquarters of] the 2nd Brigade of the 1st Division. . . . It was bitterly cold. We were billetted in a French farmhouse. . . . The British troops were opposite the Belgian frontier and they were digging [field] fortifications. . . . In that period there was the idea of not having a continuous line but having posts at strategic places. They were small posts then, not the larger company posts. That came later on in the training. I couldn't help remarking that the British soldier was enthusiastic for digging in those days just to keep warm. And yet there was a general feeling amongst the officers that, well, this [digging] is futile because if the war does come this way at all, if it comes through Belgium, we shan't stop here, we shall go forward to meet the Germans, which they did. So really it was good exercise, perhaps, in building a defensive position but beyond that it wasn't very practical.[9]

When he returned to England Pearkes passed on the impression he had received "that the enemy attack probably would come through Belgium."[10] Although the British did not expect to engage in trench warfare and thought in terms of mobility, the concept of blitzkrieg tactics had not yet been fully grasped. There was still a great deal of faith in the Maginot Line, and what had happened in Poland, it was felt, could not happen when the Germans came up against French and British troops.

Winter had kept its icy grip on the United Kingdom for months, and during the early part of 1940 training was rather limited. The mortars, carriers, vehicles, and other equipment needed arrived slowly, and more emphasis had to be placed on indoor lectures than on outdoor training. The British military authorities did everything they could. British schools and courses on everything from cooking to camouflage were opened to Canadian personnel. Ranges and training areas were allotted to the division, and the Canadians were also given every access to the results of training exercises and weaponry experiments being conducted by the British army. An experienced British army officer was loaned to each brigade for general liaison and advice. Now and then Pearkes could call on one of his British army friends to lecture to his officers. Among the first was Brig. "Boy" Browning, at this time commandant of the Small Arms Schools at Hythe and Netheravon and later commander of the British Airborne Corps.

Close to the Canadians was the 51st (Highland) Division, which was due to leave for France within a matter of weeks. Subunits from this division gave various demonstrations, and its staff officers were usually willing to help the Canadians with exercises. Its co-operation was repeated by other British formations after the 51st left for France.

Nevertheless, the training of the brigade was slow. Most of the weapons and vehicles received by the battalions were completely new to them. Before they could go on field manoeuvres, the men had to learn to drive and maintain them. Driving at night in the blackout required extra skill, and to complicate matters the drivers had to wear gas respirators periodically when driving during the day. While waiting for the full complement of their equipment, however, Pearkes kept the men busy. Physical training and route marches helped to toughen them, while arms and foot drill gave them a greater feeling of co-ordination mixed with discipline. Bayonet practice, firing on the indoor ranges, lectures on chemical warfare, map reading, and a dozen other topics helped to turn "raw recruits into soldiers,"[11] but the progress was not fast enough for Pearkes. As often as he could he would make

> his rounds of inspection of the work being carried out by the Units.
> He daily visits the ranges, lecture rooms, field craft demonstrations,
> anti-tank gun drill and offers his valuable advice in connection with
> these subjects, especially in the realm of field craft.[12]

On a typical occasion Pearkes turned up to watch the Seaforths in a rather wet and muddy training area. There, according to an onlooker, he

watched an N.C.O. demonstrating grenade throwing on a trench raid. . . . This being the general's forte, and having strong ideas on how it should be done, he handed his greatcoat to his driver and in his well-tailored barathea [uniform] got down in the mud and crawled through it to give a first class demonstration of how to raid a trench.[13]

Whether the enemy was to be found in a trench or any other fortified post, there was a right way to bomb him out of it, and, mud or no mud, the men in his brigade should know how to go about it. In a different way but with similar intent, he made sure that his own headquarters staff were soldiers first and only secondly members of the brigade staff—"I had enough experience to know that quite frequently the brigade staff might have to fight," he said later, "and they certainly did in the more mobile fighting [which came later]."[14]

Pearkes's continual drive and energy demanded a high state of physical fitness, and when he found that a group of British officers met nearby to go beagling on Saturday afternoons, he managed to get himself and his officers invited to join in the sport. "It was good sport and good exercise," Pearkes recalled, as he added with respect to the officers:

I think they rather enjoyed it. Some of them didn't run as well as others, but I thought it was a good thing to turn them all out. And then when you're running across heather and that sort of thing and looking ahead and watching where the pack of hounds are, you're developing an eye for country which is a good thing for all officers to have.[15]

It may have been partly owing to his being overly tired that Pearkes became seriously ill at the end of February. A few days earlier Brig. Kemp Welch, who had been a classmate of Pearkes in 1919 at Camberley, asked him to come to Sandhurst where he was commandant. He was aware of the reputation of the Canadians in 1914-18 for patrolling, and as that was the only activity going on between the German and Allied lines in France, he asked Pearkes to give several lectures. Pearkes also gave demonstrations showing the various methods of crawling with weapons and so forth and then returned to his headquarters. Two days later he woke up with a violent headache and was soon very ill. He was taken by stretcher and ambulance to an isolation hospital at Aldershot, where his illness was diagnosed as spinal meningitis.[16] His condition became so critical that Mrs. Pearkes was informed, and she and young John left for England as soon as they could.

By a combination of medical care and his own willpower, Pearkes began to recover so that by the time they arrived, he was able to meet them at the station. The weather had improved, and he had had several weeks convalescent leave with Col. and Mrs. Hamilton Gault at their estate in Somerset. "Looking back now," he admitted later, "I was weak. It left its mark on me, I know that. I was not quite the same man after [my illness] although I never would have admitted it at the time. I kept it quiet."[17]

As the weeks went by, Pearkes became more impatient to return to his brigade. During his absence it was under the temporary command of Col. E. W. Sansom, a regular force officer who had replaced Pearkes as Director of Military Training a few years earlier. Originally it had been planned that individual training would take place in January and February, unit and battalion training in March, and by April training on a brigade and divisional scale. Poor weather and sickness had slowed the first phase, as had the lack of equipment. By mid-March there was a steady trickle of universal carriers, Bren guns, and anti-tank rifles, but it was not until early in May that the brigade got two anti-tank guns for practice purposes.[18] Since approximately half the men who had joined up in September 1939 had no military training whatever and the other half had only militia experience, every week counted if, as expected, the division might be going to France in May.

Canada's production of warlike store had scarcely started, and the cry for equipment from British factories to satisfy British requirements had to be taken into consideration. It was not until the end of March that the Patricias were carried for the first time by motor transport, and at that a good proportion of the vehicles were civilian. Then in mid-April, unit training for most of the brigade was interrupted when, a week after the Germans invaded Norway, Maj.-Gen. McNaughton was asked to provide a small force in a planned raid on the Norwegian coast. Two battalions from Pearkes's brigade were selected for the task as they were " 'the most advanced units in training' in the Division."[19] For the Princess Patricia's and the Edmontons the last two weeks of April were taken up with the move to the north and waiting in the soggy fields of Scotland for the word to go which never came. On 10 May, three days before Pearkes returned to resume command, the Germans thrust into the Netherlands and Belgium. The long awaited storm had burst.

With the beginning of the German blitzkrieg on the Western Front, all Canadian personnel on leave were recalled, and preparations were made to move the brigade to Salisbury Plains on 20 May for its first manoeuvres. Events in France gave an immediacy to the manoeuvres during the five-day period. Before the exercises were over, the brigade was ordered back to Cove and Pearkes was told to attend immediately a conference of the brigade commanders.

En route to the conference called by McNaughton on 25 May, Pearkes expected to be told that the division would go to France. During the week the brigade had been on Salisbury Plains, the situation in France had deteriorated rapidly. By the twenty-fifth, when orders came to return to the Aldershot barracks, Calais was under shellfire and Dunkirk was assuming the status of a port under siege. Maj.-Gen. McNaughton had been requested to provide a Canadian force to assist the hard-pressed Allies, and while the 1st Brigade was being assembled to cross the Channel, he had visited both ports. His reports were not encouraging, and the 1st Brigade was ordered to remain in England.[20]

Most of this Pearkes learned at the conference. He knew that most of the 1st Brigade had been embarked and were waiting to sail. At the conference McNaughton

related his own experiences on his reconnaissance to [France]. He was not very complimentary about either [the] British or French. I gathered that McNaughton thought the situation was hopeless and had advised against sending the Divison to the Continent at this time for [it] was neither fully equipped nor trained.[21]

McNaughton also expounded on his plan to form a number of mobile columns of battalion size which would form part of the brigade groups, each of which would be as self-contained as possible and would be prepared to strike hard and fast at any enemy landing. Two days later, the divisional commander called another conference at which the brigade commanders submitted their shortages and were briefed on the latest news from France. Although Gen. Gort had requested the Canadians once again on the twenty-sixth, by the afternoon of the twenty-seventh the situation had resolved itself. The evacuation from Dunkirk had started, and as he drove through Aldershot, Pearkes saw many of the first to be taken from the beaches. "Although they were tired out and had lost much of their equipment, they were far from being downhearted and were certain they could beat the Germans if they attempted an invasion," Pearkes stated later. Meanwhile there was no time to loiter. As the British Expeditionary Force was destroying masses of equipment and supplies in France to prevent them from falling into German hands, the Canadians found themselves as one of a very few trained and fairly well-equipped divisions available for the defence of Great Britain.

So striking had been the German advance through the Netherlands and Belgium and so unexpected was their employment of paratroops and armour that there was considerable apprehension that the enemy might attack England while the nation's attention was riveted on Dunkirk and the Channel. On the twenty-sixth the 2nd Brigade was put on a two-hours stand-to, and while at the conference Pearkes was informed that the division, divided into brigade groups, was to move on 29 May to the Northamptonshire area. Aside from his headquarters and three battalions, Pearkes had the 2nd Canadian Anti-Tank Company, a company of medium machine guns from the Saskatoon Light Infantry, the 27th Anti-Tank Battery, the 5th Field Ambulance, the 2nd Field Regiment, R.C.A., the 3rd Field Company, R.C.E., "K" Section, and the 1st Divisional Signals. That evening Lt. Proctor, the brigade transport officer, started the convoy moving, but it was several hours before the last vehicle left Aldershot. By that time the head of the column was over fourteen miles away. When Pearkes saw McNaughton watching the convoy, he stopped to chat and to meet Mrs. Vanier, who had just escaped with her husband from France. Pearkes could not help smiling as the convoy went by. As he explained later:

> Each unit had such an assortment of vehicles, civilian and military, tracked and wheeled, British and Canadian, left and right hand drive. Sometimes a vehicle would stall going up a hill. Once or twice one would break down. Staff officers were stationed along the route to see that drivers were keeping their correct distance from the one in front. The troops, however, were in a cheerful mood and glad to leave Aldershot.[22]

Early in the morning the column arrived at Kettering, about twenty miles from Northampton, and the men were billeted in farms or established bivouacs in the fields in the area. Later Pearkes called his commanders together and outlined the brigade task. The warm weather was permitting the successful transfer of British and other Allied troops across the Channel. In the Midlands, however, there were extremely few troops. The Canadians were there to provide mobile columns which could be rushed to the East Coast between the Humber and the Thames should the need arise. In view of the use of paratroops by the enemy, the brigade's self-contained units were to be prepared to deal with any threat from the air as well. Slit trenches were to be dug in unit areas, anti-aircraft defences planned, far more attention was to be paid to camouflage and concealment, and above all, a thorough survey was to be made of routes leading towards the coast. Since all sign posts as well as road and route signs were being taken down to confuse enemy invaders, for the next week everyone was busy, and no one more than Pearkes himself.

He was not too happy with the battalion columns, not because the idea was unsound, but because his battalion commanders had not trained with artillery and medium machine-gun support and the opportunity for errors was considerable. He was not at all unhappy when, on 6 June, orders arrived to return immediately to the Aldershot area. It sounded as if the division might be going to France after all.

All of the British forces in France had not been hemmed in at Dunkirk, and the new British Prime Minister, Winston Churchill, hoped to bolster French morale and maintain a foothold in France by establishing in the Brittany Peninsula a British-French fortress which could be used ultimately as a redoubt against the Germans. It was decided to send two divisions, one of which would be the 1st Canadian Division. The 2nd Brigade had scarcely arrived back on 7 June when Pearkes was ordered to prepare to move. All units were to take only essential supplies. Stores and ammunition were checked, new vehicles were acquired, maps were issued, distinguishing marks on trucks were painted over, and a hundred other preparations were completed. A few days later small advance parties left "for an unknown destination," and on the twelfth the brigade headed for a port of embarkation. Even as they waited, the news from France was becoming steadily more ominous.

After Dunkirk the German armies turned with renewed vigour against the French, and even as the troops and vehicles of the 1st Canadian Infantry Brigade were landing in France,[23] the military situation was deteriorating at such a rate that it was considered advisable to withdraw. On the fifteenth, with the fall of Paris, there was a noticeable restlessness among the troops. Pearkes, if calm outwardly, waited anxiously for further orders. Blytha and John had been living in a small cottage near Camberley, and Pearkes decided they should go up to the Midlands. Blytha had an uncle who lived at Pershore, and with his help arrangements were made for her to rent a house nearby.

By 16 June the brigade's transport began to arrive back, and the men, bitterly disappointed at losing the opportunity to have a crack at the enemy, listened eagerly to the stories told by those who had been away. From them, and later from friends in the 1st Brigade, they heard something of the confusion in Brittany and of the destruction of equipment on the docks when space could not be found to take them back. Fortunately, none of the 2nd

Brigade's vehicles were disembarked. On the following day the B.B.C. announced the capitulation of France, and on the eighteenth, Churchill called upon the nation to gird itself for the Battle of Britain. Pearkes warned his men that with the Germans across the Channel, they now stood in the front line.

Twenty-four hours later the brigade was told to be ready to move. The division had been placed in General Headquarters Reserve. It was to be located near Oxford and, as part of the small British-Canadian mobile force available, was to be prepared to move in any direction "with a 360 degree front."[24] The Canadians were to be ready for a landing from the sea or the air. Once more the division was to comprise self-contained battle groups. On 23 June, two days after the advance parties from the 2nd Canadian Division arrived at Morval Barracks, the brigade was again en route northward. That evening Pearkes and his staff set up their headquarters at Wootton Park, Oxfordshire.

For the next week the brigade remained in this somewhat isolated part of England. The units dug trenches along the hedgerows, pitched tents, mounted Bren guns, and reconnoitered the roads. Several times the air raid sirens sounded, but the nearest bomb dropped over a mile away. Meanwhile, Pearkes held conferences with his officers to hammer out methods of rounding up paratroops. A few days before leaving Cove a new unit had been formed called "The 2nd Canadian Reconnaissance Squadron." This unit, commanded by Capt. F. D. Adams, consisted of some two hundred officers and men who would be mounted on three-man motorcycle combinations and armed with Bren machine guns. Attached to the brigade, it represented a very mobile force with considerable firepower. But the best way of containing and eliminating a paratroop drop had never been contemplated seriously by the Canadians or the British. Pearkes had been taken to see a demonstration of what might happen about this time.

> We stood on the hill and saw the aircraft come over. Several "sticks" [of paratroopers] were dropped and [we saw] how quickly they hid their parachutes and dispersed. They were specially trained men, almost the commando type. . . . This was the sort of enemy that you might have to deal with. It was essential that they be rounded up; you must have a drill, know what you can do and you have to move very quickly.[25]

The brigade was in Oxfordshire only a week before orders came for it to move once again. A new plan for the defence of southeastern England called for the formation of one mobile corps north of the Thames, and another, comprising the 1st Canadian Infantry and the British 1st Armoured Divisions, south of the Thames. The latter, called the 7th Corps, would also have a force of New Zealanders, the whole to be commanded by McNaughton. The brigades of the 1st Division were to move south into Surrey and Kent, one of the most likely areas of a possible invasion and one, too, which was to be on the main route of German aircraft when they started their blitz on London. On 1 July the advance parties started off, and those who remained celebrated Dominion Day by having a sports meet.

A few days later the entire brigade had moved to its new location in the Godstone-Oxted area, about twenty miles south of London. There were no barracks in the area, so after bivouacking for a day or so, Pearkes ordered that every effort should be made to get the men into billets wherever possible. Brigade Headquarters found a billet at Stockenden Farm, and other units or parts of them were soon getting settled in garages, schools, farms, barns, and houses.

Pearkes soon received word that Churchill wanted to make an informal inspection of the brigade. He wanted to see what preparations the brigade had made in order to move quickly to the South Coast or to round up parachutists who landed on any nearby airfield. Word of the visit came on Friday; the visit was to be made the next day. Never were two men busier than Pearkes and his brigade major. To arrange a brigade scheme overnight is difficult enough, but to find a staging area, prepare the units involved, and do both at night in a new area was fraught with potential trouble. What followed was termed by those who took part in it "The Battle of Winston Cross" and is best told by Pearkes himself.

We were told that Mr. Churchill would arrive at a given hour at a certain road junction which was given as a map location. It was also referred to as a crossroads at Oxted. I did my best to arrange a scheme. First of all, one regiment, the Seaforths, would be in bivouac and at a given time, they were to rush to their lorries . . . ready to drive off in a certain prescribed order. The next regiment, the Edmonton Regiment, was to be seated in their lorries and it was hoped that Mr. Churchill would walk down and would have explained to him in detail the composition of the battalion with its carrier platoon and mortars and everything. As that regiment had not had the opportunity to move, nor had I any opportunity to reconnoitre a piece of ground on which they would carry out an exercise, I asked particularly that they be not asked to move in their lorries, that they were capable of doing it but should not be asked to do so because there were little narrow lanes [in their area] and something might go wrong. The third regiment, the Princess Patricias, was to be waiting in a position near a certain large farm. . . . Here "parachutists" were to arrive and the Patricias would demonstrate a drill. . . .

Well, at the appointed hour, I went to the rendez-vous at the crossroads. Shortly afterwards there arrived General McNaughton and General Ironside, who was Chief of the Imperial General Staff at that time, and a number of other senior people. . . . We waited and it poured with rain. . . . Mr. Churchill didn't turn up and everyone got more and more concerned. Time was going on past the hour when the first unit was to be seen and nobody could locate Mr. Churchill. We sent various motorcyclists scouring the country and after waiting approximately three-quarters of an hour one cyclist came back and said that Mr. Churchill was a mile and a half up the road where he was waiting for us, and in the meantime that he had taken shelter from the rain in the local pub.

I was then told that "This is your show; you go and fetch Mr. Churchill down here to the rendez-vous." Away I went. Sure enough there was Mr. Churchill . . . talking to one or two locals. . . . I entered and gave him the smartest salute that I could and I said "I beg your pardon, Sir, but the generals are waiting at the rendez-vous for you." "Rendez-vous? What is that?" "Sir, they were to meet you at the Oxted crossroads." Then I quoted the map reference number of the "road." I said, "Would you come down to meet them?" "Oxted crossroads? These are the Oxted crossroads. I live here. I know where the Oxted crossroads are. I don't know anything about map location numbers. Better tell the generals to come up here." I said, "They're all waiting for you down there, Sir." "Tell them to come up here." So I went down and reported that Mr. Churchill was up at the next crossroads, would they please come up there.

Well, the general [McNaughton] exclaimed in no uncertain terms that the rendez-vous was where they were. However, I remember "Tiny" Ironside saying "Well I think we had better go and meet the Prime Minister." So we all drove up there. . . .

I thought, well that's the end of this. To my horror Andy McNaughton again said, "This is your party. You'd better ride with the Prime Minister."

Now Winston Churchill was not in a good frame of mind. . . . However, I got in the car and he brought out a cigar and started smoking and he said, "This is a lovely country, isn't it?" Well, I had come from the prairies and I had been looking all night long trying to arrange this scheme and trying to hunt for a place where we could carry it out, and I wasn't too enthusiastic at that moment about the country. I said, "We find it rather enclosed, Sir." He snorted and said, "This is my home." So I said, "Well, we shall do our best to defend it, Sir. Now my scheme is. . . ." And he interrupted and said, "And what are these troops?"

Quite unknown to me Howard Kennedy, who was commanding a company of Field Engineers, had been out on some sort of a working party all night and was just returning back to billets. Having heard that the Prime Minister was just passing by he lined up his dirty, unshaven company on the side of the road. They had been out all night and had been soaked and wet. "Oh, I'd like to see these men," said Churchill. "First Canadians I've seen. Stop the car." And out he got and walked down to see them and then came back to the car and said, "Not very smart troops, are they?" I explained that they had been out on a working party all night and we couldn't expect very much but that "the next unit you will see are the Seaforth Highlanders of Canada. They are in bivouac around certain fields. As we drive by the Colonel will lead the way. You will meet him in a minute, and as his car flying a flag will pass the different bivouacs, the troops will come out on the double, get in their buses which are already located along the side of the fields so that you can see how quickly they can be prepared and ready to go. The Seaforths are one of our very best militia units. Here is the Colonel now—Lt.-Col. Stevenson."

Colonel Stevenson came up and explained what they were going to do as I had done. He added, "As my car goes ahead with its flags, which everyone can see, the exercise will begin and I think you will find it a very interesting one."

"All right," said Churchill. "Drive on." "But, Sir, we've got to. . . ." "Drive on!", said Churchill. "But, Sir, we've got to let the Colonel's car go ahead so when the. . . ." "All right, all right, drive on, drive on." Well, we were followed by at least a dozen cars on a rather narrow lane. The Colonel's car had been parked in a driveway so he couldn't get ahead of us. All the staff cars came along and went sailing down. "Now, Sir, this is the field where "B" Company is on the right." We drove past and nothing happened. "Sir, something must have gone wrong here," I said. "That field over there is where "B" Company is located. You can't see them because they're so well concealed. But they should come out when they see the Colonel's flag. I don't know where the Colonel is—he hasn't come." "Drive on, drive on!" said Churchill. And so we drove through the whole of that battalion area and we never saw one single Seaforth except for the Colonel! . . . So that exercise was a complete failure.

Now the men of the Edmonton Regiment were loaded in their buses and the plan was that Churchill would get out and walk down this line of buses and everyone would say what part of the battalion they belonged to, what their role was, etc. But Churchill said, "No, I won't get out. I'll tell you what we'll do. We'll drive on to another crossroads about two miles further down the road." And he named the crossroad. He said, "I'll see them drive past." "But," I said, "Sir our plans don't call for. . . ." "Well you must be flexible; I know this country. It will be a good place for me to watch them go by at the crossroads. . . ." Well I didn't know where it was but he told the Colonel of the Edmonton. The battalion was lined up in such a way that the transport was on a little side road, and as the battalion wasn't to move, their plan was that the transport would go off first and make their way back to their billets. To them the exercise was over when Churchill had passed, and they would disperse in the ordinary way. Well, the Colonel quickly gave the order to move and the transport drivers thought they were going home, and they started out and although frantic efforts were made to get them to go the right way, in these narrow country roads with nobody except the Colonel knowing where they were supposed to go, and the Colonel himself not being at all sure where the crossroads were . . . well you can imagine what happened.

However, Churchill anyway drove on down to the crossroads and I hoped for the best. Various lorries of different troops went by this way and that, but we waited. We sat down on the green grass and shivered under a tree while it still continued to rain in torrents and not a thing happened. No Edmonton Regiment came back. I remember sending despatch riders and finally Captain D. K. Robertson, who was Intelligence Officer, and he went off to find them. He came back and reported that the troops had gone home to their billets. "Well," said Churchill, "let's go and see the next."

Well, we went to another road junction where we met Lieutenant-Colonel "Shortie" Colquhoun of the Princess Patricias. He met Churchill and explained the scheme to him—about the farm supposedly occupied by "German parachutists," and how the Patricias would come rushing up, the carriers first of all, how one section of carriers would go to the right, another to the left, and how the battalion would encircle the paratroopers and then the entire battalion advance towards the centre. When Churchill and I were ready, Robertson, who was with us at the time, would go back and tell the Princess Patricias to move.

In the meantime Churchill's valet had decided that he should change his socks. So he sat down on the roadside and put on some warmer socks because he was really wet. Then he told Robertson to move off. Do you think Robertson's motorcycle would start? Not a bit of it. Doug did everything in his power but nothing in the world would make it go. So finally he had to borrow one of the staff cars to tell the Princess Patricias.

"Well," I said, "everything will be all right this time. I'm quite certain because this is the one regular battalion I have in the brigade." I explained how they would come and how the drill would be carried out. "Here they come," I said.

There was a roar of universal carriers coming down the road. The first three turned to the left instead of the right, which amazed me. I thought there had been some slight change and that the next section would go to the right. But the first went to the left, and the second section went to the left and the whole damn battalion went all to the left. But eventually they went round the big farm and then to the far end of it. Then we heard a rattle of musketry firing from the other side. Churchill pricked up his ears when he heard musketry and then to our horror we saw troops, all dressed like German soldiers, come running towards us. Of course the battalion had entered one way and had driven all the men who were acting as parachutists towards us! Eventually an officer came up and reported the exercise was over and the question was asked, "Did you get all the paratroops?" "No Sir," he said, "they got away." So that ended the day and Churchill went back to his house at Chartwell which was nearby. I can remember saying "I shall never get knighted after this war!" I went round at once to see the different battalions and tell them that, while everything went wrong, it was just misfortune. They must not be disheartened about it. Nobody was going to be sent back to Canada because of it because there was a logical explanation. For myself, I couldn't help laughing. Had one thing gone wrong it would have been understandable. But when everything went wrong it was just too funny for words.[26]

A day or so after the brigade scheme, Pearkes and his brigade major went off to reconnoitre their new area, and what they observed further confirmed the need for harder training. When they left Pearkes mentioned to Maj. Keller that they would probably encounter security checks en route to the coast. "We got as far as the South Downs," Pearkes recalled,

and there was practically no sign of any military activity whatever. "Now when we get up onto the top of the Downs [Pearkes said] that is where we'll see the defences." There wasn't a strand of barbed wire or anything. We saw no troops; nobody stopped us. We drove right down to the sea front; there was no activity going on. There was a little bit of barbed wire strung along the shoreline, broken in many places.

On the way back ... we saw some Home Guard who were fixing up the most elementary obstacles you could imagine. There were tree trunks on wheels so that it could be swung across the road. . . . There were a few sandbagged barriers . . . but they were not manned. Infantry could have by-passed anything that there was. . . . It was appalling to think how weak the defences were. . . , and for weeks that was a cause of great anxiety to us.[27]

The Home Guard, then in its formative stages, were soon to be much more evident, and their enthusiasm for security multiplied as more accounts were published of the "fifth column" tactics used by the Germans. As the danger of invasion increased, it became a sound practice to have some means of identification handy, as Pearkes found out. He agreed with many of the measures taken, but as he travelled a lot he was stopped more and more frequently, despite his uniform, rank, and staff car. It became especially bad at night and, as he related,

It caused a certain amount of irritation. . . . We thought we had every bit as much right to pass down the roads as the Home Guards that stopped us. [In] one case Keller and I were returning from a conference at division [headquarters] and we were stopped in a not too graceful way. The man had given us the wrong signal to stop. So we stopped because there were men with fixed bayonets there and they didn't look very competent. We were asked to produce our identification. When we did I said, "May I see your identification?" The man had none. So I said "How am I to know that you are not a German agent?" He said "I am a Home Guard!" "But you're not dressed in any particular uniform," I replied. "You've got an arm band on but I don't know that you people aren't the type that we have been looking for [as parachutists]." Keller had a tommy gun and the driver had one also so I held him up and we remained there until they brought the Home Guard commander from a neighbouring town. I think they got him out of bed. There was really some fun there.[28]

In the midst of planning for local and coastal defence and setting exercises for his battalions, Pearkes was informed by McNaughton that he was to take command of the 1st Division while McNaughton assumed command of the newly created Anglo-Canadian 7th Corps. Pearkes was pleased with the news, although sorry to leave the brigade. At the same time he was not surprised. Of the three brigade commanders he was the only permanent force officer, and among the senior permanent force officers there were none who had his combination of training and experience except McNaughton himself. A year previously there was no Canadian officer who had had the experience of conducting exercises with a fully equipped regiment, much less a brigade. A major-generalship was a rank held by only about half a dozen Canadian officers since 1918, and this, almost invariably, was the most senior rank on the staff. To achieve that rank with a full division of men who represented a vital element in the possible defence of England made Pearkes both proud yet anxious that the 1st Division should be ready to fulfil its role.

Fortunately Pearkes knew most of the senior officers in the division and was acquainted with most of the regiments. Many of the younger staff officers he had helped to train, and there were a large number of junior officers he had known as R.M.C. cadets. McNaughton had told him that, of necessity, he would be taking with him to Corps headquarters at Reigate a number of his divisional staff officers. Pearkes could appreciate this, and he also wanted to transfer one or two people from brigade headquarters to fill vacancies left. Among those he took with him was Keller, who would be promoted to lieutenant-colonel to fill the appointment as G.S.O. I. Others on his staff would include Howard Kennedy as his engineer officer, Chris Vokes as his assistant adjutant and quartermaster general, Lt.-Col. C. Sanford in charge of divisional signals, and J. H. ("Ham") Roberts as his artillery officer.

Pearkes's most immediate problem was the state of preparedness of the division. Although it was at this time among the best equipped formations available for its counterinvasion task, it was not yet as well trained as it needed to be. Since it had arrived in Great Britain seven months earlier, the units were in a comparatively efficient state, but at that one regiment reported it was not until the end of June that its two-inch mortars were fired in practice for the first time.[29] This was by no means an isolated case.

Scattered around the villages and towns of Surrey, Sussex, and Kent, the Canadians worked to prepare themselves for any contingency. Twenty-five mile route marches became common, and concealing and camouflaging unit vehicles was almost second nature. The movement of a battalion became much smoother, but what it would be like if a brigade moved at night under operational conditions was another matter. Whether they were in the fields under canvas or in billets in a village, the men dug slit trenches. Overhead the air war was beginning to warm up, for already the opening strokes of the Battle of Britain were taking place.

During the late summer of 1940, as the German Air Force began to mount ever heavier raids, a distinct change was noticeable in the public's attitude. A sense of urgency and determination replaced the "business as usual" attitude of the so-called phoney war. The islands were beleaguered from the air, and German U-boats were hitting hard at the merchant marine. Householders began to grow "victory gardens," iron fences were taken down for scrap metal, more and more people were volunteering their services for war work, and an ever-increasing number of women began to assume responsibilities formerly held by men. As the British reorganized their forces brought back from Dunkirk, they began to fill in the tremendous gaps in the defence of the South Coast. In the meantime the Home Guard units, some of which had mounted elements, were growing. In time Canadian officers and N.C.O.'s were to play a large part in training these groups, for certainly in these early months their courage and determination far outweighed their effectiveness. Evidence of the concern about attacks from paratroopers could be seen everywhere. In open fields poles and wires were erected to damage gliders attempting to land in conjunction with a seaborne invasion, and an increasing number of pillboxes, anti-tank traps, barbed-wire barricades, field defences, and other anti-invasion measures were in evidence.

While everything that could be done in the way of improving the defences on the ground was being completed, overhead the Battle of Britain was gaining momentum. On 13 July Field Marshal von Brauchitsch, the Commander-in-Chief of the German Army, had submitted to Hitler proposals for the invasion of Britain, and three days later Der Fuhrer formally ordered active preparations for Operation "Sea Lion" to begin. While troops and the shipping to carry the German assault forces across the Channel were being concentrated along the coast, the German Air Force gathered together bomber and fighter squadrons from all over the Third Reich. In July there was a steady increase in the number of German aircraft flying over Southern England, and in mid-August Goering launched the full weight of the Luftwaffe against the British Isles.

The men of the 1st Canadian Infantry Division saw this battle waged over their heads day and night. The wail of air raid sirens was almost constant, as was the drumming roar of Hurricane and Spitfires climbing up from the nearby air bases to attack the enemy. Units located close to the airfields surrounding the capital, and even those further from London, all had their own experiences to relate. For the 48th Highlanders "the most infuriating situation [they] were forced to endure . . . was to remain safe down in Surrey while they watched the agony of London from afar with a feeling of awful impotence."[30] Each regiment reported daily the number of bombs falling in its area, and when a German pilot would parachute from his damaged aircraft, there was a race to reach him and put him "in the bag." Typical of the action overhead was the account written by a Seaforth sergeant on 18 August. He was driving through Edenbridge when the "Red

Alert" sounded and a bomb landed on the road. The sergeant and his friend

> went into a field where we were able to hear a tremendous hubbub in the Heavens above; furious hammering fire of machine guns, aeroplane engines racing madly, the roar and whine of diving aircraft. To our right fluttered down a Messerschmitt fighter . . . its pilot wounded, from far left a great, pale blue Hun bomber came down straight as a plummet crashing at Ide's Hill . . . scattering bombs and terror everywhere. Behind him another bomber glided down and away to our front, a Hurricane. Four men had bailed out and were in the air . . .; the action melted away then leaving Spitfires and Hurricanes hunting about for more prey.[31]

At divisional headquarters reports from intelligence sources described the weight of the air attack, the damage inflicted, the losses on each side, and, more ominously, the mounting number of German forces and invasion craft being concentrated across the Channel.

Within the divisional area the Canadians were given additional duties. Any pilot parachuting down had to be rounded up, with the British pilots returned to their bases or taken to hospital and Germans, if not wounded, taken directly to senior intelligence officers. Wrecked aircraft had to be guarded against souvenir hunters, who might strip them of valuable equipment and be unaware of unexploded bombs. High explosive oil and incendiary bombs were dropped all over the area, and on several occasions Pearkes had a close shave. On one, a German fighter, flying low, spotted his staff car and dropped a bomb just on the other side of the hedge where he passed. Later, when he was having lunch with an artillery unit, a bomb fell so close as to make everyone dodge under the table—everyone but Pearkes, who continued with his meal.

Within the division it was not possible to train beyond the battalion or, at most, brigade-group level, but what could be was done to raise the standard of all units to a higher level. Commanding officers and others at a senior level were exercised in passing verbal orders and familiarizing themselves with wireless procedure. Pearkes ordered officers who could not drive a vehicle to learn to do so and to learn how to maintain it. With the 1st British Armoured Division forming part of the 7th Corps there was some opportunity to familiarize the Canadian troops with the capabilities and limitations of tanks, but it would be some time before joint infantry-cum-tank exercises could be carried out on any scale. Every morning at 8:30 Pearkes held a short conference with the senior officers to work out questions which arose or problems which might be anticipated. What was the proper role of a machine-gun battalion in the attack? What was the best way to employ an anti-tank battery? How could a brigade deal with an attack on one of the local airports which the Canadians were to defend?[32]

With each passing week the expectation of an invasion rose. Early in September, Pearkes told his staff that British officers expected it shortly. Two days later, on 7 September, all anti-invasion forces received the code word "Cromwell," the signal to bring all units and formations to instant readiness. The movement of barges to channel ports, the concentration of Kesselring's dive bombers, information gained from German agents, and reports of enemy agents landing by parachute and small boats in Britain all pointed to the probability of an attack.[33] All units were placed on four hours' notice. Those on leave were recalled, all ranks were confined to camp, and within each unit preparations were made to move out. On 13 September a 7th Corps report estimated that "there are enough barges and light craft between Flushing and Cherbourg to carry 175,000 men."[34] All ranks now carried their steel helmets, rifles, and respirators wherever they went, the latter because German radio broadcasts were saying that the British might use poison gas in desperation, implying that Germany might do so herself. During the next week intelligence reports kept everyone tense. On the seventeenth there were predictions that "attacks between Harwich and Beachy Head might be attempted at any moment,"[35] while two days later the reports noted that an estimated 15,000 German paratroopers had already been trained. Reports of German troops training in the embarkation and disembarkation of landing craft came hand in hand with descriptions of the concentration of troops and shipping. For two weeks, with the division either on a four- or eight-hour notice basis, the Canadians waited while the air battle swirled overhead. There was little opportunity for the Canadian troops to hit back except on rare occasions when a German fighter, flying exceptionally low, might come within range of one of the six machine-gun teams sent to Tangmere aerodrome to help thicken the defences there. Pearkes had instructed his units to render every possible help to civilians who had been bombed, providing it did not interfere with essential training, and certainly at this time more than any other during the war, the relations between the Canadians and the people of southern England were very close and cordial. Although by 1 October over eight hundred bombs had been dropped in the division's area, there had been only one or two casualties among the troops. But in the cities, and even in the small villages in Surrey and Sussex, there was an ever-increasing toll of killed and wounded among the townspeople.

By the end of September, especially after the few days when tide, weather, and German preparations seemed most favourable for an attack by sea and by air, the crisis seemed to be over. For one or two days in October a warning was sent to all units to be on the alert, but the deteriorating weather, aircraft reconnaissance, a noticeable change of emphasis in German propaganda broadcasts, and various other means of measuring German intentions pointed to a reduction of an immediate threat from across the Channel.

To provide some variety from their counterinvasion role, a brigade group was sent to the coast, where it came under the operational command of the British 12th Corps. Here the brigade would be in the "front line" of defence. They relieved a British formation which had as much need of training as the Canadians and which expected to see action sooner in battles in North Africa. Even late in October, when the 3rd Canadian Brigade relieved the 10th British Brigade, the Canadians found the defences very weak. When the units of the 2nd Brigade took over from the 3rd Brigade in mid-November, for example, the Patricias were surprised that the important port of Newhaven was protected by only a squadron of tanks and one of its own platoons. The responsibility of the Edmonton Regiment "included several miles of beaches between Brighton and Shoreham and also the adjoining downs on which paratroopers might land."[36] The Seaforths, on their part, had charge of about a mile and a half of seacoast directly in front of Brighton. Here, too, the defences left much to be desired. As one of their officers wrote: "the immediate need here is to rebuild our posts which collapse every night under weather action and to strengthen the wire. A pioneer battalion on our company front for a month is needed to do this."[37]

Despite the low state of defences, the brigades seemed to enjoy their stay on the coast. Knowing the enemy was just across the water seemed to add point to their role. "I think," Pearkes recalled,

The officers and troops enjoyed the planning of the defences for the various villages which they were in. I went around a lot too [with] Paget, the commander of the south east area before Montgomery took over. There was discussion of where was the better place for [defended] localities; how could the field of fire be improved; how could the houses be fortified and what size should defended localities be? They varied from platoon to battalion and the rearranging and readjusting of these gave added interest. The men were doing some fortification and also working in close contact with the Home Guard at this period.[38]

For Pearkes the major task was to train his division as a formation.

The easing of the invasion crisis gave more time for unit and brigade training, for Pearkes discovered that there was a considerable variation in unit efficiency. Reflecting on the situation in the late summer and autumn of 1940, he stated

> When they [the Canadian regiments] left Canada they weren't even units, or they were only just becoming units. They had had no brigade training. . . . We had no training with tanks; we had really little instruction in battle practice. At that time I think the general attitude was you would just advance and that would be all. [Later] we got some tanks allotted to us and each day for a time they put one battalion through on a tank scheme at dawn. I remember getting up at three o'clock in the morning, day after day, and going out to take through each battalion. I remember so well saying to so many of the battalions: "I know you will fight bravely but your casualties will be enormous because you don't know how to move across country [or] how to take advantage of the ground."[39]

Pearkes found there was still too much of the "militia camp" attitude, and as he began to tighten the screws there was a noticeable change. "Gone were the days," wrote one regimental historian, "when manoeuvres meant blackberrying in hedges and turning up at check points in time to reach billets before the canteen opened. Training now recognized war as an intricate business and the winning of a battle as a climax only to be achieved by complete understanding of routines which had been perfected by months of drudgery."[40]

Some senior officers were somewhat shaken by Pearkes's keenness for training. On one occasion an artillery regiment was to stimulate a barrage at dawn. Nobody expected the divisional commander to be there, and when he turned up he found only one officer on duty. The gunners and N.C.O.'s were working, but the commanding officer, battery commanders, and all but the duty officer had decided to sleep in and let the senior N.C.O.'s carry on. When Pearkes let his presence be known, "there was a devil of a lot of scurrying around," and the commanding officer was relieved of his duty.

The weeding out of officers in the division was an unpleasant but necessary task which continued on into 1941. Some were lacking in leadership ability; others were inefficient owing to various faults which turned up under the strain and pressure of constant work in the field. It was becoming increasingly evident that a number of officers lacked the physical fitness which their military position demanded. Pearkes himself had always been careful to keep himself in prime condition, but there were far too many officers in their forties and early fifties, younger than he, who did not have his stamina, and this was especially true among the senior officers in the militia regiments. This, in turn, was caused in no small part by the military policy in Canada between the wars. During that period

one had to get people who were prominent in their community to command the militia unit. If they hadn't a certain position in the community they wouldn't have the spare time to devote to militia work. They contributed [also] a lot of finance to help maintain the units . . . in order to attract good troops. . . . Most officers with these qualifications were not . . . the sort of age you wanted for your [wartime] commanders . . . [but] having raised the unit, they had to take them over to England. They were keen, they thought that they were fit, they thought that they would be able to do the job. They certainly were able to attract recruits and in many cases they were capable of doing the first stages of training. When we got into the harder work . . . requiring greater fitness, they were not capable of doing it and there was a constant sending back—not through inefficiency, but lack of wartime requirements for company and battalion commanders.[41]

This drain of officers was matched by the loss of trained officers in other directions. The 2nd Canadian Infantry Division, commanded by Pearkes's old friend Maj.-Gen. Victor Odlum, had arrived in England, and it required assistance from the 1st Division to help bring it up to par. Odlum had commanded a brigade in the Great War and had remained very interested in the militia in the twenties and thirties while pursuing his business career. Thus, although he commanded the division, he had not the military experience of a permanent force officer.[42] The greatest number of trained and experienced staff officers were in the 1st Division, and just as he had to yield officers to the 7th Corps headquarters when it was formed, Pearkes had to do the same for the 2nd Division. He was also asked for officers and N.C.O.'s for the 3rd Division forming in Canada as well as for certain schools being set up there. To help offset this "brain drain," it was decided to establish a Canadian Junior War Staff School in England. The idea was excellent and the results successful, but once again, to staff the school, Pearkes lost several more officers, among whom was its commandant, Lt.-Col. G. G. Simonds,[43] a keen, promising, young permanent force officer whom Pearkes liked. The steady transfers placed a strain on his own division. There was consequently a constant need to train and re-train, for it was in England in these years that, somehow, the two decades of neglect of the interwar years had to be overcome.

During the winter of 1940-41 there was more time available to cater to the morale of the troops. The rotation of the brigades to the South Coast, the easing of restrictions on leave, greater emphasis on sport, education, and entertainment facilities, and the provision of winter billets helped to relieve the feeling of letdown, but the withdrawal of British divisions to serve in theatres of war in the Near East and North Africa made many Canadians wonder when they, too, would see action. The question whether it was wiser to send one Canadian division to a battle area to gain experience or to wait until all the Canadian formations could be sent as a group was frequently discussed at the higher levels. The Corps Commander, McNaughton[44] held firmly to the idea of the unity of all Canadian formations under Canadian command, a belief shared by many who felt they might be committed in the not too distant future. Pearkes was torn. "I would have been pleased to have taken the division in," he said later,

> [but] I also realized the national advantage of having a Canadian Corps. The general feeling was, if it was desirable that the division should be separated from the rest of the Canadians . . . we would not raise any objections about it. We came over to do our job and we would be quite prepared to go. If, on the other hand, it was considered that we had to wait until the other divisions came over and got ready —well, the feeling was "I wish they would hurry up and get trained because we're getting fed up here."[45]

During the winter of 1940-41 more attention could be given to preparing the division for major exercises and field manoeuvres which the formation had not been able to hold since it arrived. When Pearkes took over the division it was still only partially trained, and until the early winter the units and brigades had been fixed in their anti-invasion role. It was not until late September that the divisional artillery regiments reverted to divisional rather than brigade command and that arrangements could be made to have regimental shoots at the Larkhill ranges.

Within the division itself there were a number of problems, both major and minor, which were discussed at Pearkes's morning conferences. Just as some of the British divisions had put on demonstrations for the 1st Division when it arrived in England, the 1st Division was asked to arrange demonstrations for the 2nd, 3rd, and 5th Canadian Divisions.[46] Questions regarding aid to the Home Guard, security, ground-to-air communications, the use of signals sets, chemical warfare, sports, changing war establishments, staff exercises on a brigade and divisional level, traffic control, the defence of aerodromes—these and a dozen different topics were dealt with at the half-hour conferences. The need to assist the other divisions by lending them weapons came up frequently and caused some grumbling. As late as 5 November 1940, for example, the 2nd Division had less than half its war establishment in guns, and it was to be another ten months before it had all the modern 25-pounders it required. The 1st Division also lent its 2-inch and 3-inch mortars to its sister division.

Pearkes continually stressed the constant exercising of brigade and divisional staffs in their various functions and the movement of brigades by vehicles, by day or by night, under simulated operational conditions. The latter, especially, was a major problem, partly owing to the countryside for which the division was responsible and partly owing to the division's lack of previous training in mobility on a larger scale.

When the division came to its present area to take up its anti-invasion role, it had used a variety of vehicles, including impressed civilian buses and trucks, to transport men, equipment, and supplies. Since then the various regiments and battalions, including the 1st Brigade, which had lost several hundred vehicles in France, had received all of its war establishment of automobiles, universal carriers, motorcycles, and other vehicles, both wheeled and tracked. Learning to drive the vehicles through the narrow, winding lanes and roads of southern England was an art by itself, especially at night when blackout restrictions permitted only pinpricks of light in front of the vehicles and a tiny shaded bulb at the rear. The lack of road signs called for exceptionally good map reading by co-drivers. Whenever there was an opportunity, a battalion would send a convoy of its vehicles, some sixty in all, on an exercise to gain experience in moving as a body through the maze of roads between their base and the South Coast.

It was one thing for the vehicles of a battalion to move, but it was more difficult to plan to move the battalion as well, together with its weapons, ammunition, equipment, cooking facilities, quartermaster stores, and so forth. Moreover, if the battalion was to be moved tactically, priorities had to be established or the cooks might find themselves the first arrivals at the front. In an invasion no battalion would move by itself; the very least one could expect initially in the division would be a movement by an entire brigade with all its supporting artillery, medium machine-gun companies, engineer field squadrons, armoured car squadrons, and a variety of other units and subunits, each with its own complement of vehicles, and all feeding into a comparatively small area racing southward. Traffic control became extremely important, and Pearkes had his brigades experiment with an entire company of infantrymen who, leading the column, would be dropped off at crossroads and picked up again by the last vehicles in the convoy. A variety of trials of this nature were used for, as he related later:

At Camberley twenty years before and right up to the time of the British manoeuvres in the late 'thirties, we had no idea of the difficulties connected with the movement of large bodies of motor vehicles in England or anywhere else. The whole problem was being studied by the War Office and we were fed a lot of information and we were experimenting all the time. If there was an exercise, we had discussions on [it] immediately afterwards....[47]

There was a feeling at the time that you must take all your transport with you and . . . great discussions went on [regarding] what battalion transport you could take...and how much you could leave behind.[48]

In actual operations, of course, there would be no civilian vehicles on the road, and one would not be restricted from going into adjacent farmlands which, owing to the desperate need to grow more food, were out-of-bounds. It was not until Exercise "Fox," however, that the full weight of the traffic problem came to a head.

Exercise "Fox," set by Corps headquarters, was intended to practise the 1st Division in "a move by road transport to a concentration area, an advance to contact with a hostile force, and the issuing of orders for deployment and attack."[49] It envisaged an action against an enemy landing in the Dover peninsula. If McNaughton's objective in setting up the scheme was to have the division move swiftly and efficiently to the "front," it was not attained nor, according to Pearkes, was it attainable under the setting up of the scheme. "In the first place," he said,

it was ordered that units were to take *all* vehicles. This included "B" echelon vehicles. Then as the scheme progressed the Division was ordered to move through hilly country with only narrow lanes. Nobody could move heavy lorries through these lanes. A number of vehicles with heavy bridging equipment moved into the area and blocked everything. Who they were and where they came from I don't know but I saw the mix-up myself.[50]

The result was a traffic jam of memorable size, and Pearkes, caught up in it, was more than annoyed. An artillery officer who was nearby commented later:

Plate 18. Prime Minister W. L. Mackenzïe King visiting Pearkes at divisional headquarters at Holmsdale, near Red Hill, England.

Plate 19. Brig.-Gen. Pearkes accompanying His Majesty King George VI in Edmonton during the Royal Visit to Canada in the summer of 1939.

Plate 20. Maj.-Gen. Pearkes talking to the Rt. Hon. Winston Churchill at the "Battle of Winston Cross." Behind Pearkes is Anthony Eden. On the right is Lt.-Gen. A. G. L. McNaughton.

Plate 21. Canadian troops training in England. A Canadian convoy squeezes through the narrow streets of an English village.

Plate 22. Pearkes consults with Lt.-Gen. J. L. De Witt on board an aircraft en route to Adak Island, Alaska, before the joint attack on Kiska.

"Fox" ended up in the greatest schmozzle as far as movement was concerned that you ever saw in your life, with all those narrow roads. It was directed through . . . Ashford along the coast where, according to the scheme, the Germans had landed. . . . Various units and formations were supposed to go down through the area as a night move and the most terrible traffic jam anyone ever ran into developed. . . . I remember at the cross-roads—columns coming from every direction and they couldn't pass, and there was no room for anyone to pass. George was out there himself giving hell to everyone.[51]

McNaughton was along to witness the exercise, and the traffic pileup made him "livid with rage." As far as Pearkes was concerned,

Nobody could be blamed for it. Some units took the wrong turn and fouled up everything. Too many vehicles were being used. To what extent the Corps staff who had planned the exercise had reconnoitered the ground beforehand and realized the difficulties, I don't know. But the exercise had been badly planned and it was inevitable, in those roads, that there would be confusion.

I'm sure the regimental officers blamed the staff and the staff of lower formations blamed everybody else. . . . General McNaughton came around and he was blaming everybody.[52]

McNaughton was to say later that the exercises "had 'shaken the complacency of everyone participating, from the Corps Commander to the lowest private soldier.'"[53] Pearkes, on reflection, felt that perhaps the staff at Corps headquarters "may have wanted to test out and show how impossible it was to move these vehicles through that type of country." If so, they certainly proved it, "with the result that serious consideration had to be given in breaking down the transport into different echelons."[54]

"Fox" was the first of a number of exercises on a divisional scale during 1941, all of which had an anti-invasion theme. Pearkes was on the job all the time. "It was his one consuming interest . . . to make that division absolutely efficient,"[55] one of his brigadiers said later, and on the exercises Pearkes was never content with half-hearted efforts. The former adjutant of the Royal Canadian Regiment remembers one occasion during the summer of 1941.

We were starting to do these infantry-cum-tank exercises on the South Downs. General Pearkes was mad keen about the importance of digging in to consolidate on an objective. Well . . . it's hard to persuade troops to dig a hole in the ground on an exercise. Lots of people just got away with [outlining] a rectangle and saying, well, that's a hole in the ground, and that was it. But not with General Pearkes. On one particular occasion we had gone, it seemed to us, miles across very rough country, trying to keep up with the tanks. We got on to our objective and everybody just collapsed in a heap and fell asleep, including the C.O. I was . . . the only person up and about at R.C.R. battalion headquarters and from nowhere came the G.O.C. He was in a . . . rage at the R.C.R. and their very bad training of not digging in and properly re-grouping and consolidating themselves. He didn't even wait for the C.O. to be wakened up. He said: "You give him my compliments and tell him I am giving orders for all your troop carrying vehicles to return to your base. The R.C.R. will march fourteen miles home." Then pooped as we were, after giving ourselves breakfast when the exercise was over, we marched fourteen miles home for our sins.

He was a hard taskmaster. He set a pretty terrific pace and he certainly expected everybody to keep up with it regardless of age or anything else. If you weren't fit enough, then that was your fault. And this was long before Monty [Lt.-Gen. B. L. Montgomery]. Monty seemed always to get the credit for all this running and P.T. and physical fitness but, in fact, we were already doing it in the 1st Division. . . . He didn't suffer fools gladly. But then, we were training for war and that's no time for foolishness, or for fools; and we had a few.[56]

In June 1941 an exercise ("Waterloo") was held by Headquarters, South Eastern Command, in which the entire Canadian Corps took part. The 4th Corps also participated, and for several days British and Canadian divisions worked to dislodge a large "enemy" group of paratroops and glider forces on the Downs. Three weeks earlier, following their attack on Jugoslavia and Greece, the Germans had launched a successful airborne invasion of Crete, giving considerable point to "Waterloo." The 1st Division had already been engaged in a number of smaller exercises on a brigade level designed to forestall airborne attacks on nearby aerodromes. These exercises, combined with information received later from the German methods in Crete, were carefully studied by Pearkes and his staff,[57] for it was one completely new feature of warfare. Later in the year an even larger exercise called "Bumper" took place. All of the operational portion of the Canadian Corps took part in the five-day exercise which saw twelve divisions, including three armoured ones, engaged in an anti-invasion role north and west of London. "Among the satisfactory results," reported the official army historian, "was the obvious progress made in motorized movement, for despite the large numbers involved there was little congestion."[58]

"Bumper" was the last large-scale exercise in which the Canadians were involved during 1941, but there were many smaller ones throughout the year to keep the battalions and brigades fully occupied. Pearkes was able only to take an occasional weekend off to motor up to Pershore where Blytha was staying. John was attending a prep school nearby, and Blytha had joined the Women's Volunteer Services and was busy serving in canteens. Now and then she could come south to stay with friends near divisional headquarters, and George invariably had much to tell her. The visitors to his headquarters during the year ranged from the king and queen (on Dominion Day) to Noel Coward, and included British and Canadian cabinet ministers, members of Parliament, and a number of senior British officers, some of whom he had known since his days at Camberley. He was always proud to tell them of the Spitfire bought through voluntary contributions from men in the division earlier in the year and presently flying with the 41st Fighter Squadron, R.A.F., carrying the Red Patch on the port side of its fuselage.

During most of 1941 the Canadian Corps had been in G.H.Q. Reserve. The corps was growing steadily, however, and following the end of the season for invasion—a probability which was greatly lessened by the German invasion of Russia in June—it was decided to move the corps in November to take up static positions on the Sussex coast to relieve the British 4th Corps. When divisional headquarters moved on the twenty-third from Redhill to Knepp Castle, it was under the acting command of Brig. A. E. Potts.

For two years Lt.-Gen. McNaughton had been carrying a very heavy load on his shoulders, first as the commander of a division and then the corps. Moreover, as the senior Canadian officer, he was tremendously involved in a great many other matters as well, ranging from problems of organization and equipment to the relationship of the Canadian forces in Britain with British administrative and operational command. As a result there were some areas, such as training, which he tended to leave to his subordinates. "There was much more of the scientist about him than the commander,"[59] one of his brigadiers remarked, and Pearkes felt somewhat the same. He "admired him tremendously as a friend" but thought his real place should have been as Chief of the General Staff in Ottawa advising the minister. As it was, McNaughton was "too busy with the deciding of policy and conferring with the British . . . [on] the general policy of the employment of the troops rather than training the troops. . . . Someone once said to me," Pearkes added, "that he was always doing the job above his own or that five or six grades below his own in which he was fiddling about with some invention to be put on a truck, or change in a gun, or something which any Ordnance officer could have done for him."[60] Mc-Naughton's opinion of senior British officers sometimes caused Pearkes considerable silent embarrassment at high level conferences of Canadian officers. British officers, McNaughton felt, "were not sufficiently scientific soldiers. . . . I would say," Pearkes reflected, "it all sort of came down that senior British officers stressed man-management; Andy McNaughton stressed machines. He thought man-management just came along. . . . He was fond of demonstrations of equipment rather than demonstrations of an attack."[61]

These differences in opinion and approach did not mar their mutual respect, and when in November 1941, McNaughton was advised by his doctor to take a long rest, it was Pearkes McNaughton approached as the senior and most experienced officer to take his place as corps commander while he was away. McNaughton indicated that he expected that the Canadian divisions would be created into a Canadian Army comprising a 1st and 2nd Corps. He told me, Pearkes added,

> "I hope this will be a permanent appointment for you." He said: "Now I haven't got the appointing of this. It will have to come from Canada." But he said very definitely "I hope that you will be there [at Corps headquarters]." And referring to Crerar...he said: "Crerar has had no experience in command. He's always been a staff officer and I'd like him to become a divisional commander before having a corps." He said: "I think he ought to remain as Chief of the General Staff in Ottawa, but that is not what the Canadian Government wants and I know Crerar . . . is very anxious to come [over] and get into active command. I think he should take over the 2nd Division because that will give him a little bit more time to get accustomed [to command a formation]. As you know the 1st Corps, the 1st and 2nd Divisions, now, you are the logical man to go there."[62]

Corps headquarters was located at Headley Court, near Leatherhead, Surrey. Pearkes had agreed to live in McNaughton's house, situated several miles away from headquarters, and for the time he was there Mrs. Pearkes came down to be with him. At corps headquarters there was not the closely knit "family" he was accustomed to, and as he had to be away a great deal of the time attending conferences, visiting units, or observing manoeuvres, he did not get to mix with the staff as much as he would have liked.

Much of his time in November and December was spent re-examining the defensive positions now occupied by the Canadians under the operational direction of the G.O.C.-in-C. South Eastern Command. This command was taken over by Lt.-Gen. B. L. Montgomery. Pearkes had met Montgomery briefly earlier in the year when he attended an exercise at Tonbridge. On a later occasion, when Montgomery visited the 1st Division, he was being entertained in the mess and referred jokingly to an article in *The Times* which commented upon the physical fitness of "Monty's" former division. Pearkes, proud of his own men, had replied that his Canadian division would outmarch the British any day. This friendly challenge was not pursued.

Pearkes "thought a lot of Montgomery" but added that "he was at times irritating." On one occasion Montgomery came to the 1st Division and asked to see one of the brigades. "What I'd like you to do," he said to Pearkes, "would be to meet me at Brigade Headquarters and introduce me to the officers. Then I will spend the day with the brigade and you meet me in Brighton in the evening and I'll tell you what I think [of the brigade]. I don't want you to come around with me."[63] Later, when they met at Brighton, Pearkes relates

He [Montgomery] made his comments, one of which was: "I've seen the best battalion commander I've ever seen and I've seen the worst. . . . I want one promoted and the other sent back to Canada." [He mentioned their names] "Well," I said, "I can't recommend the one you want promoted. I don't think he is ready for promotion. He's an excellent training officer, a permanent force officer and has always been connected with weapon training and drawing up training programmes for camp. The other is a civilian who has been a keen militiaman and is worshipped by the men in his battalion."

What had happened was, Monty had gone to this unit and they didn't know he was coming. The one commanding officer had [his training day] all down in black and white. . . . As soon as Monty came he went and saw bayonet fighting here and mortar training or signalling here. The C.O. knew exactly where. When Monty met the other commanding officer he said: "I don't want any alterations in your training plan. What are you doing today?" He replied: "This is company training day."[64] "Fine," said Monty, "now what would 'A' Company be doing?" "I don't know, sir, as it's company training day." "Well, let's go see. Where will they be?" "I don't know, sir. I've got the best company commanders in the world."[65]

Montgomery wanted to promote the lieutenant-colonel whose training syllabus for that day permitted him to demonstrate how well he knew precisely what his men were doing, despite Pearkes's counterargument that his tactical knowledge was wanting and his performance on manoeuvres had not been up to standard. The other commanding officer's training schedule for that day was not such that he could pinpoint the exact location of his companies. Monty, in Pearkes's opinion, "jumped to conclusions very much" when it came to assessing persons, an opinion shared by others with whom he came into contact.

A somewhat stronger argument between the two men erupted shortly after Pearkes had taken over from McNaughton. McNaughton favoured the establishment of corps schools to which all units would send officers and N.C.O.'s to attend various courses. Montgomery favoured divisional schools. "I remember," Pearkes recalled,

> he came around two or three times and kept badgering me to set up these divisional schools. But I told him it was General McNaughton's policy to have the one central school for the Corps. And he said: "Oh, that's too big, too big, no good. You set up divisional schools." I said "I can't set up divisional schools. I'm only Acting Corps Commander. I've not been appointed Corps Commander yet and I know it's definitely against McNaughton's policy to have them." "Never mind all that. You go ahead and set them up." I said: "Well, sir, I'm afraid I can't and I'm not going to." On the whole we parted good friends but that's just typical. It was a difficult period.[66]

Although there were personality clashes with Montgomery to contend with, Pearkes had much to keep him occupied. By the end of the year the corps had grown to include the four Canadian divisions in England, each in a different stage of training. The three commanders of the 2nd, 3rd, and 5th Divisions—J. H. Roberts, C. B. Price, and E. W. Sansom—had served under Pearkes in the 1st Division. He knew them well and they him. Roberts was a brigadier and commanded in an acting capacity. It was this division which Pearkes expected Crerar to command, but his hopes and expectations were dashed a day or so before Christmas when he received a telegram informing him that Crerar would be arriving in England to command the 2nd Division and to assume temporary command of the corps as well.

The news that he was to be replaced came as a bitter disappointment to Pearkes. He and Crerar had long been friends. They were side by side on the seniority list, they had had a very similar training as staff officers between the wars, and they had worked well together in revising the organization of the militia in the early thirties. Since the beginning of the war,

Crerar had held several senior staff appointments. In the summer of 1940, when Pearkes gained command of the 1st Division, Crerar had been appointed Chief of the General Staff in Ottawa.

Late in 1941, a few days after Pearkes assumed temporary command of the corps, Crerar had been promoted to lieutenant-general. Nevertheless, he was anxious to get a command in the field and was willing to revert to major-general to get overseas. As a lieutenant-general and as Chief of the General Staff he would be in a strong position in Ottawa to influence those who had the final say in senior army appointments overseas. He was appointed to temporary command of the corps (it was confirmed early in 1942) on 23 December and arrived at Corps headquarters on 6 January 1942.

Pearkes's disappointment was mingled with resentment, a resentment based not so much on gaining the promotion which would come with the command of a corps, but rather that the appointment had gone to an officer who had not had command of troops in the field since the Great War.

The relations between Pearkes and Crerar were never quite the same. As Pearkes recalled later:

He displayed an unfamiliarity with the procedures in tactics that had been adopted in the past two years. I suppose I didn't cooperate as much as I should have done and I think he was a little suspicious and perhaps a little jealous or something. . . . Perhaps I was jealous. But relationships were not the happiest. They improved a little bit later but we never got on as we had done in the old days.[67]

Disappointed as he was, Pearkes was not the type of man to carry a grudge or to let his resentment interfere with his duty. There was much to do that winter, and major events on other war fronts were reshaping strategy. In Russia, following tremendous initial success, the German armies were at the gates of Moscow, and early in December the Japanese had struck at Pearl Harbour, bringing the United States into the conflict. The initial victories of the Japanese were startling. On Christmas Day Hong Kong fell, and during the early part of 1942 each week seemed to bring with it a chronicle of disaster as the Japanese reached out from the Philippines to Singapore and brought within its compass prize possessions of the British, Dutch, and French empires.

In Great Britain, Germany's absorption on the Eastern Front and the knowledge of the tremendous effort the Americans would bring caused a change of training. In December 1941, and during the first months of 1942, Montgomery had visited the various divisions in South Eastern Command, strengthening the defensive "fortresses" in his command and in many instances rearranging fields of fire and ordering new positions built. Pearkes accompanied him when his own division area was involved and was enthusiastic over the improvements suggested. Moreover, Montgomery began to place greater emphasis on offensive than on defensive training, and this too was welcome. Despite the gains made by the Germans in Russia and the Japanese in Southeast Asia, the morale of the troops began to rise in 1942, and they took keen interest in the new forms of training.

One of these was what was termed "battle drill," a type of training designed primarily for infantrymen. It was developed by the British 47th Division and copied by the 2nd Canadian Division late in 1941. In May 1942 a Battle Drill Wing of the Canadian Training School was established to spread the concept through the entire corps. In brief, battle drill was a simplified and realistic method of training men for combat, stressing physical fitness, the sounds of battle, and an "inoculation" to warfare. Initially the latter included the preaching of hate and visits to slaughterhouses, an aspect which Pearkes deplored and which later was greatly modified by British and Canadians alike.

The battalions, brigades, and senior headquarters continued to conduct exercises, including "attacks," with and without armour, on defended localities. By this time, too, Canadian battalions became "foster mothers" to the local Home Guard units, helping to train them and engaging them in weekend exercises.

As usual Pearkes seemed to be everywhere, seeking out any weaknesses and determined as ever to make his the best division in the Army. "George used to run a pretty tough show," one observer recollected,[68] and his standards were strict. His standards were well known within the divisions, and in the early part of 1942 he did not take kindly to the numerous statements on training which began to emanate from the new corps commander. An instance of this, but not necessarily a typical one, is described by a senior officer as follows:

He [Pearkes] was a real humdinger training officer . . . and he had all his division behind him. But you had to be in *his* division to be any use at all. I remember once . . . I was in George's office one day and a liaison officer from Corps came down with a whole lot of papers—instructions, etc.—and gave them to George. He looked down at them and took and chucked them straight into the wastepaper basket, in front of this liaison officer. He knew how to command *his* division without this kind of thing.[69]

During the spring Pearkes's division was engaged in several major exercises which showed up the results of the constant training and practice in which the units and brigades had been engaged. Exercise "Beaver III," carried out on 24-26 April under corps direction, envisaged the 1st Division as an enemy formation attacking the 2nd Division in the Little-hampton-Worthing area. Among the special points emerging from the exercise was "the speed with which the 1st Division showed itself able to advance by march route."[70]

A much longer exercise took place in mid-May. This was Exercise "Tiger," conducted by South Eastern Command. This eleven-day exercise, which involved six divisions, was carried out under the direction of Lt.-Gen. Montgomery. It was designed to test both troops and staffs to the limit. Transportation was reduced to a minimum, the troops lived under conditions similar to those they could expect in the the field, and problems presented to the senior commanders forced them to cope with unexpected problems and situations which might be expected in an "encounter battle" on active service. On the second last day of the exercise, for example, the corps was told that Surrey, a simulated neutral state, would "attack," unless the Canadian formations were back behind the Kent-Sussex border before five o'clock on the following day.[71] This meant a complete turnaround of the entire division and a long march by men who had been on the go all day. To accomplish the task called for unorthodox methods, and Pearkes ordered that everything on wheels should load up with marching men until they could hold no more. Using a smoothly operating traffic control system, he had the entire division behind the border by the required time, the only division which was able to accomplish the corps commander's directive.[72] Three hours later the exercise came to an end, and after a day's rest, the division marched back to its billets. Pearkes, as well as his staff, marched with them—all fifty miles. He may have been fifty-four, but he was as hard as hickory.

With Russia and the United States in the war, the probability of a German invasion of Great Britain lessened, while an Allied invasion of Europe loomed larger. Russia fought for her existence as the Germans launched their summer offensive in June, and the cry for a "second front" was heard more and more frequently in the popular press. Canadian soldiers had not yet experienced war in the field. The brief sojourn of the 1st Brigade in France in 1940 had not brought it into contact with the enemy, and the landing on Spitzbergen in 1941 was, in essence, an unopposed "attack" on an island far removed from the theatre of operations. Commando raids on the French coast were models of events yet to come and served not only to pin down German troops on the coast but also to bolster morale in Britain at a time when reverses in North Africa coupled with German submarine successes in the North Atlantic made the future look dark.

After Dunkirk, and until the summer of 1941, Canadian troops knew their role was important. After Russia and the United States entered the war, however, they felt in the backwater of military affairs, and by the summer of 1942 there was more evident expression of a desire to get into action. Pearkes was of two minds about keeping the Canadian formations together rather than sending one or more to a theatre of war under a British corps commander. He, like his men, wanted to get into action, and whether his division fought under a Canadian or British corps head-quarters would not have mattered in the short run. On the other hand, he was keenly aware of the tremendous esprit de corps which had existed in the Canadian Corps during 1914–18, and he would prefer that the Canadian identity should not be lost either at a corps or army level.

Until the commitment of a large Canadian formation on some field of battle—an unlikely event in 1942—the only opportunity open to Canadi-ans was the participation in commando raids. A number of men in the Canadian Corps had taken commando training, but they had taken no part in raids on the French coast until a few months after Crerar was placed in command. The one attempt in April 1942 by two platoons of the Carleton and York Regiment was abortive owing to poor navigation on the part of the naval personnel. Later that summer a large Canadian force raided Dieppe, but the regiments involved came from the 2nd Canadian Division rather than from Pearkes's formation, though his was probably the best trained.

When Crerar arrived in England, one of the things he mentioned at their first meeting was the need to get the corps into action. Pearkes agreed but later they had a strong difference of opinion with respect to large-scale raids on the French coast. During 1941 Pearkes had frequently discussed the possibility of using Canadians on commando raids with both Canadian and British officers. As one who had taken part in raids himself, he had some idea of their value and their cost. His interest led him to enquire into the methods used and problems encountered by the commandos. Later he attended staff exercises at Camberley directed by Lord Louis Mountbatten which dealt with large-scale raids from the sea. At these exercises opinion was "very, very divided." "Some people felt," Pearkes related,

that these raids would be valuable and that they should be under-taken. I was never enthusiastic about that. I thought if there was any large scale raid it would take up so much equipment, it would require so many men and [employ] so much equipment and artillery support if it was going to be effective, that it wasn't worth doing until the real invasion came about. It was only wasting effort. If we withdrew after a couple of days we would only give the Germans an opportunity to laugh at us and say here was an invasion which failed. I was never in favour of it. Small raids with a hundred men or so might be all right. [They had] a nuisance value and kept German troops guarding the coast. I was in favour of small raids [in which] you weren't going to lose many men and which didn't require a great expenditure of . . . resources. But the bigger raids such as . . . the Dieppe raid I was all against. I couldn't see that any lessons could be learnt which couldn't be learnt from the study of past experiences . . . or that it might gain any experience which was really worthwhile, which you couldn't foresee.[73]

Pearkes told Crerar quite bluntly how he felt. "I was anxious enough to get into battle—nothing would have given me greater pleasure at that time to have led the 1st Division into battle—but I was thankful my division wasn't asked to go [on the Dieppe Raid]. My views were well known."[74]

On 30 April 1942 Lt.-Gen. Crerar selected the 2nd Canadian Division to provide units for the Dieppe raid, and during the next few months those selected underwent special training for the assault. Three months later Pearkes visited Maj.-Gen. Roberts who described the training going on, but the time and place of the raid, still wrapped in secrecy, were not mentioned. Two weeks later, on 14 August, Pearkes had lunch with McNaughton who told him some details about the proposed raid. Pearkes did not hear the full story until the actual day of the raid, 19 August, when he was returning with Gen. Sir Bernard Paget[75] from an Army-Air Force cooperation demonstration. On his arrival at 1st Division headquarters on the following day Pearkes learned that over half the force had been killed, wounded, or captured. The "lessons" of Dieppe were gained at a very expensive price.

Eight or nine days after the Dieppe raid the Army commander called in Pearkes, and two days later Pearkes was en route back to Canada. McNaughton pointed out that the formation of the 2nd Canadian Corps, which Pearkes hoped to command, was being delayed. "He [McNaughton] was disappointed," Pearkes related,

and he said that he had received word from Canada and they had asked for me to come back. He said there was considerable hysteria on the West Coast, a Japanese submarine had shelled the [Estevan] lighthouse, the Japanese were still in Kiska and Attu, and that I would have two divisions under my command as well as corps troops. [McNaughton added] that I was to take over and be responsible for all the defences of the West Coast, and that the Air Force and the Navy would come under me in an emergency. . . . He indicated, although he did not definitely say so, that "I expect you will be made a lieutenant-general as soon as you arrive in Canada because [in your command] there are two divisions, the coastal defence troops and a lot of training establishments. You will have the whole of British Columbia, Alberta and the Yukon under your command." He said that it was a very big job. I naturally said "Well, I would infinitely rather remain in command of the 1st Division whether I get a corps or not at some future date. I'm not concerned so much about that but I would rather take my division into action." General McNaughton said: "I hope you won't insist on that attitude because I think it is your duty to take this other appointment and return to Canada." He didn't say I had to return to Canada. He added "You are not being returned to Canada for inefficiency or anything, it's because they're asking for you. You [know] Western Canada and we've got to have a new command out there."[76]

Of all the things McNaughton said, his appeal to Pearkes's sense of duty was the deciding factor.

Pearkes was told that space on an aircraft going to Canada would be made available to him in two or three days. This gave him no time to say goodbye to his men, and even his own staff had only one day to arrange a farewell party. As for Blytha and John, they would have to come home by ship about ten days later. She was accustomed to move quickly and with a minimum of luggage, so they had a leisurely trip back on the *Queen Elizabeth*, which was carrying many wounded men back to Canada.

11

Pacific Command

Shortly after nine o'clock on the morning of 1 September 1942 an air force bomber left London for Montreal by way of Prestwick, Iceland, and Labrador. On board was George Pearkes, taking the longest flight he had ever been on and relishing the thought of crossing the ocean by air. It seemed incredible that McNaughton had first spoken to him about the new appointment only two weeks before. After Pearkes had agreed to serve, McNaughton had wired Lt.-Gen. Kenneth Stuart, who had replaced Crerar as Chief of the General Staff, that Pearkes could be available in a week's time. Two days later Stuart recommended Pearkes to the Honourable J. L. Ralston, Minister of National Defence. Stuart noted that the person holding the appointment of General Officer Commanding-in-Chief, Pacific Command should be acceptable to the other two services, should have overseas experience, should "be one who already has the confidence of the Canadian people as a good fighting soldier," and finally, should "have the energy and knowledge needed to train and fight this important Command."[1] Stuart added that he had cautioned McNaughton that Pearkes "would be useless in Canada if he returned a disgruntled man" and that Pearkes must be told "he had been specially asked for by name from Canada." Stuart mentioned that he had consulted the Deputy Chief of the Naval Staff and Deputy Chief of the Air Staff, both of whom, he wrote, "consider the appointment an excellent one."[2] As a double insurance, Stuart had Maj.-Gen. H. F. G. Letson, the Adjutant General, then on a visit to England, interview Pearkes himself, and he reported that Pearkes "looks forward with enthusiasm to making his new command second to none." While Pearkes was still airborne over the Atlantic, Ralston released the news of his appointment.[3]

When Pearkes arrived in Esquimalt on 6 September he assumed charge of a command which encompassed all of British Columbia, Alberta, the Yukon Territory, and the District of Mackenzie of the Northwest Territories. In this one million square miles of territory there was a population of slightly over one and a half million people, over half of whom lived in British Columbia. From a glance at the map at headquarters, Pearkes could see that most of the troops in his command were stationed in the Pacific province. During the next few days, while he met his new staff and familiarized himself with the operational and administrative aspects of his new responsibilities, Pearkes was briefed on the series of events which culminated in his recall from England.

The stunning successes achieved by the Japanese armed forces had sent a wave of fear and apprehension through British Columbia. The capture of Guam and Wake Island, the destruction of H.M.S. *Prince of Wales* and H.M.S. *Repulse* and the surrender of Hong Kong in December, the seizure of most of the Philippines in January, the penetration into Malaya and capture of Singapore in February, the evacuation of Rangoon in March, the conquest of Java—indeed the whole series of Japanese victories in Southeast Asia brought with them alarms all along the Pacific Coast of North America. In March 1942 John Hart, the Premier of British Columbia, discussed the situation with the senior officers of the three services. Although it was pointed out to him that there was little probability of any strong Japanese forces attacking Canada, he stated that the people were "obsessed with the necessity of adequate protection of British Columbia from any possible eventuality and until this can be assured did not appreciate the necessity of sending weapons and equipment abroad."[4]

The alarm felt in British Columbia was increased by the large number of Japanese-Canadians living there. Of some twenty-three thousand people of Japanese descent resident in Canada, over twenty-two thousand lived in the Pacific province. Three-quarters of these lived within a fifty- to seventy-five-mile radius of Vancouver.[5] Following Canada's declaration of war, pressure was placed on the federal government by trade unions, veterans' organizations, service clubs, municipal and provincial governments, and others to disperse these Japanese-Canadians to the other side of the mountains. As a result they were evacuated early in 1942 to areas in the interior.

Still, as the outer reaches of the British, French, and Dutch Empires fell to Japanese troops, the people of British Columbia demanded more and more protection from the armed forces. In March 1942, the Chief of the General Staff recommended the completion of the 6th Division and the mobilization of brigade groups of a 7th Division. This was approved by the War Committee, which also authorized a large increase in R.C.A.F. squadrons in Canada. Under continuous pressure it was decided a few weeks later that the 7th Division should be mobilized and brigade groups of an 8th formed. "That the expenditure on the armed services for the fiscal year 1942- 43 was nearly double that for 1941- 42," wrote the official army historian, "was due in no small part to the excitement in British Columbia."[6]

A further stimulus to the alarm felt in British Columbia occurred in mid-June 1942 when, as a diversionary action to draw off American naval forces from the planned Battle of Midway, Japanese forces invaded the Aleutian Islands, occupying Kiska and Attu. Among those who predicted this action was a prelude to an attack on British Columbia was Howard Green,[7] a well-known member of Parliament from Vancouver. Soon the War Committee authorized the formation of an 8th Division.

During 1942, therefore, there was a tremendous buildup of troops, weapons, and equipment in Pacific Command. In May of that year there were only 8 3.7-in. and 12 Bofors anti-aircraft guns in British Columbia. By November 1943 there were 56 3.7-in. and 142 Bofors guns protecting cities and vital installations. The number of operational air force squadrons in Western Air Command doubled. The army buildup was spectacular. Under Pearkes were the 6th Division, commanded by his old friend Maj.-Gen. A. E. Potts, and the 8th Division, commanded by H. N. Ganong, who, like Potts, formerly had commanded a brigade overseas. Potts and his division were responsible for Vancouver Island, while Ganong, who had his headquarters at Prince George, had northern British Columbia. By the spring of 1943, when the number of troops in Pacific Command reached their peak, Pearkes was to have command of some thirty-five thousand officers and men.[8]

There were also thousands of others in the Reserve. The efficiency of the reservists was reaching hitherto unattainable standards since usually they were able to make use of the skill, weapons, and equipment of battalions located nearby. One of the more interesting formations which came into existence just prior to Pearkes's arrival, and one which he fostered from the outset of his command, was the Pacific Coast Militia Rangers. This organization was composed of rangers, trappers, miners, woodsmen, loggers, and others in 137 companies scattered over British Columbia. Many smaller communities were difficult to reach from the main centres. To provide them with some measure of protection, it was decided to form and arm a body of "irregulars" or "home guard" units composed of men who were familiar with their area and accustomed to the climate and conditions of the mountains and bush country. Like the American Minutemen, they could be called upon at very short notice to leave their civilian jobs to defend their localities. They served without pay and selected their own officers and N.C.O.'s. Their role was to provide local defence against minor raids, to gather intelligence, and to operate, either by themselves or in conjunction with active units, to repel a major attack.[9] The P.C.M.R. was to grow into a force of approximately fifteen thousand officers and men.

Pearkes was somewhat surprised at the degree of precautionary measures in force. When he left England German bomber squadrons were located fifty to a hundred miles away, and continual raids had necessitated a high standard of passive air defence. Japan, however, was six thousand miles away, and even Kiska was about two thousand miles from Vancouver. Nevertheless, the air raid protection system was very active, and periodic tests of the sirens were held to practise volunteers in their various tasks. There was a "dim-out" but no "blackout" in the larger coastal cities, but on board ship travelling between Victoria and Vancouver all external lights were blacked out, and passengers travelling by air between the two centres had to draw blinds over the windows. There was also a sense of unreality about the situation. Although British Columbians demanded more anti-aircraft guns and air force squadrons, few if any went to the trouble of building air raid shelters or, for example, of taping large windows in downtown stores. There were numerous volunteer organizations, but apart from rationing there was little official compulsion on the population in Canada to contribute to the war effort.

Perhaps the most outstanding example of this was that in 1942 about 65 per cent of the men in the 6th and 8th Divisions were N.R.M.A. soldiers. The National Resources Mobilization Act introducing conscription had been passed in June 1940 as a result of Germany's sweeping victories over France and the Low Countries. Conscripts, however, were not obliged to serve overseas, and as the war continued, more and more volunteer servicemen joined units sent overseas in 1941 and 1942, so that an ever-increasing proportion of the new divisions created to serve in the Pacific and Atlantic[10] Commands was made up of home defence soldiers. It was the first time Pearkes had come into contact with them, but at this stage he was primarily interested in the level of training and competence of the regiments and brigades in which they served rather than in whether or not they might be persuaded to "go active." He felt no antipathy towards them but rather was of the opinion, as he expressed it in the following year, "that when the time comes for these men to take their place in the battlefield, they will do so without coercion and will do justice to their unit and formation."[11] Events were to prove him partially wrong in this respect, but by that time too the military situation on which he based his opinion had changed as well.

On his way to Victoria, Pearkes was briefed in Ottawa by Stuart, who for the past several months had been acting as G.O.C.-in-C. Pacific Command as well as holding the position as Chief of the General Staff. Stuart drew up a document to define Pearkes's authority.[12] In essence, Pearkes

Plate 23. Canadian troops disembarking from American ships for the assault on Kiska.

Plate 24. Aerial view of the military camp at Terrace, B.C., July 1942.

Plate 25. John G. Diefenbaker (left), G. R. Pearkes, and Howard Green (in front of the door).

Plate 26. John G. Diefenbaker (centre) meeting with some members of the Progressive Conservative caucus, Ottawa, 1956. Pearkes is seated second from the right.

BRITISH COLUMBIA

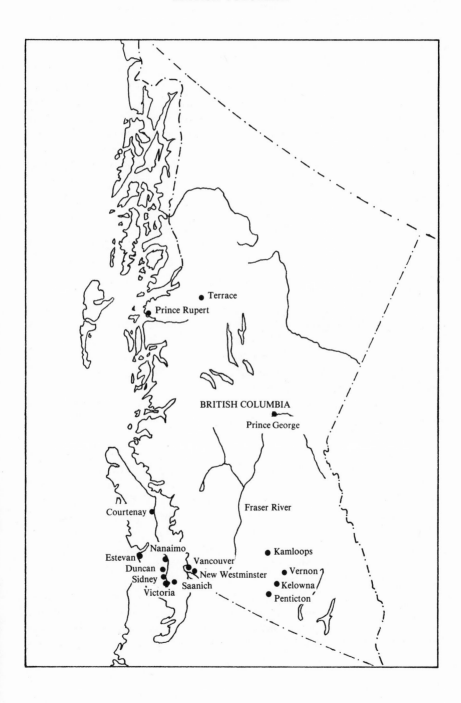

Terrace

Prince Rupert

BRITISH COLUMBIA

Prince George

Courtenay

Fraser River

Nanaimo

Kamloops

Estevan

Vancouver

Duncan

New Westminster

Vernon

Sidney

Kelowna

Saanich

Victoria

Penticton

was to "exercise command through District Officers Commanding and Formation Commanders over all units and establishments of the Canadian Army, both Active and Reserve" in Military Districts Nos. XI and XIII. He could, with the consent of N.D.H.Q., exercise direct command over units, formations, and garrisons should the need occur. Pearkes was also charged with co-operating with the senior naval and air force commanders in the preparation of plans and conduct of combined operations under the general instructions issued by N.D.H.Q. It was his task, too, to initiate and control all measures requiring "the preservation of internal security and the protection of vulnerable points which were military responsibilities in his command."

One of the first documents he studied was the defence plan which had been prepared by his staff and based, presumably, on Stuart's appreciation of national strategy. With respect to the defence of the Pacific Coast, it was felt that the main enemy objectives would be the Victoria-Esquimalt-Vancouver area, the lines of communication between that area and Eastern Canada, the Prince Rupert area, which had become an important port and railhead for American servicemen and supplies going to Alaska, and, finally, Vancouver Island north of Victoria. The scales of attack anticipated varied with the target. They ranged from a medium-scale air attack from Japanese aircraft carriers to a maximum seaborne destructive raiding force of some two brigades. There were other dangers which could not be overlooked such as the establishment of refuelling bases for Japanese submarines in some isolated inlet along the long coastline of the province or perhaps an attempt to sabotage vital communications by elements of the fairly large alien population.

During the first months Pearkes was concerned with completing a number of tasks started by his predecessor and initiating a number of his own ideas. Although Work Point in Esquimalt had been the site of district headquarters for well over half a century, it was vulnerable to a seaborne raid. On 8 September Pearkes had his first meeting with the Joint Services Committee. This committee, chaired by Pearkes, was composed of the three senior commanders of the navy (Rear-Adm. V. G. Brodeur), army, and air force (A/V/M L. F. Stevenson). They met regularly to co-ordinate plans and policy with the G.O.C.-in-C. acting as *primus inter pares*. Here Stevenson ·gave a résumé of the negotiations for acquiring the property of the Jericho Country Club in Vancouver and the progress of construction for housing and headquarters of the three services at Jericho Beach. Originally the plan had been that the design of Combined Operations Headquarters would permit close physical contact between the operations staffs of the three services, but it was considerably modified by National Defence Headquarters.[13] When Pearkes and his staff moved to Vancouver at the end of November, however, it marked the beginning of a long period of harmonious association with his opposite numbers in the other two services. This experience illustrated to Pearkes something of the extent to which the three forces could be successfully integrated. It was to remain in his mind as a model of what might be accomplished in other spheres of military organization.

The move to Vancouver, incidentally, also meant that for the first time in three years George and Blytha could settle down with some measure of permanency. In Victoria she stayed with her parents, but when Pearkes moved to Vancouver, she went with him. As usual, Blytha quickly became involved in a number of women's volunteer organizations, which, added to the calls made on her time as the wife of the senior military officer in the command, kept her almost as active as her energetic husband.

One of Pearkes's initial problems was the difficulty in transporting troops rapidly from one point to another in B.C. The lack of roads in some of the regions led him to request Ottawa to provide buses and cars which could travel on both roads and railroads.[14] In some places, such as the area between Terrace and Prince George, there was also a need for horse transport, should any action take place away from the few gravel or dirt roads. There was no decent connecting link between Prince George and the Alaska Highway, then almost completed. In an emergency, the ability to pack supplies over this gap might have considerable importance.

On Vancouver Island north of the capital, there were several roads constructed by military forces. One road connected Menzies Bay to the head of steel of a logging railroad which ran up from Sayward. Shortly after he arrived Pearkes found that some two hundred conscientious objectors working on the roads were to be moved from Vancouver Island to Alberta to cut wood for internment camps.[15] He put a stop to that. There was also a detention camp in the area, and military prisoners were used on the road as well. Another important route to be opened up was a road from Shawnigan Lake to Port Renfrew, where there was a small but important naval establishment. The small scattered communities of Ucluelet, Tofino, and Alberni were important both from a commercial and military point of view, and here too military roads were established which were to be developed as highways in the postwar period. Carving these roads out of the virgin bush, building bridges, and blasting rock was done under the supervision of the Royal Canadian Engineers. It gave both the engineers and the troops working under them good experience.

This isolation made many of these ports and towns prime areas for attack. As a result R.C.A.F. aerodromes in such places as Tofino, Comox, and Cassidy were prepared for demolition should they be seized by a raiding party and any attempt made to use them, even briefly, for raids on the larger centres to the southwest.[16] Local army commanders were also charged with preparing plans for the evacuation of civilians from certain coastal communities. These plans remained in effect until late in 1943. Thus the military roads constructed had the dual purpose of getting troops in to a threatened area and providing an escape route for civilians.[17]

One of the most unusual defensive measures was an armoured train which, until its role ended in November 1943, ran between Terrace and Prince George. Once a week it made its seventeen-hour-long trip from its permanent railroad siding in Terrace where it came under the operational control of the brigade stationed there. Together with a small crew, it was allotted a force consisting of a company of infantry, forty-four artillery officers and men, and a handful of engineers, medical corps, and a signaller. Aside from the normal weapons carried by the infantry, the train carried two 75-mm. guns and four Bofors anti-aircraft guns with a brace of searchlights.[18] Its role was to provide a mobile striking force which could support any infantry action between the two towns, engage enemy landings on the coast or on the banks of the Skeena River between Tyee and Prince Rupert, and transport detachments of infantry in an emergency.

Reports of "unknown enemy aircraft" and Japanese "periscopes" came in almost daily during 1942, and even in the interior of the province there were demands for protection. One of the latter, for example, was from the Consolidated Mining and Smelting Company of Canada whose smelter at Trail supplied more than half the lead and zinc used by the British Empire during the war. Many evacuated Japanese were located in small towns in the valleys carrying the road and rail routes to Trail, and a senior executive wrote to the Prime Minister that there was nothing to prevent the Japanese from overpowering their guards, cutting the telegraph and telephone communications, seizing a Canadian Pacific Railway train, and leading a type of banzai attack on the power plant in the West Kootenays to sabotage the smelter. He also felt that there was a possibility of an air attack from the Pacific. To cap his requests for a show of military force he wrote, "Our workmen, of whom there are well over six thousand in the Kootenays, are inclined to feel that our effort could not be as important as we tell them it is or the government would take steps to protect it. . . . The effect of the odd anti-aircraft practice would do a great deal to stimulate the idea that we were actually in the war and that our production was important." When the matter was passed on to Pearkes, he pointed to some of the difficulties which an aircraft carrier would encounter in sending its planes over three mountain ranges and getting past the R.C.A.F. fighter squadrons. He was also able to quieten the fears of a threat from the Canadian Japanese whose plight was bad enough without further confinement.

A variety of methods to speed up movement of troops to counter

Japanese raids were discussed by Pearkes and his colleagues at the Joint Services meetings. One idea which received attention was the establishment at Prince George of a large collection of gliders which could lift a counter-raid force to a threatened area. One of the difficulties was the lack of open spaces where such an airborne force might land. The committee recommended an amphibian rather than a wheeled type of glider since there were innumerable lakes.[19] Nothing came of this scheme, but it does serve as an example of the concern to meet the challenge which distance and geography placed on the three services.

When Pearkes had been a staff officer at Work Point Barracks, he had been interested in the challenge of the mountainous territory, and shortly after he arrived back on the Pacific Coast he found that a few officers had recently attended a course on mountain warfare. The idea had originated with E. C. Brooks, president of the Alpine Club of Canada. In April 1942 he proposed to extend the facilities of the club's mountaineering camp in the Little Yoho Valley to train about twenty officers. As he wrote later:

In view of the Japanese menace and the need for adequate defence plans for our western mountain passes, it would seem that immediate action should be taken to train a highly specialized "corps d'elite" who would be highly mobile to operate in difficult terrain. The adequate defence of our mountain passes and of the chain of air fields now being completed between British Columbia, the Yukon and Alaska could be best assured by well trained mountain and ski troops, and if Canada is not in a position to supply them, it will be unfortunate. Even if we had only a *token force* of troops specially trained in mountain warfare, it would at least be a move in the right direction and would not leave the onus of the defence of our mountain passes on the trained American mountain troops in the not at all impossible event of a sudden invasion by the Japanese.[20]

A letter from the Minister of National Defence thanking Brooks suggested that the course might be repeated from time to time, and when Pearkes received a copy of it, he immediately arranged to meet with the club president and agreed that "we should . . . have some men we could get hold of quickly who would be trained should it ever be necessary to undertake an operation in mountainous country."[21] Pearkes received permission to repeat the course but this time on a much larger scale. Ottawa agreed to his proposal to send an entire rifle company and to have the instruction increased from two to three weeks. The second course went extremely well, and late in July 1943 Pearkes paid a visit to the camp. "He stayed long enough," wrote an observer,

> to witness the exercises in some of which he actually took part, being quite attracted to the long rappel which one platoon was doing. He, himself, made the rappel, about 60 feet over rock cliffs, as well as one of lesser height, besides visiting all the platoons on the ground and making interesting enquiries concerning methods of training. . . .
>
> In the evening . . . he expressed his complete satisfaction with the work in hand. So much was he impressed with the value and possibilities of the Course that he determined to extend the length of the Camp by another three weeks and requested the Club to accept the training of another group of equal number to the first, from other units. Before his departure he suggested that the training might be continued through the winter in some convenient area, and that next year the school might be enlarged to 500 or possibly 1,000 trainees.[22]

With Pearkes's approval and backing, this type of training was taken over by the military authorities and organized, late in 1943, as a Mountain and Jungle Warfare School at Terrace.

During the early period of his command Pearkes was, of necessity, concerned with the defence of the province. Soon, however, he began to think of the offensive. Obviously, if the Japanese forces on Attu and Kiska were dislodged, the threat to British Columbia would be greatly reduced. Since these islands belonged to the United States, the initiative had to come from the Americans. Moreover, there were insufficient naval forces available at Esquimalt either to transport assault troops over the two-thousand-mile sea voyage or to provide the necessary protection and bombardment. However, the initiative for Canadian participation came from Pearkes.

On 10 October 1942, accompanied by the United States liaison officer attached to his headquarters, Pearkes left for a visit to Lt.-Gen. John L. DeWitt, the commanding general of the United States Fourth Army and the Western Defense Command at San Francisco. He commanded the American forces both to the north and south of Pearkes, and since Pearl Harbour the Canadian and American governments had been co-operating in a number of joint enterprises. In Pacific Command, for example, the 1,671-mile Alaska Highway was being pushed to completion under the direction of the U.S. Army Engineers at a cost of $138 million. In Prince Rupert the population had almost tripled as a result of the "invasion" of American military forces using the port as a base. Here, too, Canadian and American troops worked jointly on completing a road up the Skeena

Valley. Coastal defence artillery batteries on both sides of the border co-operated to control the entrance into the Strait of Juan de Fuca, and in a variety of other ways there was a considerable amount of joint effort and planning between the two commands.[23] In San Francisco Pearkes

> spent a very informative, interesting two days. . . . General DeWitt was an elderly man, small and wiry in structure, had a very keen brain [and was] obviously an excellent administrator. I don't think he'd ever had any command in operations . . . but he was a very hard worker. . . . I wanted to find out all I could about the [American] defences . . . and I gave him all the information we had.[24]

Pearkes and DeWitt became warm friends and during the winter of 1942-43 kept in touch by telephone.

On 13 April 1943 DeWitt visited Pearkes in Vancouver and informed him that he had received permission the previous month to attack Attu and that the assault was planned for mid-May. He also mentioned the possibility of a later attack on Kiska. They had talked about the steps which might be taken to dislodge the Japanese in October 1942, some five months before DeWitt had received authority to undertake the operation. Pearkes was interested then and was more interested now that the Americans were planning on action. He discussed with DeWitt the possibility of Canadian participation later in the year when, if all went well, Kiska would be attacked. The American general welcomed the idea and promised full co-operation when the time should be ripe.[25] Meanwhile, Pearkes, looking to the future, asked whether it would be possible to send a small group of Canadian officers to act as observers, and DeWitt agreed. Pearkes reported to Stuart, but he did not say anything about their private discussion regarding Canadian participation at Kiska. At this point Pearkes and DeWitt felt that an American approach through military channels to feel out the Canadian authorities might bear more fruit.

About a fortnight later, on 10 May, Lt.-Gen. Stuart received a wire from Maj.-Gen. Maurice Pope in Washington saying that J. D. Hickerson, secretary of the American section of the Permanent Joint Board on Defence, "had suggested to him that it would be eminently appropriate if Canadian forces cooperated in removing the existing threat in the Aleutians."[26] On the following day Stuart wired Pearkes to ask whether it was " 'too late to consider some form of army participation.' " The bread cast upon the American waters by Pearkes was returning. Stuart's enquiry, unknown to him, came on the same day that the Americans attacked Attu, an assault which was not made public for several days. Pearkes told him about his private conversations with DeWitt and about the enthusiasm of the American commander for Canadian co-operation. Stuart favoured the idea, for he had been advocating the need to give Canadian troops battle experience. He believed, too, that if the N.R.M.A. soldiers took part in a campaign which would help remove the Japanese threat, it would reduce the growing prejudice against them.[27]

Stuart immediately began to press directly and indirectly for Canadian participation in the Kiska campaign both in Ottawa and, through Maj.-Gen. Pope, in Washington. Pope was instructed to see Gen. George C. Marshall and put to him Stuart's enquiries. Marshall promised to relay the message to DeWitt, and on 24 May Marshall informed Pope that DeWitt had expressed delight at the prospect of having Canadians participate. Marshall added that he had authorized General DeWitt to confer with Pearkes and work out the necessary plans.[28] It was not until two days later, at a meeting of the Canadian War Committee, that Mackenzie King was informed of the proposal. King was irritated that the idea had been initiated by the military authorities and routed through American channels. He felt that, basically, the idea was good but was quick to ask whether the planned action would make it any more difficult to get reinforcements for overseas. Stuart assured him it would not. The Prime Minister, once he arranged that the whole matter was placed on a ministerial level, and although his annoyance at the way things had been handled was only slightly mollified, agreed to Canada's participation.[29]

Three days before the War Committee met, Pearkes wired Stuart and asked if permission could be granted for official talks with DeWitt. Provided no commitments were made, Stuart agreed. On 25 May, therefore, Pearkes and DeWitt again discussed the situation. DeWitt proposed that the Canadians supply an infantry battalion and an anti-aircraft battery for garrison duties at Amchitka to strengthen the counteroffensive potential for the American forces already there and a brigade group to be employed with the American task force in the capture of Kiska. After the meeting Pearkes immediately wired Stuart indicating that the requisite force could be found within his command and requesting permission to proceed. DeWitt at the same time informed his superiors in Washington, who agreed to his first suggestion subject to Canadian approval and submitted the second to the Joint Chiefs of Staff in Washington. It was a week before Pearkes received authority to act. Since DeWitt had wanted the force for Amchitka to be ready by 15 June, the delay had cancelled any hope to provide assistance for the Americans, and in any event Ottawa rejected the suggestion. Approval for the brigade group to prepare for the attack on Kiska was granted, however. With only six weeks available before its embarkation, there was a great deal to be done.[30]

When Pearkes received permission to proceed with the formation of a brigade group at noon on 3 June, he immediately called Maj.-Gen. H. N. Ganong to tell him that the Winnipeg Grenadiers and the 24th Field Company, R.C.E., had been selected for special training.[31] He had already telephoned Maj.-Gen. A. E. Potts in Victoria asking him to report immediately. The 13th Canadian Infantry Brigade of Potts's division was to be used since it was the senior brigade in the command. Ganong and Potts selected the units on the basis of their strength and efficiency. Each was recommended as "well enough trained for combined operations provided a period of intensive training was authorized." Pearkes was very careful in this respect. A year and a half previously the Canadians sent to Hong Kong were neither sufficiently experienced nor trained to cope with the task given to them. If the Japanese defending Kiska fought as hard as those on Attu, those in the attacking force would have to know their business. Moreover, it was necessary to bring the units up to strength immediately. The Canadian Fusiliers, the Winnipeg Grenadiers, and the Rocky Mountain Rangers had all contributed drafts for overseas service. Further withdrawals were forbidden, and other units in the division were tapped for men to make up deficiencies in manpower. Pearkes also informed his officers that those units occupying the Nanaimo Military Camp must be moved out immediately to make way for the 13th Brigade to start its training for Operation "Greenlight." At the meeting he held with his staff and senior officers on 4 June, Pearkes stressed the need to start intensive training immediately. The staff was also told to examine closely the information coming in from the Canadian observers in Alaska as well as from the conversations held with American staff officers sent by Gen. DeWitt.[32]

Two days later Pearkes flew to Ottawa to meet with the Chief of the General Staff and his senior officers. Here the entire plan of the operation was discussed and several decisions taken. Pearkes had recommended Brig. D. R. Sargent to command the force, but Stuart agreed that his low medical category had to be considered. When McNaughton was asked for recommendations he suggested Brig. H. W. Foster. Pearkes knew him well both as an officer in the Lord Strathcona's Horse in prewar years and later as a senior officer in the 1st Division. He welcomed this appointment and was pleased that Maj. W. S. Murdoch, who had also served on his staff overseas, was to be appointed brigade major.

Pearkes pointed out that the American equivalent of a brigade group included a far larger number of engineers and pioneers. These men were needed especially to land supplies on the beach and move them forward. Since the battalions in the brigade represented British Columbia, Manitoba, and Ontario, Pearkes suggested using Le Régiment de Hull from Quebec. Stuart agreed. "It was a wise decision to take," Pearkes said later. "When they [Le Régiment de Hull] were in Kiska they were the life and soul of the whole party during the period of occupation."[33] To strengthen security, a press release stated that two brigades from Pacific Command would be engaged in special training, one at Wainright, Alberta, and the other at Nanaimo, B.C. Troops were sent to Wainright to give weight to the cover story, and the 13th Brigade assembled at Nanaimo. Close by at Courtenay a combined operations training school had been established which worked closely with the air force squadrons located farther to the south and a naval establishment nearby. Here the battalions in the brigade alternated between battle drill training with live ammunition and practising the various drills and manoeuvres associated with an assault from the sea. Transportation of the brigade group, of course, would be provided by the Americans, and it was also decided that certain items of American equipment would be used. Brig. Sherwood Lett, an old friend of Pearkes who had recently returned from England after being wounded at Dieppe, was appointed liaison officer between Vancouver and Ottawa and, at the same time, was to lend his assistance to the planning staff.

Pearkes flew back to Vancouver on 8 June highly pleased with the conference in Ottawa, but on the day he returned he received a telegram from Gen. DeWitt. It had been understood that the brigade would not leave Nanaimo until 1 August, permitting it to have at least six weeks' training. DeWitt now requested that the training and equipping be completed by 15 July. Pearkes was in Vancouver only two days before he flew to San Francisco with Brig. W. N. Bostock to see DeWitt. There were a number of decisions to be made and action taken on them immediately—American weapons, certain items of American dress and equipment, the loading of both troops and equipment, and a variety of administrative problems ranging from rations to the payment of the troops in U.S. funds. Pearkes also had a long talk with Maj.-Gen. C. M. Corlett, who was to command the entire Task Force.[34] It was decided to modify the organization of the Canadian brigade to give more independence and self-sufficiency to the Canadian battalions or "combat teams" as they were to be termed. After discussing the general operations plan of attack with Corlett and DeWitt and following a side trip to San Diego where he observed the American troops training in combined operations, Pearkes returned to Vancouver on 14 June.

The day after Pearkes arrived he assembled his staff, briefed them on the changes to be made, informed them about the decisions made regarding weapons and equipment, and brought them up to date on administrative matters. To Brig. Lett and one or two others he gave the outline of the operational plan. Unit censorship on the "Greenlight" forces was imposed immediately. He also gave orders that the battalions or "combat teams" at Nanaimo should live, eat, and train together. This would bring the engineers, medical staff, artillery, and other arms supporting the infantry into a closer combination. He also told them that Brig. Foster would be arriving in a few days to take over command of the invasion forces and that the Chief of the General Staff was expected shortly to observe the progress of their training.

Two days later Pearkes was airborne again, this time heading north to visit Lt.-Gen. S. B. Buckner, Jr., at his headquarters in Anchorage and to visit Adak where both the American and Canadian forces would carry out final training in a climate similar to Kiska. As usual Pearkes gained as much information from Buckner as he could about training facilities, the type of climactic conditions the Canadians could expect if they remained in Kiska for some months, and so forth. He was given the latest intelligence available, gleaned primarily from air force squadrons bombing the island, which estimated some eleven thousand Japanese on the island. Despite the blockade of Kiska by American naval forces and the bombing it received by both American and Canadian squadrons, it was felt that the Japanese would put up a desperate struggle as they had at Attu. At Anchorage as in San Francisco, Pearkes was struck by the whole-hearted co-operation of the Americans. Aerial photographs, maps, officers familar with Japanese methods, weapons experts, mechanical transport, indeed every facility the Canadians requested was given in full measure even to the provision of Japanese interpreters.

When Pearkes arrived back in Vancouver on 22 June, he met Brig. Foster and Lt.-Gen. Stuart. Stuart seemed pleased with his inspection of the brigade and the training they were getting. Pearkes brought him up to date on the information he had and drafted an official letter stating his own satisfaction with the force as well as an outline of the plan of operations.

When DeWitt and his staff arrived in Vancouver on 5 July, Pearkes took them over to Nanaimo to observe the training of the brigade. "The Americans," he stated,

> were extremely pleased with our Canadian troops. [DeWitt] was very impressed by their smartness and their manner of marching. . . . These troops were physically fit and well trained. They had had pretty rigorous training in preparation for this operation and I had some good regimental commanders who put their heart and soul into it.[35]

DeWitt was able to see the men wearing the mixture of Canadian-American equipment which had recently been issued to them, and both senior officers, after talking to the officers and men, would have agreed with the brigade war diarist when he claimed that the "morale of the troops is high and all are anxious to get on the move."[36]

It was a cold, dark morning when the 13th Brigade formed up on the parade square, laden down with sixty-pound rucksacks besides their weapons. At five in the morning of 12 July they began to march to the wharves where American ships which had been loaded the previous day were waiting to embark them. Pearkes was there with his senior staff officers to wish them good luck. Later that day the ships moved off to rendezvous south of Discovery Island before sailing in convoy towards the north. It was not until the thirteenth that Brig. Foster informed all officers of their first destination and final objective. The type of training they were carrying out, the censorship of mail, the tight security measures taken around the wharves during embarkation, and the fact that there was only one Japanese base on the North American continent had led many to make an intelligent guess, however, but no word leaked to the newspapers.

After seven days at sea, the Canadians reached Adak on the evening of 20 July. Having come so far north, most of the men

expected a bare, rocky country with a little coarse grass in the lowland near the shoreline. Everybody gasped as the low mists parted now and then to reveal beautifully verdant hills [and] rocky valleys in which all rocks seemed to be moss covered, but the mists closed in and we turned our thoughts to the harbour itself. Adak harbour was like the roads of Southampton water. Ship after ship lay at anchor [of] all types and description; not to forget the little tugboat that steered us past the final opening in the submarine boom and laid us alongside a wooden jetty.[37]

For the next three weeks the battalions trained. They became thoroughly familiar with their weapons and had several major rehearsals in combined operations by "attacking" Great Sitkin Island which was nearby. They found, too, that while Adak might have looked like a jewel from the sea to live there was something else. "The air is like a Scottish mist, the ground like a quagmire," the war diarist wrote at the beginning of August, and a week later he experienced something of what was to come.

Tonight the wind rose to 40 miles per hour. The rain was torrential, roads washed out, our small vehicle park (we have only five vehicles) melted into the side of a coal dump and small rivers ran through tents;

in some places it required a considerable effort to lift our feet after standing in one spot for a couple of minutes.[38]

No matter what the weather the training went on. The more the men worked together the greater their confidence grew in each other.

Pearkes had made arrangements to establish an advanced headquarters in Adak, but for several weeks he remained in Vancouver concentrating his attention on those regiments which might be called upon to reinforce or replace the "Greenlight" units. There was a need for replacements among both officers and men. These units also had to be brought up to strength and their training altered to conform with northern conditions. If they were to develop the regimental spirit which Pearkes emphasized, the sooner they were brought up to war establishment and reached the highest possible standard of efficiency, the better. His ideas in these matters were well known by his staff, and Pearkes knew Brigadiers W. H. S. Macklin and W. N. Bostock, his two chief staff officers, would carry out his orders and suggestions with zest and energy.[39]

A week before the Canadians embarked for Kiska, Pearkes flew up to Adak to his advanced headquarters. The full-scale amphibious exercise on nearby Great Sitkin Island was just ending. He visited the units every day to see for himself that everything that could be done to ensure the success of their task had been done. "I was satisfied," he said later,

> that the troops would be able to give a good account of themselves, particularly in close combat. I was satisfied with the overwhelming strength that the forces had. With the five big battleships and cruisers there they could have blown the island off the face of the map almost. . . . The weather was more our greatest concern than actually the fear of the fighting but we knew the Japs would fight to the end if they were there.[40] They had demonstrated at Attu . . . [that] many of them were prepared to fight to the very end. . . . So we had stressed the importance of individual combat and the use of the rifle and bayonet. Our men were fit . . . and would have given a good account of themselves.[41]

On 11 August the Canadians began to embark. The scene on the dock was a memorable one with newspaper correspondents and cameramen interviewing and photographing the American and Canadian senior officers. One of the Canadian public relations officers who was present recalled the scene:

As the Canadian troops marched aboard their transports . . . General Pearkes, in the pouring rain, stood at the gangplank and spoke to and shook hands with scores—perhaps hundreds—of soldiers. General Buckner stood a few paces behind and watched the embarkation. In several instances General Pearkes would ask me to have such soldier photographed and send the photo to his mother. He would ask the man his name and the name of his hometown and wish him all good luck.

Some months later in Vancouver [I met Buckner] outside the Vancouver Hotel. We chatted about the Kiska experience and then General Buckner said: "Major, you remember that day on the dock at Adak?" "Yes, sir, I shall never forget it." "Well in all my years of service, I have never seen a senior commanding officer reach his men as General Pearkes did that day. I venture to say that every man to whom the general spoke really felt himself a soldier. What is his secret of reaching the men like that?" "It is quite simple, sir. He loves soldiers and they respond."[42]

In a sense, Pearkes was only doing something which came to him quite naturally. When he was an N.C.O. and later an officer in the Great War, he worked his men hard and did everything in his power to ensure that his platoon, company, or battalion was well trained and provided for prior to going "over the top." Just as he moved among his men before leading them on the attack at Passchendaele, so he got close to the men who would attack Kiska.

As the transports were loaded, they eased out into the harbour, now packed with ships of all sizes. It seems remarkable in retrospect that with almost five thousand Canadian soldiers on board ship as part of a large invasion fleet, Pearkes did not have the authority to permit them to sail. All during the period from the time "Greenlight" force was raised up to and including this point, the Canadian government had been very cautious about committing the troops to action. It was not because this was the first time a Canadian force would be operating in the field under senior American officers, but rather owing to the fact that a large proportion of the force was composed of home defence men. Amendments to the conscription act had widened the scope of their service to Newfoundland, the United States, and, with the decision to partake in the Kiska operation, to Alaska. Under this amendment, passed on 18 June, the Minister of National Defence "issued on 11 July a 'Direction' permitting the despatch of the 'Greenlight' force for 'training, service, or duty' at Adak or points in Alaska 'east of Adak'—i.e., those parts in the Aleutians then firmly in

American hands."[43] All the training and preparations to date had assumed that the Canadians would, in fact, be engaged, but the political caution in Ottawa, stemming probably from the Prime Minister, was illustrated not only by the appointment of Brig. Lett as a liaison officer but also by the visits to the west coast by the Chief of the General Staff, the deputy minister and, latterly, Maj.-Gen. J. C. Murchie, the Vice-Chief of the General Staff, who was at Adak with Pearkes. These officers, as well as Pearkes and Foster, kept Ottawa fully informed, and at each stage of the 13th Brigade's training, Pearkes and a senior officer from Ottawa assured the military authorities in Ottawa in writing of their satisfaction that the force was properly equipped and trained. Kiska was not to be another Hong Kong or Dieppe. Murchie had been a major under Pearkes when he was the Director of Training in Ottawa so they knew each other well. It was not until the day before the brigade began to embark, however, that Murchie sent a telegram to Ottawa stating his satisfaction with the training, morale, and equipment of the force. He added that relations with the American commanders were good, that along with Pearkes and Foster he felt the plans represented a practical operation, and that he could "recommend with Pearkes' and Foster's concurrence that authority be granted for the Canadian force to proceed and undertake proposed operations."[44] This telegram was sent on the evening of the tenth, the same day Murchie left to fly back to Ottawa.

Meanwhile the troops were embarked, the plans laid, and Pearkes waited with growing impatience for authority to send the brigade forward. As he stated later:

> I was in a terrible predicament. . . . The plans the Americans had drawn up were based on Canadian cooperation. The troops had to embark [and] embarkation went ahead. I felt confident that Ottawa would approve; I didn't see how in the world they could back out. I wouldn't have backed out anyway—I couldn't. . . . I just made up my mind that if the message didn't come through that they were going. If it had come through with a definite order they were not to go, I'd have had to carry it out. But I couldn't upset the plans of an ally because communications were so bad [at Adak].
>
> It was very worrying. . . . If I had carried out literally the instructions which Murchie gave me, those troops couldn't have been embarked. It was most unfair to put a commander in such a position.[45]

It was not until the early hours of 13 August, when the first ships of the invasion force were beginning to leave the harbour, that Pearkes received the telegram giving the Canadian force permission to proceed. He asked to be taken out to the *David W. Branch*, the headquarters ship, and handed Brig. Foster his final instructions. Late that afternoon the Canadians, too, slipped out of the harbour and sailed westward.

The story of the attack on Kiska is told in detail elsewhere.[46] Unknown to the Americans or Canadians the Japanese garrison had been evacuated under the cover of fog late in July. Extremely poor weather conditions together with faulty information from intelligence sources combined to lead the American commanders to believe the Japanese had only abandoned their main bases and had taken up positions in the hills. As it was, when the assaults on Kiska were made on 15 and 16 August, the combat teams found a deserted island. As the 13th Brigade war diarist put it, while the Canadians were pushing south over the island to meet up with the Americans: "Reports continued to stream in pinpointing caches of Jap parachute bombs, rifles, L.M.Gs., ammo., food, clothing, etc.—also reports that every hill, more especially every high ridge, was alive with Jap positions and dummy positions. This would have been a terrific fight."[47] Fortunately for everyone concerned, it was not. A few casualties, including some killed, were suffered from booby-traps as well as from trigger-happy soldiers firing mistakenly on their comrades. Aside from these misfortunes, the worst the troops were to endure was the winter weather of the Aleutians.

As soon as he heard of the occupation, Pearkes set out by destroyer to visit Kiska and spent the nineteenth with Foster[48] and his battalion commanders. All spoke very highly of the behaviour of their units in the assault and in their patrolling activities. Meanwhile, all ranks were engaged in unloading stores, preparing a site for a tented camp, and trying to make themselves comfortable on an island which was beginning to become daily more bleak as winter weather approached. Pearkes did not doubt that the brigade had benefited from the operation. He was also pleased at the cordial relations and close co-operation which existed then and continued to exist all during the months ahead.[49] A day or so later he left for Vancouver, after informing Foster and his battalion commanders that they should expect to remain there on garrison duty for several months.

Since the 13th Brigade was not engaged in combat, the time it spent on Kiska has rarely been mentioned in official histories. In Europe at this time the 1st Canadian Division was battling in Sicily and Italy. Naturally, interest in the struggle of this first Canadian formation in combat in the major theatre of war was far greater than the difficulties encountered by a brigade in the remote Aleutians. Although the 13th Brigade did not have to contend with the enemy, it did have to contend with the elements.

Something of this may be gained from the following comments extracted from the war diary:

August 27th, 1943—The wind last night rose to a full gale. In the new camp many tents, even those dug in four feet, were ripped or blown away. This morning several people . . . were actually blown off their feet by sudden williwaw gusts.

September 15th, 1943—It seems that each month we may expect at least four blows exceeding 50 miles an hour and one exceeding 80 miles an hour. . . . Last night's gale drove the torrential rain through every seam in the tent. . . . The noise in the tent was unbelievable. When morning came bedrolls were wet and stoves were full of sodden ashes.

October 28th, 1943—Last night at 2345 hrs the meteorological office recorded an east wind of 50 m.p.h. with very strong gusts reaching 70 m.p.h. At 0730 hours this morning exactly the same reading was recorded for a west wind. At 1445 hrs. the R.C.O.C. phoned the information that one marquee and six tents had just become airborne and when last seen were heading for Amchitka.

One of the best, brief summations of the brigade's activities on Kiska was made by Pearkes in a letter he sent to Stuart following his visit to the island during 7-11 November. "Since the occupation of the island last August," he wrote,

the brigade has been employed continually in manning outposts, constructing defence works, unloading ships, building wharves and piers, constructing a camp and creating roads over the tundra. Plans for the defence of the northern portion of the island which has been allotted as a Canadian responsibility have been carefully worked out. . . .

Whenever opportunities have arisen, serious efforts have been made to carry out some forms of training. . . .

During the first four weeks of the occupation practically the entire brigade lived and slept in foxholes but now all personnel are accommodated in [American] tents. . . . Usually two tents are placed side by side and in order to obtain some additional protection against the high winds . . . these are either sunk in the ground or earth banks are built around them to a height of six feet. (A storm which occurred the day before my arrival registered a wind velocity of 90 knots and dislodged forty tents in the brigade area.). . . .

The provision of adequate lighting for these tents has proven a matter of considerable difficulty for the ration of candles is totally inadequate. Fortunately there were a number of Japanese generators left on the island and these have been reconditioned. . . .

Ingenuity has also been shown in the construction of shower baths, e.g., the Winnipeg Grenadiers constructed a dam and thus formed a reservoir to hold 30,000 gallons. With salvaged pipe they established a flow of water to a bath house constructed of corrugated iron from an old Japanese dugout. The heating arrangements consisted of the air tank from a dismantled U.S. torpedo found embedded in the runway of the Japanese seaplane base. [It] had a capacity of approximately 120 gallons and was heated by an ingenious oil burner, the whole being enclosed in a tin sheath covered with mud to maintain the heat.

When Allied troops arrived on the island the only roads existing were narrow, hand built trails. The Canadian camp area is now being connected to the main beach by road. . . . During the period I was [there] two to three feet of liquid mud covered the entire surface of the road—I am told this is a normal condition. . . .

Discipline has been excellent and the morale of the troops still remains high. They feel they have a difficult and disagreeable task to do which has not provided opportunities for glory but that the task has to be done and they are proud of the fact that they have done a good job.[50]

Pearkes's trip to Kiska reinforced an idea which he had had for some time, that is, that Canada should continue to co-operate with American forces fighting the Japanese in the Pacific. As this concept became a reality, Pearkes gave more thought to the potential use of the large number of Canadian units then doing little more than garrison duty in British Columbia. When speaking to Lt.-Col. G. S. Currie, the Deputy Minister (Army) of National Defence, at Nanaimo in mid-July, Pearkes mentioned to him that "he thought . . . this [attack on Kiska] was one of the first steps on the road to Tokyo and that Canada should be prepared to follow it up and stay with it to the end."[51] Three weeks later, he wrote to Brig. Bostock from his advanced headquarters at Adak. He mentioned that from his talks with the Americans, it was apparent that "Generals DeWitt, Buckner, Admiral Kincaid and all the senior officers are terribly anxious to get on to the Kurils." Pearkes agreed completely with their reasoning. Having seized the initiative in the Aleutians, it should be retained. An attack from the north would force the Japanese to split their fleet and divert a large number of men from the South Pacific. Airfields could be created in the north Kurils just as they had been in the Aleutians, and these would be in striking distance of the Japanese Empire proper. It would also deprive the Japanese of their very important fishing grounds off Kamchatka. "I haven't the slightest idea," he continued,

> as to what will be the intention of the Canadian government. My own view is, as you know, that it is of the utmost importance that we get in this battle if we are to be considered as a Pacific power. The fact that Canadian troops are fighting here will be the indication to all the united nations that the British Empire is prepared to go on and defeat Japan as well as dealing with Italy and Germany. . . .
>
> I am more than ever convinced that this northern route is the right approach, especially if it can be coordinated with operations from the south. We shall have a true pincer movement on Japan. . . .
>
> If we start offensive operations against Japan and if the attack on the Marshall Islands is successful, an adequate defence will be provided for British Columbia. I should feel quite happy to leave it to the reserve army and the P.C.M.Rs., because with all the out positions held, Japan could not possibly launch a serious attack upon the mainland of America until she had recaptured the Marshalls, Midway and the Aleutians.[52]

At the time he wrote, the senior American officers had no indication from Washington as to future military operations in the North Pacific. Pearkes, however, had no desire to be placed in the position he had been in with "Greenlight Force," which had only the minimum amount of time to train. Should the Americans decide to push on, the sooner he knew what the Canadian policy would be the better. Four days later, on the same day the invasion fleet was leaving Adak, Pearkes wrote to the Chief of the General Staff informing him of the speculations on future operation among American officers[53] and suggesting reasons why Canadian troops should participate in the endeavour against Japan if Washington agreed to the proposed plans. He stressed the need for an early decision from Ottawa. Moreover, he added, an attack on the Kurils "will probably require rather larger forces than those employed against Kiska, and for this reason the United States authorities might appreciate a larger Canadian contribution should the Canadian Government decide to participate." Pearkes thought in terms of three brigade groups. The personnel of Le Régiment de Hull had made such a good impression that Pearkes felt one of the brigade groups might be composed mainly of French-speaking

Canadians. Should Ottawa agree to the participation of such a force in the North Pacific, Pearkes admitted that he did not know to what extent N.R.M.A. soldiers would be considered eligible to take part, but he added that the morale of "Greenlight Force" as a whole was such that he felt "sure a very high percentage of N.R.M.A. personnel would volunteer to go Active provided they knew that they were going to remain in their own Battalion and that the unit was to be employed on operations against the Japanese."

Pearkes received no firm guide from Ottawa regarding a military policy for Canada in the Pacific. In 1943 the attention of the Canadian government was on the Italian campaign and plans for the second front. With her limited resources, Canada had to concentrate on one major theatre of war, and for the present that was Europe. The Pacific Theatre was put aside and not until late in 1944 was more serious attention given to it. It is rather interesting to note, however, that when Ralston requested advice from Lt.-Gen. Murchie, who by that time had replaced Stuart as Chief of the General Staff, regarding the role Canadian troops might play in the Pacific after the collapse of Germany, Murchie submitted a memorandum containing many of Pearkes's ideas.[54]

All of this, however, was in the future, and although Pearkes received no encouragement, he kept very much in mind the possibility of Canadian involvement in the Pacific and, within his command, did what he could to prepare for it. One example of this was the wholehearted backing he gave to the Japanese Language School. Early in 1943 Ottawa requested fifteen candidates from Pacific Command who had a basic knowledge of the Japanese language. These were to be sent to the U.S. Military Intelligence Service Japanese Language School in Minnesota. None were available, nor were there any facilities for teaching Japanese in B.C. The need for training men in this language became more apparent when American interpreters were loaned to "Greenlight Force." Among his staff, however, Pearkes had as his G.S.O. I (Intelligence) Lt.-Col. B. R. Mullaly, who had lived in the Far East, spoke Japanese, and was interested in establishing a Japanese language school. In May the G.O.C.-in-C. wrote to Stuart strongly recommending such a school which would be supervised by Mullaly and partly staffed by two Canadian-born Japanese.[55] Originally the idea was to provide Canadian students going to the American school with a better grounding in Japanese which would, in turn, give them the benefit of the more advanced instruction there. In June Ottawa gave its permission for the undertaking on a temporary basis, and the first class of eighteen students met at the Vocational Training Centre in Vancouver in August.

As the semi-official school developed, efforts were made to place it on a permanent basis, increase its staff, and give additional instruction to the candidates, especially in military and intelligence subjects. Pearkes once again strongly recommended to Ottawa the expansion of the school. As its director reported,

These recommendations were adopted and the result has been [the] extension of the scope and drastic revision and streamlining of its syllabus with the object of attaining maximum results in minimum time, and laying the foundations of an organization for the provision of a specially trained and competent front line interpreter-interrogator teams for any Canadian formation which may take the field against the Japanese army.[56]

During the course of its existence the school accepted a total of 232 students, of whom 137 were able to complete the course. By far the greater number of these were from the army, but there were a few representatives from the other services as well. In time most of the successful graduates were sent to South-East Asia Command where they were engaged in psychological warfare, document translation, intelligence and counter-intelligence work, and war criminal control measures. Considering the limited time it was in operation, as well as the length of time, usually a year, it took a candidate to master the language, the school performed a unique and successful function.

During 1944 there was another, much smaller, group of soldiers under-going intensive training in British Columbia for intelligence and sabotage work in South-East Asia Command. It originated with F. W. Kendall, a Canadian mining engineer, who in the early 1930's established himself as a consultant in the Far East. His business in southern China was interrupted by the steady advance of the Japanese Army. In the years before Pearl Harbour, Kendall had been approached by the British to undertake several undercover roles, among which was the establishment of an intelligence network with radio communication covering all the Japanese-occupied territory from Taiwan to Hainan. In 1940 he underwent special training for duties he was to perform should Hong Kong be attacked. After the capture of that colony, he was in charge of the planned escape of some seventy senior military and civilian personnel to mainland China. In 1943 Kendall was in India where he was attached to a S.O.E. (Special Operations Executive) school training groups of Indians, Malayans, and Chinese to infiltrate into Japanese-occupied territory in Southeast Asia.

Some time later Kendall was sent to London to discuss the possibility of forming a group to re-enter the Hong Kong area in operations against the Japanese. Working through the New York headquarters of the S.O.E., the

Canadian ambassador to the United States, Lester Pearson, and finally the Canadian Intelligence in Ottawa, Kendall ultimately arrived in Ottawa and then Vancouver. He was given permission to establish a small, tented camp at Lake Okanagan on the shore opposite Summerland. There he collected together a number of Canadian Chinese who had volunteered for special duties in the Far East. Some, like Capt. Roger Cheng of the R.C.C.S., were already in the Canadian Army and had training in wireless communication. Others had military experience in various other corps as privates or N.C.O.'s.[57] None, however, had the specialized training they would need, and during the summer of 1944 Kendall and the small group of specialists he had with him worked them intensively, teaching them every trick they knew to enable them to survive and operate behind the Japanese lines.

The story of the groups who trained at this secret camp cannot be told here, but until they left in the fall of 1944, Pearkes—one of the very few who knew of the existence of the camp—did everything to assist them. He arranged for their supplies, equipment, tents, food, explosives, and so forth, provided a boat for transportation, and saw to it that special facilities were made available to permit the groups to practise sabotage "raids" on certain military establishments in their final phase of training. In August Kendall invited him to visit the camp and Pearkes eagerly accepted. "We were more than halfway through training," Kendall recalled,

> and I was very proud of the progress these boys had made. We put on a special exhibition for him—a midnight attack against an encampment. . . . He was fascinated. He was like a Boy Scout. But we were using stuff that he had never heard of before and of course we showed him everything, illustrated everything and took him through our war games. . . . Oh, he was back in action again and having the time of his life. . . . He fired all our weapons, made up his own explosive charges and fitted his own timing devices. He was just one of the boys.[58]

Sitting around the campfire Pearkes had the opportunity to talk at some length with the men and learned a great deal from them. They were anxious about their status upon their return to Canada and especially concerned about the franchise which had been denied them for many years. They were bitter about the anti-Oriental feeling prevalent in British Columbia for decades. They felt themselves to be Canadians, they had volunteered to fight for Canada, and it was only right they should expect the privileges as well as the duties of citizenship. After listening to them, Pearkes promised that after the war he would do everything in his power to get them their full rights as citizens, a promise he was to keep.

The requirement for Chinese-speaking personnel to be used for special assignments in Southeast Asia was a continuing one, and as the largest proportion of Canadian Chinese lived in British Columbia, it was natural that Pearkes would be especially interested when Ottawa announced that those men were to be called up for service under the National Resources Mobilization Act. There were many who had joined the services voluntarily, and although all had been registered under provisions of the N.R.M.A. authority, it was not until September 1944, that call-up notices were served. Defence headquarters issued instructions for the call-up in August, at about the same time as Pearkes was visiting the secret camp in the Okanagan. He ordered a committee, chaired by Lt.-Col. B. R. Mullaly, to study the implications of the call-up, having in mind the potential benefit there might be if they were gathered together, given special training, and employed in the Pacific Theatre.

The committee met early in September and made the following suggestions. Of the Canadian Chinese in British Columbia, it was estimated that between two and three hundred would be accepted into the army, and another one hundred might be available from the rest of Canada. When one considered the demands of industry, applications for postponements, and so forth, it was felt that some two hundred men might be available for active service. The committee, which was attended by Lt.-Col. F. L. Hill, a specialist on the needs of the Pacific Theatre, was made aware of the great need for men of Asiatic origin with a knowledge of Japanese. When it was suggested that Canadian Chinese should be trained together at a special camp at Milnes Landing, Hill felt it would be a good recruiting ground for the Japanese Language School, and others stressed the aptitudes of these men as signallers, engineers, and other specialist training.[59]

Pearkes forwarded the report of the committee to Ottawa with his enthusiastic endorsement, adding that if such a training centre was formed, it should hold not only new recruits but others in Canada who had volunteered previously. After they completed their basic training, he thought some would be available as ordinary reinforcements, but there would be a considerable proportion who would qualify as specialists. "It is obvious," he wrote, "that men of Chinese racial origin would be of more value serving in an Asiatic than a European theatre of war."[60]

It may have been a good idea, but Ottawa was unwilling to accept it. Murchie pointed to the small number of men involved, the difficulties attendant on a separate reinforcement stream, the desirability of merging recruits of Chinese origin with Canadians of European stock, and, finally, stated that "specialists" could be screened and selected from present basic training centres in Pacific Command. As a result there was no special training centre formed. However, there was merit on both sides of the argument.

Pearkes's promotion of the Japanese Language School, his support of Kendall's group, and his attempt to establish his own special centre for Canadian Chinese in Pacific Command are examples of some of the sidelights of his interest in preparing for the day when Canadian troops would be used against Japan. However, his desire to arouse Ottawa to the potential of Canadian participation in the war against Japan in 1944 was to be frustrated by the demands for reinforcements in the European Theatre.

12

Frustration and Resignation

In the early hours of 3 January 1944, the United States Army Transport *David W. Branch* slipped quietly into Esquimalt Harbour. On board were over one thousand officers and men of "Greenlight Force" who had left Kiska ten days earlier. The men had spent Christmas and New Year's at sea, but nothing could dampen their enthusiasm when they left Kiska. "To a man," wrote one officer, "we prayed that as long as we might live and as far as we might travel we would never again land on these desolate shores."[1] Within a week officers and men were scattered all across Canada on furlough. The brigade, they were told, was to be concentrated at Vernon. Many would have preferred to go to Victoria or Alberni—in fact the further south, the better. Nonetheless, Vernon was far better than Prince George or Terrace.

The return of the 13th Brigade brought approximately five thousand officers and men back under the control of Maj.-Gen. Pearkes, but whereas once he had two understrength divisions to command, he now had only the 6th Division as well as thousands of men on various types of garrison duty ranging from coastal defence artillery to units guarding aerodromes and vital communications links throughout British Columbia and Alberta. In the spring of 1943, the two divisions in Pacific Command, the 7th Division in Atlantic Command, and the units on garrison duty in both commands, had reached a total of some sixty thousand "other ranks."[2] Of this number about 63 per cent were N.R.M.A. men, but the remainder were "G.S." or General Service men who had volunteered for overseas service and could be siphoned into the reinforcement stream.[3]

During 1943 it became increasingly obvious that the large home force was no longer necessary. The year had seen the war turn very definitely in favour of the Allies. Although much remained to be done before Germany,

Japan, and their satellites were defeated, as far as Canada in particular was concerned, the U-boat menace in the Atlantic had been greatly curbed and the Aleutians had been cleared. As the danger lessened at home and more Canadian troops became involved in the fighting overseas, the military authorities in Ottawa proposed a severe reduction in home war establishments. Two weeks after the occupation of Kiska, the Chief of the General Staff recommended the disbandment of the 7th and 8th Divisions as well as the reduction of garrison units which would result in the release of almost fourteen thousand all ranks. This proposal was accepted by the Cabinet War Committee and the minister announced it officially a fortnight later.

Pearkes was informed on 13 September that he would have available as operational troops three infantry brigade groups, each of four battalions, as well as Headquarters, 6th Division. In addition, for coast defence duties, he would have four additional infantry units and the 31st Reconnaissance Regiment. The three brigades in Pacific Command were to be equipped similarly to the brigades overseas, and moreover all officers and men were to be re-examined to ensure that only personnel of ages and category similar to the requirements for overseas reinforcements would be employed. The reorganization of the 6th Division[4] "was designed to permit the use of one or more of the brigade groups in 'further operations against the Japanese in the North Pacific Area' in cooperation with United States forces,"[5] an idea Pearkes had been proposing for almost a year, but at this early date there was no indication from Ottawa when, or indeed if, these operations would take place. The result, as Pearkes noted later, was that

> the policy changed, as far as I was concerned here in Pacific [Command], from keeping the 6th and 8th Divisions keyed up as much as we could against the possibility of an attack, to one in which the 6th Division was to prepare itself for any commitment which might occur in the Pacific. . . . Up to that time my main interest had been to try and maintain the units and the divisions for the defence of this coast. Now I made a distinct switch as far as the 8th Division and other units were concerned to try and get as many men to volunteer. I went around to unit after unit . . . and urged the N.R.M.A. men to volunteer. I spoke to battalion after battalion on parade. I remember going to Gordon Head [camp]. . . . I went to Terrace. I went to Prince George. I went to Vernon. I remember going to Port Alberni. . . . [My theme was that it] was your duty now to volunteer. Reinforcements are urgently required, and while the government isn't going to take the step to order you overseas, as many men as possible should volun-

teer. That applied to all units other than the 6th Division during the winter of 1943-44.[6]

During this winter and throughout most of 1944, therefore, Pearkes did what he could to make sure that one portion of the troops in his command reached as high a standard of training as possible and that the remainder, excluding those units needed to man important coastal defences, would be redirected into the reinforcement stream or other appropriate areas as their units were struck off strength.

The list of regiments in Pacific Command which were to cease to function was issued in mid-October, and from that time until the end of the war there was a steady reduction of forces. Towards the end of the month the Pacific Coast Militia Rangers were ordered to reduce their numbers to ten thousand all ranks. In November, the complement of No. 1 Armoured Train was reduced to nil strength, and during the early part of 1944 a number of small units and subunits in garrison along the coast became superfluous. In March 1944, Military District No. XIII (Alberta) ceased to form part of Pacific Command, and in July, when the fighting in Normandy was reaching its climax, Ottawa authorized further reductions in the defences of B.C. At the same time there was a steady relaxation in the civil defence measures. No longer were blinds required to be drawn in aircraft using airports located on the Lower Mainland, and in August hoods were discontinued on locomotive headlights.[7] An event which was especially welcomed was the authorization of commercial wireless stations to disseminate weather information in clear.[8] The end of the danger of enemy landing on the Pacific Coast except nuisance raids was accepted by even the most cautious.

While these reductions in strength and the closing down of some of the camps were in progress, in certain other areas connected with the future employment of the 6th Division, there was a buildup and strengthening of existing facilities. Pearkes's interest in establishing a school to train men in mountain warfare was based on the need to defend British Columbia. As a possible role for Canadian troops in the Pacific began to loom larger in his mind in 1943 and 1944, Pearkes took a number of steps to prepare for training such a force. Thus in 1943 he established a jungle warfare school at Prince George to "train personnel of the 6th Canadian Division in bush tactics, bush travel, river travel and river crossings in all types and conditions of low-lying countries."[9] Several of the instructors had been sent on a special course in Hawaii, an arrangement Pearkes made through Gen. DeWitt. Later those attending the school were instructed from time to time by officers who had seen service with Australian or American forces. During the first seven months of its existence the thirty or forty infantry candidates taking the month-long course, exercised in the Prince George area and conducted their water crossings and travel on the Fraser and small adjacent rivers. In the spring of 1944 the Mountain and Jungle Warfare Schools were amalgamated and relocated at Terrace. By this time the "jungle wing" had increased its capabilities and was training a company at a time. Much of the training carried out by the combined schools would be as useful in British Columbia as in the Southeast Pacific. Pearkes by no means went beyond his authority in training men for a theatre of operations in which the government had not indicated its future policy. Rather he was preparing the ground should an active Canadian policy in the Pacific be approved—and he hoped and thought it would.

It was for this same reason that the scope of the Combined Operations School at Courtenay was greatly increased. This type of training in British Columbia had originated early in 1942 when there was some fear of the Japanese securing some isolated foothold along the coast. A hundred small wooden landing craft were ordered by the army and manned by reserve personnel of the Royal Canadian Navy.[10] These craft were stationed at strategic points along the coast, and in October 1942 combined operations began on a small scale. In the summer of 1943 "Greenlight Force" had received its preliminary training at Courtenay. During the autumn there was an increasing demand for naval personnel trained in combined operations to serve overseas, and, as a result, the Naval Service had to reduce its commitments on the West Coast, leaving almost the whole responsibility for combined operations there to the army.

During the latter part of 1943 and for most of 1944, Pearkes worked to put all the units in the 6th Division through the Combined Operations School as well as to improve the capabilities of the school itself. By mid-January 1944, all of the 14th Brigade Group had completed combined operations training, and the 15th Brigade Group was under orders to send its battalions to Courtenay. Pearkes wanted to send the 14th Brigade Group on to a training area in the Pacific for advanced instruction, but Ottawa again reminded him that training of brigade groups for possible Pacific operations was to be of a preparatory nature only and within the resources of his command.[11] The resources, however, were not good enough for Pearkes. In California he had seen American troops train with far better, larger, and more modern craft than his wooden boats. Moreover, these were wearing out; the difficulties of maintenance were increasing, and the problem of keeping sufficient craft operating to meet army requirements was considerable.[12] In December Combined Operations had requested ten new landing craft, but after hearing more about their difficulties, Pearkes wrote to Ottawa requesting almost a hundred landing craft of various types which, he was informed, would cost over $2.5 million.[13]

However, Pearkes had made his point. If the 6th Division was to train seriously in combined operations, it had to have better equipment. Lett got permission to send out to Pacific Command Lt.-Cmdr. Wadsworth, who had experience in combined operations in Sicily and Italy and was familiar with the famous Inveraray School of Combined Operations. Lett also said that action was being taken in Ottawa by all three services to improve the situation and that Pearkes's request to send six officers for attachment to an American division about to start amphibious training had been approved. When Wadsworth met with Pearkes and some of his senior staff officers in Vancouver early in February, he found Pearkes still enthusiastic about amphibious training despite the estimated cost. Pearkes "expressed his opinion that cost is a secondary consideration as, if combined operations training is . . . necessary, equipment must be provided unless training is to remain of an elementary nature." Moreover, Pearkes now "expressed his desire to send a brigade complete with transport to San Diego to experiment and develop loading plans, etc., to adapt procedure to suit Canadian equipment while gaining practical experience."[14]

Whatever Wadsworth reported to his seniors in Ottawa, he could not help but have been impressed by Pearkes's enthusiasm. If there was any way the 6th Division could be trained for Pacific operations, the G.O.C.-in-C. was determined to find it. The Japanese Language School, the Jungle Warfare School, the desire to form special Canadian-Chinese units, his success in sending Canadian officers to serve with American and Australian formations in Southeast Asia to gain experience, his desire to give brigades in his command training experience in Hawaii or San Diego, the attention he began to give to problems in the Pacific Theatre during staff studies[15]— these were only some of the steps he took to prepare for the day when Canada would join with American or British Commonwealth forces fighting the Japanese. Certainly from his point of view the possibility of a raid on the British Columbian coast became increasingly remote in 1944 with every passing week. At the same time it was inconceivable that the division should be used merely for garrison duty. He was determined that the brigade groups' standard of efficiency should not slump. Pearkes felt the disbandment of the 8th Division had been a proper course of action, but the highly trained 6th Division now needed more direction. In essence he had two choices. He could wait until a more definite policy statement came from Ottawa and relax his pace or assume that Ottawa was serious and work the brigade groups hard so that the formation could enter into battle with Japanese veterans.

Pearkes naturally made the second choice. He did not believe that the Canadian divisions in Europe would be ordered to the Pacific while there was a trained division in British Columbia which had never seen action or suffered any casualties. In 1943 and early in 1944, he still believed that the

N.R.M.A. men could and would be persuaded to "go active." There might even be the possibility of conscription, and although Pearkes never mentioned this verbally or in writing, he remembered that it had happened before. Whether the men in his command were volunteers or conscripted for home defence was of minor concern to him. They were all soldiers, there appeared to be a reasonable likelihood they would see battle in the Pacific, they needed to be trained, their officers needed as much experience as possible, and someone had to do something about it.

Canada's participation in the Pacific Theatre was not overlooked by the military authorities in Ottawa. Pearkes's various requests had to be approved by the senior officers as well as by the minister, and possibly they stimulated further enquiry. Two days before Lt.-Comdr. Wadsworth met with Pearkes and his staff in Vancouver, for example, Brig. R. B. Gibson, Deputy Chief of the General Staff (Administration), wrote to the Chief of the General Staff an appreciation summing up the various factors affecting Canada's participation. After posing a number of possibilities, he stated that "all these questions can only be considered intelligently if information is available to the planners as to the strategic plans for operations against the Japanese." In brief, he suggested that once a political decision was made, Canada should participate in the planning stages and have some decision as to where, how, and in what numbers Canadian forces would be used. The decision was not forthcoming, however. In June 1944, Murchie mentioned to Stuart[16] that "up to the present the only expression of policy by [the] Canadian government is that the extent and nature of Canadian participation will be decided when the appropriate time comes and [the] nature and extent of any participation of land forces have not been discussed except in a most preliminary and general way."

Not until the first week in September, when the Allied forces in Europe were rushing towards the borders of Germany, did the Canadian government decide to participate actively in the war against Japan.[17] As far as the army was concerned, a contribution of one division, to be used in the North or Central Pacific, was considered appropriate. King, who had been so anxious to declare war on Japan following Pearl Harbour, was hopeful that this division would not be used. If it had to be, he preferred that it not be sent to help the British recover former possessions. He told Churchill at the second Quebec Conference that the Canadian government was considering a general election, and as he put it in his diary, "no government in Canada once the European war was over would send its men to India, Burma and Singapore to fight with any forces [*sic*] and hope to get through a general election."[18] When, in October 1943 the Chief of the General Staff gave Ralston a memorandum suggesting Canadian participation in either the North or Central Pacific, a memorandum which incorporated many of the ideas suggested by Pearkes a year earlier, presumably it found favour in the War Cabinet.

The story of the deliberations and negotiations with the British and American governments regarding Canada's role in the Pacific Theatre need not be retold. Pearkes was given neither direction nor encouragement in his preparations, but his superiors in Ottawa could not be blamed for the government's indecision. The European Theatre of War had priority. Under these circumstances, and following directions which were at first vague and then essentially contradictory, Pearkes did his best to accomplish what he thought Ottawa wanted and what appeared to him reasonable.

Early in 1944 the pressure on the districts and commands in Canada to convert more N.R.M.A. conscripts into volunteers for overseas service increased. For the past two years the number of conversions had decreased. In 1942 there had been 18,274, but in 1943 only 6,560. In December 1943, while the 1st Division was in Italy battling for Ortono and suffering heavy casualties, only 294 N.R.M.A. men converted. The stream of reinforcements had to be maintained, and as a result even more volunteers were siphoned from the 6th Division. Pearkes advised Ottawa that the loss of General Service men from Pacific Command "would seriously retard [the] more advanced training of remaining personnel in companies and units."[19] The need for reinforcements, however, could not be denied. Pearkes was well aware of the situation at the front from correspondence he had with friends in the 1st Division, and as the months went by he began to hear more and more about understrength platoons and companies on the Italian front.

In March the Adjutant General, Maj.-Gen. H. F. G. Letson, suggested that one way to encourage conscripts to go active would be to propose to a regiment that it would be sent overseas as a body if all the N.R.M.A. men became volunteers. He proposed to Gen. Stuart that the 13th Brigade would be especially suitable for this tactic. Stuart agreed, as did the Chief of the General Staff. Letson conferred with Pearkes and the brigade commander[20] at the end of the month. They received his proposals "in an enthusiastic and most cooperative manner," Letson reported, and within a few days the attempt at mass conversion was under way.

The attempt to get all the N.R.M.A. men to "go active" played no small part in Pearkes's life later in the year, and it deserves more than passing interest. There was probably no formation in his command which Pearkes respected more than the 13th. He had selected it for the Kiska operation, brought it up to strength, saw to it that it had the best training and equipment available, received good reports of its assault on Kiska, and had admired the way its battalions had kept up their morale despite the exceedingly miserable weather and living conditions. The brigade, therefore, was probably the best in Pearkes's command when it returned to B.C. He looked upon it as one of the three which might be used against the Japanese later in 1944 or possibly in 1945. That he was both willing and enthusiastic that it should be used as a formation which might be sent to Europe is also indicative of his belief that the Canadian forces in active operations in Europe must have first call, even if it meant stripping his command of its best troops.

After Kiska the men were given 30 days' furlough, and in late February the last group to return from Kiska reported back to camp. Brig. Macklin, who took over active command of the brigade, was the fourth person to command the formation since Foster had assumed command some seven months earlier. He noted that there had also been a tremendous turnover among the staff and senior officers. Macklin, who had visited the brigade in Kiska with Pearkes, soon became aware of a considerable drop in the men's morale. In Le Régiment de Hull over sixty men failed to return from furlough and were classified as deserters. The other regiments had fewer absentees, but it was indicative of the lowering of morale in general. As Macklin reported later,

the lowering of morale was not due to bad quarters, bad food, bad clothing or lack of amusement. It was almost entirely due to deep rooted belief among other ranks that they would never be sent to fight, and their intense desire to get out of the army and get back home to the farm or the factory. One padre said, accurately enough, that it was due to a complete absence of any spiritual or moral driving force.[21]

There were other factors working on the 13th Brigade during February and March. While the brigade had been training for the Kiska operation in 1943, an order had been issued[22] concerning compassionate farm leave. The order, in brief, cited the "unusual difficulties in connection with agriculture" owing to the shortage of farm labour. It gave to General Officers Commanding-in-Chief and District Officers Commanding permission to grant compassionate farm leave or release men for farm duty providing it would not "result in substantial interference with essential army activities." This order had no effect on the brigade while it was in Kiska, but shortly after the men returned from furlough, the senior officers in the units were besieged with requests for release, requests which were accompanied by sheafs of supporting letters from parents, parish priests, and others.

While Brig. Macklin stressed the need for units to train for future battle, his words were undermined by orders from Ottawa in March instructing him to gather together officers who would volunteer to serve with the British Army which was short of junior commissioned officers. This order reinforced many soldiers' opinion that their regiments would never be called upon to fight overseas as a unit. It also made officers question the value of the training they were giving the men. Macklin himself was in a dilemma, for if he tried hard to get officers to go on the "CanLoan" scheme, he realized that he could probably siphon off junior officers anxious to get overseas. In brief, he was being asked to bleed his battalions to an extent which would make them close to inoperative, or at least third-rate. At this time, the end of March, he was called to Vancouver and told about the scheme to send the brigade overseas if all the men in the battalions would "go active." Pearkes promised "that the whole resources of Pacific Command would be put behind the scheme to ensure success."

It is likely that Pearkes's enthusiasm for the scheme was greater than Macklin's, for the latter was closer to the men. Nevertheless, he agreed to back the scheme and set about the task with a will. To say that it was an uphill fight would be a massive understatement. Resistance to volunteering for overseas service was strong in all units, but in some it was stronger than others. The outstanding example was Le Régiment de Hull, which had recently been reinforced by some 180 N.R.M.A. men "who had, in nearly all cases, done nothing but fatigues and [administrative] duties for anything up to two years." Most of the N.C.O.'s were not volunteers, including two of the company sergeant-majors. The commanding officer's appeal in this unit, and to some degree in other units, received little support from this influential group.

The small number of volunteers in the brigade's infantry battalions was reinforced by volunteers transferred from other infantry units. While the officers in the 13th Brigade were cajoling the men to go active, Brig. Macklin supported the commanding officers, who suggested that a number of hard core N.R.M.A. soldiers be transferred to other units. He also favoured the reduction in rank of senior N.C.O.'s who were not active service men. Drafts of men from other units to bring the brigade's units up to strength helped to convince many that the authorities were actually serious about sending their regiments over as an entity, but the daily rate of conversion was slow all during April.

Pearkes himself was doing what he could to stimulate conversions. Early in April he sent Lt.-Col. John MacGregor, V.C., to Vernon to talk to the men both formally and informally. "He . . . was of great help," Macklin reported later. A week later, on 11 April, Maj. Paul Triquet, who had recently won the Victoria Cross in Italy while serving with the Royal 22nd Regiment, arrived in Vernon to speak to Le Régiment de Hull. Only about a dozen men responded on the spot to his appeal to go active. It was disappointing, but at least it was a crack in the concrete-like resistance to date. The mayor of Vernon is reported to have said at the time of Triquet's visit that it was "a humiliating duty imposed on a good soldier."[23] Pearkes, when questioned about the action, gave a characteristically blunt reply. "I have spoken along the same lines many times myself," he said. "I see nothing humiliating in trying to do my duty or encouraging others to do theirs. I did not win my V.C. by keeping my boots clean at Passchendaele, nor has any other officer recipient of that decoration won it by leaving things to the sergeant-major."[24]

From the beginning Pearkes visited, frequently more than once, all of the major army camps in his command. Early in April, for example, at Gordon Head, after praising the work done by N.R.M.A. soldiers in Kiska, he spoke to the men of the need for trained volunteers in the Canadian forces poised for the invasion of Europe. He stressed their patriotic duty to "go active" and used all his arts of persuasion. Speaking to a newspaper reporter later he said:

> We ourselves must be inspired to give these men the impelling faith that will drive them to make the supreme effort. We must give them the spirit of confidence . . . and a clan spirit. . . . Our job is reclaiming lost citizens to Canada . . . boys who have grown up for twenty years without any spirit of patriotism . . . and our reward will be an increasing number who volunteer to join their comrades in storming the bastion of Europe.[25]

A week and a half later, after addressing other units, Pearkes was in Vernon and was brought up to date on the latest strengths in the four battalions in the 13th Brigade by Macklin. Aside from the officers there were now 1,835 volunteers plus another 138 from subunits. Of this number, however, 927 had been transferred from other units. Thus, in approximately three weeks, starting with a nucleus of 370 volunteers in the brigade, the intensive drive had resulted since 1 April in only 876 conversions, or about ten per day per unit on the average. Pearkes talked to the regiments here also—the third Victoria Cross winner in as many weeks—but the response was only fair. "I tried principally to appeal to their pride in Canada," he said later, "and to the fact that the outcome of the Second Front might rest upon the number of home defence men who are ready to back up the troops already overseas."[26] In spite of the modest results, Pearkes kept hammering away at the conscripts. He said publicly at one point that no man should wear a "khaki uniform unless he is willing to wear it anywhere,"[27] which was certainly an expression of his own opinion rather than government policy. In general, his appeals, although vigorous, were never made in such a fashion as to alienate the wavering N.R.M.A. soldier. If these men were stigmatized, none would have converted, but with constant prodding, cajoling, and appealing, the number of volunteers grew steadily.

Within the 13th Brigade, meanwhile, there was an interesting psychological effect of the announcement that the brigade might go overseas. Up until February 1944 about 80 per cent of the N.C.O.'s and men were not volunteers. Nevertheless, there had been little open rancour between the volunteers and draftees. What distinction existed was further submerged during the long months spent in Kiska. "I had hoped," Brig. Macklin reported, "that it [the alienation of the two groups] would not re-appear but this hope was not fulfilled." He continued:

The instant the announcement was made the 13 Infantry Brigade would mobilize on a volunteer basis the active personnel mentally ranged themselves in a body on one side and the N.R.M.A. ranged themselves on the other. . . .

On the one hand we started with a cadre of officers and N.C.Os. and a few men whose highest ambition was to get to grips with the enemy in the shortest possible time. The disappointment of this group at the obvious reluctance . . . of the N.R.M.A. soldiers to enlist was intense. The feeling rapidly changed from disappointment to scorn, and even to anger, mingled with incredulity. . . .

The volunteer is conscious of his position. He is proud of it. He is anxious to work. He salutes his officers and speaks to them with self-confidence. The N.R.M.A. soldier slouches at his work. He tends to become sullen. He nurses his fancied grudge against "the Army." He hates "the Army."

I have seen this feeling developed to an amazing degree in 13 Infantry Brigade through the month of April, as men enlisted and new drafts of volunteers arrived. On 1 April the 13 Brigade was a unified formation even though Esprit-de-corps and morale were none too high. . . . But three weeks later 13 Brigade was rent into two distinct bodies of men poles apart in feeling and outlook. By 1 May there were some 2600 active personnel of high morale, fine bearing and excellent spirit, and on the other hand there were about 1600 or 1700 N.R.M.A. soldiers discontented and unhappy; a solid mass of men who had resisted successfully every appeal to their manhood and citizenship, despised by their former comrades, and finally rejected even by their officers as hopeless material out of which to make a fighting force.[28]

As arrangements had been made to send all volunteers for overseas in the brigade on embarkation leave by 5 May, the beginning of May in essence marked the end of the recruiting campaign. The remaining N.R.M.A. men were transferred to other units, and final drafts of volunteers added to the numbers. By 1 May, when Pearkes made his final inspection in Vernon, there were approximately 2,500 officers and men on parade. About half were reinforcements from other units, about one-third had volunteered from the N.R.M.A. men in the brigade, and the remainder had been volunteers already serving in the brigade. It was a stirring moment as they marched past accompanied by the bands of the Rocky Mountain Rangers and the St. John Fusiliers, and in a brief but emotional speech Pearkes wished them all goodbye and good luck. On the following day he received a telegram from the Minister of National Defence congratulating him for "a very excellent job. I realize that you made the suggestion that these battalions be given the opportunity to go as units knowing that you were undertaking a piece of hard work for all of you," Ralston wrote. "The way you have stuck to it and seen it through is typical of Pacific Command. I congratulate you and appreciate the leadership which you yourself are furnishing."[29]

The recruiting campaign was not only hard work for Pearkes and all others concerned, it was also a revelation, in many respects, of the attitudes of the N.R.M.A. soldiers. A year earlier Pearkes had felt that, when the need was serious and the N.R.M.A. man knew it, there would be little difficulty in getting him to volunteer. Now, he had seen how difficult it had been to get conversions. In his report Macklin had spelled out the reasons for the limited response, and Pearkes was in agreement with most of them. The fact that there were some ten thousand unapprehended deserters in Canada was, as Macklin noted, "known to every soldier and has a most devastating effect on discipline and morale." The scars left by a decade of economic depression had its effect. Thousands of men, unemployed for years, were able to get jobs when the war brought an upsurge in the economy, and they resented bitterly being drafted into the forces. Many, therefore, deserted, and frequently their employers did not enquire too closely into their military commitments.

The same thing applied in a different way to the various extended leaves for farming, mining, logging, and so forth. "Almost every N.R.M.A. soldier firmly believes that he is entitled to extended leave if he wants it," Macklin noted, and added:

The pressure from outside sources to get men out of the army on leave is unending and relentless, and has a continuously unsettling effect.

The volume of applications is so huge that any attempt to arbitrate between the deserving and undeserving is utterly impossible. . . .

It does not suffice that G.O.C.-in-C. Pacific Command announces severe restrictions on leave as long as other responsible authorities continue to make contrary statements. A recent example, the latest of many, was a statement by various Western meat packing interests that they mean to ask the army (not the Navy or the R.C.A.F.)—to release men to relieve their labour shortage.[30]

Perhaps more than any other factor which accounted for the resistance to volunteering was a lack of patriotism. Macklin pointed out that most N.R.M.A. soldiers were not of British origin and most came from farms. Their education was "deplorably low," their knowledge of British or Canadian history skimpy, "and in fact [they] are typical European peasants, with a passionate attachment for the land." It would be a slow but necessary process to convert these men into patriotic soldiers. It could only be done by educating them to see beyond their immediate surroundings and making them realize that the tyranny of dictatorship must be wiped out if they were to retain the freedom they accepted so casually.

Pearkes was still optimistic about the future, for this was part of his nature. "While admittedly the going was much harder than we expected," he wrote to the Adjutant General, "I do not think we really did too badly, and an encouraging sign is that there is a feeling abroad amongst other units in the Command that more N.R.M.A. soldiers are likely to go active."[31] Three commanding officers had asked him if their units could go overseas within the past week on the same basis as units in the 13th Brigade, which inclined him to believe that lasting good had been obtained. Recruiting figures for the first eleven days in May were good, but the transfer of 2,500 volunteers had left large gaps in all units, particularly among N.C.O.'s. He suggested that "these wounds be allowed to heal" and that a level of volunteers be built up again among the battalions remaining to influence the N.R.M.A. men and to serve as a basis to build on for the future.

Pearkes was also aware that priorities within his command were changing. "It has become necessary to emphasize the importance of the role of reinforcing the Canadian Army overseas," he wrote to his commanding officers towards the end of April, "while at the same time continuing to plan and prepare for other tasks assigned to the Pacific Command."[32] Indeed, all units should be brought to the highest efficiency "because at any time additional forces may be ordered overseas, and the period of training in England reduced to a minimum."[33] It was generally realized that the invasion of France was only a few weeks away. Time for further training would also be brief if the government brought in conscription, a possibility which still seemed rather remote in May 1944.

During the summer, therefore, Pearkes worked hard both to provide the reinforcements for overseas and to maintain a reduced but well-trained operational force for the Pacific or any other theatre. He attempted to have the 13th Brigade replaced by cutting the two extant brigades from four to three battalions and having another battalion sent from Eastern Canada to complete the complement. Maintaining high standards was by no means easy, for increasing pressure was being placed on Pearkes to release men. As he put it:

> The Department of Agriculture was always urging me to release soldiers for seeding and harvesting operations and at the same time the Department of National Defence was urging me to get these soldiers trained and to go active and go overseas. I was between the devil and the deep sea. Time and again the Deputy Minister of Agriculture would ring me up [and say] "We've got to have more men released; we've got to get this crop in." Some men went practically for the whole summer. They went home for seeding, they stayed for haying and they were again granted leave for harvesting—only too anxious to come back in the winter because there was nothing to do on the farms. And these men never did get trained and they formed the hard core of the resistance movement against volunteering and against going overseas. They were not trained because during the winter the training couldn't be as active as in the summer. It was more limited. . . . They were all right during the wintertime—they were happy. . . . And then came the appeals from local politicians, from the clergy, from mayors of towns and from the Department of Agriculture in Ottawa. One day I'd get a telegram asking for men to be released immediately to go on the farms in Saskatchewan and frequently including men by name.
>
> The conflicting policies of these two departments [Agriculture and National Defence] made it extremely difficult for me. Naturally I had Murchie and others urging me to get them trained men. But the government was weak in that respect; it never gave us a clear instruction. . . . I put requirements of the Department of National Defence first, and [yet] Jimmy Gardiner [the Minister of Agriculture] says that I never did understand the importance of producing food.[34]

On 15 May, the same day the 13th Brigade left British Columbia for overseas, Pearkes held a conference with all his commanders and senior officers of the rank of lieutenant-colonel and above. He outlined his plans for an educational programme for N.R.M.A. soldiers. He felt that these men should become more familiar with the fighting in Europe and the Pacific and with the long struggle which yet lay ahead. Too many home defence soldiers seemed to feel that victory was just a matter of time and that somehow it would fall to the Allies without too much more effort. It was not an attitude which promoted a desire or need to convert from home to overseas service, and Pearkes was determined that every unit and sub-unit in his command should organize an information centre. These were to be designed "to stimulate the interest of all ranks in Pacific Command in current war development and world affairs generally." He stressed at a later meeting that he expected each commanding officer would give the matter his personal attention.[35]

Meanwhile National Defence Headquarters had decided to conduct an intensified campaign both to recruit men into the army and to convert more N.R.M.A. soldiers. At the end of May Pearkes again called his commanding officers together and once more outlined the situation. The various roles given to Pacific Command had not changed, he noted, but the Canadian Army was on the brink of major operations in France. "The maintenance of that effort at the highest possible peak of efficiency is our major role at the present time," he told his officers. He realized that withdrawals of General Service men in any sizeable numbers would necessarily postpone any involvement in the Pacific. He pointed out that the Canadian government had made no definite commitments for military operations there. Furthermore, it was now likely that only General Service soldiers would be used in the Pacific and only when the European situation cleared. Thus, although Pearkes wanted to maintain a nucleus of officers and men for a potential Canadian force in the Pacific,[36] he stressed the need to recruit reinforcements. "Success can be obtained only by the concerted action, unselfish efforts and whole hearted co-operation of all concerned," he said and added: "These I know you will give."[37]

The campaign during the summer and autumn of 1944 was the most intensive ever undertaken. Newspaper recruiting advertisements urged young men to volunteer, and editors added their voices. On the radio there were regular half-hour recruiting programmes with a mixture of martial music, patriotic songs, and appeals stressing the need to maintain the pressure on the enemy. On 6 June, when the Allies invaded Normandy, there was tremendous enthusiasm from which recruiting officers benefited, but the pace never slackened. There were window displays in stores, military ceremonies and mobile recruiting vans at town fairs, parades and band concerts in towns and cities, and honour roll ceremonies in villages.

Restaurants printed recruiting messages on their menus and public utilities enclosed them in their bills. Theatres showed recruiting "clips." Recruiting posters and cutouts were placed in as many public buildings as possible, while in the rural areas army projectionists showed army films to service clubs and any other audience they could gather. Militia regiments put on tattoos and displayed equipment in public parks. With the co-operation of civic officials street decorations and sidewalk stencils carried the message. Journalists were urged to visit the training centres and encouraged to write up what they saw. Recruiting stickers were carried on automobile bumpers and windshields, and if a person travelled by bus or tramcar, he or she was bound to see advertisements with a recruiting theme. In the churches many clergymen spoke out in no uncertain terms about the necessity to defeat the dictators. On every occasion likely to gather an audience, one was bound to see an army float, plastered with displays, with a nearby sound-truck adding the vocal to the visual message.

Pearkes himself, of course, was as involved in the campaign as deeply as anyone. Each week he had a detailed report made to him and held a conference with his staff and heads of services to plan ways of improving the campaign. He spoke to as many·groups and clubs as he could. He gave his support to "The Green Patch,"[38] a command publication designed to give information about recruiting and stimulate the conversion of N.R.M.A. men. By 11 July he was able to advise Ottawa that over 2,000 soldiers had converted during June, but as the summer months went by and the casualties in Italy and France mounted steadily, the imbalance between the reinforcements needed and those available permitted no letup.

The drying up of the reinforcement stream was becoming a very critical matter to Col. Ralston, the Minister of National Defence. The enthusiasm engendered by the Normandy landings had resulted in 3,259 N.R.M.A. men throughout Canada converting. This figure had been reduced by about 60 per cent in July, and by October there were only 967 conversions. General service enlistments and appointments also dropped, though not as dramatically. In June 7,062 enlisted but in October only 5,304 men were available. The optimistic forecasts of the mid-summer regarding infantry reinforcements were soon proved to be inaccurate,[39] as were other forecasts regarding the early collapse of Germany. As a result there were increasing complaints from formations in the field regarding the difficulties they were encountering in keeping their infantry battalions up to strength, despite measures taken to remuster into infantry men who had been trained for other corps. Late in August Stuart advised Ralston through the Chief of the General Staff that a serious problem in infantry reinforcements was looming. He indicated, however, that it was primarily an administrative problem. It was not until the latter part of September, therefore, that

Ralston, disturbed at the conflicting reports, both official and unofficial, regarding the true nature of the situation in the front lines, decided to visit Italy and France.

Ralston arrived in Italy on 26 September and did not return until 18 October. His tour of the battlefronts and his discussions with army officers convinced him that the reinforcement situation could be solved only by a reassessment of policy. He cabled the Prime Minister a few days prior to his return intimating the results of his investigation, and Mackenzie King believed Ralston would suggest the conscription of N.R.M.A. soldiers. In this case, King would face the same crisis he had seen rip apart the Liberals in 1917. He recorded the depth of his feeling in his diary that evening:

> I could not bring myself to being the head of a government which would take that course—a course which might, after five years of war in Europe, and preparation for a year and a half of another war in the Pacific—lead to spurts of civil war in our own country. It would be a criminal thing, and would destroy the entire war record, as well as to help dismember the Empire, for I am certain that its after effects would be all in the direction of demand for complete independence, if not annexation with the U.S. Anything to be separated from being in wars because of Britain's connection with them. I want to see the Empire endure. It can only endure by there being complete national unity in Canada. This is going to be a trying experience. . . . Ralston has been a thorn in my flesh right along. However, I have stood firm before and I shall do so again. . . . It is a repetition of the kind of thing that led to the creation of the Union government after Borden's return from England [in 1917]. That will not take place under me.[40]

If King entertained any hope that Ralston might have found some other means of providing reinforcements, it was shattered when, at a meeting of the War Committee on 19 October, Ralston asked that trained N.R.M.A. soldiers should be sent overseas. The fat was in the fire. The issue was placed before the full cabinet five days later, and as King feared, it was divided. Those favouring conscription were in the minority, but it was a very impressive minority. During the last week of October the conscription issue dominated their attention. King's attitude from the beginning was summed up in his diary notes dealing with the meeting on 24 October. "If we were driven to the extreme indicated [i.e., conscription], the Liberal Party would be completely destroyed and not only immediately but for indefinite time to come. That the only party that would gain would be the

C.C.F. who would be handed . . . complete control of govt."[41] King and his supporters made a variety of suggestions coupled with dire warnings to the conscriptionist element. There was the suggestion that, with certain financial inducements, more N.R.M.A. soldiers might be persuaded (bribed would be a better word) to volunteer. King suggested that he might make a personal tour of the N.R.M.A. camps, and at one point even proposed that the gaps in the ranks of French-Canadian battalions overseas might be filled with Frenchmen. King stressed the dangers of a conscriptionist policy; not only would national unity be shattered, but there might even be civil conflict. He suggested reductions in the establishments of the Canadian forces in the field. He cabled Churchill enquiring about the possible length of the war and the need to impose conscription, but his hope for a reply which would undermine Ralston's arguments was not fulfilled. There seemed to be no denying the need for trained infantrymen, and the greatest source of these was among the numerous battalions in Canada filled with trained N.R.M.A. men who had no desire to go overseas.

The intensity of the Prime Minister's desire to avoid having to impose conscription led him to seek out Gen. A. G. L. McNaughton. He had relinquished the command of the Canadian Army in December 1943 and since that time had been living in Ottawa. Apparently King felt that there was a conspiracy in the cabinet to oust him, a conspiracy led by Ralston. Ralston, the source of his problems, must be replaced by a person who felt that means could be found to supply reinforcements without conscription, and McNaughton seemed to be the man. While King was secretly conferring with the former army commander, Ralston sought some way to meet the Prime Minister's plea to avoid conscription. He was well aware of the long, hard campaign carried out during the spring and summer to get N.R.M.A. soldiers to volunteer, but on the extremely slim hope that a final, massive yet short campaign might possibly work, he decided to telephone Pearkes late on the morning of 1 November. Ralston asked Pearkes to give absolutely straightforward opinions on his questions and then enquired about the possibility of getting a substantial number of conversions quickly. Pearkes told him that the officers in the command "have gotten much of the cream away already." He added that most of the units had been stripped of their General Service N.C.O.'s and that the men had a very negative attitude and wanted only to return to civilian life.[42]

A short time later, during a discussion Ralston apparently told Angus L. Macdonald[43] the depressing news he had received from Pearkes. In any event, Macdonald decided to phone Pearkes himself. Pacific Command contained the greatest number of N.R.M.A. personnel, and its commander's advice was of prime importance in the political crisis. It was two o'clock in the afternoon in Ottawa, a little more than an hour before the cabinet was to meet. An outline of the telephone conversation between Pearkes and Macdonald was kept and is given below as recorded.

Notes of telephone conversation between Hon. A. L. Macdonald and Maj.-Gen. Pearkes, 2 p.m., November 1, 1944.
Re appeal to NRMA men to become G. S.

Macdonald— Would an appeal of ten days be long enough?

Pearkes— doubts whether it would. The camps are scattered. One would have to go to Vernon, Prince George, Terrace and Nanaimo.

Macdonald— Have there been any appeals by civilians?

Pearkes— No. The men question if the army is giving them the true picture. There is a feeling that the army officers may be exaggerating. There will be no mass conversion among the men. They will take time to talk it over.

Within a week after the visit most of the men would have made up their minds.

Assuming you started your appeal on the 6th November and finished, say on the 15th, you should know the results by November 30th.

Thinks it would be dangerous to have the Prime Minister make any appeal. If the Prime Minister came, they could not allow the appeal to fail. Col. Ralston might get better results. You might get 2,000 – 3,000 in three weeks. At present getting 10-20 recruits a day.

It might be well to say that if this appeal fails, we will resort to conscription, but Pearkes doubts it. If this were said, the men would say "We will hang back and wait until the government tells us."

It would be well for the Prime Minister to make a radio address or a written appeal supporting the appeal made by Col. Ralston at the camps.

Re question as to attitude of the men towards active service.

Pearkes— In the first place most of them will not be moved by any desire to go active. They will say the war is nearly over; "We have been told that there are enough reinforcements for this year. Some people don't want us anyhow. We want to go back to civil life as quickly as possible and think the chances of getting back are much better if we do not go overseas."

Most of them say, "If the government tells us to go, we will go."

> If we said we intended to invoke conscription there
> would be no trouble in the camps. There would be a
> few deserters but probably less than there were before
> the departure of the Kiska operation. In fact the men
> would heave a sigh of relief and say, "Well, that has
> been settled for us."[44]

At the time this conversation was going on, the Prime Minister was putting the final touches to his plan to get rid of Ralston should he not agree to withdraw his demand for conscription. Ralston, having questioned Pearkes and presumably others about the merits of a last appeal, was still unable to see any way of meeting the overseas requirements. Shortly after three o'clock the cabinet met, and in one of the cleverest manoeuvres in his political career, the Prime Minister managed to dismiss Ralston and replace him with McNaughton without splitting his cabinet.

By placing so much trust and confidence in McNaughton, who had been out of service life for almost a year and who was not in touch with military affairs in Canada, King really was placing his trust in the unknown. The ruthless tactics he used when ridding himself of Ralston, however, were indicative of the action he would employ towards anyone who, in his mind, might attempt to frustrate the new minister's grand design to fill the reinforcement stream without conscription.

The announcement of Ralston's resignation on 1 November and of McNaughton's appointment on the following day made banner headlines across the country. Moreover, it brought the conscription issue into the political sphere. To Pearkes it came as a great surprise. "I don't think it was an appointment that I regarded with enthusiasm," he recalled. "I didn't think that he would bring in conscription and I didn't see how he could get the men by voluntary enlistment."[45] McNaughton, however, had evidently been impressed by the dark picture painted by Mackenzie King. Among the evils the Prime Minister saw in conscription was the possibility of an insurrection among the N.R.M.A. men. Much was made of McNaughton's popularity, and indeed from 1939 through 1943 he had had an extremely good press. Probably, as McNaughton's biographer states, he really did think that the voluntary method would work if he told the nation how great the need was. At the same time, when he accepted his new position, he had not studied the situation as Ralston had. McNaughton, as one shrewd observer pointed out at the time," has said that he does not agree with the military authorities."[46]

The new Minister of National Defence was only a day in his office when, after studying the charts and figures available, he concluded that the fifteen or sixteen thousand trained reinforcements needed in Europe by the end of December would have to be obtained from among the N.R.M.A. personnel. He formed a committee on recruiting to consider how to make voluntary methods work, and apparently they considered the strongest weapon available to them was McNaughton's reputation. If *he* told them the need was great, then surely the N.R.M.A. men would respond and the crisis would be over. It was decided, therefore, that the new minister would speak on 5 November at Arnprior at a victory loan rally and on the following day to an Ottawa branch of the Canadian Legion. The speech at Arnprior was not well received, and his talk to the seven hundred veterans in Ottawa was a near disaster. The veterans, as might be expected, could not see why trained N.R.M.A. soldiers should be sitting idle in Canada when overseas soldiers who had been wounded several times were being ordered back into the line. Two days later the Prime Minister gave a radio speech on the need to maintain unity and called for everyone to co-operate to make the voluntary system work. King was rarely, if ever, inspirational; he left the public somewhat puzzled about various vague points, yet at the same time not entirely dissatisfied with their interpretation of his speech. Its effect in the camps of the N.R.M.A. men, however, was not noticeable.

McNaughton's next move was to call together in Ottawa all his senior army officers. His plan was to order them to approach the home defence soldiers once again. He knew almost every one of the senior officers personally, and, as his biographer relates, he counted on inspiring them with some of his own zeal and enthusiasm.

On 9 November, when Pearkes received the call to attend a conference of all G.O.C.-in-C.s and District Officers Commanding in Ottawa, he left almost immediately by train and was in Ottawa a day before the meeting started on the fourteenth. It was the first time he could remember when all the D.O.C.'s were gathered together, and he had the opportunity to speak to many old friends. A few minutes before 9:00 General McNaughton came into the room followed by his senior staff officers.[47] After a brief welcome, the chairman introduced McNaughton. He was blunt and to the point. He emphasized especially the short term requirement for infantry reinforcements while men, both in Canada and the United Kingdom, were being converted and retrained for infantry. He intended to reduce the size and numbers of units in Canada and to cut to the bone the number of soldiers working temporarily in civilian occupations. Even those who remained in civilian jobs would henceforth be paid only the usual army rate. The main thrust of his speech, however, was his announcement that it would be government policy to continue to reinforce the army overseas with volunteers and that obviously it was the duty of the senior officers to use "every means . . . to enlist the support of the public and to emphasize to N.R.M.A. personnel the opportunity and public responsibility which is theirs in this time of national emergency."[48]

Having completed his speech, McNaughton put his papers in his despatch case and began to leave the room. For a moment there was a complete silence. Other officers as well as Pearkes must have wondered whether or not McNaughton had any idea of what had been done already. It appeared, as one District Officer Commanding put it later, that "McNaughton thought he could tell us what to do and we'd do it and it would be all right."[49] He had just about reached the door when several officers rose. Among them was Pearkes who called out "Don't you wish to hear the reports from the District Officers Commanding?"[50] McNaughton hesitated but turned back and heard some of their comments. They told him briefly of the tremendous efforts to get the home defence men to volunteer, the limited success they had had, and the poor prospects for the future. They gave him some indication of the difficulties encountered in trying to overcome the influences on the N.R.M.A. men from their families and other sources. They pointed out, too, that time and time again, in answer to pleas to go active, the N.R.M.A. men would respond that if the government really wanted them, it should compel them to go, and if this was the law they would go willingly.[51] McNaughton listened, repeated his declaration that the former generous leave to N.R.M.A. men to work in the farms and fields would be restricted and then left. Certainly his senior officers left him in no doubt whatever about the chances of getting a quick, substantial response which would somehow make the "new" governmental policy a success.

The remainder of the morning was taken up by the Chief of the General Staff and in the afternoon the Adjutant General held forth. There were a number of points to be made about home war establishments, the disbandment of certain artillery units, speeding up the training of volunteers in Canada, and other matters. But the main worry of most of the officers there was how to carry out successfully a policy which for the past six months, with the exception of June, had shown consistently decreasing returns. Pearkes, perhaps, was especially concerned. McNaughton had made pointed reference to the fact that in his Pacific Command were the greatest number of trained N.R.M.A. infantrymen. Pearkes and all his officers had been working on them to volunteer since April; possibly, given time, more could be coaxed to volunteer. But the shortage of reinforcements overseas would be extreme by December. He had warned Ralston earlier that, under the best conditions, it would take a month to get a few thousand even if they were lucky. He also felt that the policy would not produce the wave of volunteers which McNaughton felt the magic of his name would bring. However, as Murchie pointed out to the rather disgruntled gathering later, "it was not for them to discuss the Government policy . . . but rather to apply themselves to implement the policy."

Although Pearkes held considerable reservations, he did not for a moment feel that he should not do his utmost to carry out the duty imposed on him. Immediately after the conference was over, Pearkes wired his headquarters to call together all his senior officers to meet in Vancouver on 20 November. His staff officers were to attend the meeting also, and he let it be known that he would announce the minister's "new" policy at the meeting and would, at the same time, welcome any suggestions from the battalion commanders regarding new approaches to get home defence soldiers to go active.[52]

Pearkes was back in Vancouver by Saturday. On the previous day the local newspapers carried a statement made by General McNaughton which implied that, as a result of the conference on the fourteenth, the voluntary policy would provide the reinforcements the government was seeking. A number of the district officers commanding were so incensed that they wired the Chief of the General Staff protesting the minister's statement and requesting a retraction. Newspaper reporters in Calgary, Vancouver and elsewhere sought confirmation of McNaughton's optimism[53] from the district commanders, but they could say nothing publicly. It appeared, therefore, that McNaughton was expressing the consensus of opinion. Pearkes was among those who protested. A rather weak excuse was sent him by telegram on the nineteenth. It was followed by a telephone call from McNaughton on the same day during which he said he would clarify the situation by another press release on Monday. This reassured Pearkes and, presumably, some but not all of the others.[54]

Early on Monday morning Pearkes went to the Seaforth Barracks in Vancouver to meet his senior officers. They had been gathering in the city during the weekend. The concentration of so much "brass" in the major hotels had not gone unnoticed by the local press. When Pearkes arrived, he found to his surprise a number of reporters talking to officers in the hall outside the room where he was to present McNaughton's policy. Pearkes had not called a press conference, nor did he particularly want them there at that time. Maj. Gus Sivertz, the command's public relations officer and a former newspaperman, had acquiesced to the reporters' request that they attend, and, indeed, they requested Pearkes through Sivertz to be allowed to attend the conference. Pearkes refused. Since they were there, since the conference had not yet started, and since the reporters had already been talking with the officers, Pearkes "said that they might ask the various Camp Commanders what the situation was in their areas insofar as recruiting had been proceeding." "I did not allow officers of Pacific Command to criticize the government's policy at any meeting with the press," Pearkes added. "In fact it was in order to avoid the possibility of policy being criticized that I allowed the press to talk with the officers regarding the situation in their own camps."[55] In view of later events, it would have been wiser if Maj. Sivertz had arranged a formal press conference. Pearkes knew he would need the newspapers' help to promote McNaughton's policy, and if the reporters wanted to get an idea of what the situation was like in the camps before he held the conference, he could not see how it would violate any security or confidence since, with a little bit of digging, they could have found out themselves. He had neither anticipated nor planned the situation, but he could not have ordered the press to destroy their notes or their memories. It would have created a great deal of suspicion and adverse comment.

At the conference itself Pearkes outlined the critical need for trained infantry reinforcements, the need to maintain the formations in the field, the decision to retain the voluntary system, and the additional effort necessary to get volunteers from among N.R.M.A. soldiers. He made a hardhitting appeal to them all to try once more and assured them of his full support. He handed out extracts of the speech made by the Prime Minister on 8 November as well as that made by McNaughton a week earlier. The words of these two men were to be made known to all the home defence soldiers, and every battalion and camp commander was to ensure that they were publicized.

That evening, before he went to bed, the Prime Minister heard on the radio some of the statements made by the senior officers in Vancouver. He felt that there was a conspiracy in the West. The next day, in an article which was picked up by other newspapers across Canada, Alan Morley stated that "at a press conference" a number of senior officers in Pacific Command, whom he named, intimated that N.R.M.A. soldiers would probably go active only if they were ordered to do so. In their opinion (and these were personal opinions the reporter quoted), the plan to reinforce adequately the overseas divisions could not be met through the voluntary method. This report, reproduced in the Ottawa papers on 21 November, came as a thunderclap to King and McNaughton. McNaughton, according to his biographer, was not only surprised but, believing what he read, began to feel that the army in Canada "was full of rotten stuff" and questioned the loyalty of some of his senior officers on the Pacific Coast.[56] He had his adjutant general wire Pearkes asking for an explanation. Pearkes replied that there was no formal press conference, that he had "granted permission to officers concerned to state progress . . . in response to P.M. and Minister's appeals," and that he read no statements in the papers "which could possibly be considered improper." His telegram was brief, and he did not go into details as he doubtless would have, had he appreciated the growing suspicions aroused in the minds of King and McNaughton.

McNaughton had shown the Prime Minister copies of the telegrams which had been sent from some of the District Officers Commanding protesting the optimistic press release McNaughton had given earlier. The minister "felt there was a real conspiracy right in the department itself not to have this voluntary system work." He believed that instead of helping, "everything possible was being done from different sources to enforce conscription."[57] He added that he thought Pearkes was at the bottom of the "conspiracy" in the West, presumably owing to his friendship with Stuart whose resignation[58] McNaughton requested, as well as to "certain situations" which developed in the United Kingdom which forced McNaughton "to allow Pearkes to come back to Canada." King, on his part, reminded McNaughton that a day or so ago he mentioned to him that "our men were suspicious of Pearkes" and that "they felt he had never tried to make the voluntary system go." This feeling of suspicion, together with McNaughton's growing belief that there was a conspiracy within the Defence Department, gave far greater weight to the news from Vancouver. The Prime Minister thought that the army was defying the civil power and wrote in his diary that "these men in uniform have no right to speak in ways which will turn the people against the civil power."

It is against this background of strong but completely unfounded suspicions of events in Vancouver that the next steps in the conscription crisis can be understood. Pearkes's brief explanatory telegram to Murchie, which would have been shown to McNaughton, was unacceptable. Lt.-Gen. Murchie, the Acting Chief of the General Staff, was ordered to pursue the matter further, which he did on the following day, 22 November, with the Adjutant General and the Judge Advocate General. Walford submitted a memorandum to McNaughton stating that Pearkes's reply by telegram did not establish any basis for judgment as to the true nature of the incident. Aware that a military court of enquiry could not compel the attendance of civilian witnesses, they proposed that Lt.-Gen. E. W. Sansom be sent to Vancouver "to prepare a report on all facts relevant to the determination of a firm course of action." McNaughton, who was under tremendous pressure that day, agreed with the suggestion. Maj.-Gen. Walford wrote a rather lengthy letter to Sansom on the same day outlining the problem and adding that Sansom was being given the task as it was considered "that the desired information can best be obtained by an investigation . . . rather than through the medium of a formal enquiry."

On this same day in Vancouver Pearkes was engaged in writing a detailed report. Before it was completed, Pearkes received a wire informing him that Sansom was flying to Vancouver to investigate and report on the "press conference" and to interview the officers who had made statements. To Pearkes it was like a stinging slap in the face. "The circumstances connected with this investigation," he wrote later, "have been the most humiliating experience of my military career." He was so incensed that he offered to retire to pension immediately should the minister find it embarrassing to relieve him as G.O.C.-in-C. Pacific Command and find him another appointment.

The decision to send Sansom was but one of several weighty problems McNaughton had on his mind. On 22 November, he also received the resignation of Brig. R. A. MacFarlane, commanding Military District No. X (Manitoba), who had earlier protested McNaughton's press release. McNaughton feared that this might be only the first of a number of resignations, and if this happened "the whole military machine would . . . begin to disintegrate and there would be no controlling the situation."[59] What was more unnerving was the advice he received on the same morning from his chief military advisers in Ottawa. Two weeks had passed since McNaughton and King had made their national appeal, and the N.R.M.A. soldiers were not volunteering. Murchie, backed by his senior officers, told the minister this unpleasant news, and, at his request, it was written and signed. McNaughton immediately informed the Prime Minister. With the last possible alternative to conscription dashed from his hand and facing the bleak prospects of a vote of confidence in the House of Commons, King now felt it expedient to use coercion to maintain reinforcements to the army overseas. On the evening of 22 November the Prime Minister met with his cabinet, informed his colleagues about the new situation, and said that McNaughton was thinking in terms of conscripting a limited number of men. He outlined the proposal he would announce publicly in tne House of Commons on the following day supporting McNaughton's stand. By this act he saved the Liberal party from splitting asunder, and presumably by ordering the conscription of only a limited number of men he prevented, according to his light, a military revolt in Canada. Conscription, now, was necessary—but even in this serious situation, only to a limited extent.[60]

In Vancouver, meanwhile, Pearkes had acted immediately on receipt of the message from the Adjutant General on the twenty-second. He had held his conference on Monday. It was now Wednesday. The 130 officers who had attended his conference had all returned to their units. Some, such as Brig. A. R. Roy, who commanded the 15th Brigade at Terrace, as well as his senior officers, were still en route. Pearkes warned the Adjutant General early on Thursday that it would be impossible to assemble all the officers Sansom wanted to see on Friday morning, but he assured him that he would call them back immediately. Shortly after noon, three hours after he had wired the Adjutant General about the steps he had taken to comply with instructions from Ottawa, Pearkes received a telephone call from Murchie. It was late afternoon in Ottawa and Pearkes was told that the government had passed an order-in-council making sixteen thousand N.R.M.A. personnel available for overseas. Pearkes's reaction to this news may be imagined. He was concerned, however, with the repercussion which might occur in the various camps in his command when news of partial conscription reached them. He felt the senior officers should remain with their troops at this time, and thus he wired the Adjutant General asking that Sansom's investigation be postponed until the twenty-seventh. Sansom, however, was already en route to Vancouver by air, and Pearkes did not receive a reply from the Adjutant General in time to delay the departure of many officers from their stations. As a result the investigation started on time on the twenty-fourth. At the same time, by both radio and news-papers, word of partial conscription had spread in Pacific Command. The scene was set for trouble, and trouble soon came.

News of the government's decision to conscript sixteen thousand N.R.M.A. soldiers for overseas service first reached the military camps in British Columbia in the late afternoon of 23 November. The soldiers in the camps of the three infantry brigades at Nanaimo, Vernon, and Terrace all knew about it by dinner time. In every battalion almost every soldier was concerned, for there were few which, by this time, had more than a dozen General Service soldiers in the ranks. Few battalions had their full comple-ments of officers, and with normal absences for furloughs, sickness, attend-ance at military schools, and so forth, there were a number of instances where lieutenants, rather than majors, had acting command of companies. There is no need to describe the result of the announcement of conscrip-tion in all the major camps, but its impact on the 15th Brigade in Terrace is worth noting.[61]

Brig. A. R. Roy was due to arrive in Terrace to take command of the 15th Brigade shortly after 6:00 on the evening of the twenty-third. In his absence the brigade was commanded by Maj. R. W. MacMillan, who was also second-in-command of the Prince Albert Volunteers. None of the commanding officers of the three battalions was available as all had been called to Vancouver and, like Roy, were en route home. The brigade major, Maj. R. L. Williams, had received instructions from Vancouver to arrange for Brig. Roy and the senior officers in the brigade to return im-mediately to attend the investigation at command headquarters. In most instances, therefore, it was a matter of remaining on the train with only the briefest stop to receive their transportation warrants. There was no trouble in the units, but Brig. Roy told Williams to advise the acting com-manding officers to be on the alert for fire sabotage and to check the ammunition dumps and stores just in case. It was not until after noon on the following day—the same day as Sansom was conducting his investiga-tion in Vancouver—that the situation began to deteriorate. The second-in-command of Les Fusiliers du St. Laurent, Maj. H. J. Thuot, was en route to a conference called by the brigade major when he was told that two companies refused to go on parade. This was the first intimation of trouble to the other acting battalion commanders. That night Maj. Thuot was told by his quartermaster that the ammunition hut had been broken into and that a large quantity of ammunition had been taken as well as four boxes of grenades. This information was given to the other units in the brigade—the Prince Albert Volunteers and the Prince Edward Island Highlanders—and an officers' guard was placed immediately on their ammunition stores.

On Saturday, the twenty-fifth, the men in Les Fusiliers du St. Laurent refused to go on parade or to obey their officers. The situation was similar in the other two regiments, but it appeared, both then and later, that a considerable amount of pressure and coercion was being used by the leaders of the mutiny in the Fusiliers on the other units. Shortly after noon over three hundred Fusiliers, all armed, paraded to the camps of the neighbouring battalions, gathered a number of sympathizers, and continued on into Terrace. They carried banners proclaiming their resistance to conscription. On the same day, Lt.-Col. W. B. Hendrie had come to Terrace. He commanded the Mountain Warfare School located nearby and was the senior officer in the area. He immediately assumed command of the brigade and warned all officers not to try to stop the demonstrators by force except when the men might attempt to molest citizens or damage property. He asked the chief magistrate to close the liquor shop and beer parlours, ordered the paymasters to put their money in the bank, and had two railway cars containing ammunition and beer moved out of the railroad yards. He ordered his officers to keep him informed and to continue their attempts to persuade the men to return to duty. Hendrie then telephoned command headquarters and asked Pearkes to send a large flight of aircraft over the camp to intimidate the mutineers.

In Vancouver Pearkes was receiving news of disturbances and demonstrations in Vernon, Terrace, Prince George, Courtenay, Chilliwack, Nanaimo, and Port Alberni. In most cases the reaction to the news of partial conscription was limited to the troops marching in an organized manner to the nearby town. Some banners were carried, but generally speaking those parading were unarmed and orderly and made their demonstrations with considerable feeling but no violence. Pearkes immediately sent the senior officers in Vancouver for Sansom's investigations back to their stations. Most could reach their camps by automobile within twenty-four hours and the situation was soon under control.

In Terrace, the most distant of the major camps, the danger was greater. November weather prevented flying the senior officers back, but they were ordered to return with all the speed which an erratic railroad timetable allowed. Meanwhile Pearkes kept Ottawa informed. On Sunday, 26 November, the men in camp refused to attend parade and a group of fifty to seventy privates had entered the sergeants' mess ordering the senior N.C.O.'s to remove their stripes and join them. More machine guns were taken from the quartermaster stores, but in most cases these weapons had had their breech blocks removed and were harmless. There were rumours that a 6-pounder anti-tank gun was mounted in a commanding position, and it was also evident that the subversive elements in the units were in close contact. The situation was potentially dangerous, but still not ugly, and the combination of tact and firmness displayed especially by Col. Hendrie and the other officers was commendable. Pearkes, meanwhile, took such action as he could. He was informed that the men in Les Fusiliers du St. Laurent had assured Maj. Thuot "that they intend no violence" but stated that the unit would not move until it was either disbanded or conscription cancelled. Pearkes felt that it was necessary to move the units not only as part of the overall plan to concentrate N.R.M.A. infantry units in Eastern Canada, but he also hoped that the knowledge of the movement of French-Canadian units back to Quebec would have a salutary effect. He was also interested in segregating the small, but obviously dominating, number of subversives in each battalion from the main body of men. He asked for two hundred additional military policemen to be sent from other commands and also requested that steps be taken to censor the news media. Later, too, having considered the request for a demonstration by R.C.A.F. planes over Terrace, he agreed but warned the officers there to inform the men that the planes were coming and were not armed. In the end the aircraft were not sent owing to poor flying weather as well as to an order from Ottawa that no further attempt should be made.

Within a few days, despite one or two tense moments, when the mutiny seemed to be at a specially dangerous stage, the troubles in Terrace were over and the situation returned to normal.[62] The arrival of Brig. Roy and his senior officers late on Monday evening, the onset of colder weather, the knowledge that their end of the month pay would be withheld until they reassumed normal duties, the feeling of isolation as word filtered through that everything was quiet elsewhere, the obvious refusal of the government or military authorities to follow their wishes, with the consequent loss of confidence in the leaders of the mutiny—these and other factors all contributed to a progressive improvement in the situation so that by 1 December everything was in order and troop movements to Eastern Canada were in progress.

When he made his full report to National Defence Headquarters on 5 December, Pearkes made a number of points which throw additional light on the week-long events following the conscription announcement. He wrote:

As investigations continue it becomes increasingly evident that action was instigated in each instance by a comparatively small group of men who did not want to go overseas in any way, and that the great majority of the men took part in a spirit of bravado and horse play. Only at Terrace did intimidation become evident.

The situation at Terrace was of a much more serious nature than at other camps. At this station . . . the men, not having the same easy access to current news . . . were under the impression that similar affairs were occurring elsewhere in the country, and were encouraged by this erroneous belief, to continue action to a state of mutiny.

Indiscreet handling of new releases by the Press had a decided contributory effect. The first news story of the Vernon demonstration stated that 1000 men took part, whereas less than 200 were actually involved. Such exaggeration was obvious encouragement to malcontents in other camps. . . .

Recent heavy withdrawals of GS NCOs had a marked effect on maintenance of discipline, as it was on these NCOs that Commanding Officers had relied. In their absence NRMA NCOs, while efficient administratively, were either unable to control the dissidents or were more or less sympathetic to the anti-conscription movement.[63]

Investigations and reports to date show that the first reaction to the announcement of conscription for overseas, was distinctly favourable —generally speaking an expression of satisfaction that the question was at last decided. Later news that only 16,000 NRMA men were to be sent reacted unfavourably, and caused discontent in that it appeared some would be allowed to stay at home, and the cry of "discrimination" quickly gained volume. . . .

Senior officers being absent, the men did not have sufficient confidence in the Juniors left in charge to discuss with them their doubts and worries, and malcontents found it easy to persuade the doubters that demonstration was the only weapon available to them. . . .

While disturbances occurred in several places, involving hundreds of men in camps where thousands were stationed there was no serious bodily harm caused nor was any material damage caused. This is due to the high standard of morale which had previously existed in all units; to the discretion used by Regimental Officers, and to the innate common sense of the majority of the men, which enabled discipline eventually to be restored.[64]

In the years since these events numerous writers have attempted to read into them some sort of military conspiracy or underhanded manoeuvring designed to frustrate the civil government. Nothing can be further from the truth. In a sense, Pearkes had the same opinion of the N.R.M.A. soldiers as McNaughton, only at a different time. It was really not until the spring of 1944 that Pearkes began to realize the degree of resistance towards volunteering for overseas service that existed. The summer-long propaganda campaign further convinced him that if reinforcements for overseas were to be maintained at a rate the Chief of the General Staff felt necessary, then the N.R.M.A. men must be conscripted. He had reached that conclusion several weeks before McNaughton became minister, and it would be fair to estimate that almost every other senior officer in Canada felt the same. He did not, as is sometimes intimated, attempt to help sabotage McNaughton's plan by calling together his officers rather late at a moment when time was of the essence. Train schedules, the distances involved, and the unpredictable flying weather in British Columbia in November were such that he could not have collected together 130 senior officers faster than he did. Pearkes and others, at the time and later, were accused of giving the authorities in Ottawa a false impression when they suggested there would be no trouble once conscription was invoked. Officers all across Canada had heard for months if not years the same refrain from the N.R.M.A. soldiers—"if the government really wants us, they must tell us by ordering us overseas." For many this was merely a convenient shield used as the ultimate argument against serving overseas, but certainly it had been used long enough and widely enough for it to gain credence. At that, such trouble as did arise in British Columbia came in large measure as a result of political decisions in Ottawa. It was McNaughton's decision to investigate the so-called "press conference" in Vancouver which resulted in senior officers being absent from their units at a critical time. It was Mackenzie King's decision to switch suddenly from a voluntary to a conscription policy, so sudden a decision indeed that in numerous instances the N.R.M.A. soldiers in barracks heard about it over the radio even before their own officers. In passing it is interesting to note that only a few days earlier the Prime Minister had visions of American troops crossing the border to restore order in Canadian camps if conscription was imposed, and McNaughton was extremely concerned that there were insufficient G.S. soldiers available to handle any mutiny among the ranks. These dark and foreboding thoughts were forgotten when political expediency demanded the imposition of conscription. One can only assume that these were phantoms of the imagination of both men, or surely they would have ensured that everything possible would be done to prepare the draftees for the reception of the news.

On the same day Pearkes completed his report on the disturbance in British Columbia, the Adjutant General, Maj.-Gen. A. E. Walford, had completed a memorandum for the Minister of National Defence based on the report he received from Lt.-Gen. Sansom. The report presumably lifted any remaining suspicion from the mind of McNaughton. It read in part:

There is no evidence from Lieut. Gen. Sansom's report of any lack of loyalty on the part of the G.O.C.-in-C. or any officer concerned, to the policy laid down by the Minister. On the contrary recruiting results subsequent to the D.Os.C. Conference at Ottawa . . . testify to most energetic action. During the six weeks ended 11 Nov., Pacific Command secured an average of 36 conversions per week. This figure rose to 84 during the week ending 18 Nov. and 170 in that ended 25 Nov. I feel that the officers should be fully exonerated from any charge or suspicion of disloyalty to the policy of the Department or of lack of cooperation.[65]

The Adjutant General further stated that, according to Sansom, the public relations officer should have been more careful as to the conditions under which the officers came into contact with the press, but the error having been made, "it was to meet this situation that the G.O.C.-in-C. authorized the press interviews on which the newspaper reports were based." There were "grounds for criticism of both the G.O.C.-in-C. and the P.R.O., Pacific Command for failing to appreciate the very dynamic state of public opinion on this subject, and the consequent danger of casual press interviews."[66] Aside from this light rap on the knuckles, however, the report had little to say other than to stress the loyalty of all concerned.

On the same day Sansom was investigating the "press conference" in Vancouver, another incident occurred which caused Pearkes considerable annoyance. On 24 November there appeared in the Vancouver *News Herald* a second article written by Alan Morley, who was reporting from Ottawa. In it he described the recent dramatic political impact of the conscription crisis. At one point he wrote: "What part the open revolt of B.C. army officers against the plan last Monday played in the final decision will probably not be known until he [McNaughton] writes his memoirs in some far-off, post-war years."[67] Pearkes was incensed at the suggestion that he or any of his officers were disloyal. He wired Murchie asking permission to release an emphatic denial to the press in Vancouver or, as an alternative, asking if Murchie would prefer to do it from Ottawa. When no reply was received, Pearkes wired again on the following day. He pointed out that the Morley article had received widespread publicity throughout Canada. The matter, he added, "was of great moment to many officers under my command who feel that their reputation as officers and their loyalty as Canadians has been questioned." He ended by saying that the officers concerned hoped the department would initiate legal proceedings on their behalf. Murchie's reply was to ask for a copy of the article which was sent the same day.

For a week there was no further word. Pearkes was busy with the events of his own command, but when he returned to Vancouver he again enquired of Murchie whether he or the Chief of the General Staff should refute the charges of there being an "open revolt." By this time, 2 December, both Murchie and McNaughton had seen Sansom's report. The report, however, was also being examined by the Privy Council and the Judge Advocate General, so Pearkes's enquiries were put off for the time being with a note that the minister hoped to be able to make a statement on the fifth. By the ninth, Pearkes was furious. Once more he wired Murchie, pointing out that a number of his officers were scheduled to go overseas within two days' time. "It is intolerable," he wrote, "that the character of these officers should not be cleared before leaving." In a burst of anger he added that "at this distance this procrastination appears [to be a] contemptible evasion of responsibility."

This was probably the strongest language Pearkes used in any letter or telegram he ever sent. If he wanted to arouse the Chief of the General Staff to action, he certainly succeeded—but the wrong way. Murchie evidently showed it to McNaughton, and the Judge Advocate General was asked to examine the message with the view, if he saw fit, of pressing charges against Pearkes for an action prejudicial to "good order and military discipline under Section 40 of the Army Act." As the Adjutant General surmised, the telegram was designed to get an answer to Pearkes's previous enquiries rather than stir up trouble. When by the twelfth Pearkes had still not received word, he waited no longer and gave a statement to the press claiming that his officers had never been in revolt but on the contrary had loyally supported government policies. The following day he received word that he and the officers whom Sansom had investigated were exonerated of any infringement of regulations regarding the statements made on 20 November.

The series of events which had resulted in publicity calling into question Pearkes's loyalty and the honour of the officers under his command made a profound impression on him. He was unable to strike back, and the refutation of such charges by the authorities in Ottawa over two weeks later was small comfort. He had thirty years of service in the army, and in those three decades he had devoted himself to his profession without stint. A year previously, before the conscription crisis came to a head, he had been made a Companion of the Order of the Bath. Part of the citation for this award read: "In every appointment which he has held he has given outstanding service. His unflagging devotion to duty and his great ability in the training and handling of troops have contributed greatly to the war effort of the Canadian Army at home and abroad."[68] To receive such an award from the government on one hand and to be investigated on suspicion of disloyalty on the other was more than he might be expected to accept with equanimity.

Of greater importance, however, was the effect on him of the method used by the authorities in Ottawa to fill the reinforcement stream. Pearkes was amazed when the government brought forth the "appalling policy of sending over 16,000 N.R.M.A. men . . . without bringing in overseas conscription for others." That, to him, was "the stupidest thing . . . they had done." He realized full well that it would not be possible or desirable to send all the N.R.M.A. men overseas at once, but to conscript only some was to raise an immediate outcry. The reason for it, of course, was political expediency, but the brunt had to be borne by the military officers.

To make things worse, the telegram confirming the order-in-council stated that there was to be no letdown in the efforts to obtain conversions of N.R.M.A. soldiers to General Service status. The reason behind this request was to ensure the most favourable reception of the conscripts once they had arrived with the battalions at the front and to simplify administration.[69] Pearkes's plan to carry out this order differed from the earlier methods which had met with only limited success. He issued orders that the men should be interviewed individually or talked to in small groups rather than addressed in large gatherings. All were to be told of the need of their services as well as the practical benefits to their own future of becoming a volunteer and enjoying the full opportunities for successful re-establishment in civilian life. With the experience he had over the past nine months, he felt that at this stage those who were conscripted for overseas service would see the wisdom of converting without additional pressure.

At the same time he had reached a decision regarding his own future. He had come to Pacific Command at a time when there appeared to be considerable danger of a Japanese attack. Later he had worked to train a force which the government might wish to use against the Japanese. Now it was clear that the government would not consider the employment of such a force until the end of hostilities in Europe, and, further, the brigade groups which had been trained were being sent to Eastern Canada prior to the men being sent overseas. As a result, in his mind, Pearkes was now little more than a senior recruiting officer, and nothing in his background, training, or character made this task appealing. On 5 January, therefore, he wrote requesting to be relieved of his appointment as G.O.C.-in-C. He would have liked another appointment—anything which would get him out of the recruiting business—but realizing the difficulty there might be in finding another which called for a man of his seniority, he added that he was willing to retire to pension. Certainly the reduction in the strength in the command during December made it unnecessary to have a senior major-general in command.

Two weeks later the Adjutant General replied that there was "no present intention of reducing the status of Pacific Command" and indicated it would not be until the end of the war that the authorities might dispense with the need of a senior experienced commander as G.O.C. At about the same time he received instructions urging "energetic and continuous efforts" to persuade N.R.M.A. soldiers to convert.

These instructions convinced Pearkes more than ever that he should be relieved of his command. The best and most conscientious home defence soldiers had gone active, and generally the most undesirable were left. The continual pleading by officers after conscription had been ordered was now proving to be an error. As Pearkes put it:

> the effect of this policy has been disastrous in that discipline has been ruined and the authority of officers undermined by the refusal of large numbers of men to accede to their officers' requests. In consequence men have failed to distinguish between a request and an order, and gradually the impression permeated among certain sections of the men that only those orders which appeared necessary or attractive to them need be obeyed. The mutinous behaviour of the troops at Terrace last November . . . and the huge number of N.R.M.A. soldiers now away without leave or declared deserters, are the visual and undisputable results of the policy which I am now ordered to repeat.

He went on to say that the troops available to him for operational duties were at a minimum. Units were considerably understrength and contained a very large number of recently transferred soldiers. "The esprit de corps at present is negligible," he continued, "and their standard of discipline is low." He concluded:

> If these men are now to be appealed to again and again to go active after they have turned a deaf ear to all previous entreaties, any hope of restoring discipline or building efficiency will be destroyed and the men will only accept those orders that appeal to them, thus reducing the units to a group of disgruntled individuals.
>
> To ask N.R.M.A. soldiers of low medical category to volunteer for general service when they know that they will never be permitted to go overseas is making a mockery of the volunteer system and is regarded as a sad joke by officers and men.[70]

He stated that he was fundamentally opposed to a policy of asking the regimental officers to appeal repeatedly to their soldiers, and, as this was to be followed, he said he could no longer assume the responsibility for maintaining discipline among the units of his command nor for the fulfillment of their various operational roles. He again requested that he be relieved of his command or be retired according to his previous requests. Pearkes knew that if he was retired at this time it might embarrass McNaughton, who was standing as the Liberal candidate for a by-election in an Ontario riding. To avoid this, and especially to avoid giving McNaughton's Conservative opponent any political ammunition, Pearkes suggested that an effective date for him to be relieved of his command might be in mid-February, after the election, and that there should be no announcement prior to that time regarding his future.

No word came from Ottawa. Pearkes waited with growing impatience, but he waited until the campaign was over and the results were in. When, five days later, he still had no answer he wired the Adjutant General. When informed that his requests were "under consideration,"[71] Pearkes asked if he might take two weeks' leave since he had had none since 1938. It was refused. The situation was now intolerable. He was forced into a position whereby he had to enforce a method of applying governmental policy which he felt was ruining the discipline of his units. "I am therefore in an utterly dishonourable position," he wired Maj.-Gen. Walford, "as I will not issue instructions to my junior commanders placing them in impossible situations." In such circumstances, he concluded, he felt it was his right to demand to be relieved of his command. This time he got action. On 15 February he was relieved. Three weeks later the Cabinet War Committee decided that he should be retired as there was "no suitable employment" for him in the Canadian Army at his present rank.

The announcement that Pearkes was being retired on 16 February was noted in the press across Canada. One of the persons who saw it was Colonel Ralston, the former Minister of National Defence. He wrote to Pearkes in part:

> This isn't the time for words. I was impelled, however, to tell you I was sincerely sorry to hear that the Pacific Command and the army generally is apparently no longer to have the benefit of your most competent services. I can only guess at the circumstances and if my guess is correct I can only say that I would have taken the same course as you have. . . .
>
> I don't know what your plans are but I want to say this to you that, if you do leave the army, you can feel here is one individual who appreciates and values all you did, and who has some conception of the devotion to duty and the selflessness you displayed in your unflagging effort to make the system work. No one knows better than I that the job was tough and not a particularly attractive one.[72]

For Pearkes it was, in many ways, the end of an era. Less than three months after he received official word that he was to be retired, the war in Europe ended. He was fifty-seven years old and had served the government from the time he was a constable in the North West Mounted Police. He had no future mapped out, but he knew that he did not want to retire. He had six months accumulated furlough coming to him, and for the present he looked forward merely to a period of rest and relaxation.

13

Member of Parliament

When Pearkes gave up his appointment as G.O.C.-in-C. Pacific Command, he looked forward to being out of the limelight which the conscription crisis had brought to him. Although he regretted the circumstances which resulted in his request for retirement, his sense of duty was as strong as it had been when he joined the army in 1915. In a statement he made to the press on 15 February, he said he hoped "opportunities would arise in which I can still render some service to [the men in the Command], to the men who are returning from the three services overseas and to the country as a whole."

This part of Pearkes's statement immediately led to speculation that he would enter politics. In Ottawa when James Gardiner, the Minister of Agriculture, heard about it, he was moved to say that Pearkes had been "acting for the Tories ever since he came back from overseas and there's no reason why he shouldn't run for them." The Canadian Press report added:

> "I'd say further, that statements by General Pearkes and some of his officers have done more than anything else I know of to cause the high incidence of absenteeism in the army."
>
> He added without elaboration: "The story has been continuously coming out of British Columbia that the Troops in the camps had been advised not to volunteer; that the act of volunteering would only be playing into the hands of the Government and they ought to make the Government compel them to go overseas."[1]

Gardiner's statement was printed in most of the major newspapers in Canada, and it was condemned in most of the editorial pages. The Toronto

Globe and Mail and the Montreal *Gazette* were only two of the major newspapers demanding to know why Pearkes was retired, while the Winnipeg *Tribune* characterized Gardiner as going "to work with a bucket of mud and a smear brush" to strike "a new low in ministerial mud slinging."[2]

While the newspapers took up cudgels in Pearkes's defence, Pearkes himself wanted to bring a libel suit against Gardiner. He first asked his superiors in Ottawa if the department was going to take any action and, if not, whether he might be permitted to do so. He was informed, indirectly, that there was no need for the department to make any statement and, directly, that he could consult his solicitor respecting any personal action. However, Pearkes was also told that if he chose the latter course, it did not mean he or his lawyer could use military files to substantiate his case. Thus, Pearkes could only take comfort in the newspaper support he received as well as the large number of personal letters containing expressions of support and sympathy.

Within days of the announcement of his retirement, Pearkes was approached by a number of people who suggested that he run in the next federal election. Pearkes had never considered the idea. As a serving officer before and during the war he had kept completely clear of political involvement. He belonged to no political party, and although he had voted for the Conservatives in the federal elections, he had not attended a political rally of any sort since he was a young man. Even when the Vancouver newspapers began to speculate, they were at first unsure whether he would run as a Conservative or as a candidate for the Co-operative Commonwealth Federation.

Among those who approached Pearkes were two well-known former Conservative M.P.'s, Leon Ladner and Brig. Gen. J. A. Clark. Another was Howard Green, who had been representing a Vancouver riding for the Conservatives since 1935. At this time Green was responsible for his party's provincial organization and had been serving as the Conservatives' chief defence critic in the House of Commons. It had been Green and John Diefenbaker who had grilled McNaughton in the House over the conscription issue.[3] Green and one or two others went to see Pearkes at his home. As he said later:

We were considering having him run either in Vancouver Centre or in Nanaimo, both of which seats . . . he could have won. . . . He was a natural in public life. People liked him, he spoke well, he had an excellent personality and hundreds of friends. . . . [People] admired the stand he had taken in the conscription crisis. He had risked his career . . . and we admired his action very much [as it] was right in accord with our views for what should be done.[4]

There were a number of things which Pearkes had to take into account before he made up his mind. Physically he was in excellent condition, and he did not like the idea of retiring. The soldiers who had served under him would soon be coming back from overseas, and as a member of Parliament he felt he could help the veterans get re-established. However, if he was elected it would mean being away from his family while the House was sitting, and he preferred to live on the West Coast. On the other hand, in a few years John would be going to study at the university. Pearkes's pension, after his thirty-three years of service, came to only about $5,600, and he had little other income. As a member of Parliament he would have an additional $5,000, though he would have to maintain homes in British Columbia and Ottawa. Although the financial enticement, therefore, was modest, the chance to serve made him decide to offer himself as a candidate.

The next question was where he should run. Green and others had suggested Vancouver Centre, then being represented by a Liberal cabinet minister, Ian Mackenzie. Pearkes found that the area had a large proportion of apartment dwellers and a record of changing its party support frequently. The Nanaimo constituency, however, seemed more appealing. It included at that time Saanich, rural Esquimalt, the Gulf Islands, and the farming, fishing, and logging area which stretched up to Nanaimo. The former Conservative contestant, Frank Cunliffe, a Nanaimo lawyer, was not anxious to run again. If Pearkes was accepted as a candidate, he could live in Saanich, not far from the dairy farm where his mother and sister lived.[5] Although he had travelled all over Canada during his career, Pearkes had considered the area his home ever since he returned from the Great War.

Before he made any commitment, Pearkes went to Victoria and Nanaimo where he discussed the matter with a number of prominent Conservatives. The Nanaimo riding was then being represented by a Liberal M.P., Lt.-Col. Alan Chambers, who was serving overseas. Cunliffe confirmed that he did not intend to contest the seat.[6] Pearkes also talked to Sir Henry Drayton, Frank Davie, the president of the Nanaimo Progressive Conservative Association, Robert Wootton, Hugh Henderson, William Haldane, C. R. West, and others, seeking advice and support. He gained a very good idea of the political aspects of the riding. At the same time these men, whose support he would need, had the opportunity to question Pearkes and to judge him as a potential candidate. From the outset there was a meeting of minds, and Pearkes agreed to let his name stand.

Late in March, the Pearkeses decided to buy a house on Tattersal Drive in Saanich. Until they could take occupancy, they moved into the San Sebastian Motel. It was from these cramped quarters that he was to run his campaign. These moves gave added weight to newspaper speculations that Pearkes would be a candidate. When it was announced that nominations for the Nanaimo candidate would take place on 14 April, most of the local political pundits were taking it for granted that Pearkes would throw his hat into the ring. That evening, at the Knights of Pythias hall in Duncan, the local Conservative Association gave Pearkes a rousing reception and voted unanimously to nominate him as their candidate.

The change from being a major-general in charge of a very large military establishment to a retired army officer seeking votes impressed itself on Pearkes from the very beginning. It had been ten years since the Conservatives had been in power in Ottawa and five years since the last election. Locally, the party's organization needed attention, and fortunately Pearkes, in time, was able to gather a number of enthusiastic, hard-working volunteers. It was a large riding, so Pearkes divided it into various areas. For example, the Nanaimo area came south to embrace Ladysmith, and there, led by Frank Cunliffe and Dr. Stanley Morrison, a group of supporters soon got organized, rented an office in Nanaimo for a headquarters, and prepared to advertise the merits of their candidate. In Saanich Maj. Hope McQueen and Arthur Frane organized the area, while in Sooke, Capt. P. W. de P. Taylor gave a great deal of assistance. In the Cowichan area Thomas Gillespie and C. R. West acted as official agent and campaign manager respectively.

Since Pearkes was already a well-known public figure, there was no need to raise large sums of money to make him known to the electorate. As he recalled later:

I didn't know anything about the financial support other than I was assured . . . that there would be assistance both from the provincial and the federal associations as well as from the local association. . . . They said I wouldn't be expected to put up more than my own personal expenses of travelling around the constituency; that all the advertising and the hiring of halls and that sort of thing would be provided, which it was. I think we ran a very, very cheap campaign. In fact none of my campaigns ever cost me more than a few hundred dollars.[7]

Funds for the campaign came from a variety of sources. The gathering and disbursing of these funds was carried out by the campaign agent, and Pearkes left the finances completely in his hands. The executive of the local association gave direction in such matters—how much money would be devoted to newspaper advertising and in what newspapers, how many posters should be run off, how much radio time they could buy for their candidate, and so forth. The agent, in turn, had to file with the returning officers an account of all monies received and spent on behalf of the candidate, and this in turn was subject to public scrutiny.[8]

The campaign manager, especially in Pearkes's first attempt to get elected, was invaluable. Frank Davie, who volunteered his service in 1945, had been a former president of the local association and knew the constituency well. He arranged for Pearkes to speak in all the polling divisions and made provision, when necessary, for friends to take him by motor launches to visit the numerous islands and talk to voters in rented halls. Local supporters would give tea or coffee parties. Davie could advise Pearkes about the areas where he should campaign hardest and about the topics which he should stress in particular areas. In the Esquimalt district, for example, he spoke in favour of returning district headquarters back to its prewar locality once the war was over. At the same time he voiced the complaint of many in Esquimalt when he spoke about the large amount of nontaxable Department of National Defence property in the municipality. In a different locality, where the fishing industry was important, Pearkes spoke out against the Japanese returning in large numbers to the coast to regain the hold they had had on the industry. He was by no means anti-Oriental, but it should be remembered that the war with Japan was approaching its climax and that every week brought an increasing number of Japanese war atrocities to light. Nobody in the province wanted the Japanese back at that time, and it was "good politics" to beat that drum when there was a large number of fishermen in the audience.

The campaign manager also accepted on Pearkes's behalf an invitation to an all-candidates meeting sponsored by the Nanaimo local of the United Mine Workers of America. It was probably the largest up-Island meeting during the campaign. The crowd, which eventually reached an estimated seven hundred people, soon outgrew the U.M.W. hall and the debate, which continued for three hours, was moved to the Nanaimo Arena.[9] This was the only time all the candidates met. The Liberal incumbent, Lt.-Col. Alan Chambers, was campaigning in uniform. He praised the people's war effort and King's leadership. Pearkes, who was the second speaker, agreed that the nation's war effort was excellent but, as might be expected, found little to praise in Liberal war policies. Among other things he denounced the government's announced policy of sending only volunteers to the Pacific Theatre. He stressed the need for an equality of sacrifice, and since the government now accepted conscription as a policy, they should use it. The C.C.F. candidate was Dr. J. M. Thomas, the principal of Mount View High School in Saanich. He is reported as suggesting that Canada was living under an economic fascist society and would continue to do so if either the Liberals or Conservatives were returned to power. He added that Gen. Pearkes did not know what he was talking about when he said the C.C.F. would impose state socialism and in general gave a good account of himself. The fourth candidate was George Greenwall of the Labour Progressive Party. He was against reactionary elements, which seemed to include most people not within his own party. It was, in all, quite a meeting. As Pearkes said later: "I believe I made a good impression because years afterwards I met the chairman and he said that meeting won me the election because I seemed to be honest and straightforward and not much of a politician!"[10]

Mrs. Pearkes frequently travelled with her husband and did what she could to help him. She was not enthusiastic initially about George entering politics. The personality involvements and the public debates were foreign to her, but after she had talked over the matter and knowing her husband's desire to assist veterans after the war, she put her heart into it. She was to prove to be an invaluable asset. She combined charm with a remarkable memory, a sincere interest in people, and an ever-ready dry wit.

As a vote-getter, Pearkes himself was his own best advertisement, whether he was on the platform or talking to individuals. Despite his former senior rank in the army he had the common touch and was equally at home talking with a berry-picker on a Saanich farm, a logger in the Lake Shawnigan area, or a businessman in Nanaimo. As a public figure his life was an open book, and as a newcomer to politics, he had no broken promises to explain nor past favours to fulfill. There is no doubt that, in the first instance, his Victoria Cross may have gained him some votes. It was almost universally known that he was a hero of the Great War, and one may assume that many veterans favoured him. More important, though, was the real interest he showed in everything that went on in the community. Moreover, he never missed an opportunity to make himself known as a candidate. When Howard Green came from Vancouver to speak on Pearkes's behalf in this campaign he related: "when the boat was landing at Nanaimo, I looked through the window and there was George Pearkes standing on the wharf shaking hands and sharing in laughter with one of the dock hands who was waiting to catch the rope, and I thought to myself 'They're never going to beat that fellow!' "[11]

Pearkes was at his best when he talked about constituency and military matters and tended to play down some of the national problems on which, at this stage of his career, he had formed no firm opinion. Every candidate, of course, favoured the return of peace and prosperity, but Japan had to be defeated, and both Pearkes and Chambers wanted the numerous military camps on Vancouver Island to be used to their full extent to train the force Canada planned to send overseas. Pearkes wanted to use conscripts as well as volunteers for the task, and at one point spoke in favour of retaining some form of compulsory military training in the postwar era.[12] He was to change his mind on this subject later.

Since the major industries on Vancouver Island depended on exports for their prosperity, Pearkes favoured any and all help which might be of benefit to them. As the international economy was such that all the lumber, fish, and coal which could be produced had a ready market, there was no need to dwell a great deal on that topic. He did speak, however, of the desire to maintain a healthy trade with Great Britain. He felt the British had suffered a great deal during the war and needed Canada's help. Six years of wartime prosperity had not erased the memory of the Depression, and there was a considerable amount of apprehension among the ranks of labour in B.C., not only about the possibility of a postwar slump but also about the impact of hundreds of thousands of veterans to be absorbed. Pearkes's platform statements on labour and unions followed those outlined in his party's political handbook. What was to trouble him in later years was how to solve the problem whereby one labour union going on strike had the effect of throwing out of work thousands of men in associated or allied industries. Strikes which had a cumulative effect were both uneconomical and unfair. He felt the best solution was to have some sort of a joint labour-management court or committee which could reach a solution and ward off the need for a strike. Failing that he thought in terms of a "labour court" which could enforce mediation between the two. He was strongly in favour of any means which could prevent a situation arising which labour felt must be resolved by a strike, however, and held to this agreeable but ill-defined concept throughout his political career.

By the first week in June the campaign was reaching its climax. Pearkes found it easy to talk, received very little heckling, explained the Conservative platform, and listened carefully to the questions from his audiences. By 10 June the final speeches were made, and on the following day the votes were cast. Pearkes drove to Nanaimo that morning and made his way south to Victoria during the day, visiting polling stations and calling in to thank his supporters. That evening the returns began to come in, and it became apparent that it would be a close race, the closest Pearkes was to have. Dr. Thomas, the C.C.F. candidate, turned out to be the strongest competitor, but Pearkes surged ahead and ended with a plurality of 1,639 votes. The results were sufficiently close, however, to make Pearkes reflect that if there had been no Labour Progressive candidate skimming off votes from the C.C.F., Dr. Thomas would have likely won.

The final results when the returns from the soldiers overseas had been tabulated, were: Pearkes—11,181; Thomas—9,542; Chambers—8,223; and Greenwall—2,707. Of B.C.'s fifteen federal ridings, five went to the Liberals, five to the Progressive Conservatives, four to the C.C.F. and there was one independent. Of the five Progressive Conservative M.P.'s, two (E. Davie Fulton of Kamloops and C. C. I. Merritt, V.C., who won Vancouver-Burrard) had been former officers in Pearkes's division overseas. The other two (Howard Green of Vancouver-South and Grote Stirling of Yale) were respectively a veteran of the Great War and a former Minister of National Defence. Of the 245 seats in the House of Commons, the Liberals gained 125, the Progressive Conservatives, 67; the C.C.F., 28; Social Credit, 13. Eleven other members represented various independent groups. Overall the Liberals had lost seats and the Conservatives had gained, but the King government was still firmly in the saddle.

When Pearkes first agreed to accept the invitation to be a candidate, he thought that if he was successful, he would remain an M.P. for the length of the Parliament. He felt that most of the legislation respecting the rehabilitation of veterans would be passed in the immediate postwar years, and then he would yield to a younger candidate. When he left to attend his first Parliament in September, therefore, he had no idea of carving out a political career, nor did he harbour secret aspirations for high political office. When the train stopped in Calgary en route to Ottawa, Pearkes was delighted to meet two fellow Conservative M.P.'s. One was Douglas Harkness, whom Pearkes had last met overseas when Harkness was an artillery officer in his division. The other was Arthur L. Smith, a Calgary lawyer who had long experience in the Conservative party and who was to provide the two freshmen members with a great deal of good advice during the trip.

After taking the oath in the Speaker's office on the morning of the day Parliament opened, Pearkes and other Conservative freshmen had to find the office of the party whip, Col. A. C. Casselman. The Speaker allotted offices to the various parties, but it was up to the party whips to say which members would be in which offices. Pearkes was to share his office with John Hackett, who had been re-elected for Stanstead. Casselman also showed the new members where they would sit in the House, and Pearkes found he would be beside Lt.-Col. Merritt. Two holders of the Victoria Cross seated next to each other would have been a rare situation in any Commonwealth parliament.

The forms of parliamentary practice and procedure took some time to learn before Pearkes really began to feel at home in the House. But it was not long before Pearkes's daily life in the capital became fairly routine. When he first went to Ottawa, Pearkes, like many other members, took advantage of the reduced rates which the Chateau Laurier offered to members of Parliament who would be in permanent residence during the winter months. After his first session, however, he rented a private bedroom with bath in a house on Gilmour Street. It was sufficiently close for him to walk to and from the office, but the bitter cold of the Ottawa winter, which reminded him of the Yukon, often made him wish he was back in the milder climate on the Pacific Coast.

In Saanich, meanwhile, he had had to buy a second house. Owing to the postwar housing shortage and the tremendous demand for rented premises, laws had been passed which prevented him, as the owner of the Tattersal Drive house, evicting the family renting it. Pearkes's son, John, was attending Shawnigan Lake School, so George and Blytha decided to take advantage of the Veterans Land Act and bought a house in the Brentwood area, some seven miles further out from Victoria. Occasionally Blytha would be able to visit George for a few days, and, of course, he would return for the Christmas holidays. The long months of separation were trying, however, and despite the various activities in which she was engaged, time did not go by quickly. To the extent that she could help him politically she did so. People would telephone or write asking for information or action on a variety of subjects, and these she would send to George, together with newspaper clippings and comments about constituency matters and concerns.

For Pearkes the dullest times were the weekends when the House was not in session. "It was grim," he stated later, and added

> Sometimes local members would invite you to stay the weekend. John Hackett and Colonel Casselman were particularly kind to me. But on the whole, weekends dragged. . . . Saturday you might go back to your office, get some correspondence done, and [later] play a game of bridge or two but that's about all.[13]

Being a "grass widower" in Ottawa probably led Pearkes to go out seeking company more than he ever did before. He had some friends in Ottawa from the years when he had been on staff at Defence Headquarters. As he gained experience and more prominence as a leading member of the Opposition, invitations came to him from the foreign diplomatic corps. Pearkes liked going to the embassies and meeting the cross-section of other countries' representatives in Canada, senior Canadian civil servants and military officials, prominent citizens of Ottawa, and so forth. He felt that as a member of Parliament it was desirable to attend the "national day" receptions or cocktail parties held by the embassies, and one might pick up some bits and pieces of useful information. Social life among the M.P.'s as a group was very limited—indeed, about the only time the majority of them would meet socially would be at the annual National Press Gallery dinner.

Getting information was always a difficulty for M.P.'s, especially since members did not have any research staff. Since Pearkes knew quite well most of the senior officers at Defence Headquarters, some people thought he could establish a direct pipeline into the department. Such was never the case. "I was always diffident about speaking to service people about the conditions of their service," he said later, and added:

It seemed to me that I, having been a soldier, should not embarrass
my old friends by asking them to be critical of the government policy
and I kept away from them. I never went into the [Defence] Headquarters during all those years, and it was only at social meetings that
I saw the people. My source of information was always the legitimate
source, that is, from printed matter, or if I wanted information I asked
the Minister or the Deputy Minister or the . . . [services] public relations officer.[14]

There were other areas where information was more readily available.
Certain industries kept offices in Ottawa and were more than willing to
supply members of Parliament with material. Also major industries and
firms in British Columbia, as elsewhere, published "house organs," and
from these journals Pearkes was able to keep in touch with major trends in
the fishing, forestry, and other industries. His letters of inquiry to companies, unions, organizations, or associations usually resulted in plenty of
material relevant to his questions, and naturally groups or associations
seeking his assistance would include supporting evidence.

It was agreed among the Progressive Conservative members from British
Columbia that questions relating to the province beyond the boundaries of
their own ridings should receive attention according to areas for which
they were generally responsible. For example, Pearkes would pay special
attention to the Islands, Davie Fulton would look after the Interior,
Howard Green, the Vancouver area, and so on. The party members were
also divided into committees whose task it was to pay special attention to
the activities, policies, and proposals of the various government departments. Thus, there was a P.C. defence committee, finance committee, trade
and commerce committee, and so forth. Pearkes was asked to be chairman
of the defence committee with Merritt as his vice-chairman and Harkness
as secretary. As Harkness recalled later: "George was always . . . reading
and keeping up on what was happening from the military point of view . . .
as we all were. . . . In that particular group we constituted quite a bit of
experience."[15]

The experience of the veterans, however, centred on conventional warfare. The first atomic bomb was dropped only a month or so before Parliament met. No one doubted that a new era had been ushered in, but the
scope and speed of technological change was still hidden in the mists of the
future. Periodically, with the consent of the Minister of National Defence,
the party's defence committee might meet with one of the senior service
officers who could brief them on military developments. As a result of these
and other sources, Harkness related, "we learned a good deal about a very
large number of problems and questions . . . both in order to put up any

reasonable criticism in the House and to suggest alternatives [to the government]."

It is important that a member of Parliament should have available as much information as possible on a subject before talking about it in the House. It is also important that the voters in his constituency should be informed about the efforts he was making on their behalf. In this respect Pearkes was fortunate. During his first years as a member, one of the senior reporters in the Ottawa Press Gallery was Tom Green. He was a Conservative who worked for the Victoria *Colonist*, a Conservative newspaper. He was pleased to see a P.C. member come from Vancouver Island, and he used to visit Pearkes's office, have a drink of Scotch, and talk politics. "In those days," Pearkes added, "he played things up very well for me."[16] There were a variety of other methods, of course. For example provision was made through the party association for members to make a recording of a ten-minute talk to their constituents. The best advertisement for any member of Parliament, however, is the manner in which he serves his constituents, whether they voted for him or not.

One thing an M.P. in the Opposition could do much easier than an M.P. whose party was in power was to gain favourable publicity by asking the government to pay more money to those already being supported by government funds. In 1946, for example, Pearkes spoke out in favour of increasing the thirty dollars per month old age pension, and for some time he was able to contrast the Liberal government's slowness in implementing the raise with the speed with which it passed the "baby bonus" law. There were a large number of retired people in the Victoria-Nanaimo area, and it was an excellent chance to help these people as well as others in the province and the Dominion. He made a similar plea for a younger group, the student veterans. The idea of the government sending veterans to take university training "was a splendid move, and it will reap wonderful dividends for Canada." However, he noted that a married veteran received only eighty dollars a month as a living allowance, and consequently the average student was going into debt on the average of $43.50 per month. By September 1946, over one thousand student veterans in Canada had to leave university for financial reasons, and Pearkes came out strongly for an increased allowance for them.[17] There may have been only three or four hundred student veterans living in his riding, but most of them would remember that he had spoken on their behalf. When, ultimately, the students' allowance was increased by ten dollars a month, Pearkes would gain as much credit as the Liberal member in the adjoining riding.

Pearkes worked hard in the postwar years to help veterans. He kept in close contact with the Canadian Legion, and this organization, in turn, found in him one of its strongest supporters. In his own riding, for example, Pearkes was very active in championing the cause of those veterans who, under the Veterans Land Act, had contracted to buy several dozen houses being built on the Braefoot estate. From the very beginning there were complaints to the Department of Veterans' Affairs. Poor drainage, inadequate sewage, poor construction, high costs, delays, and other problems had made the plight of the thirty-eight veterans' families a local issue. Pearkes visited the area several times to see the situation himself and had both spoken to and written the appropriate officials in the Department of Veterans' Affairs. He badgered them so much that even the Honourable Ian Mackenzie, the minister, came over to examine the problem and promised to take appropriate steps. This he did do eventually, and Pearkes in the process managed to reduce costs and payments by the veterans by many thousands of dollars.

In Ottawa Pearkes was a member of the Parliamentary Committee on Veterans' Affairs. This committee consisted of sixty members representative of all parties, all provinces, all services and service ranks from private to general. After hearing evidence from representatives of the Canadian Legion, auxiliary services, Department of Veterans' Affairs officials, and others, the committee sought to compile a "veterans' charter" which would incorporate all orders-in-council relating to veterans which had been made under the War Measures Act. Among those matters with which it dealt were the War Service Grants Act, the Veterans Land Act, the Pensions Act, Imperial Pensions, Veterans Rehabilitation Act, and many other similar items. Pearkes considered it the most important committee on which he served, and indeed it was perhaps his major concern in the immediate postwar years. Since the committee was non-partisan, he was able to have a strong voice in recommendations sent to the government for approval. This was especially important when, during the winter of 1945-46, there were few opportunities during the session to discuss the affairs of the returned men. The non-partisan approach to questions in the committee began to change in 1946, however, and Pearkes and other non-governmental members found they had to work harder to get their recommendations accepted. As he described the situation at the time:

> In the first place the government [i.e. Liberal members] would revive the questions which had been settled; the Liberal "whip" would appear at the committee and "count heads"; then, in time to vote and steamroller the recommendations of the government [members] to the committee, Liberal back-benchers and cabinet ministers would slip into the room. The only thing that counted was their vote.[18]

As the years went by the veterans melded into civilian life and society. Many M.P.'s who, like Pearkes, had agreed to serve initially in parliament to ensure that war veterans would get a "square deal" from the government had their attention diverted to more immediate affairs which made the decade one of the most interesting in Canada. Pearkes, too, was caught up in the new issues which arose, but he never forgot the veterans. The long and quiet battles he waged on their behalf, in the House and in the offices of the Department of Veterans' Affairs, were recognized many years later by the Canadian Legion when he was appointed Grand President.

Pearkes was also a member of the Fisheries Committee, and this too served as a platform which he could use to promote the interests of fishermen in his own riding and British Columbia in general. Many aspects of the fishing industry affected the federal government. The sale of fresh fish by Canadian fishermen to American firms had an impact on employment in Canadian canneries, for example, while government support or assistance to British Columbian salmon canneries to export their product could bring prosperity to fishing villages along the coast. The combination of navigational aids, radar stations, and an adequate coastguard service to aid B.C. fishermen was a theme Pearkes hammered on time and again and so too were harbour development and the need for additional wharfage. He was to find out that if the squeaky wheel did not always get the government grease, it nevertheless paid to keep the needs of his riding and his province in the public eye. He knew that a firm, polite and steady reminder in the House, the press, or over the radio was an effective, if rather tedious, method of getting action.

Early in 1957, when a railway strike was in progress and threatening hardship to the people on Vancouver Island, Pearkes came out strongly for facilities to be established at the northern end of the Saanich Peninsula so that a fast freight and passenger ferry service could be provided between Victoria and Vancouver. At that time he thought of Sidney as being the western terminal. Later, when the provincial government established a ferry service to replace the Canadian Pacific connection, the ferry wharves and terminal were located only a short distance away at Swartz Bay. Both Pearkes and Howard Green were strong advocates of Canadian control over waters between the Queen Charlotte Islands and the mainland where fish originating in British Columbia waters would have to pass to reach the Pacific Ocean.[19] This concern over conservation and the depletion of fishing grounds off the B.C. coast anticipated a later and much stronger public attention to the problem. Pearkes was to bring it up repeatedly during the 1950's, and it was but one more instance of his attempts to improve the conditions for those in the fishing industry both in his riding and in the province.

There were few matters affecting British Columbia in general and his riding in particular which did not bring forth some comment from Pearkes. There is no need to list them all here, but a few will indicate the breadth of his interests. The forest industry, of course, received as much attention as the fisheries, and one of the things he attempted to do was have the federal government establish a Pacific Forest Research Centre on Vancouver Island. He came out strongly for reforestation, but if there was any one theme he held to it was his demand that the federal government, which siphoned off millions of dollars annually from the forest industry, should be spending more than it was to help the British Columbia industry meet the strong American competition.

Agriculture was another industry which Pearkes helped whenever he could. Traditionally the farmers' vote usually went to the Conservative member, but there was no one major segment of farmers in Pearkes's riding which dominated the group. Fruit growers, seed and bulb farmers, diary farmers, vegetable and berry farmers, chicken farmers—there was variety coupled with the independence of the small operator. Pearkes made it a habit to visit the fairs in his riding, especially at Saanichton, and his own love for farming coupled with his interest in their problems meant that he was there for hours on end, easily available to his constituents and anxious to do what he could for them. One small example will suffice. Between 1939 and 1947, the value of the egg crop in the province had increased from $4 million to $16 million. This leap in production was caused not only by wartime demands, but also by the decision of the federal government in 1942 to aid B.C. poultrymen by a freight assistance policy. Almost all the feed grain had to be imported from the prairies, and by 1947, 179,000 tons were being used. The government decision in 1948 to remove the price ceiling of grain going to B.C. together with a raise in freight rates led to one authority predicting that egg production would decline by two-thirds. This, of course, affected many poultry farmers in Pearkes's riding, and he, in turn, was quick to take up the matter in the House.[20]

Those engaged in fishing, forestry, agriculture, and other major industries could usually count on support in Ottawa from their industrial or union organizations, but there were other groups who had little voice in the nation's capital. Among those Pearkes championed were the native Indians. His interest in the Indians dated back to the time when he was a constable in the R.N.W.M.P., and later, when he was a scoutmaster in Calgary, he had established a warm relationship with local bands and frequently had some of their leaders come to the camp to talk to his scouts. His interest in their problems was genuine, and whenever the opportunity arose he would bring their plight to the attention of the minister in charge of their affairs. Something of this may be seen in the following excerpt from a speech he made in the House in June 1948:

I wish to express my regret that such a meagre amount is being provided for the improvement of Indian reserves. . . . I object to only $500,000 being spent for the maintenance of the reserves and provision of houses for our Indians. Furthermore, right in the heart of Nanaimo is Nanaimo Reserve No. 1. I went there last Fall at the invitation of the chaplain of the reserve. I drove up to the boundary line and was told that I would have to leave my car. I stepped off a paved road onto a dirt track full of potholes. I left houses where there were electric lights, sewers and water and I went in among hovels where there were no lights, no water, no sewer. This is right in the heart of Nanaimo. . . .

I pleaded with the Department to do something to improve the roads and they generously granted $100, making it $300 instead of $200 for maintenance of roads. This enabled the Indians to bring in a few cartloads of cinders to put in the worst mudholes. This is all I have been able to get from the Department and it is not good enough.

Another matter I brought to the attention of the Department was the fact that the children on Nanaimo Reserve No. 2, some eight miles away, had not been able to obtain any education for the last five or six years simply and solely because the Department will not bring the few Indian children on that reserve into the school at Nanaimo.[21]

Pearkes's concern for the native Indians was mixed with an appreciation of their ancient culture and the difficulties they were having in adapting to a white man's society. In the 1960's he could do more to attract public attention, and the services he rendered were recognized by the various bands in the province.

There was another group in the province—the Chinese-Canadians—to whom Pearkes gave his full support when, in 1947, the question of their being given the franchise came up. He had not forgotten his promise to the Chinese-Canadian soldiers who had trained in the Okanagan Valley. On 2 May 1947, when he rose to support the measure, he spoke of their service and sacrifice and how they deserved all the rights of Canadian citizenship. He was more cautious about opening wide the door to the wives and families of Chinese living abroad. In British Columbia alone, he pointed out, there were some 13,174 Chinese-Canadians who had wives living abroad, many with children. The return of the Canadian soldiers from overseas, the large numbers of European displaced persons pouring into Canada, the consequent severe shortage of housing, and the overcrowding in the Chinese sections of Vancouver and Victoria made him suggest that families should come to Canada only at a rate at which the available housing, educational, and similar facilities could absorb them.[22] He sympathized with them, and later, especially after mainland China came under Communist rule, Pearkes aided many Chinese-Canadians in his riding attempting to gain entry for their close relatives.

In the postwar years Pearkes reflected the feeling of his constituency with respect to the Japanese-Canadians and their possible return to the coast. Indeed, in his first speech in the House in September 1945 he stated, when talking about British Columbian fishermen, that "never again must Japanese be allowed to capture the fishing industry of British Columbia."[23] The intensity of feeling against the Japanese was not lessened after the defeat of Japan, especially as the stories of their maltreatment of Allied prisoners of war were spread by returning Canadians. In the following year the situation had not changed. "I have had letters," Pearkes said, "from individuals, from farmers, from fishermen, from employers of labour, from churches and organizations all containing this plea: Do not let the Japanese come back to this territory after the war. They do not want them to come back...the main reason being that they are not assimilable."[24] Even as late as 1948, when the government was considering whether or not to permit the Japanese to return, Pearkes still spoke of the continuing bitterness in the Pacific province and hoped another year might pass to allow passions to cool down. There is no doubt he was somewhat embarrassed when he considered that he was requesting that Canadian citizens should not be permitted to live in certain sections of Canada. Nevertheless, in this case he was expressing the sentiments of his constituents, and there is no doubt that those living in his and other B.C. ridings felt very strongly about the subject.

As Pearkes gained experience as a member of Parliament he spoke on a greater variety of subjects. Once his initial shyness had worn off, he entered into debates with considerable zest. His speeches, according to one of his colleagues, were generally courteous and reasonably gentle. Rarely would he lash out and slip a verbal knife into a Liberal member across the floor, and perhaps for that reason he was seldom heckled. At the same time, he was forceful, tenacious, well-prepared, and ready to question the government's arguments.

He was also learning more about the provincial and federal Progressive Conservative associations in British Columbia. When Pearkes was first elected there was a considerable harmony between Howard Green, the leader of the federal association, and Pat Maitland, the provincial leader. At that time, and until 1952, the province was governed by a coalition of Liberals and Conservatives, a situation which could be and sometimes was awkward when federal and provincial party members attempted to join their actions or to reach agreement on issues. Following Maitland's death in 1946, Herbert Anscomb was elected leader of the provincial Conservatives. Green soon found that Anscomb had his own ideas about how the two levels of the same association should operate, and the tension between the two groups increased.

While the struggle for dominance became more bitter, there was also dissension within the ranks. At the federal level, George Drew replaced John Bracken as leader, while on the provincial level there was growing disenchantment not only within the ranks of the coalition but between Anscomb and some of the senior Conservative leaders. Originally Pearkes was on the periphery of these affairs, but he was drawn into them further each year. In the immediate postwar years he was approached by the provincial association to speak on behalf of various candidates running for election. For example, when Grote Stirling decided to retire in 1948, a by-election was called and a former Conservative M.L.A., W. A. C. Bennett, was nominated to contest his riding. Among those who came to the Okanagan to campaign on his behalf was George Pearkes.

The friction between Anscomb and Green was responsible in large measure for Pearkes accepting the presidency of the Progressive Conservative Association in British Columbia in October 1947.[25] Reflecting on the situation as it existed at the time he said:

> I felt that Anscomb was in a difficult position. He didn't have the loyal support of the federal branch. . . . I think it was a clash of personalities. . . . Bracken had appointed Howard Green as his representative and [he] was trying to separate federal activities in the Association from provincial. I think that he, and perhaps other people . . . welcomed the fact that I would become president . . . thinking that I would be able to place more emphasis on the federal side of things. I think as things turned out I was inclined to work perhaps more with the provincial people than [they] expected I would have done.
>
> It wasn't a happy period because there was this dog-fight coming on between the provincial and the federal people. I felt that the position of president of the Association should have rather more influence, or position of responsibility, than was given to him. Anscomb . . . told me a good deal of what was going on. He objected very much to the practice of the leader in the federal house writing to Green, and Green carrying out certain instructions [or] suggestions from the [federal] leader without ever consulting the president of the Association or the leader of the Conservative Party in British Columbia. Anscomb . . . felt that as leader of the Conservative Party in the provincial House that he was leader of all the Conservatives in British Columbia, whereas Howard Green took the attitude rather that the federal people were quite separate from the provincial. Although they had one asso-

ciation and at that association's meeting any member attending could talk on either provincial or federal affairs, yet when it came down to taking action . . . the two were quite separate.[26]

Although Pearkes did what he could to maintain peace and unity, the bitterness continued. One of the Progressive Conservative members of Parliament, who was elected vice-president of the association in 1950 when Pearkes was serving as president, described the situation in part in these words:

[It] was not a conflict of personalities, although personalities were injected into it. It was a conflict over principle, as to whether the national leader and the national Association should have any direct responsibility for Federal organization, and for the direction of Federal affairs, within the province.[27]

Matters came to a head between the two contending points of view when Deane Finlayson became leader of the provincial party.[28] At an annual meeting in Vernon in 1954, he allowed a vote of censure to be passed against George Drew, the federal leader. This led to the formation of the British Columbia Co-ordinating Council for federal organization. "It was created," Fulton observed,

by Conservatives in B.C. who saw the necessity of having some organization within the province, loyal to the National leader and National Party, exercising under the National Association a co-ordinating influence on Federal organization within the 22 Federal ridings in the province. The National Association has merely recognized and approved what British Columbia has done, at long last, to get Federal affairs and organization in the province on an even keel after two Provincial Leaders in succession have created an impossible situation.[29]

Altogether Pearkes was more than pleased to turn over the office which had a small measure of prestige and very little power. It was some years before the breach was healed, and in the meantime the Progressive Conservative voice in the B.C. legislature faded to a mere whisper.

During this period the national party association also had a change of leadership. For some time, owing to ill-health combined with a strong element within the party who wished to see him replaced, Bracken had been unable to weld the party into a dynamic, unified, and hard-hitting force. Late in 1948, therefore, the Conservatives held a national convention to choose a successor. Among the strongest candidates for the office were a westerner, John Diefenbaker, and an easterner, George Drew, the Premier of Ontario. Pearkes knew both men and played a minor role during the contest. "I was very fond of George Drew," Pearkes said later.

> He had a strong personality and he was a very hard worker. He was a good speaker in the House and if he were more popular in the country he would have made an excellent prime minister . . . [but] I never felt he could get elected. I think he was considered too closely associated with the Toronto financiers and too far removed from the average man. . . . He was dignified, he had amongst his friends a pleasing personality, was very easy to get on with and talk to, but to the average man . . . he would seem too reserved and too far away. . . . I think the average person would have thought that he was too much a socialite. . . . But he had all kinds of ability and he would have made an excellent prime minister.[30]

John Diefenbaker, whom Pearkes nominated for Conservative leadership in the 1948 convention, had quite a different personality. Pearkes had known him for some three years, and he respected his ability in the House, his concern for the "man in the street," and his reputation as an orator in promoting Conservative interests. Diefenbaker was not one of the group who, for example, gathered in Earl Rowe's office for a social drink after a hard debate in the House nor would he be "one of the boys" at a bridge game whiling away a dull Sunday afternoon. A Baptist and a lawyer, he had a passionate interest in politics, a long record of service, a growing reputation among parliamentarians, and a strong following in the party, especially among the westerners. Despite Pearkes's admiration for Drew, he did not think he would be able to bring the party to power, but he felt Diefenbaker would succeed. Some felt that his name might be a drawback, but Pearkes believed it might garner votes from the ethnic groups. At the same time Diefenbaker was a fourth generation Canadian whose roots went back to United Empire Loyalist stock in Ontario and the Selkirk settlers in the West. Faced with choosing between a candidate who Pearkes felt would have a wide, popular appeal and one of proven ability whose support came primarily from Ontario, Pearkes chose Diefenbaker. Nominating his fellow westerner, Pearkes gave one of the best speeches he had ever made.[31] Nevertheless, the delegates chose Drew, by an overwhelming majority.

Eleven months earlier Mackenzie King had resigned as prime minister and the office was assumed by Louis St. Laurent. This break in political leadership was matched, in a sense, by a change in Canada's pace and development. The switch from a wartime to a peacetime economy and the absorption into civil life of almost a million veterans had taken up most of the attention of the government. At the same time the steady pressure exerted by the Soviet Union in Europe which culminated in the blockade of Berlin, together with the realization by Canadians of their postwar economic strength, resulted in challenging initiatives being taken by the St. Laurent government. On the domestic front the evidence of growth and prosperity were to be seen everywhere. Canada's population in the period from 1948 to 1958 increased from 12,883,000 to 16,589,000, while the gross national expenditure went up from $15.45 billion to $31.773 billion. Newfoundland entered into confederation with Canada, the St. Lawrence Seaway project was completed, the discovery of new huge oil fields and mineral deposits stimulated industry, wartime controls were dropped, the Trans-Canada Highway was being built, construction was at an all-time high—no matter where one looked there was evidence of an economic boom which made the late 1920's look pale in comparison.

The surging economy helped to maintain the Liberals in their comfortable majority. In the elections of 1949 and 1953 they gained 193 out of 262 seats and 173 out of 265 seats respectively. Pearkes did extremely well in his own riding, winning a majority of almost 8,000 votes over his nearest rival in 1949 and about 5,500 votes in 1953. He never forgot that his power lay in the voters and service to them was a prerequisite of his future. Among the Liberals, however, two decades in office were developing an attitude among many that parliamentary office was theirs almost by right. Cabinet members especially became more arrogant. Among those who typified Liberal arrogance and personified the "bullying" tactics in the House in the mid-1950's was C. D. Howe. No one instance brought this more to the notice of the public than the Trans-Canada Pipeline Debate in the early summer of 1956. In order to ram through a bill which would permit construction of the pipeline, the Liberals decided to use closure, which was not only unusual but which was announced even before debate began. The debate soon developed into a vicious party fight. Every parliamentary device was used on both sides, and possibly the climax came when the Speaker, apparently influenced by senior Liberal members, reversed his own decision to favour the Liberals. This not only resulted in an uproar in the Commons, but also added to the unfavourable image of the government and led to a 10 per cent drop in the rating of the Liberals in a public poll. The Liberals' rating sank again as a result of the Suez affair, and increasing inflation, high taxation, and a variety of other irritants made it obvious that if an election were held the Conservatives had a better chance of winning than had existed for decades.

In September 1956 when George Drew resigned as leader of the Progressive Conservative party, the selection of the new leader gained added importance. Almost from the beginning John Diefenbaker became the chief contender at the leadership convention, which met in Ottawa on 12-14 December.[32] Donald Fleming and E. Davie Fulton were the other two main contestants. Ever since the contenders had started their campaign for nomination, Pearkes had backed Diefenbaker. At the same time he was on good terms with Fleming and Fulton. Fleming, he felt, "lacked something in personality. He was too serious. He could never relax. He was a terribly hard worker . . . had sound judgement but . . . I don't think would have made a good leader." Fulton, although a fellow British Columbian, was considered by many in the party to be too young and ambitious. He was making a strong appeal to the younger element in the party as well as to the Quebec element, but Pearkes felt he did not have the following either in the party or among the electorate generally which was essential to victory. At first Pearkes did not expect to do more at the convention than vote for Diefenbaker. It was known that H. J. Flemming would nominate him, and it was expected that he would be seconded by a French Canadian, probably Pierre Sevigny.[33] Politically it probably would have been astute. Diefenbaker did not speak French, he had no strong following in Quebec, and he did not have an influential "lieutenant." However, he preferred to have Pearkes second his nomination. As Pearkes explained later:

> He [Diefenbaker] said he wanted someone from the West. He didn't want two people from the East. He wanted me personally because I had nominated him before and he said unless I seconded it, it would look as if we had had a row or something. . . . I told Diefenbaker repeatedly that my feelings would not be hurt if he asked a French Canadian to second his nomination . . . but he wouldn't hear of it. I think his attitude was: "well, we need not bother too much about Quebec; Quebec will go in on the winning side anyhow."[34]

Probably Diefenbaker lost some support from the Quebec delegates by the choice he made, but it is impossible to estimate how many. In any event, when the first ballot was taken, Diefenbaker swept to victory with a 60 per cent majority. The Progressive Conservatives had a new leader, one who could bring the party to power in the next election. For eleven years Pearkes had been the Conservatives' chief spokesman on defence matters and had made himself an authority on veterans' affairs. Should his party win power, it was highly probable that he might be selected for a cabinet appointment, and as such he would have the opportunity to bring into force some of his own ideas on defence. Pearkes's attitude towards military affairs during the period he was a member of the Opposition is an interesting study for the next stage in his career.

14

Defence Critic

George Pearkes was first able to speak openly about Canadian defence policy during the 1945 election campaign. Although Germany had been defeated, the conquest of Japan was still to be completed. The furious battles in the Pacific and Southeast Asia indicated that there would be a great deal of hard fighting before the Japanese forces were overcome. Early in April 1945 the Prime Minister had announced that the forces which Canada proposed to send to the Far East would be composed entirely of volunteers. Pearkes, as might be expected, was among those denouncing this policy on the basis that it represented an inequality of sacrifice. His view, in brief, was that there were thousands of trained soldiers who had never been sent to the field of battle and that the volunteers had already done their duty. In May, when questioned on the subject, he suggested that in peacetime it might be advisable to retain "a form of conscription and [the] calling up of young Canadians for eighteen months to two years."[1] Later, Pearkes changed his opinion, and he was never to propose conscription in peacetime, mainly owing to the costs involved. Nevertheless, he and a number of his Conservative colleagues would have favoured such a measure should Canada have become involved in a major conflict.

The war had brought about profound changes in the relationships of the Great Powers. Germany and Japan now lay in ruins, while even the victors had been hard hit. National economies had been warped by the demands of war, transportation and communication facilities had been shattered, mines and factories had been laid waste, as had other huge areas whose production had helped to feed and clothe large populations.

Canada, fortunately, had been spared such damage, and now interest in things military was focused primarily on the return of the veterans and their absorption into civil life. For a short time a Canadian Occupation

Force remained in Europe, then it, too, was brought back and disbanded. Naval, air force, and army bases were declared surplus and closed down, warehouses bulged with arms and equipment, and immense amounts of military stores, vehicles, and ships were sold off.

Even while Canada was eagerly disbanding most of its military forces and disposing or dismantling most of the large infrastructure it had created to service them, there were those who felt that the nation should not, and indeed could not, return to its prewar state of pitiful military inadequacy. The development of new, more efficient, and more effective weapons made it obvious that the Atlantic and Pacific Oceans were no longer moats behind which Canada could live with her customary serenity. Between 1939 and 1945, for example, bomber aircraft had quadrupled the bomb load they could carry and doubled the range of operation. The air bridge across the Atlantic could carry traffic both ways. Moreover, something of future weaponry could be seen in the V-I and V-II rocket attacks on England in 1944 and 1945. Most impressive was the development of the atomic bomb which, almost overnight, brought a new dimension to warfare.

The importance of air power was stressed by Pearkes in his first talk on military affairs outside the House of Commons. In a speech in Toronto in November 1945 he discussed the possibility of a third world war and concluded that Canada might become the Belgium or Poland in such a conflict. "Invasion would be launched by air," he said, "with a great weight of bombs followed by . . . attacks from airborne troops." No longer could Canada be immune from attacks. "Our isolated approaches . . . are no longer a protection. Rather they provide secret approaches for the enemy." He suggested a need for changes in the nation's defence forces, and came out strongly for an effective intelligence service "which could provide warning of attack from seemingly friendly countries" as well as "unremitting research that will make surprise less likely."[2]

By the end of 1946, both internal and external events reinforced the decision to increase the size of the three services and to modify, in some degree, their structure. It was apparent that Canada could no longer count almost automatically on military assistance from Great Britain. It was also fairly obvious that Great Britain herself, strained by two major wars would no longer be able to maintain her former dominance. Canada would have to rely on the United States. At the same time, if it was to maintain its sovereignty, the nation would have to display its willingness to play the role of a junior partner and maintain a creditable defence force.

This need became all the more evident as interest shifted from the Nuremberg war criminals' trials to Communist attempts to reap a political harvest in Europe. Apprehension over Russian aims and successes was greatly increased in Canada, when, as a result of the defection of Igor Gouzenko from the Russian Embassy in Ottawa, the extent of Russian espionage was spread across the newspapers. When Pearkes had alluded to the possibility of war between two major powers in which Canada would be involved a few months earlier, he had Russia and the United States in mind.

By the end of 1946 it was decided to place the three armed services under the direction of one Minister of National Defence. The Honourable Brooke Claxton assumed this appointment in December of that year, and during most of the time when Pearkes served as the chief military critic of the Opposition, his shafts at the Liberals' defence policies were aimed at Claxton. Among the services, the army underwent the greatest changes in organization. The old "Permanent Militia" now became the Active Force of the Canadian Army, while the Non-Permanent Active Militia was renamed the Reserve Force. The old military districts were reorganized into commands and areas, and the greater number of civilian employees permitted all services to employ more military personnel in strictly military pursuits. The number of all ranks in each service was increased four to five times from its prewar figures, and each was to have a large reserve force with equipment and Active Force assistance on a scale undreamed of in the 1930's. Still, the total number in the Active Force was only 32,610. As to the role they would be expected to play, Claxton suggested the requirements would be:

1. to defend Canada against aggression;
2. to assist the civil power in maintaining law and order within the country;
3. to carry out any undertakings which by our own voluntary act we may assume in co-operation with friendly nations or under any effective plan of collective action under the United Nations.[3]

Pearkes spoke more frequently on military matters as time went on. His interest in a degree of integration of the three services was expressed as early as October 1945 when, in the debate on demobilization of the air services, he asked:

when we come to the administrative services of the army, the navy, and the air force, is there not an opportunity whereby the services, perhaps the medical, dental, pay or commissariat services, might not in some respects be combined.[4]

A measure of integration was one of his main themes. In the same speech

Pearkes, looking to the future, recommended "a careful study of jet propelled aircraft and of radio controlled aircraft." He added:

> it may be no more fantastic than other developments would have seemed a few years ago to suggest that the air forces of the future will be launched from subterranean runways and guided towards their objective without a single airman being on board or in the air.[5]

In this early period Pearkes touched upon other themes which he was to elaborate later. One was the creation of a committee to review Canada's military requirements, a committee composed of representatives from both civil and military life. The Industrial Defence Board was established a few years later, and a standing parliamentary committee on defence expenditure made its appearance in 1951. Pearkes had spoken strongly for placing the three services under one minister, and he also favoured strong forces-in-being since he felt there would no longer be time for comparatively leisurely mobilization.

Although 1946 and 1947 had given mounting evidence of Soviet intentions in Europe, events in the following two or three years made it seem obvious that Russia was embarked on a campaign to establish her hegemony over Europe and other parts of the world. One after the other the countries of Eastern Europe fell under Communist domination, while at the same time Russia, where she could, stripped the productive capacities of eastern Germany, Hungary, and other states. By 1948 the number of displaced persons who had fled from Communist control was nearing one million. Early in the same year the Communists seized control of Czechoslovakia by a coup d'état, and at about the same time, as a counter to the attempt to restore economic and political stability to western Germany, imposed a blockade on Berlin.

This series of events, accompanied by the harsh and repressive measures on religious and political freedom imposed by new Communist régimes, led Western European nations to consult to find means of uniting their collective strength. The strength of the conventional armed forces of what came to be termed the Western Allies was dangerously low, and among those who were compelled to review their state of preparedness was Canada. The reduced level of Canada's ability to contribute to the defence of the Western Allies gave Pearkes an opportunity to criticize Claxton. However, his criticism was on the whole constructive and, at times, helpful to Claxton himself. The two men got along well together, and Pearkes said later:

> I think Claxton was a very capable minister. He was energetic, he

knew what he wanted and went around visiting [military] establishments. He wasn't an orator at all [but] he answered questions. I liked
Claxton. I had to oppose him, of course, but we were good friends
actually. [He] was one of the best ministers we had. He got a lot done.
He built a lot of barracks and he was maintaining a defence force
which was more efficient than it has been ever since.[6]

Politically Pearkes had to suggest both in the House and out of it that
his party could and would perform better. If the army was small, one could
always say that it should be larger. If it was increased in size, then the
Opposition could say it should be more efficient or blame the minister for
its lack of heavy weaponry. If the navy built ships, the Opposition might
question their design, speed, or purpose. If, through some miracle, the
minister could present the soundest possible argument for having the
armed forces in the shape, size, location, and balance they were, then the
Opposition could always bring up a subject such as civil defence. "It was
quite fun being in Opposition," Pearkes reflected later, and added: "I said
a lot of things [in the House] which were ideals, a goal which Claxton
couldn't reach nor could I reach. We had to modify our desires and had to
change them."[7]

Opposing the government's programme merely for the sake of opposing
was not characteristic of Pearkes. Not infrequently he proposed changes in
defence matters which Claxton favoured but which he was finding difficult
to implement. It is always good politics if the government can undercut
the Opposition by adopting their policy ideas. If, for example, Pearkes was
demanding more money be spent on modern weaponry, and if Claxton at
the same time was trying to secure funds for the same purpose, then Claxton had, in essence, additional power to his voice in the cabinet.

As chief military spokesman, Pearkes spoke in the House not only for
himself but also for the party. Once the Conservative caucus defence committee was formed,

> it went about its own organization and its own tasks. The primary
> responsibility . . . was to take under consideration any bills introduced
> by the Minister and the departmental estimates, to discuss the matter,
> to make recommendations to caucus . . . and then to organize the
> debate in Parliament. The chairman . . . was responsible, for instance,
> for working up the list of speakers, submitting it to the Whip who in
> turn submitted it to the Speaker of the House. . . . it was his job to see
> that he and his committee worked out what aspect of the subject
> would be covered by what speakers.[8]

The number of veterans among the Conservative M.P.'s elected in 1945 meant that there was no lack of informed opinion. The party leader (in 1948), George Drew, was a veteran who held strong views on the value of the reserves, and Pearkes sometimes had to make more favourable reference to them than he felt necessary. Members of the committee such as Lawrence Skey (a former wing commander), Douglas Harkness (a former artillery officer), and Davie Fulton (a former company commander and staff officer) all contributed to the House debates on defence. Other party stalwarts such as George Hees (a former brigade major), Leon Balcer (a former naval officer), and the redoubtable Howard Green (a Great War veteran)—and these are only a few examples—all added to the variety of experience available to the Opposition.

Implicit in the debates on defence and Canada's role in a future conflict was the idea that the nation would be fighting in an alliance. Pearkes, like so many others, placed considerable hope in the United Nations, but his expectations began to wane as Russia used her veto power to negate joint action. Pearkes regretted the decline in stature and power of Great Britain and with it the loosening of the strong ties between the countries of the Commonwealth. In the two world wars men from the self-governing dominions fought side by side for common ideals. The comradeship welded in wartime, Pearkes felt, was slowly ebbing as the postwar problems weakened the wartime unity. Pearkes felt that whereas Canada had been "a strong dominion in a strong empire or commonwealth and in that way was able to exercise more influence," now that situation was changing and the new power base for the democracies was in the United States.

Unlike many native-born Canadians, however, Pearkes never saw the United States as a potential threat to Canadian sovereignty. This was probably owing to the long and very friendly relations he had with the American military authorities during the time he was G.O.C.-in-C. Pacific Command. Thus, despite his strong pro-British feelings, Pearkes faced with equanimity the fact that the United States now surpassed Britain on the world stage. Canada, like Western Europe, sheltered under the American nuclear shield. The shield covered the continent, and as he considered continental defence to be indivisible, Pearkes favoured close co-operation with and support of the United States whenever Canada's defence was debated in its wider aspect.

Thus, in the immediate postwar years Pearkes favoured the continuation of military co-operation between Canada and the United States. The Permanent Joint Board on Defence never stopped functioning, and early in 1947 Mackenzie King made the first official statement of a policy of joint defence co-operation. This co-operation envisaged an interchange of individuals to familiarize them with the defence establishment of the other country, the exchange of observers for exercises and development and tests of material, the encouragement of standardization of arms, equipment, armament, organization, and methods of training, and the mutual and reciprocal availability of military, naval, and air facilities in each country. In June of the same year the government introduced a bill authorizing U.S. forces in Canada to try their offenders before U.S. courts without recourse to Canadian law. Pearkes supported the measure and questioned only the anticipated size of the American forces which might be on Canadian soil.

The form of Canada's future military co-operation with either or both of its former senior allies was imposed by external events. As the ominous encroachments by Russia continued in Europe, encroachments which were matched in the Far East by Communist victories on mainland China, the democratic nations of Western Europe began to reforge the chain which had helped them contain and then overcome Nazi Germany. Talks between the Western nations had led initially to a reassessment of the military status and preparedness of the occupation forces. In mid-March 1948 a five-power treaty of mutual assistance was signed in Brussels by the United Kingdom, France, Belgium, the Netherlands, and Luxembourg. This treaty, designed to facilitate their collaboration in economic, social, and cultural matters and for collective self-defence, was widely acclaimed in the United States and Canada. In the following month, during a speech reviewing Canada's external affairs, Louis St. Laurent stated in the House:

> Our foreign policy must . . . be based on a recognition of the fact that totalitarian communist aggression endangers the freedom and peace of every democratic country, including Canada. On this basis and pending the strengthening of the United Nations, we should be willing to associate ourselves with other free states in any appropriate collective security arrangements which may be worked out under articles 51 or 52 of the charter.[9]

This statement by the Secretary of State for External Affairs was well received in Canada. In the United States the plan to participate with other nations to add weight to the defence of Western Europe was also gaining support. There is no need here to describe the various steps which led to the creation of the North Atlantic Treaty Organization. It is interesting, however, that Canada was an early and strong proponent, one which hoped to see NATO evolve with strong economic and cultural ties as well as with sufficient military power. The fact that Canada, with its history of apathy towards things military and its well-known mistrust of committing in advance its forces beyond its borders, agreed to participate also gives an indication of the mounting fear and feeling of insecurity.

Following the signing of the NATO treaty in April 1949, the various signatory powers prepared to implement its aims as soon as it had been ratified. These preparations were spurred by the announcement by President Truman that Russia had exploded a nuclear device. This unsettling news was followed by an even greater incentive to take action when in June 1950 the Communist forces of North Korea invaded the Republic of Korea and, within two days, had seized its capital and were thrusting south.

The war in Korea created an atmosphere of crisis in Canada and elsewhere. Expert opinion had held that Russia would pursue its policies by all means short of war. A deterrent force, such as that being planned by NATO, would show the U.S.S.R. that war was impracticable and unprofitable. With the outbreak of hostilities in Korea, many strategists felt that the need for a counterforce was immediate. Would Russia be willing to wait while the NATO countries built up armed forces, and, meanwhile, what was to be done in Korea?

In Ottawa, as in London, Washington, and elsewhere, the news of the Korean invasion came as a shock. In New York the Security Council, acting with unaccustomed speed and vigour in the absence of the Russian delegate, condemned the aggression and decided to establish a United Nations force to assist the South Koreans. Prime Minister St. Laurent and a number of his ministers were away from Ottawa that weekend, but when the cabinet met, it was decided to send three Canadian destroyers to assist U.N. naval forces en route to the theatre of operations. On 14 July the Secretary-General of the United Nations appealed to member states to render more effective assistance, especially ground forces. Despite the semi-isolationist editorials in many of the French-Canadian newspapers, the Canadian government decided to make available a squadron of long-range transport aircraft to the commander of the United Nations forces. Neither the naval vessels nor transport aircraft could be expected to have any bearing on the conflict, however, and in both Canada and the United States there was mounting criticism of Canada's limited contribution. Public pressure had its effect. Early in August, having called a special session of Parliament, St. Laurent announced his government's intention to raise a special force for service in Korea. Within a month almost thirteen thousand men had volunteered, of whom some eight thousand were accepted.

In 1948, well before the NATO treaty was signed, Pearkes was criticizing Claxton for implying that Canada was prepared to meet any emergency. He pointed to the limited number of men, the poor training of the under-strength reserve forces, and the changing situation in the world. "The government has consistently refused to recognize our changed position in the general make-up of the world organization for defence and the changed geographical position of Canada in view of the new inventions which have appeared on the defence scene in the last years," he said. Warming up to his subject, he added:

I do not believe it is likely that a push-button war could be initiated by any country in the immediate future. But I am equally convinced that countries may spring a strategic or tactical surprise which, without going to the length of push-button warfare, might find us in an extremely unfortunate position.[10]

He also stressed the need for a greater degree of efficiency and integration in the services. Pearkes welcomed the suggestion by St. Laurent in the previous month that there should be a single, mutual defence system including and superseding the Western Union Defence Organization. However, whereas Claxton felt that Canada should not join in any pact to help defend Western Europe unless the United States joined also, Pearkes felt that Canada should act on her own accord. "All I can say in that respect," he said, "is that it is a very good thing for Canada and a very good thing for this world that we did not wait for the United States in 1914 or in 1939."[11]

In June 1949, two months after Canada decided to join NATO, a federal election gave the Liberals a comfortable majority under St. Laurent. George Drew, the new Conservative leader, was both more dynamic and more aggressive than John Bracken, and also more interested in defence matters. When the treaty was debated in the House, all parties supported it, especially, perhaps, as they saw it as more than a strictly military alliance. It placed Canada in an alliance with both Great Britain and the United States, thus maintaining the traditional ties with the former while gaining the support without the complete dominance of the latter.

During the latter part of 1949, especially after the September announcement that Russia possessed the nuclear bomb, the Defence Minister did what he could to increase the strength of the armed forces, planned for the acquisition of new fighter aircraft for the R.C.A.F., and arranged for a greater measure of integration and administrative efficiency among all the services.[12] Pearkes and the Conservatives stressed that the nation could no longer depend upon a period of grace for reserve units to mobilize and train. The need was for a greater number of men in the services now. Primary attention, Pearkes felt, should be given to the R.C.A.F. "I consider that the lack of R.C.A.F. reserves is the weakest point in our whole defence armour." He went on to explain:

it is a well known principle of war that force is concentrated against the vital objectives at the right time. . . . If the U.S.S.R. are ever to achieve victory in the foreseeable future, they must strike at the United States. The time that they will decide to strike will be of their own choosing. It may be after the war has broken out for some time; it may be after they have lured American and Canadian forces from this continent on some major diversionary operation which is being conducted in Europe. . . .

On the other hand it is quite possible that they might decide to attack their strongest opponent, the strongest country of all the free nations, right at the commencement of the operations at a time they considered opportune. . . .

We should like to attack as far away from Canada as possible the enemy forces that are attacking us, but we may not have very much to say about that.[13]

The concept of Canada as a steel helmet protecting the United States was to remain basic to Pearkes's thinking on defence policy all during his parliamentary life. During this early period, when the obvious threat seemed to be from Soviet bombers, he stressed the need to provide the necessary complex of radar stations and modern interceptor squadrons which would be Canada's and the continent's first line of defence. Claxton appreciated his suggestions but pointed out the vast funds required to implement them.

In the spring of 1950, when the budget for the defence department was increased to $425 million, Pearkes was pleased to see that the R.C.A.F. was to get the lion's share, approximately $169 million, or an increase of $31 million. The R.C.N. was also to benefit considerably, but with both services much of the additional money would go towards the purchase of new weaponry. The cost of both modern aircraft and naval vessels was spiralling, and thus the increase in manpower was only modest. Moreover, the steady and sometimes startling technological and scientific advances in armaments were mainly features of the larger and more varied industrial nations. Thus, purchases were a considerable drain, and more effort was to be directed to obtaining an agreement with the United States to stimulate reciprocal armaments purchases.

Meanwhile, as summer approached, the Conservatives learned very little about possible Canadian defence commitments to NATO. Numerous meetings had been held, plans were being laid, and arrangements were being prepared to co-ordinate the various forces, but there was no statement regarding Canada's specific contributions other than a decision to increase facilities in Canada to train NATO air crew. Parliament adjourned a few days after the Republic of Korea was invaded, but was called into special session in August.

Pearkes was in Victoria when the invasion took place. He was among the thousands of people who watched the three destroyers move out from the naval base at Esquimalt en route to Korean waters. He applauded St. Laurent's decision later to offer a squadron of transport aircraft, but he criticized the government's initial reluctance to send ground troops. The inability of the government to provide trained men brought into focus a disagreement over manpower policies—that is, the question of compulsory military training.

Among those who were favouring some form of conscription as the Communist menace became more threatening in the late 1940's and early 1950's was General H. D. G. Crerar.[14] In an address to the Military Institute in Quebec in February 1949 he stressed that only the ability of Canada and the United States to move large, well-trained forces to Europe quickly would provide a worthwhile guarantee to the democracies facing Russia and her satellites. Russia had conscription for all three services and could mobilize a large, efficient force. This gave them a great advantage. Canada, he felt, should accept compulsory military training in peacetime if she was to make a worthwhile and creditable contribution. Crerar repeated his warning after the Korean conflict had broken out.[15] Another former officer also favoured at least a measure of conscription after the Korean War started, but in attempting to avoid the inevitable political implications, he suggested that it should not be imposed in Quebec.[16] Generally speaking, however, the Canadian public, tended to feel, like Lt.-Gen. E. L. M. Burns, that Russia would not commit her forces to aggression, fearing that it would provoke an atomic counterattack by the United States.

Pearkes felt the government should contribute troops to Korea, especially as the request came from the United States, a country "to whom we have been turning and so frequently mentioning in the last few years saying that we counted upon her to come to our help if we should be in trouble."[17] Unlike Crerar, the Canadian Legion, and others, he did not suggest conscription, but when Claxton announced the raising of a special force for service in Korea, he pointed out the difficulties which would arise when the small regular force attempted both to train this force and still to carry out its role of defending northern airfields. The airborne brigade itself, although "composed of magnificent units with long traditions," was not as efficient or as well trained as the minister would have the public believe. "No headquarters have been trained to command the various units," Pearkes declared. "There is no staff appointed. There is no signal section working with the units. Those units have never been brought together . . . to take part in any formation exercise."[18] He drew the attention of the

House to how open Canada was to an attack by a diversionary raid by airborne troops or raids from the sea. Although welcoming the government's proposals to build up and re-equip the services, he felt that Canada had been caught unawares and that the crisis was being handled by measures which should have been taken earlier.

The tremendous demands made on the regular army units to carry out their normal tasks and to recruit, equip, and train the men for Korea tended to throw into relief the deficiencies of the reserve forces. They had never reached the low ebb of the post-1918 years, but nevertheless the level of training of the non-veterans was not satisfactory. Drew, with his special interest in the reserves, hammered on this theme and Pearkes supported him. The climate of the times demanded more "forces-in-being," however, and Pearkes was more interested in increasing the size of the regulars.

One of the problems faced by the Conservatives, was the limited amount of military intelligence available. Improvements in armaments were growing rapidly year by year. Naturally the capabilities of these new systems were classified information, limited to a few people even in the Department of National Defence. It was, therefore, frequently difficult for the Opposition to make constructive criticisms of expenditures on defence. For some time Pearkes and others had been requesting standing committees, composed of persons from all parties, which could enquire more deeply into expenditures of the defence department, question senior officers, and inform themselves more completely. Pearkes had asked for such a standing committee as early as 1946, and almost every year thereafter he brought up the subject again. Eventually such a committee was formed. While it lasted, the Opposition used it to good effect.

When the special force for Korea had been raised and was in training, Pearkes's comments on the brigade group and its subsequent action tended to be uncritical. In January he visited the brigade training at Fort Lewis, Washington. He pointed out that if the enlarged Canadian forces which Claxton envisaged were to be trained at home, thought should be given immediately to securing a sufficiently large camp site to permit larger formations to train. Pearkes approved the type of training the men were receiving; in fact, on the platoon and company level he thought it was better than that given to American soldiers. Necessary as it was for Canada to send the force, Pearkes expressed the hope that the conflict in Korea would not turn into a "Spanish ulcer," a term used in Napoleonic days to describe the drain on the French army attempting to subdue Spain and Portugal. By the time the brigade group in training at Fort Lewis sailed for Korea in April 1951, however, Claxton had announced the government's plans to expand the armed forces to an unprecedented size and the outline of Canada's contribution to the NATO alliance.

The defence measures made public between February and May 1951 reflected the concern felt during the winter of 1950-51 when Chinese armed forces joined those of North Korea to make another striking advance down the Korean peninsula beyond the thirty-eighth parallel. Early in February Claxton stated the country's defence objectives. There was to be a large buildup of every service with new equipment. A civil defence system was to be organized, a Department of Defence Production created, and NATO allies supplied with masses of equipment. Later he added that some six thousand troops would be placed under General Eisenhower, the Supreme Allied Commander, Europe, of the NATO forces, along with eleven squadrons of aircraft, mainly Sabres. Special emphasis was to be placed on the manufacture of modern jet fighter aircraft in Canada. In a projected three-year programme the strength of the armed forces was to be increased to one hundred and fifteen thousand. The $5 billion to be spent on defences between 1951 and 1954 would permit not only the increase in strength and new equipment for the army and air force, but also the increase of the navy's antisubmarine fleet from forty to one hundred ships. Early in May Claxton gave further details regarding a third Active Force brigade, which would be Canada's contribution to NATO's land forces.

There was much in the government's programme to commend itself to the Conservatives. For years they had been suggesting that the services should be strengthened and re-equipped. Pearkes was "encouraged to hear the Minister admit that . . . [a danger from Russian bombers existed] and that he places as the number one requisite for our defence forces the need of protecting the cities of this country against such raids."[19] He had frequently brought up the need for more and better fighter aircraft based far to the north and linked with radar stations. The lack of protection afforded to some of the major civilian airfields, such as Whitehorse, had not passed his notice, and originally he feared a sudden descent upon such potential bases for refuelling enemy bombers.

When technological advances made it possible for enemy bombers to refuel in the air, the time available for warning of an impending air strike was lessened. Radar stations and fighter squadrons defending the north retained their value, but civil defence became more important. Pearkes had drawn the need for civil defence measures to the attention of the government early in 1948. Later, in October, Claxton had appointed Maj.-Gen. F. F. Worthington as the Co-ordinator of Civil Defence. Worthington had made some progress in the two and a half years since his appointment, but his budget was small, his staff limited, and his work confined mainly to planning, co-ordinating the efforts of volunteers on the municipal level with provincial and federal staffs, preparing films, pamphlets, and other material for instruction, and, more latterly, organizing a school at Arnprior. Pearkes had brought the subject up several times in 1949 as the international situation deteriorated. As the stockpile of nuclear bombs increased, it became obvious that if the United States and Russia became involved in war, it was almost inevitable that the air war would be fought in part over Canadian territory.[20] Thus, when Claxton announced early in February 1951 his intention to improve Canada's civil defence, Pearkes agreed wholeheartedly but suggested the organization might be placed under a less burdened minister. Later that month the responsibility for civil defence was given to the Department of Health and Welfare, where it was to remain for the next half dozen years.

Pearkes's main interest in the early 1950's centred upon Canada's NATO commitments. In December 1951 he made his first trip to Europe since 1942 to attend the sixth session of the General Assembly of the United Nations as a parliamentary observer. He acted in the same capacity at the Consultative Assembly of the Council of Europe. During this time he watched the 27th Canadian Infantry Brigade Group arrive to take its place in the NATO forces with the British Army of the Rhine. Later he visited bases in Germany where the army and air force units were stationed as well as Berlin and a number of major German cities.

Pearkes had favoured the formation of the 27th Brigade Group, although he had earlier suggested that an "air mobile" or specialist brigade might be better. He hoped that this third brigade, and indeed the enlargement of the three services, would bring with it a drive to recruit more officer cadets at the universities, more standardization of arms among the North Atlantic powers, and more unification among the three services. After his visit to Europe, however, he began to question the type of brigade Canada should send over. In 1952 Pearkes expressed his views about the brigade.

> I could not help but be impressed by what seemed to me hindsight, if you like, as being the unsuitability of the composition of our contingent . . . for instead of supplying a very mobile, fast-moving, hard-hitting formation of armoured and technical units, we had dispatched a formation built around three infantry regiments. This Canadian infantry brigade would operate, should war break out, in the great plain of Central Europe . . . a territory flatter than our western prairies traversed by great strategic highways and intersected by innumerable crossroads.[21]

Pearkes did not think it was best for Canada to send an ordinary infantry brigade, especially as Europe had a great reserve of manpower. He felt that a comparatively small force, equipped with new and superior weapons, could change the course of a battle or an entire campaign and stressed that "the importance of our contribution to N.A.T.O. [should be] that of a mobile and thoroughly modern organization." Pearkes could appreciate the value of Canadian troops serving in Europe, the training they would get with larger formations, the chance of going on manoeuvres with allied brigades and divisions, the measure of defence their presence would give to European diplomats, and the added attraction the chance to serve overseas would give to recruiting. However, against this was the cost of transporting the brigade to Europe, the additional costs of providing for their maintenance and supply, the expense of sending over soldiers' families, and the rotation every two years or so of the brigade. Thus, if a brigade was to serve overseas, surely it should be a very special one.

Pearkes, incidentally, was not among those who feared a rearmed Germany. Germany had had no army for seven years, he noted, and it would take some time before a reorganized German Army would be ready to take the field. "Personally," he added, "I feel that the immediate danger of the next two or three years, so far as the possibility of a Russian advance through Europe is concerned, outweighs for the time being at least the dangers which might be foreseen in the creation of a German army."[22]

Two and a half years later Pearkes spoke out in favour of German rearmament. By this time Russia's arsenal of atomic weapons had been greatly increased, and there was considerable pressure by the senior officers of NATO to secure more conventional ground forces. German rearmament, even ten years after the war, was still a matter of very serious apprehension. Pearkes's remarks in the House, as he admitted, savoured "somewhat of a military appreciation," but they are indicative of the way he approached a problem.

To Pearkes the concept of a neutral and defenceless Germany did not make sense. Now that the Russians had a stockpile of atomic weapons, would they be more willing to use them? Pearkes did not think so. However, he explained,

> The large Soviet forces with more or less conventional arms . . . constitute a threat if we do not possess a deterrent and I do not see how we can rely solely upon a weapon such as the H-bomb which quite possibly we might never dare to use. We are, therefore, obliged to provide ourselves with the means of defeating with conventional arms as well as retaining the power to retaliate against thermo-nuclear attack.[23]

Western Europe could not be defended without including the territory of West Germany. "It . . . surely makes sense for us to defend West German territory," he said, "and to have that defence provided with, rather than without, the assistance of West German manpower."

Pearkes appreciated the apprehension felt by those who, directly or indirectly, had suffered from the results of German militarism. He pointed out, however, that the German divisions would be under the command of NATO's supreme commander, that the Federal Republic's democratic government seemed firmly established, and that the Nazi spirit had been stamped out. "I have to be realistic," he concluded. "I am not elated at the prospect of seeing this field gray army once again in existence, but if the participation of Germany in the Western European union will make that system effective, I am prepared to accept the risks."

Despite his long association with the army, Pearkes considered the air force to be Canada's first line of defence. In 1949 he suggested that there should be three dollars spent on the air force for every one dollar spent on the army. He felt the R.C.A.F. was especially deficient in aircraft suitable for fighting in the far north and in transport planes for carrying the airborne brigade. The R.C.A.F. never did have sufficient aircraft to carry all three battalions of the airborne brigade simultaneously, and the demands of Korea and NATO ultimately made such inroads into the formation that the question became academic.

The government's promise to provide an air division for NATO coupled with the huge gaps in Canada's own air defence, gave Pearkes cause for concern. He considered the greatest attribute of the R.C.A.F to be its flexibility. He questioned whether any excessive commitment of the air force to Europe might not find Canada "once again shackled to continental and land-bound operations."[24] He favoured a periodic review of the policy of despatching jet fighter squadrons to Europe. Moreover, he doubted whether it would be wise to send over the first twelve squadrons Canada raised. In 1953 he again stressed that most of the R.C.A.F.'s operational squadrons were in Europe. Speaking in April on the need for Arctic air defences, he noted that there were in Canada one squadron of CF-100's, three squadrons of Sabre jets earmarked for NATO, and nine auxiliary fighter squadrons equipped with Second World War Mustangs or worn out Vampires. The auxiliary squadrons were certainly not sufficiently equipped to support the government's claim to possess the means to repel an air attack. He suggested that, with almost half the defence budget going to the air force, the proposal for an associate minister of national defence might be amended to provide for an associate minister for air. This would permit special attention to be given to the R.C.A.F. without over-burdening the minister, for, as Pearkes noted, there were not only aircraft to consider, but "there is the vast field of guided missiles . . . which must be explored and developed."[25]

During the next four years the Conservatives continued to stress the need for a sound air defence and a balance among the three services. "The time has not yet come when war can be won solely by air power," Pearkes said late in 1953,[26] but he urged Claxton not to lose sight of the need for Canadian air defence. He suggested Canada should have available not only modern interceptor aircraft, but also air-to-air and ground-to-air guided missiles, all backed by a modern warning system. But he appreciated Claxton's difficulties. With defence planning at the crossroads, Pearkes in 1954 could only advise that the forces be kept flexible, efficient, and up-to-date.

Pearkes made a significant speech on air power in June 1955. The new minister, Ralph Campney,[27] had said that the government intended to place more emphasis on continental defence. Referring to the recent "White Paper" on defence, he also indicated that, in co-operation with the United States, Canada was providing "additional warning networks and increasingly effective and co-ordinated air defence forces on this continent."[28] Pearkes thoroughly agreed with this policy and added:

> We believe that Canada is making a contribution to NATO by taking part in the joint defence of this North American continent. . . . We are not a country which can provide all the defences required. . . . But we do want to pay our fair share. . . . We cherish certain sovereign rights . . . although we recognize as a fact that to a certain extent sovereignty must be surrendered in order to play our part in . . . continental defence.[29]

Canada did not have, nor could she afford, fleets of bombers such as the Americans had in Strategic Air Command as a retaliatory threat, nor did she possess nuclear warheads. Her contribution had to be in the provision of the most modern interceptor fighters, and even in this area Pearkes felt that "Canada cannot produce all these air forces."

The idea of indivisibility of continental defence, the need to assist in the defence of the United States, and the consequent recognition that this entailed some surrender of Canadian sovereignty was firmly entrenched in Pearkes's mind by the mid-1950's. He preferred that, wherever possible, Canadians should man installations on Canadian territory which were then in whole or in part being manned by American military forces. However, if these installations were vital to continental defence and if Canadians were as yet unable to provide the skilled manpower to carry out the task, then he saw no reason not to accept their aid with gratitude.[30]

Pearkes did not have as strong views about the navy as he did about either the army or air force. Following the war, the Royal Canadian Navy was greatly reduced and most of its ships either sold or laid up. By 1948 the navy's strength was about seven thousand all ranks. After the formation of NATO and the war in Korea, the navy's manpower ceiling was doubled, but for most of the 1950's, the senior service received only 15 to 20 per cent of the defence dollar. Although the percentage was small, the tremendous increase in the budget did permit the navy to expand and engage in constructing new ships. The Canadian navy's role in NATO was a continuation of her primary role during the Second World War, that is, anti-submarine warfare.

The concern of Pearkes was whether or not the reserve ships which the navy placed into active service were capable of performing their tasks. The rapid advances being made both in submarines and the torpedoes they carried were making it more difficult for even the new surface vessels to detect and destroy them. Moreover, the cost of refitting the older ships and of building the new ones was spiralling. As Claxton admitted in 1954:

Our anti-submarine escort vessel is designed . . . to be able to hunt . . . high-speed submarines. On that account it must have the very expensive characteristics of great speed, lack of vibration, low noise level, non-magnetic features and the like as well as a very full set of electronic and electrical equipment.[31]

These engineering problems added to the delay in the government's naval programme and provided ammunition for the Opposition. Pearkes stressed the need for better anti-submarine hunting teams and for a second aircraft carrier on the Pacific Coast. He felt such a vessel would bring considerable benefits to his constituency. More especially, owing to the limited number of service airfields on the Pacific, it could help keep watch on the Pacific approaches, assist the navy in its anti-submarine work, and generally help fill the gap of the continental defences between Alaska and continental America.[32] Although the concept of anti-submarine warfare had suggested almost automatically the idea of keeping the sea lanes clear for commercial shipping on the high seas during wartime, by the mid-1950's Pearkes began to speak about the changing role of submarines. "Modern submarines," he noted, "can come within a reasonable distance [of our shores] and from those submarines can be launched missiles or even aircraft."[33] To improve the means of locating the submarines, "the fullest possible use of reconnaissance planes and helicopters working with the fleet air arm" should be considered.

The changes both in the balance among world powers and in the means of exercising military power in the decade after the war made it extremely difficult for any nation to plot a firm course in defence matters. During this decade Pearkes's opinion on some matters changed. Some of his ideas, however, seemed to grow stronger over the years. He continued to favour the regular over the reserve forces. He did not feel that, in any major war, there would be enough time available to bring the reserves up to a state of efficiency sufficient for them to be committed to battle. This did not mean that the reserves should be eliminated, as some extremists thought. They had their value as reinforcements provided their training was improved.

He also believed that civil defence was being neglected. In 1955 he said:

> I think that the armed forces must play an increasing role in civil defence and that you cannot divorce civil defence entirely from the rest of the defence of the country. I believe that part of the training of all regular personnel and of all reserve and auxiliary personnel should be in civil defence duties as well as military training.[34]

In this era aircraft carrying nuclear bombs were still the most dangerous weapon. Pearkes felt, as did many others, that no power would resort to thermonuclear warfare except under the most extreme provocation. The knowledge that any attack on the United States would bring about inevitable retaliation in kind resulted in an almost complete trust in the value of deterrence. But the deterrence must be able to function. An air attack on North America would permit at least some degree of warning, sufficient to enable some civil defence measures to be taken. If these were to be even partially efficient, an organization had to be in readiness, and Pearkes felt the best organization must include the armed forces.

This concern to maintain the deterrence which preserved the peace, that is, to maintain the ability of the United States to retaliate against a nuclear attack, led Pearkes to reiterate the importance of Canada's role in continental air defence. Pearkes and his party had welcomed NATO and appreciated its demands on Canada's armed strength, but Pearkes never forgot where the citadel of defence was located—and that was south of the border.

In the summer of 1956 and in the spring of 1957, Pearkes made major speeches in the House of Commons which summarize his ideas on defence prior to his leaving his role in the Opposition. He saw the armed forces as having four major roles. The first was to join with other NATO powers in contributing to the deterrent. "We have got to make it very clear to any would-be enemy that it is not worth that would-be enemy's time to consider the possibility of launching a war." Another role was to shoulder its share of the burden in the cold war by contributing to the support of Canada's allies by means of mutual aid, continuing the air crew training scheme, and similar measures. A third role Pearkes suggested was to be able to play a part, under United Nations auspices, in helping to combat "bush fire" wars or wars of a limited scope such as the conflict in Korea.[35] Finally he said that Canada must be prepared "for the war of survival if all our efforts to deter the enemy should fail."

Early in 1957 Pearkes returned to his theme of deterring the enemy. "At the present time," he said on 30 March, "we can only insure peace through strength and I think we must adhere to that axiom just as much as we adhere to our desire for peace." As far as he could see, there appeared "to be very little change in the overall desire of the Russians to achieve the objective which they set out many years ago."[36] Recent reductions in the numbers of men in the Russian forces were more than made up for by additional firepower. Moreover, there had been recent reductions in the NATO lineup, with France withdrawing troops to meet the crisis facing her in North Africa and Britain reducing her force from seventy thousand to fifty thousand men. If the NATO forces continued to be weakened, Pearkes warned that Russia might be tempted to move through Europe in the first instance rather than initiating a war by a nuclear strike at the United States. Under these circumstances, it seemed that the Western powers had no option but to maintain conventional weapons as well as nuclear deterrents. "There are so many things the forces need now that we are entering upon an atomic era," he said, and continued:

> Field Marshal Montgomery said last October that in his opinion fifty per cent of all strategic tasks would be performed by missiles in less than ten years, and about 75 per cent of the present type of aircraft used for the support of land armies will have been replaced by nuclear weapons in the hands of land forces. Some of these weapons now urgently required are short-range missiles, guns and howitzers with small atomic heads. There is also the whole field of guided missiles, vertical take-off aircraft, etc., weapons which science has developed and is rapidly making available for those who would use them.[37]

Several weeks after this speech, Prime Minister Louis St. Laurent announced there would be an election on 10 June. Public opinion polls showed that 47 per cent of the electorate favoured the Liberals as against only 32 per cent for the Progressive Conservatives. After twenty-two years in office the Liberals could call a great many accomplishments to the notice of the public. However, many Canadians were dissatisfied with the Liberal government for a variety of reasons. For example, Walter Harris, the Minister of Finance, had recently granted a meagre six-dollar increase to old age pensioners and had been promptly labelled "six-buck Harris." In Pearkes's riding, where there were a large number of pensioners, it was good ammunition. Charges of arrogance and complacency in the Liberal government were common, and C. D. Howe's autocratic and seemingly dictatorial attitude in the House were used to good effect. Prairie farmers were annoyed at the government's failure to advance money on stored-up grain, while in the Maritimes there was an underswell of resentment about lack of economic growth. Many people, including a large proportion of people in Pearkes's riding, were disenchanted with the government's stand on the Suez crisis of the previous year, and some of St. Laurent's remarks were interpreted as being almost anti-British.

In his own riding, Pearkes was opposed by Alistair Fraser, a thirty-four-year-old former executive assistant to the Liberal Minister of Fisheries, James Sinclair. The Social Credit party's candidate was Noel Bell, a former New Zealander who had emigrated five years earlier. The C.C.F. candidate was Dr. J. M. Thomas, who campaigned against Pearkes in 1945. They were all good men, but Pearkes, who showed little sign of his sixty-nine years, had a record of service to his riding which was hard to criticize. The new party leader, John Diefenbaker, was campaigning all across Canada, and every week, as his audience grew larger, it became more apparent that the campaign was becoming a crusade. In British Columbia so many came to hear him speak at the political rallies that they could not get inside the halls. His oratory and indeed his entire presentation of the Conservative appeal captured the imagination of tens of thousands, and his indictment of the Liberal government convinced even more people that it was time for a change.

The voting on 10 June 1957 was one of the heaviest in Canada's history, and the Progressive Conservatives were swept into power. In Esquimalt-Saanich, one of the last ridings in the country to announce the results, Pearkes gathered more support than ever before; for the second time in a row his opponents lost their deposits. But his personal victory was made all the more pleasant by the results from Eastern Canada and then the Prairie provinces during the early evening. Liberal losses were severe. Nine Liberal cabinet ministers were not re-elected, and many former "safe" Liberal seats were captured. In British Columbia the electors voted in seven Progressive Conservatives, seven from the C.C.F., six Social Crediters and only two Liberals. On the national scene, the Conservatives captured 112 seats to the Liberals' 106, despite the fact that the Liberals received slightly more of the popular vote. The C.C.F. gained 25 seats, Social Credit, 19, and there were 3 independents. Four days after the election St. Laurent met Diefenbaker, and following the tabulation of the vote from the armed services, when it was made evident that there would be no change in the number of seats, St. Laurent prepared to hand over the reins of power. Meanwhile, John Diefenbaker was selecting the members of his cabinet. One of the first persons he called to Ottawa was George Pearkes, whom he asked to serve as his Minister of Defence.[38]

15

Minister of National Defence

The days following the June 1957 election were among the most exciting George Pearkes had experienced for many years. There was the anxious waiting for the services vote to be counted, the concern over whether St. Laurent would resign in the face of the Conservatives' small majority, and the need to form a government, if called upon, which would confirm the party's election claim that it had both the ability and men to guide Canada. Pearkes saw Diefenbaker daily during this tense period, and it is safe to assume that he was a sounding board as the party leader prepared his list of cabinet ministers.

The changeover in government took place in a simple but moving ceremony on the twenty-first. Within minutes of St. Laurent and his cabinet handing their seals of office to Vincent Massey at Government House, Diefenbaker and his colleagues arrived to receive them. An hour later the new cabinet members were en route back to their offices, ready to attend their first cabinet meeting.

The change from being a member of Parliament in Opposition to his appointment as Minister of Defence brought certain benefits as well as vast responsibility. Pearkes had an increase in salary and expense allowances from $12,000 to $27,000, together with certain perquisites, such as an army car and driver for official use, a modest expense account, a large but by no means luxurious office in the defence department as well as one in the Parliament Buildings, and certain other privileges. In return he was given the responsibility for a budget of about $1.7 billion, an armed force of some one hundred and twenty thousand officers and men, and a departmental civil service of a little over fifty thousand. Added to this, of course, were the large resources of his department, which ranged from the army brigade and R.C.A.F. squadrons in Europe through the Distant Early

Warning (DEW) stations in the Arctic to the naval ships in the Pacific. Scattered even further afield were Canadian troops with the United Nations Emergency Force in Egypt, military observer teams in Kashmir, and a handful of Canadians serving with the International Control Commission in Indochina. In all, the immense department consumed approximately one-third of the total national budget, an amount which was a constant worry for the Minister of Finance, Donald Fleming, and a steady target for others.

It now became necessary for Pearkes to establish himself in Ottawa, and Mrs. Pearkes decided to join him. During this period, therefore, he made a quick trip to Victoria to tend to domestic details. Shortly he had to fly back and move into his new offices, meet his Deputy Minister, Frank R. Miller, confer with his senior civilian officials, and be briefed by the Chairman of the Chiefs of Staff and the chiefs themselves.[1] Here, for the first time, he received a briefing on Canada's defence posture, secret information regarding Canada's commitments to NATO, and an outline of all up-to-date information covering such subjects as troop dispositions, warning lines, weapons being developed, and intelligence reports.

Pearkes would have liked to delve deeper into the department's past plans and present capabilities, but for the moment it had to be deferred. A meeting of the Commonwealth prime ministers had been called, and he was to accompany the Prime Minister to London a few days after being sworn in to office. Gen. Foulkes, whose task it was to brief the new minister, had only the shortest time to prepare the position papers and discuss with Pearkes Canada's military affairs. At the same time there were several problems requiring decisions by the government when the conference in London was over. On 23 June, the Prime Minister and Pearkes, accompanied by a small group of advisers, left Uplands Airport for London.

At the meeting Pearkes had the opportunity to become acquainted with most of the leaders of the Commonwealth both during the sessions held at No. 10 Downing Street and, more informally, at the social functions held in their honour at Windsor Castle[2] and elsewhere. Around the long table, presided over by Harold Macmillan, were the prime ministers of the old dominions, as well as those who had been elected to high office in recently independent states such as Pakistan, Ghana, and Ceylon. The open discussions and the candid expression of conflicting views when they occurred made it, for Pearkes, one of the friendliest meetings he was to attend as minister. There was, as he expressed it later, "a good feeling" at the conference, with a sympathy and understanding among those attending which made him feel that the Commonwealth, despite the divergent interests of its parts, could still play an important role in world affairs.

Although there was no aspect of Canadian defence policy planned in Commonwealth terms, Canada and Great Britain were partners in NATO.

Moreover, Canada's geographic position made her role vis-à-vis North American continental defence of more than passing interest. Both Diefenbaker and Pearkes favoured close co-operation with the Commonwealth wherever possible. Canada saw no change in Russia's attitude and expressed the view that, although efforts should be made towards disarmament and the cessation of atomic tests, no consideration could be given to a significant reduction in her armed forces. Pearkes pointed out that Canada was spending a large amount of money to build and maintain the warning system and other defences of the nuclear retaliatory forces. This heavy burden he felt necessary since the United States was the bastion of the NATO countries. This additional cost, however, would not lead to a withdrawal of Canadian troops serving with the United Nations Emergency Force on the Egyptian-Israeli border.[3] Presumably Pearkes and Diefenbaker also assured their colleagues that Canada would continue to favour Commonwealth and NATO countries in the openings in military and technical training facilities in this country.

Britain's defence posture was given close attention by all the delegates, for not only did she have the strongest forces, but also her interests, if no longer imperial, were worldwide. Pearkes was aware that, owing to Britain's need to conserve foreign exchange, her commitments overseas, and the steadily increasing cost of maintaining forces, she wished to reduce her troops in Europe, but he also realized that this was a NATO rather than a Commonwealth matter and steered clear of questions. Duncan Sandys, with whom Pearkes was soon to be on intimate terms, gave an excellent résumé of the scope of Britain's commitments and something of the plans she had to improve her weaponry while molding her army into a compact, mobile, all regular force. The latter especially interested Pearkes as he stressed the importance of "forces-in-being" for the Canadian Army.

During the course of the meeting Pearkes, who had made a two-day flying visit to the Canadian NATO army brigade group and the R.C.A.F. No. 1 Air Division in Germany and France, made a brief trip to the Netherlands. There he represented the Prime Minister when Prince Bernhard officially opened the new Canadian Embassy in the Hague. Perhaps the most interesting social gathering Pearkes attended was the dinner given by the British Prime Minister at his Downing Street residence on 2 July. Here, for the first time since he had had his brigade on manoeuvres early in 1940, he had an opportunity to chat briefly with Sir Winston Churchill. The old warrior was visibly aging, but his zest for life and interest in the Empire and Commonwealth were very evident.

By 5 July the Canadian delegates were en route home, and on the following afternoon in Ottawa the Prime Minister gave a résumé of their trip to London, and Pearkes reported briefly on his visit to the Canadian forces. By the seventh, Pearkes was in his office, meeting with his staff and, among other things, making arrangements to accommodate his new executive assistant and private secretary. For the former position Pearkes chose one of the masters at Shawnigan Lake School. Larsen had been active politically, he knew the riding, and, as his new responsibilities would not permit him to give his constituents as much attention as before, Pearkes felt Larsen would be suitable. As it turned out, Larsen left before he completed a full year. His place was taken by Richard H. N. Roberts, whom Pearkes met in London when he visited Defence Liaison Staff.

At that time Roberts was doing graduate work at the London School of Economics. As a lieutenant in the naval reserve working part time with the Defence Liaison Staff he had met Pearkes, mentioned casually that he knew his son John, at U.B.C., and soon found that the new minister was asking him a number of probing questions. Soon afterwards Pearkes offered him the post of private secretary. When he became executive assistant Roberts was only twenty-six and lacking the patina of experience which would have been valuable to a new minister.

Among the major problems facing Pearkes when he became minister was the question of the integrated air defence of Canada and the United States. It was first brought to his notice when he was briefed prior to his leaving for London, and to understand the decision reached by Pearkes, something of the background of the question might be given here.

The wartime military co-operation between Canada and the United States had not withered away. Among the instruments which were maintained was the Permanent Joint Board on Defence which met four times yearly as an advisory body to both governments. One of the new postwar committees to be formed was the Military Co-operation Committee (1946), which as early as 1949 prepared a plan for emergency defence that outlined the major joint actions necessary and principles of common defence operations. Early in 1954 the appearance of high-performance Soviet jet bombers stimulated more need for integrated planning. Later that year, a combined air defence planning group, located at Colorado Springs, was directed to prepare a plan for the best single air defence of the two countries. The group's plan envisaged a combined defence, with forces of both countries operating under a single commander responsible to both countries.[4]

In December 1955 the Joint Chiefs of Staff in Washington approved in principle the need for peacetime integration of the two air defence forces. The Canadian Chiefs of Staff expressed interest, and a Canadian-American Military Study Group was formed to consider methods of uniting operational control. By the end of 1956 their report recommending air defence integration had been completed. In February 1957 the American Joint Chiefs of Staff approved the report, providing that integration of operational control be limited to the continental elements of air defence. The U.S.

Secretary of Defense, Charles E. Wilson, gave his approval shortly thereafter. In April the Canadian Chiefs of Staff recorded their agreement and
put the matter up for governmental approval. Then the election was called.

Gen. Charles Foulkes, the Chairman of the Chiefs of Staff, briefed
Pearkes on the background of the proposal during that busy day before he
left for London. Foulkes gave his minister written reports on several
defence matters which he urged Pearkes to read and discuss with Diefenbaker during their flight. Until this time, Foulkes recalled later, the
proposed plan had been progressing favourably towards a political settlement. "On the 15th of February, 1957," he added,

> it was discussed and agreed to on the level of the Chiefs of Staff,
> including a representative of External Affairs who happened to be
> Ronnie Macdonnell . . . and the Clerk of the Privy Council, R. B.
> Bryce. In the Chiefs of Staff Committee we always included the Clerk
> of the Privy Council and the Undersecretary [of State] for External
> Affairs because there is such a close link between military matters and
> external affairs. And Bryce, as the Secretary of the Cabinet . . . is the
> man responsible for putting all these things to the government . . . we
> always had him in to ensure that he would give us advice as to the best
> way it could be put up . . . for approval.
>
> The next step was to prepare . . . a submission to cabinet defence
> committee. This was prepared, Mr. Campney signed it and I then
> called . . . Bryce. . . . He informed me that the Prime Minister was so
> busy he doubted whether we would get a date. . . .
>
> On the 15th of March I prepared . . . copies of the cabinet defence
> paper [on air defence integration] which was approved by Campney
> and it went to Bryce for distribution. He actually went as far as get-
> ting it into his office ready for distribution when the Prime Minister
> called me in with Campney. . . . "Well," he said to Campney, "we're
> coming back [into office] aren't we, and then we'll deal with this." And
> he said to me: "General, is that going to upset you?" "Well," I said,
> "the only thing that worries me is that the United States Chiefs of
> Staff have approved this and I am expecting to hear any day that their
> Secretary of Defence has approved it."[5]

Foulkes himself was not only behind the proposal, but he was also appre-
hensive lest there be a leak in Washington before the matter was decided
upon in Ottawa. However, there was nothing Foulkes could do for the
moment except to explain to Admiral A. W. Radford[6] the delay caused

by St. Laurent's unwillingness to deal with it in cabinet prior to knowing the election results and promising to re-submit the proposal to the new government. On Pearkes's return from London, Foulkes was told that the matter had been taken up with the Prime Minister who gave his tentative approval. Foulkes was most anxious to get a decision and, with Pearkes's consent, asked Bryce to get the Prime Minister's approval to discuss it at an early meeting of the cabinet defence committee. Despite his attempt to do so, Bryce was unsuccessful, adding that Diefenbaker felt that the Conservative government could perform its duties expeditiously without the assistance of committees or prompting of Liberal public servants and General Foulkes.[7] Foulkes, somewhat surprised, saw Pearkes later, told him about the telephone conversation, and gave the minister the key paper relating to proposed agreement for what was called the North Atlantic Air Defence Command (NORAD). "That afternoon," Foulkes continued, "Pearkes took the paper with him... up to the Prime Minister's office and he came back about an hour afterward and walked into my office, threw it onto my desk and said, 'There it is, approved.' I was stunned."[8]

There is little doubt that Foulkes exercised all the influence he had, which was considerable, to convince Pearkes that the NORAD plan was a good one. He laid heavy emphasis on the possibility of a leak in Washington, and certainly he stressed the need for haste without dwelling on possible political repercussions. He indicated to Pearkes that Campney had approved the scheme, and very likely Pearkes felt that, since the scheme had progressed as far as it had with Campney's blessing, the Liberals in Opposition would have little to say should the Conservatives continue what was apparently their course of action.

Pearkes, of course, had known Foulkes for several decades. They had been in the permanent force together, and Foulkes had been a staff officer in the 1st Division overseas. Although Foulkes felt that the Prime Minister was suspicious of him owing to his close friendship with Lester Pearson, Pearkes trusted him as he would one of his staff officers. "I relied very largely on him," he said later, "I think that he was loyal to me all the way through."[9] Moreover, in the department at this time there were no advisers to the minister outside the Chiefs of Staff, and Pearkes was content that they were eminently suitable. "I didn't believe in going out and getting other advice," he related. "It would not have seemed loyal to the Chiefs of Staff if I had gone out and tried to get a few other people, more junior officers, to come. I thought it was up to the Chiefs of Staff to get . . . ideas and pass them on."[10] He would have liked to have more time "to have sat down in a retreat and thought out some of the problems," but "the demand of cabinet meetings and House of Commons work was so great that one didn't have all that time. It was a continual rush and Diefenbaker liked to have his cabinet about him."[11] Pearkes expected loyalty from his Chiefs of Staff, and in turn he felt he should be loyal to them. The ideas he had he put to them for consideration and asked their advice. Sometimes it became necessary politically to disagree with them, and he would say so. At other times he would receive conflicting advice based on honest differences of opinion, and he then weighed the matter and handed down his decision.

Some writers have suggested that he was dominated by his Chiefs of Staff and their chairman. It is probably closer to the truth that very frequently he agreed with their conclusions. The plan for NORAD not only made sense militarily, it was something which he had been advocating strongly himself since 1955. "I always felt," he said, "as I've said time and time again, that the defence of the North American continent was indivisible. You couldn't divide it into Canadian responsibility and an American responsibility. . . . I had no qualms about NORAD . . . and I don't think there was any surrender of sovereignty."[12]

Since he was in full agreement with Foulkes's proposal, Pearkes took action. He had never worked with a cabinet defence committee, and obviously the Prime Minister, who would normally chair the committee, had neither the time nor the inclination to attend one. So Pearkes went to the Prime Minister's office to discuss the matter. At this time Diefenbaker was also Secretary of State for External Affairs.[13] The meeting of Pearkes and Diefenbaker, therefore, represented a meeting of three of the usual four ministers at a cabinet defence committee. The Prime Minister agreed to the proposal for an integrated air defence command after consulting with a senior member of the Department of External Affairs. Pearkes then returned with the document to Foulkes.

Shortly thereafter the American ambassador called upon the Department of External Affairs to suggest that, prior to the joint announcement of the approval of NORAD, a joint communication should be sent to NATO headquarters. Unfortunately, he came at an inopportune time. The Undersecretary, Jules Léger, was absent owing to serious illness in the family. Ronald M. Macdonnell, the Deputy Undersecretary, who had sat in as an invited member of the Chiefs of Staff Committee and was familiar with the background of the negotiations, had just left for Cairo to take over the Canadian ambassadorship left vacant by the tragic death of Herbert Norman. This left John W. Holmes, the Assistant Undersecretary, who was aware of the negotiations but unfamiliar with the details. As he wrote later:

As Acting Under-Secretary I would certainly have been briefed if the Defence Liaison Division had known that this was going to be pressed in the new government. By misfortune Paul Tremblay had just arrived to become head of the Defence Liaison Division and he was not in-

Plate 27. The Honourable G. R. Pearkes, Minister of Defence, on a visit to SHAPE headquarters, Versailles, France.

Plate 28. The unveiling of the Arrow, October 1957. The cancellation of this interceptor aircraft was one of the first crises Pearkes had to face as Minister of Defence.

Plate 29. The new Minister of Defence,
G. R. Pearkes, arriving at the
Parliament Buildings, Ottawa,
July 1957.

Plate 30. Pearkes laying a wreath at the
Canadian memorial,
Vimy Ridge.

formed either. Jim McCardle, as I recall, came in to see me with Paul Tremblay, having heard what happened and Jim, who was the one person in the Department well briefed, expressed dismay at the speed with which this was done. I don't think our officials were disposed to oppose the NORAD agreement but they felt it was very important it should be discussed . . . and recorded in a more formal agreement, and also that we should take advantage of the agreement to press hard for better forms of consultation. In the end this is what we got.[14]

On the weekend of 27 June, the American Secretary of State, John Foster Dulles, visited Ottawa and Diefenbaker and Pearkes discussed the NORAD arrangements with him. Subsequently, prior to the public announcement, the Prime Minister explained the agreement to the cabinet and some discussion on it took place.[15] Considering the newness of the ministers and their tendency to concentrate on matters which affected their own departments, it is likely that the long term impact of the agreement, made public on 1 August, did not impress itself on their minds. Probably it appeared to them, as Foulkes was to describe it later, as "the last step in co-ordinating the whole of the air defence of the continent which had been developed over the past fifteen years."[16]

Following the announcement by Pearkes and the American Secretary of Defense of the agreement on an interim basis, events moved quickly. Air Marshal Roy Slemon was appointed as the senior Canadian officer and Gen. Earle Partridge as the senior American officer. Early in September it was agreed that, as of 12 September, NORAD headquarters at Colorado Springs would become operational. The Commander-in-Chief of NORAD, Gen. Partridge or, in his absence, A/M Slemon, the Deputy Commander, would be responsible to the Joint Chiefs of Staff in Washington and the Chiefs of Staff Committee in Ottawa, each of which in turn would be responsible to their political superiors.

Pearkes considered the NORAD agreement to be one of the highlights of his career as minister. At the same time, it was to be attacked both in the House and to some extent in the press as well. As the months went by and as NORAD became involved more and more with technological changes in weapons systems, the debate became warmer. To the extent that one can isolate this agreement from other defence matters, however, it might be well at this point to outline the major criticisms levelled against it.

On the Liberal side of the House Lester Pearson and Paul Martin began by asking whether or not there was any written agreement between Canada and the United States respecting NORAD. Pearkes replied that, to date, there had been only a joint public release by the American Secretary of

Defense and himself together with an order-in-council, dated 31 July 1957, appointing Slemon as Deputy Commander. "It was considered desirable," he added, "that the two commanders should get together and work out the exact details of their relations before any more formal agreement should be made defining exactly the role of the two commanders in relation to the civil power, and that note is now in the course of study."[17] Soon Pearson began to question the procedure by which the interim agreement was brought about. The C.C.F. was somewhat less concerned with procedure. Stanley Knowles was in the first instance favourable to the idea of joint defence and for the need to establish prior arrangements for NORAD headquarters to act. He felt, however, that Pearkes had not shown that Gen. Partridge or A/M Slemon drew their authority from any civilian or political body and expressed his concern over Parliament's lack of control over decisions made at Colorado Springs. Pearkes pointed out NORAD was operating "on an oral and verbal agreement" and again outlined the structure of authority which came jointly from Washington and Ottawa.[18]

Other questions came up as well. Some felt that Canada was tying itself too closely to the United States. The degree to which an American general might control Canadian forces came up in a variety of ways, and Pearkes had to explain repeatedly the concept around which NORAD was being formed. Gen. Partridge did not command any Canadian armed forces. This was vested in the commanding officer of Air Defence Command at St. Hubert, Quebec. Nor did Partridge's authority extend to the disposition of Canada's nine fighter squadrons or any other Canadian squadrons. "In peacetime," Pearkes said,

> NORAD will be responsible for the development of plans and procedures to be used in war. These . . . are . . . to be ready for immediate use in an emergency. They will be approved . . . by the chiefs of staff of the two countries . . . and governmental approval will be sought before the plans are implemented. . . . In time of war NORAD will be responsible for the direction of air operations in accordance with the plans which have been agreed to in peacetime. . . . I emphasize the fact that the decision to go to war must rest with the government of this country and not with any general, of Canadian or any other nationality.[19]

It was not until a week after the signing of the exchange of notes regarding the principles to govern the future organization and operations of NORAD that the new Secretary of State for External Affairs, Sidney E. Smith, tabled them in the House. Smith emphasized that part of the Canadian note which described integrated headquarters exercising operational control over assigned forces in the NATO area as being a well-established precedent to NORAD. As the Canada-United States region was an integral part of the NATO area, he suggested that the exchange was little more than an amplification of and extension under the North Atlantic Treaty.[20] When Prime Minister Diefenbaker, on 10 June, brought the exchange of notes to the House for parliamentary approval, he also stressed NORAD's connection with NATO, and to those who had claimed that Canada's sovereignty was being impinged said flatly that "survival knows none of the fineries of a nationalism that used to exist." He spoke of the defensive nature of NORAD, noted that the principles agreed to were basically those worked out when the Liberals were in power, and added that as a further co-operative measure with the United States the Canadian government had decided "to permit the establishment of facilities at certain Canadian bases for use by tanker aircraft of strategic air command."[21]

Lester Pearson welcomed the chance to debate the NORAD agreement. He agreed that the principles behind it were sound, but he did not miss the opportunity to criticize the procedures. He also scorned the Conservatives' attempt to tuck NORAD under NATO's wing. NORAD was a bi-lateral agreement between two countries, and although the NATO authorities were kept fully informed, the direct lines of communication and authority went to Washington and Ottawa, not Paris. Pearson then went on to query the possibility of American aircraft under NORAD's command crossing into Canadian skies if armed with nuclear weapons. Herridge of the C.C.F. supported Pearson's argument and went further. He felt that the NORAD agreement was tied in with the Strategic Air Command, which he termed an offensive or at least a retaliatory force. Thus, Canada might, accidentally, become entangled with American military policies beyond North America. He disliked the idea of Canadian forces coming under the command of an American general which he felt was the surrender of sovereign rights "to a single country under a bilateral agreement." He also foresaw closer Canadian-American air defence leading to an increasing reliance by Canada on American technological and scientific skills.

As other major decisions were made which affected Canadian air defence, criticisms changed from the principles of integrated air defence to the methods employed in accomplishing it. These ranged from Harold Winch's claim that Canada's sole duty was to prevent undetected hostile flights over Canada to Maj.-Gen. W. H. S. Macklin's statement to the Canadian Club in Guelph, Ontario, that NORAD was "the most gigantic military swindle in military history."[22] As for Pearkes, he continued to believe that "the right thing was done in forming NORAD," although "possibly the approach might have been in a different way."[23] He was pressed by Foulkes who was "so concerned about the possibility of a leak from the U.S.A. that, had this occurred, the whole plan might have fallen through. . . . Perhaps we didn't realize the political difficulties," he reflected, but added "I felt that it was in the interests of Canadian defence that we get it approved. It would take a long time anyway to get things working, and I wasn't at all certain that there might be some opposition in Cabinet."[24] Pearkes had acted quickly, but for him it was not to be a question of acting in haste and regretting at leisure. The later criticisms levelled at NORAD had anti-American overtones with which he thoroughly disagreed, and the idea that by voluntarily sharing sovereignty one lost sovereignty he never accepted. With those who later claimed that if there were a massive bomber attack from Russia, there were bound to be a large number breach the air defences, Pearkes would agree. But the essence of NORAD was the protection of the nuclear retaliatory force, the Strategic Air Command, and if this potential counterstroke could not deter a Soviet strike, then indeed the game was lost. As he put it later:

> We couldn't be strong everywhere. We had to rely upon Americans. . . . We couldn't begin to defend Canada as a whole. . . . I could see nothing from the defence point of view but the closest possible liaison with the Americans. . . . If the North American continent was going to be attacked the United States and Canada had to be in it as one. . . . I couldn't see why we couldn't have . . . American squadrons stationed right in Canada but the government wouldn't agree to it. Yet they were quite content to have Americans manning some of these [radar] lines, but . . . they were far away and were hidden.[25]

In retrospect, it seems Pearkes might have used different tactics, but he might also have gone further than he did. There were fields in Western Canada prepared, allocated, and supplied so that American squadrons could move in and use them in an emergency. More than this Pearkes could not do owing to the probable effect on public opinion, which, by the late 1950's, was beginning to squirm under the unaccustomed, visible reliance on American power while, at the same time, British power continued to wane. Pearkes looked analytically at the military situation without traditional prejudice. All he could do for the moment, however, was to push the air defence of the continent as far to the north as he could and help to make it efficient.

It was one thing having cabinet approval of the NORAD agreement, but it was another to exercise the weapon which had been forged. When the Conservatives came to power, there existed an agreement to allow United States Air Force overflights of Canadian territory with aircraft carrying air-to-air atomic weapons in the event of the highest emergency and subject to previously agreed rules of operational procedures. Naturally this would not normally be done except in the case of the highest alert, when war was anticipated or had been declared, or for some other particular reasons relating to operational efficiency. Nevertheless, plans had to be made beforehand. The original agreement had been made on a six-month basis, and as the first period had been found satisfactory, a one-year extension had been proposed. This would end on 1 July, only days after the Conservatives assumed office. Pearkes favoured the continuation of the agreement, but under the Aeronautics Act aircraft carrying atomic weapons flying over Canada had to be approved by the Secretary of State for External Affairs and the Prime Minister as well. A number of such flights had already received permission from the Liberal ministers, some taking place just after the Conservatives had taken office. In 1957 there was no trouble having the agreement renewed, but by 1959, when Howard Green held the external affairs portfolio and when there was increased concern over atomic weapons and the Strategic Air Command in general, it was not easy to achieve Canadian consent even to a joint air defence exercise.

In 1959 it was decided that a large-scale test of North American defences, code-named Operation "Skyhawk," should be held involving the use of Canadian airspace. Planning for the exercise began in June, with the hope that it could take place late in October. Both Americans and Canadians were involved in the planning, and things went smoothly until it reached the political level.

The Canadian cabinet considered the scheme late in August and decided against it. The cabinet felt that the exercise could not be considered routine, that it would be interpreted by the public as being inspired by extraordinary circumstances, and, further, that the timing was bad as a major diplomatic move to reduce tensions between East and West was underway. The Canadian reply shocked the Americans, especially as personnel from the Department of National Defence and Department of Transport had been involved at a very early stage. President Eisenhower had given his approval, and the Americans felt the Russians recognized firmness and strength. Millions of dollars had been spent on the system, and surely it was time to test its efficiency. If the exercise was cancelled and it became known to the press, the publicity would more likely hinder Eisenhower's discussion with Premier Khruschev than help it.

Despite a personal visit by the American ambassador and a later message on the subject from Eisenhower, Diefenbaker refused to change his mind, although he suggested that if civil aviation could continue uninterrupted, the cabinet might reconsider its position. There had doubtless been a breakdown in upward consultation and communication from the military regarding the exercise, a fact which annoyed Eisenhower but which reinforced Diefenbaker's conviction that it was an illustration of a tendency on the part of military officers to extend their authority. Early in December both governments finally decided to cancel the exercise.

The frustrations encountered attempting to mount "Skyhawk" gave way to caution and longer preparation. In October 1959 Gen. Partridge requested permission to prepare a large-scale NORAD test called "Skyshield." Pearkes recommended it, for he was concerned that the integrated air defence command should be tested. In November, there was agreement in principle with the Americans to the exercise, and it was emphasized that there should be ample prior warning. It was felt advisable that Pearkes should prepare public opinion for the need of such an exercise. Early in June 1960, after consulting with Diefenbaker and Green, Pearkes prepared a statement for the newly formed Committee on Defence Expenditure and then had Arthur Smith, a Conservative M.P. from Calgary who was on the committee, ask him a question which would permit him to express his views publicly. When it was evident that Pearkes's statement caused no upsurge of public opinion against the idea, the Chairman of the Chiefs of Staff was permitted to notify Washington that "Skyshield" could proceed. No public announcement was made until three weeks later, and when the exercise itself took place, official press reports on it were kept to a minimum.

The change in attitude towards NORAD by the government from one of wholehearted co-operation to cautious collaboration was a trend against which Pearkes fought both in the House and in the cabinet. It was indicative of a change of public mood brought about by the realization of Canada's increasing reliance on her powerful neighbour. The economic impact of this change, together with the growing fear of nuclear warfare, was to have political consequences which affected Pearkes throughout his tenure as minister.

Associated with the active air defence of the country was the protection of the population from bombing. The civil defence organization which had been built up to deal with any possible suicidal German or Japanese attack lapsed until it was reorganized and placed under the Department of Health and Welfare in 1951. Here it tended to excite little interest, and, had war broken out, the effectiveness of its operations would have been doubtful. During the 1950's, Pearkes and others in the Opposition began to criticize the government's civil defence preparations. In 1955 Pearkes was advocating an increased role for the armed forces:

I believe that part of the training of regular . . . reserve and auxiliary personnel should be in civil defence duties. . . . It should not necessarily take second place in their training. Due importance should be attached to the training of regular personnel in civil defence duties. After all, a lot of these men will be taking their discharge and then they will go into civilian life. If they have had a thorough training in elementary civil defence problems, they will be a valuable contribution to the civil defence organizations of this country.[26]

Pearkes was especially keen on the part which the militia could perform. "I would go so far as to say," he added, "that the prime role of the militia in the future should be civil defence." He realized that the militia, or parts of it, would be called upon to assist the regular forces, but he argued that in all likelihood in a future war Canada would be assaulted from the air and that consequently all three services must be prepared both to fight in their normal roles and to assist the civil population.

In office, Pearkes began to implement some of his ideas on civil defence. As the months went by, however, he found that he was embarked on one of the most unpopular courses of action he ever undertook. Shortly after the new Parliament met in 1957, Pearkes, in answer to a question regarding the role of the reserves, stated that on 1 October a training directive had been sent out stating that one of the primary aims for training for the year 1957-58 would be "to prepare the militia for its role to assist in any future mobilization for active service and for civil defence. Emphasis will be given to civil defence."[27] Later, in a letter to the Minister of Health and Welfare, he elaborated on his reasons for the new emphasis.

It has for some time been the established policy in Canada that the armed services, co-ordinated by the army, will come to the aid of civil defence. In the initial stages of nuclear attack on this country, the assistance available to the civil defence organizations in the armed forces will mainly be from the regular army and the reserve forces of the three services. It was therefore decided that, should such an attack occur, the first duty of the latter forces will be aid to civil defence organizations should it be unable to cope with the situation. . . .

Since civil defence is . . . organized on a local basis of self help with few, if any, mobile reserves capable of being moved from one area to another, the two main tasks in aid of civil defence for the armed services are providing mobile support groups and assistance to local civilian effort with technical units and equipment.[28]

Pearkes elaborated in his first major speech on defence policy in the House on 5 December 1957. As far as the army was concerned, he anticipated two types of possible battles. One would be in Europe, "fought by forces in being and in position"; the other would be in Canada, "to assist in restoring order out of the terrible chaos that may result from enemy attacks with long range nuclear weapons."

Pearkes's announcements during 1957 and in 1958 were received with some apprehension. "It is perhaps unfortunate," his private secretary wrote to one reserve senior office, "that the notion of civil defence has dreamed up in people's minds a vision of men in overalls with stirrup pumps. . . . It would perhaps be more realistic to call the function assigned to the militia . . . a role of strategic survival."[29] The Toronto *Globe and Mail* defended Pearkes's position and demanded that even stronger action be taken by the government. In an editorial the newspaper commented:

> Mr. Pearkes has attempted honestly to answer questions about civil defence so far as they were within the scope of his department. Unfortunately, there has been a dearth of action and information on civil defence from Health Minister Monteith. For instance, the co-ordinator of civil defence, Major-General F. F. Worthington, resigned in September. No successor has yet been appointed. General Worthington's deputy, Major-General G. S. Hatton, has carried out the administrative duties of the co-ordinator; neither he nor Mr. Monteith has offered the Canadian public any policies, proposals, plans or predictions.[30]

Part of the problem certainly rested with the divergent opinion on the role civil defence should play in the army. Gen. Foulkes had originally persuaded Brooke Claxton to transfer civil defence to the Department of Health and Welfare, and he did not welcome its return. In May 1958 Monteith suggested merging the federal civil defence organization with the nucleus of the new Emergency Measures Organization, joining both under the control of one of the ministers without portfolio. At about the same time, Monteith also asked the retiring Chief of the General Staff, Lt.-Gen. H. D. Graham, to undertake a comprehensive survey of all aspects of civil defence. While Monteith hoped to unburden himself from civil defence, Pearkes did not want to assume the full responsibility. Moreover, owing to the emphasis then being placed on forces-in-being (or regular forces), the role of the reserves was being questioned, and there were some who felt that they should be reduced to a bare minimum. If they were given a civil defence role as well as their traditional role, Pearkes felt there would be less criticism of their place in national defence.

The new Chief of the General Staff, Lt.-Gen. S. F. Clark, supported Pearkes's basic ideas. Clark felt that as both sides in the cold war built up their missile armoury, there would be a greater possibility of conventional warfare on the scale of a Korean War. In such an event the militia might be called upon as reinforcements. "At that time," he added, "there was a feeling . . . that the militia should be cut to the very bone because the chance of training them ready to go in the early phase of the war just wasn't on. . . . We felt, on the other hand, that they were very loyal, intelligent people and that they should be trained. . . . Our worry was, that if you ever needed them in the future [and] had them down to too small an organization, it would take many years to gain their confidence and build them back up again."[31]

Most important, however, was the practical problem Pearkes faced as minister. "I think he was worried," Clark recalled, "that if a crisis arose, possibly followed by a conflict, it would be very difficult to explain to the public why there were no defensive arrangements for them." He added:

> What was involved primarily was to teach not only the militia but the regular force how to rescue and look after people if our country was hit. . . . If the war broke out quickly, we might be so damaged that we couldn't move a brigade or a division outside the country. We had at this time about 120,000 servicemen and 40,000 in the reserves. Now why shouldn't these people be highly trained in either role? Most of them are concentrated in camps like Petawawa and Gagetown, so they were reasonably mobile. If they are well trained soldiers, it was my view they could be trained also in this other [civil defence] role.[32]

Foulkes, meanwhile, was doing what he could to make sure that the armed services should not have the prime responsibility for civil defence which the Graham report proposed. He discussed the matter with Robert Bryce, the secretary of the cabinet, who was keenly interested in the general problem of the survival of government in case of a nuclear attack, and Foulkes stressed that the matter was one which affected all government departments. After a great deal of further study a compromise plan was agreed upon, and in March 1959, the Prime Minister announced major changes in civil defence. "The principal change proposed," he said, "is that the army should undertake primary and direct responsibility for a number of the technical civil defence functions heretofore carried on by civil defence organizations at provincial and municipal levels." He then elaborated on the new responsibilities for army personnel, outlined the tasks he envisaged for provincial and municipal governments, and gave a brief account of the role to be played by the Emergency Measures Organization attached to the Privy Council office.

Initially the press seemed to favour a stronger civil defence system. The

Saskatoon *Star-Phoenix*, for example, felt that although "this change in the role of the militia may cause many wailings and heart tugs among the traditionalists, its new mission could equal or even surpass in performance, and therefore in importance, the past glories of the army services' various branches."[33] This view was by no means shared by the regular or reserve forces. The latter, especially, were more vocal as their ranks were filled with civilians who were soldiers only by inclination. Training in first aid, rescue work, traffic control, radiation monitoring, emergency communications, and similar tasks was met with little enthusiasm. Those who thought seriously about the need for these skills accepted the new direction but reacted unfavourably to the time such training took from their "normal" military training. The reaction was especially strong since the number of training days (and thus pay days) permitted the militia had been reduced in 1958–59 as had the number of days allowed at summer camp. Moreover, news reports seemed to indicate that the reserves would be turned into a civil defence organization, and this was affecting recruiting. Despite Pearkes's reassurance that they would "still be trained for their traditional role as reinforcements for the active service in the event of war,"[34] many were disturbed that their main role appeared to be as some sort of a survival corps.

To some extent their feelings were reinforced by a growing criticism of the plans in the press during the summer of 1959. As long as there was some warning of an attack, the rapid evacuation of the population from the cities had been considered feasible. The growing possibility of a nuclear attack by intercontinental ballistic missiles, however, threw increasing doubt on evacuation procedures. People began to ask whether it would not be better to build bomb shelters than to evacuate, and one newspaper suggested that "a shelter programme is the only alternative to no defence at all."[35]

The argument was in full swing as the army was perfecting its organization of mobile support columns designed to perform re-entry and rescue tasks as well as to assist in maintaining law and order, guarding vital points, and so forth. The argument was widened by those who pointed out that most reserve force armouries in the larger cities were centrally located and thus liable to be in the city's devastated area after an attack and by others who argued that the most likely targets on the continent would be the large American industrial cities, in which case Canadian cities should plan to receive massive numbers of American refugees. The two policies, "hide" or "run away," one newspaper editorial pointed out,

> could not reasonably be combined without the expense of much more money than the nation could afford. Thus the policy of the Dominion

government has been sketchy. . . . Even the Minister of Defence who, strangely enough, has only this month been invested with the complete responsibility for it, is happily floundering among the opinions of generals and civilians from Canada and pundits from the United States. In the various communities which have tried civil defence, civil defence workers have been treated with the same kind of distrust as temperance advocates and social workers.[36]

There is no doubt that previous civil defence plans, based on a possible attack by comparatively slow bomber aircraft, would become in large part outdated with the advent of the Intercontinental Ballistic Missile (ICBM). Even though it would be some years before the U.S.S.R. had sufficient missiles to launch an attack, the Canadian public felt that new plans should be ready at once and reacted unfavourably to delay. Dividing the responsibility among three cabinet ministers was criticized by some members of the Opposition. It was also one of the reasons leading to the resignation of Maj.-Gen. G. S. Hatton, the deputy federal civil defence co-ordinator. Added to the problem, of course, were the regional responsibilities of the provincial governments.

In the autumn of 1959 a federal-provincial conference on civil defence was held in Ottawa. At its end Pearkes made a brief press statement which indicated a considerable change in policy. Stress was now to be laid on partial evacuation and the use of bomb shelters. Pearkes stated that there would be no hope for citizens in an area hit directly by the blast of a nuclear bomb, but he said those beyond the immediate area could be saved, especially if they were shielded from radiation. To build major shelters to protect all citizens was beyond the financial ability of the government, so Pearkes stressed "do-it-yourself" basement shelters.[37]

The reactions to Pearkes's summary of the new policy—a policy which, incidentally, the provincial delegates approved—were as varied as they were widespread. The Ottawa *Citizen*, even when the conference was in progress, felt there was "little point in talking about fall-out shelters, evacuation routes and warning systems in the hope of enlisting public support at a time when people are more interested now in the outcome of the world series or closing up the summer cottage."[38] The Toronto *Globe and Mail*, although it claimed that "an element of realism is . . . seeping into the Dominion government civil defence plans," nevertheless felt that many households could not afford the "luxury" of bomb shelters which ranged from three hundred to one thousand dollars.[39] The Toronto *Star* scorned what it termed Pearkes's "every man for himself" approach and suggested that the government should consider spending $2 or $3 billion on a national shelter programme.[40] Although advice to the public on the adequacy of shelters, and even shelter policy, was the responsibility of the Emergency Measures Organization and not the Department of National Defence, Pearkes received a flood of letters concerning home bomb shelters. Some complained that the municipality would impose additional taxes if they improved or enlarged their home to include a shelter; some wondered if the sketch of a shelter shown in a local paper would be of any use for a family of four or five, and others wanted the government to either raise their wages or permit a deduction in income taxes to help them pay for a shelter. Coupled with these letters were those from small construction companies seeking government approval and sponsorship for their particular shelter design. Still others complained that it was impossible to draw up the design of a shelter for national acceptance owing to the conflicting municipal construction by-laws.

The amount of adverse editorial comment in the press led Lt.-Gen. S. F. Clark to suggest in November that steps should be taken to correct misapprehensions. As he wrote at the time:

> There have been a good many releases and quotations from talks by various ministers and officials but it seems to me that a comprehensive statement tying the activities of the various departments together is still needed. . . .
>
> The preparation of this statement would involve several departments: the Department of National Health and Welfare, covering their matters; the Department of Justice, in respect of the R.C.M.P. responsibility; the Department of Defence Production, dealing with the War supplies agencies; the Office of the Privy Council on behalf of all the Emergency Measures Organization responsibilities.[41]

Statements on national survival by government leaders, either in or out of the House of Commons, apparently had little effect on the Canadian public. Later, in June 1960, when the Prime Minister tabled a pamphlet on building fallout shelters entitled "Booklet for Survival," the Canadian Institute of Public Opinion went to work in every province "to get the first factual report on what Canadians would do should the warning of a nuclear attack be given." The results were not encouraging. "Vagueness and fatalism" was the strongest reaction. Forty-two per cent said they had no idea what they would do to protect themselves or said they would do nothing. The next largest segment, 26 per cent, said they would head for the basement, go underground, or "get into a hole somewhere." After this, the report added, "ideas dwindled away into vagueness, with three per cent saying they would pray and only five per cent suggesting they felt they were prepared for the emergency."[42]

It was little comfort to Pearkes that, basically, both of the opposition parties agreed with the proposition, as Paul Hellyer expressed it, "to try and take such steps as we can to protect the largest possible proportion of our civilian population."[43] The public was apathetic, the press was unsympathetic, the armed forces by no means enthusiastic. Lifeboat drill is not the most popular activity on an ocean cruise, especially if it is known there are more passengers than the lifeboats can handle. In some ways Pearkes's position was similar to that of the ship's captain, and his duty was to ensure that there were some survivors as the ship forged ahead in unpredictable waters.

There are few new governments which are elected to office which do not promise to achieve greater or better results for the same or less money than their predecessors, and the Conservative administrations elected in 1957 and again in 1958 were no exception. Pearkes promised to reduce defence spending while achieving maximum results. He was able to reduce the defence budget considerably, but he was subjected to no small amount of criticism in the process.

Prior to the election, the Liberal Government had spent a net cash outlay on defence of approximately $1,806,934,000. In 1957-58, this was reduced to $1,695,872,000, then to $1,661,830,000 in the following year, and by 1959-60, to $1,512,209,000. This represented a drop in spending from 36.3 per cent to 26.4 per cent of the government's total budget.[44] Much of this decrease can be accounted for by the completion of construction on major items ranging from radar warning sites to storage depots and barracks, but Pearkes waged a constant battle also to limit or reduce the number of civilian and military personnel in his department while maintaining a high degree of efficiency. This battle was fought against the background of high unemployment, which in turn made the situation more sensitive politically.

From the time he assumed office Pearkes, along with his cabinet colleagues, was sent constant reminders by Donald Fleming, the Minister of Finance, stressing the need to reduce to a minimum the number of civilian employees in his department.[45] On the other hand, he was constantly beset by appeals against layoffs from individuals, unions, members of Parliament, and municipalities.

Pearkes gave instructions that the reductions in personnel should be carried out as humanely as possible, but each year, faced with the constant demands for retrenchment, he cut away, consolidated, or combined units and subunits to achieve the maximum efficiency and the least cost.[46] The problem was, of course, what constituted the "maximum efficiency" and, further, efficiency to do what? Something of the conflicting views between finance and national defence can be illustrated in the exchange of letters between Fleming and Pearkes in 1960, while the army, exemplified by the Chief of the General Staff, might provide the example of the service affected.

In March Fleming wrote Pearkes mentioning the concern of the Treasury Board over the unhealthy proportion of the defence budget going into operation and maintenance, with particular emphasis on personnel costs. The board had examined, among other things, the proportion of military to civilian personnel in headquarters in the three services and noted that it varied from about 75 per cent for the R.C.A.F. to 63 per cent for the R.C.N. It noted that 12 per cent of army military manpower was engaged in support services but only about 2 per cent in the navy. It pointed out that in June 1959 almost 36 per cent of the total naval personnel were engaged in training or were at training establishments. Further, although Air Material Command had eliminated 174 civilian positions, it had added 279 service positions.[47] This was followed by a later letter asking whether it would not be possible to reduce the total number of servicemen by substituting civilians for them.

Pearkes's reply to the above illustrates the problem as seen from his office.

It has been my policy to concentrate on achieving manpower economics by reducing civilian establishments and maintaining our military manpower within the approved military manpower ceilings. This policy . . . concentrates efforts to achieve manpower economies in the area where there has been the gravest criticism. It maintains . . . needed military manpower for meeting defence needs in any kind of an emergency. It provides positions through which military personnel may be rotated from isolated posts, from overseas and from sea duty. It enables temporary minor fluctuations in work load to be met without increased costs by way of overtime pay, and provides training in skills which could prove beneficial in a time of national emergency. Trained military personnel cannot be engaged as and when required, and the building up of adequately trained military staff takes time. From the point of view of training and development of military personnel, it is therefore not desirable to vary total military manpower on the basis of individual establishment changes.[48]

Pearkes ended by noting that civilian staff in his department had been reduced from the 1956-57 total of 54,371 to 49,637 and added: "We can't have it both ways. If I am to reduce civilian staff I cannot, at the same time, substitute civilians for military personnel."

Fleming, who was a member of the cabinet defence committee as well as Minister of Finance, felt that even more might be accomplished. He suggested a review of the validity of the authorized ceilings of military personnel to see if the essential tasks could not be carried out with fewer men. He wondered if the fourth brigade, established as a result of the Korean War, could still be considered essential;[49] and whether all the air squadrons then in operation were necessary. He suggested further that reducing the total number of servicemen from one hundred and twenty thousand to one hundred thousand might be considered. Pearkes had already asked his Chiefs of Staff about the effects of a 20 per cent reduction. He summed up his own opinion to Fleming as follows:

A 20 per cent cut in personnel in the navy would have the following consequences: disbanding of the remaining two air reserve squadrons in Toronto and Vancouver; shutting down the supply sub-depots at Vancouver and Longueuil and the naval base at Sydney, N.S.; eliminating the fighter aircraft squadron on the carrier; laying up four destroyer escort ships of our NATO commitment and our entire fleet of ten minesweepers; an arbitrary cut of ten per cent of the ships' crews, thereby reducing the manning level . . . to 75 per cent of the fighting complement; and a reduction of ten per cent of headquarters training and support staffs ashore. In addition there would be smaller, consequential actions such as the discharge of approximately 600 officers.

In the army a 20 per cent reduction would be borne largely by the forces that are not committed to Europe, to the Middle East, to the Congo or Indo China. The deletion of the 4th Brigade which you mention in your letter would mean that there would only remain the three brigades that are committed to NATO and we will not have a formation from which to provide for any emergency in Canada or for employment with the United Nations. The Alaska Highway maintenance would have to be handed over to another agency and there would be a general reduction across the board. Certain units and establishments would have to be closed, approximately 1,100 officers would have to be discharged.

In the air force a 20 per cent reduction would involve the following principal actions: disband all auxiliary squadrons based at Montreal, Toronto, Hamilton, Winnipeg, Saskatoon, Edmonton, Calgary, and Vancouver; close the supply depot at Moncton, N.B.; close the flying training school at Gimli, Manitoba; hand Goose Bay and Tor Bay over to another agency; close the repair depot at Calgary; close the joint training school at Rivers, Manitoba; close station at Edmonton; and possibly disband one maritime and one transport squadron. In addition, there would be major reductions at continuing units and approximately 2,000 officers would have to be retired.

Pearkes ended by stating in no uncertain terms: "You can see from the above that a reduction of the order that you have suggested would have a major impact on the defence position of the country and it would be one I could not accept."[50]

Although there was constant pressure on Pearkes to reduce the numbers in the services, there was no corresponding desire to reduce commitments. To use the army as an example, Lt.-Gen. S. F. Clark was approached to see if the numbers of headquarters and staffs might be cut. Clark pointed out that in 1945, the then Chief of the General Staff, Lt.-Gen. Foulkes, established a command structure of five command and six area headquarters to train and administer some twenty thousand soldiers with no overseas commitments and no clearly defined defence of Canada tasks. In 1960, he noted, with four command and ten area headquarters, the army trains and administers almost forty-eight thousand soldiers and more reserve forces than in 1945-46. "Our commitments," he added, "include a brigade group overseas in peacetime, survival operations in Canada requiring far more men than we have in the regular army and militia, and approximately 1,000 [servicemen] a year rotated annually to undertake our UN and military Truce Supervisory Commission commitments in Egypt, Palestine and Kashmir."[51] As he commented later:

It seemed to me that the only logical and proper way . . . was to review the role of the services. My concern was the army, to see what one needed in manpower and equipment to carry out the task assigned to it and then you either reduced the tasks or reaffirmed [them]. Once you affirmed it, then it would be the responsibility of the service concerned to prove . . . that the numbers asked for to carry out the tasks were reasonably accurate. . . .

There is some minimum of support staff you have to have for operations, administration and training. . . . It's a matter of judgement whether we ask for too many or too few people. . . . If there was an error it was a small percentage. If you start saying "let's chop 10 or 20 per cent off" any of these things, then you have to readjust the whole programme. This means the government must decide what commitments it intends to make. It must say we can't do this in the U.N., or

Plate 31. G. R. Pearkes inspecting veterans of the Canadian Scottish Regiment, Victoria, B.C., June 1973.

Plate 32. Lt.-Gov. Pearkes with Her Majesty Queen Elizabeth, the Queen Mother, at Government House, Victoria, B.C.

Plate 33. Lt.-Gov. Pearkes lighting a ceremonial fire with Chief Sewid at Alert Bay.

Plate 34. Lt.-Gov. Pearkes taking the salute on the steps of the Parliament Buildings, Victoria, B.C. Premier W. A. C. Bennett is in the centre behind him.

we can't send more people to Kashmir; . . . or we can't send more to Suez.[52]

Clark was to stress this point to Pearces's successor late in 1960, pointing out that whereas he had to cope with a budgetary limitation of 47,799, the existing commitments called for 54,871 men. The problem of the army being given more commitments than it could meet was by no means new, and indeed the problem was to grow progressively worse in the next decade in all three services.

While coping with attempts to maintain the strength of the armed forces, Pearkes received a constant stream of requests which, if acceded to, would have increased the non-military use of the three services. A certain number were permitted as it helped to improve relations with the public. On the other hand, if all the requests had been followed, it would have cost millions of dollars and hundreds of thousands of man-hours.

More serious, of course, were the demands which had to be met and which tended to increase rather than diminish. Search and rescue operations by the R.C.A.F. placed a considerable work load on that service. Between January 1957 and January 1959, for example, there were eighty-five searches for lost aircraft, and of these only twelve were R.C.A.F. aircraft. Calls for help could not be ignored, but as in the calls to enlarge and improve air-sea rescue works, the demand had to be met from a decreasing budget. Requests for aid to the civil power, of course, had to be met in whatever form it assumed. In October 1958, for example, the services assisted in the Springhill mine disaster. Three months later they were helping the city of Winnipeg dig out of a major snowfall. Later that year preparations were made in case military assistance was required in the loggers' strike in Newfoundland, and, of course, there were calls for help to combat forest fires or to rescue people in flooded areas. Extending assistance often went beyond the national boundaries. Requests for service to the United Nations received the highest priority, and during the Korean War thousands of Canadian servicemen were involved. By the time Pearkes assumed office, these commitments had been greatly reduced. Nevertheless, in the summer of 1957 there were still well over a thousand officers and men engaged in U.N. peacekeeping or supervisory duties.[53] These, of course, had to be rotated back to Canada periodically as had the men in the brigade group and air division serving with the NATO forces in Europe. To maintain morale, it was preferable that a sergeant in Egypt, for example, should not be posted in Germany without having some time in Canada. It was also preferable that all Canadians posted abroad should be professionals and, if possible, with a minimum of three years' experience. As a good proportion of the services personnel was constantly changing, the "pool" available for overseas duties was much smaller than one might expect, and one can more readily understand the attitude taken by Pearkes in the light of the commitments assumed by the government.

When Pearkes felt he could cut down, he did so. The old Northwest Signal System, which for years was operated by the army, and the navy's icebreaker, H.M.C.S. *Labrador*, were both handed over to the Department of Transport. The Canadian Officers Training Corps was reduced in numbers as many of the militia units already had too high a proportion of officers to men. He tried, but with little success, to reduce the number of military attachés which the Department of External Affairs wanted for their embassies. He closed a number of military stations, but at the same time he was anxious, wherever possible, to replace American servicemen in Canada with Canadians. He managed to reduce their number from approximately 15,000 to 9,500, but to the extent their tasks were assumed by Canadians, reductions in one area were absorbed by increases in another.

One of Pearkes's disappointments while in office was his inability to gain any but modest savings in manpower through integration or amalgamation of the services. Integration had interested previous ministers. Following the Second World War, the three services had been placed under one minister. Shortly thereafter the Defence Research Board had been organized to look after all three services; the military colleges trained cadets for the navy, army, and air force; and, of course, the army's Dental Corps, even during the war, had served the dental needs of all servicemen.[54] The Korean War had slowed movement in this direction, and there was a varying degree of resistance on the part of some of the corps. Pearkes, while in Opposition, had favoured continued action along these lines, and so did the Chairman of the Chiefs of Staff, who would have gone further and faster and in a somewhat different direction.

As early as January 1958 Pearkes mentioned in the House that "serious study" was being carried out as to the advisability of amalgamating several of the administrative services such as the medical service. He added that although the means of ending duplication was being examined, he was finding "it was not an easy matter."[55] It was not until August that Pearkes was able to meet with the Canadian Forces Medical Council and direct them to plan to unify the medical services, effective at the beginning of the new year. A few days after announcing this measure in the House, Pearkes was able to add that the chaplain service was to be integrated under a Roman Catholic and Protestant chaplain-general. In the same year Pearkes ordered that recruiting centres were to combine their activities under one roof.

These were minor accomplishments in Pearkes's view, and he wished he could have gone much further, although not to the extent of later years. He reflected later:

My thinking was that any army unit, air force unit or naval unit . . . which could help a kindred unit in one of the other services should . . . be required to serve with that other unit. . . . I couldn't see why, if the army said "we're short of signallers," they couldn't acquire naval or air force signallers if they had a surplus. . . . That's putting it in rather simple terms. . . .

If I had remained minister, I would have started the reorganization of Commands in which senior officers of any service might be in command. I was uncertain about these functional Commands.[56] I would have certainly amalgamated far more closely the headquarters. . . . I would probably, in doing so, have been forced to accept a modified system of functional command . . . but I would like to have kept some form of command structure. . . . I wouldn't have touched regiments [nor would I] have gone into providing a [uniform] dress for some time. . . . I don't know if it would be necessary for [servicemen] to wear the same uniform [but] it might have come to that.[57]

Basically, Pearkes's idea of integration stemmed largely from his experience as G.O.C.-in-C. Pacific Command. Here he had what was essentially a combined headquarters where senior and staff officers of the three services worked together smoothly and efficiently. He wanted to avoid competition among the services but without destroying their traditions. Although he implemented some of his ideas at the lower level and had committees working on others, Pearkes's primary concern was integration at the top. To an extent he practised this himself. He had weekly meetings with his Chiefs of Staff Committee and looked on Foulkes as something more than chairman of the committee. "As Chairman," he explained,

Foulkes was responsible for presenting the Committee's views but nothing prevented me from saying to him "Now this is what the Committee thought; what do you think?" He had much closer entree to me than any of the other Chiefs of Staff. . . . He did present a paper [on integration] to me and I think that he was disappointed that I didn't go ahead faster. But the pressure of other business prevented me from doing so as did the difficulty of getting the Cabinet to go along with radical changes which had to be made. Also, the rest of the Chiefs of Staff didn't go along with Foulkes.[58]

Foulkes probably would have agreed with Pearkes in part, for his plan envisaged a major change within the three services which would have given priority to functional command. He was concerned with the administration of the integrated corps, and he had bumped into the problem of inter-service rivalry over earlier ventures. This had led him to believe that one could not introduce integration piecemeal, which he felt Pearkes was attempting to do. "I think that if George had stayed [in office] he would have had a real try at doing something more," he said, "but I don't see how it could be done without going into the whole thing." At the same time he appreciated the difficulties Pearkes was having. "With the problems he had to face, integration was always one he could push off . . . and by the time he had faced the Arrow, the re-equipping and the nuclear role for the [NATO] Air Division, the civil defence problem and nuclear weapons, he had enough on his plate."59

Most senior military and civil service officers in Ottawa at that time would probably agree with Foulkes. The NORAD Treaty, civil defence, manpower, and integration—these were matters with which Pearkes could deal with one hand. But at the same time he was dealing with these, he was far more involved with matters of greater importance. Nuclear weapons were more important than integration, and the decision on the Arrow had far more impact than closing down a few military stations. It is to these major decisions in his career as minister we must now turn and attempt to see them against the background of fear over a Russian attack on the one hand and the growing influence in the cabinet of those who put their faith in sweet reason, mutual trust, and God. Pearkes was a practising Christian, but as the minister responsible for his country's defence, his duty was not to turn the other cheek.

16

Hawks and Doves

When George Pearkes took office in June 1957, he assumed he would be able to bring about many of the reforms which he had advocated. He quickly found out that to advocate a line of action was far different from carrying it out as a minister. The Conservatives had claimed that they would reduce defence expenditures. However, communities across Canada depended on the money brought in by a local air force station or naval dockyard, and to cut military strengths meant placing more men on the labour market at a time of heavy unemployment.

Pearkes would have liked to increase the amount being spent on defence research. In this he had only modest success, for balancing this need was the necessity to find money for the overdue pay raises for servicemen. Even a modest pay raise for one hundred and twenty thousand runs into millions of dollars annually. The Minister of Finance, although generally helpful and sympathetic to the Department of National Defence, had also to find money to finance the numerous measures the government brought in to assist Western farmers, old age pensioners, and others. At a time when modern weaponry was doubling and tripling in price every few years, money—or the lack of it—was going to be a determinant of defence policy to an extent he never anticipated.

Defence policy was based on the country's external or foreign policy, and here too Pearkes found it impossible to reduce expenses by having the government reduce commitments. Canadian servicemen in Egypt, Kashmir, the Congo, and elsewhere cost the department millions of dollars. Pearkes also found Canada's commitments to NATO more definite and demanding than he anticipated, and, consequently, although he was able to make certain changes in the structure and administration of the Canadian brigade in Europe, he found it politically as well as militarily inadvisable to carry out some of his earlier ideas about the reduction of troops in Germany.

Overshadowing the entire spectrum of defence policy decision making in his early months in office was the fact that the Conservatives were a minority government. It was considered most likely that the Conservatives would have to go back to the country again within a year. This, together with the fact that the party had not been in power since 1935, imposed a considerable caution in policy making. Ironically, after their overwhelming victory at the polls in 1958, the government continued to be cautious in many areas, for its leaders not only wished to avoid being labelled arrogant (as the Conservatives had accused the Liberals) but also to show the country that the Conservatives were able to govern well despite their long sojourn in the political wilderness.

Thus, as far as Pearkes was concerned, the major decision he took in 1957 was to commit Canada to NORAD. At that great consideration had been given to the fact that the Liberals would not violently oppose a measure which they had brought to the brink of fruition. There were other major decisions which had to be faced in 1957, however, which ultimately were to lead to rifts within the cabinet as well as to considerable public unrest with defence policy. One was whether or not to continue with the production of the Arrow aircraft; the other was the agreement in principle by Canada to the use of nuclear weapons. These stories will be told in detail once the relevant documents are open to the public. Here we can describe the events only as they affected Pearkes.

As weapons improve and their striking power becomes more accurate and more deadly, the planning and production for their use takes an increasing amount of time as well as financing, and this in turn means the time-gap widens between the year when the idea for a weapon is discussed and the year when the weapon is placed in the hands of the armed forces. In a lecture on "Strategy and Defence Science" to a symposium held by the Defence Research Board in Ottawa in December 1957, R. Cockburn noted:

> The timescale of development is a critical factor in planning. It is not sufficiently appreciated just how long a period is involved in the consecutive steps of research, development, production and training. Even during the last war it took up to five years to achieve a new weapon in quantity, but in peacetime it is more nearly ten years before a new concept becomes available to the Services. . . . New requirements must be based, therefore, not on current military doctrine, but on the strategic situation which will arise in ten years' time.

When Pearkes assumed office, he was briefed by the Chief of the Air Staff on the progress of a new aircraft, the CF-105 (or the Arrow). At that time there were nine squadrons of CF-100 Mark V fighter aircraft in Air Defence Command. These formed the main line of defence. As early as 1950, however, the Royal Canadian Air Force, the Defence Research Board, and the Department of Defence Production were studying the type of aircraft needed to counter the improved capabilities of the Russian bomber in the future. In July 1950, the A. V. Roe Canada Company (or Avro) received authorization to commence design studies on an advanced supersonic all-weather interceptor aircraft. After many months of study, planning, changing specifications, and so forth, the company was asked to proceed. Because its main role would be the interception and destruction of enemy jet bombers flying at a high altitude, during the day or night, in all weather conditions, the specifications demanded an engine, weapons and fire control system, and a tactical direction and control system suitable to the Canadian environment which, in turn, required the very best scientific and technical capabilities available in Canada and elsewhere.

During the early 1950's the scientists and engineers worked steadily, and after delays, innumerable submissions of designs, testings, and examinations the CF-105 programme began to reach a stage where an ever-increasing amount of money was required each year to construct and develop the pre-production aircraft. By 1955, for example, C. D. Howe announced in the House of Commons that the government had paid out about $30 million towards the development of the Arrow and intimated that, by the time it was completed, the programme would cost about $100 million.[1] This estimate was quickly revised upward until the development costs were close to $300 million with about $1.5 billion needed to supply fifteen squadrons.[2] The rising costs had worried the Liberal government which began a six-month review of the programme and, even in 1955, informed the A. V. Roe Company that a major part of the programme could be halted or abandoned at appropriate stages if this was found necessary. At the same time "Ralph Campney visited Washington and endeavoured to get the United States air force authorities interested in the CF-105. He received encouragement to go ahead but received no commitment at all from the United States to purchase the aircraft."[3]

The mounting costs of the CF-105 were offset, in part, by other considerations. The CF-100's, even though their performance had been improved upon, were becoming outdated, and with the appearance of a new Russian supersonic intercontinental bomber in 1954, it became apparent that the need for an aircraft like the Arrow, originally promised by 1958, was urgent. Moreover, the CF-100 was an all-Canadian fighter which had given a tremendous boost to the Canadian aircraft industry. It had ranked among the best all-weather fighter aircraft when it was first made available to the NATO squadrons. As the Arrow developed it, too, gave a tremendous stimulus to the Canadian industry as more and more of its components were designed and produced by Avro. No aircraft with the Arrow's capabilities was on the drawing boards in either the United States or Great Britain, and even if the Americans had not committed themselves to buy the Arrow, it was felt by many—and it was wishful thinking—that they *might*.

By 1956, the amount of money being poured into the Arrow project was criticized by Lt.-Gen. Guy Simonds, the recently retired Chief of the General Staff, who now could speak publicly about the large proportion of the defence budget being absorbed by the R.C.A.F. "The wisdom of embarking upon the development of the CF-105 fighter is open to serious military objections," he wrote, and added:

It should be abundantly clear by now that the ground-to-air missile offers the only prospect of eventually counter-balancing the existing ascendancy of the offensive in terms of aerial warfare. If as many believe, there may be a dangerous time-gap to be covered by some form of defence, after existing fighters are obsolete and before a really reliable ground-to-air guided missile is available in operational quantities, then it would have been both more sensible and economical to have adopted a prototype fighter developed by the United States or Britain as a gap filler rather than to embark on an expensive venture of our own, the product of which at best will have a very short, if any, useful operational life. The combined vested interests of the air force, the aircraft industry and defence research scientists, burning with zeal to participate in a project they could call their own, coupled with the known desire of ministers to maintain a defence effort with a strict manpower ceiling, swept aside any opposition to this venture.[4]

Simonds, perhaps, was expressing publicly what some senior naval and army officers were expressing privately in 1956 and 1957 as the costs of developing the Arrow threatened to take an even larger slice of the defence budget. They had favoured the idea originally for, despite interservice rivalries, it was generally understood that when one service wished to develop a new tank or undertake the construction of a more efficient ship, the other services had to wait for the next fiscal year to place their own requests to the minister. But the cost of the Arrow programme was exceeding every expectation, and although senior R.C.A.F. officers and others waxed eloquent about the progress being made as well as the tremendous potential of the aircraft, enthusiasm was waning among the other services, especially as their own commitments to NATO, the U.N., and elsewhere remained constant. By the end of 1956 another factor had to be considered. Then it was learned the United States Air Force was planning to produce an aircraft with capabilities approaching those of the Arrow although of lesser range and unable to operate beyond the limits of semi-automatic ground control.

Such, in brief, was the position when the Conservatives assumed office. The Arrow programme was running later than planned and was costing a great deal more than expected. There was comparatively little publicity about the Arrow prior to the 1957 elections. Less than four months later, however, Pearkes was invited to the Avro plant at Malton to take part in the ceremonies when the Arrow was shown to the public for the first time. Speaking to the large crowd in attendance, Pearkes said in part:

> Much has been said about the coming missile age and there have been suggestions that the era of the manned airplane is over. . . . They suggest we should put our faith in missiles and launch straight into the era of push-button war.
>
> I do not feel that missiles and manned aircraft have, as yet, reached the point where they should be considered as competitive. They will in fact become complementary. Each can do things which the other cannot do, and for some years to come both will be required on the inventory of any nation seeking to maintain an adequate deterrent to war.[5]

Basically, Pearkes's prediction was to be valid, but that evening an event occurred which made the missile age seem much closer than it was. Moscow radio announced that it had put into orbit, some 550 miles above the earth's surface, the first man-made satellite, "Sputnik." The implications of this scientific breakthrough in the Cold War received immediate attention in the NATO countries and elsewhere. Two ideas appeared to be uppermost in the minds of many. First, to place such a satellite in orbit, the Russians must have developed an operational ballistic missile driven by a rocket engine at least as big and as efficient as the best in the United States, and consequently the Russians probably had a workable intercontinental missile. Second, apparently Russia's scientific capability had been seriously underestimated, and the comforting thought that the United States led in the technology race was no longer tenable. This was the start of the belief, later proved false, that there was a "missile gap" between Russia and the United States. This belief, widely held by American intelligence agencies at the time, was to have a very decided effect on the Arrow programme.

Later that month and during the period until the new elections in the spring of 1958, Pearkes announced the government's intention, "upon the advice of the chiefs of staff," to continue to support the development of the CF-105. "The best advice that I have," he told the House in December, "founded on the judgment given by our own military advisers and military advisers from our N.A.T.O. partners, is that for many years to come there will be manned bombers."[6] He felt, however, that if an attack came, it would be "a combination of intercontinental missiles and manned bombers." Questioned again in January 1958 about the Arrow, he was slightly more hesitant but answered that "the future of that aircraft will depend entirely on the nature of the threat. The matter is constantly under examination, and as long as the threat exists, development and production of the CF-105 will continue."[7] He was also careful to state that the programme might be cancelled should the situation warrant it.

During 1958 Pearkes found himself in an increasingly difficult position. For a variety of reasons, many connected with the desire to make the Arrow the most efficient weapon in an era of rapidly changing technology, the cost of the aircraft continued to escalate. Originally it had been estimated that the aircraft, when developed, would cost about $1 million per unit, or about 25 per cent more than the CF-100. By the end of 1958, that estimate had quintupled to at least $5 million per aircraft, and that, of course, did not include the huge sums the government had paid towards its development. It also did not include the cost of the missiles each airplane would carry, nor the expensive guidance-control network which would have to be established throughout the area where the aircraft was expected to operate. Despite the obvious excellence of the Arrow, the financial burden of trying to develop and produce an aircraft which, hitherto, only the major nations could afford was becoming unbearable.

In July, when Pearkes and other cabinet ministers had the opportunity to have a meeting with John Foster Dulles, the American Secretary of State, Canada's growing concern about the role it could play in NORAD was one of the topics discussed. Pearkes noted that about one-half of the nation's defence budget was now devoted to air defence. There was good operational co-operation between Canada and the United States; what was now needed was more co-operation in production. Because Canada's requirements were small, Pearkes emphasized, the unit cost of producing complicated weaponry was high. Moreover, American-made components in Canadian-manufactured defence items was increasing an already adverse balance of payments. The Argus aircraft, for example, was being built in Canada, but about 35 per cent of its components were from the United States. Twenty per cent of the electronic equipment needed for the Arrow had to be purchased from the United States, and the aircraft was to be equipped with the American "Sparrow" air-to-air missile which meant a further drain. Further, if Canada was to build more radar stations, obtain the Bomarc surface-to-air missile, install the SAGE (Semi-Automatic Ground Environment) equipment needed for the new sophisticated weapons, and push continental defence some 250 miles to the north, the cost to Canada would be about $350 million. These considerations argued strongly for increased cost-sharing between the two countries, and Pearkes also emphasized to Dulles that it would be extremely helpful if the United States could buy some of the Arrow aircraft. Dulles was sympathetic. He told the Canadian ministers about some of the problems the United States was attempting to cope with and felt that a number of the points brought up by Pearkes should be brought up when the newly-created ministerial Canada-United States Committee on Joint Defence met.

Sympathy did not solve the problem of the Arrow. In August, therefore, Pearkes flew to Washington to talk to the American Secretary of State for Defense, Neil McElroy, to examine the possibility of American purchases of the Arrow.[8] "While proposals were exploratory, and no communique came from the conference," one source reported, "Pearkes apparently left little encouraged."[9] By this time the United States itself was developing an advanced supersonic aircraft with many features of the Arrow and the aircraft industry's lobbyists in Washington were a very powerful group. Furthermore, since "Sputnik," more attention was being paid to the "missile-gap," and consequently there was polite interest but again no commitments forthcoming from Washington.

During part of the time Pearkes was away, the House of Commons' Standing Committee on Estimates had been considering the 1958-59 estimates of the Department of National Defence and Defence Production. The committee, although taken aback at the $175 million set aside for the CF-105 programme, reluctantly concurred in the need for money but expressed its concern about the government entering into any subsequent weapons programme "without first negotiating for some cost-sharing agreement with either NATO member countries or the USA under the NORAD agreement."[10] Pearkes, when he returned to Ottawa to answer questions in the House, admitted the dilemma in which he was placed. By this time, in fact up to the end of the previous fiscal year, $220 million had been spent on the Arrow. The additional $175 million allocated for further research would carry on the programme until 31 March 1959, although, as he noted, "we have the right to discontinue it at any time."[11]

The concern over the apparent Russian lead in the missile race grew to the extent that military intelligence estimated that the manned bomber would be phased out sooner than expected. The first of a series of successful American satellites had been launched early in 1958, and as the Arrow was not expected to be ready for operational service for another three years, the potential length of its operational service was questionable. As Pearkes recollected later:

> As the pendulum swung from the possibility of bomber to intercontinental ballistic missile attack, the requirement [for the Arrow] seemed to me to decrease and become of secondary importance. Yet while there might be an ICBM attack . . . it might easily be followed by . . . waves of bombers come over to destroy special targets. However, looking back at it now . . . I doubt whether the international situation was as grave, and the likelihood of a Russian attack was nearly as probable as we thought.[12]

Military planners were overly impressed by the potential of Russia's military capabilities, as a number of them admitted later.[13] Nevertheless, Pearkes had to consider and weigh the intelligence he was getting from British and especially American sources. Although usually good, in this instance it was not reliable, and indeed one American has termed the U.S. Air Force's exaggerated estimate of Soviet intentions and capabilities "an outstanding instance of costly miscalculation."[14] Trying to peer into the 1960's, Pearkes felt "that the bomber was rapidly becoming obsolete and that we shouldn't invest this large proportion of the defence vote into a weapon which was useless against the ICBM."[15] Moreover, not only did it seem that the Russians were deeply committed to ICBM's, but intelligence reports also indicated at the time that their production of jet bombers appeared to be lessening.

Yet there was a major consideration which had to be faced. The missile age might indeed by "around the corner"—but how far around? It took years to develop a modern aircraft, and even after a successful test flight, there was a long time-gap before sufficient aircraft were manufactured and became operational. The same held true with missiles. The jet bombers of the Strategic Air Command and their Russian counterparts would continue to be the major threat to each country in case of all-out war for many years to come, and indeed even after both had built up their ICBM arsenals, the role of jet aircraft would not be over. The new ground-to-air missiles, of which the Bomarc was one of several, would doubtless play an increasing part in air defence, but one still needed swords as well as shields in air warfare as it would be fought for some years to come.

The pressure on Pearkes was tremendous. "We were besieged by the A. V. Roe people," he recalled later. If the Arrow was to continue, Pearkes had to have more money, but working with a limited defence budget, he faced the problem of either reducing the effectiveness of the other two services or admitting that the expensive programme must be halted. He might have demanded more millions for defence, but his arguments would have been questionable, and he was well aware of the needs of other departments to implement many of the measures the Conservatives had promised. To scrap the Arrow completely would be a risk, but a first step had to be taken and a last, strong effort could be made to find buyers before the final decision.

In September 1958 a press release from the Prime Minister's office stated that the government had decided to introduce missiles into the Canadian air defence system and that the number of supersonic interceptor aircraft required for the R.C.A.F. would be "substantially less than could have been foreseen a few years ago, if in fact such aircraft will be required at all in the 1960's, in view of rapid strides being made by both the United States and the U.S.S.R." The press release noted that "the preponderance of expert opinion" held that by the 1960's manned aircraft, "however outstanding," would be less effective in meeting a threat than previously expected. With the introduction of the Bomarc as part of Canada's anti-bomber defences, fewer manned, supersonic interceptor aircraft would be needed, and thus "the government had decided that it would not be advisable at this time to put the CF-105 into production." However, the impact on the aircraft industry if the development of the Arrow was discontinued abruptly, together with the uncertain international outlook, made the government decide as "a measure of insurance" the development programme for the aircraft with its Iroquois engine should be continued until March 1959 when the situation would be reviewed. Contracts for the Astra fire-control system and the Sparrow missile, however, were to be terminated and modifications made to allow substitution of a fully developed missile and control system which would save a considerable amount of money. Nevertheless, even with this saving, up to the end of September 1958 the Arrow had cost $303 million. "To finish this development of the CF-105 and its components, including the Astra and Sparrow," the press release noted, "and to produce enough to have about 100 aircraft for squadron use would cost about another billion and a quarter dollars."

The six months following the announcement regarding the Arrow put more pressure on Pearkes and caused him more sleepless nights than any other period of his career. Almost immediately there was a flood of letters to him, to the Prime Minister, and to members of Parliament from organizations and individuals expressing alarm at the possibility the Arrow might be scrapped. In November A/M Slemon, the Canadian Deputy Commander at NORAD headquarters, stated publicly that the manned interceptor would be an "unescapable requirement for as long as we can see." Both he and Gen. Partridge were reported to have recommended to the Canadian Chiefs of Staff that manned interceptors be retained, and

Slemon particularly pointed out that the Arrow would have more speed, better altitude, longer range, and greater manoeuvrability than its closest rival, the American F-106. It would be the best in the air until the American F-108 came into production in about six years, and meanwhile NORAD "needed very long range manned interceptors to carry out interceptions as far north as possible."[16] Another critic of possible cancellation was John Gellner, a former R.C.A.F. officer, who pointed out that the real issue at stake was Canadian independence. If the Arrow was not built, he felt Canada would rely on the "Nike" or "Bomarc" ground-to-air missile. These, of course, were unmanned, and, since it appeared that Canada would not purchase a foreign-built fighter, Canadian air surveillance would be in the hands of American fighter pilots.[17] Pearson, sensing the difficulties facing the Conservatives, was quoted as saying in Edmonton "that if his party had been in power when the first ICBM was fired, a decision would have had to be made at that time to cancel the CF-105," and he suggested that the government should cancel the production of the Arrow in the fall.[18]

Meanwhile Pearkes was extremely busy. If he could get promises from the Americans or the British to purchase the Arrow, there was a bare possibility the huge financial burden might continue to be economically tolerable, thousands of highly skilled technicians would continue their employment, and the Canadian aviation industry would enhance its growing prestige and possibly widen its market. Unfortunately, the hoped for purchases were not forthcoming. In December 1958 at the NATO meeting of defence ministers, Canada was told finally and definitely that the United States would not purchase the Arrow. Two months later a similar reply was received from Great Britain. The cost of the aircraft, the demands of their own aircraft industries, the delays in production, and the uncertainties surrounding the role of the manned interceptor versus the coming generation of missiles were some of the main arguments.

The A. V. Roe Company was intensely interested in the ultimate decision. When the Conservatives came to power, the Arrow programme was running about a year late. Nevertheless, Avro officials were confident that the Arrow would not only be more than a match for any supersonic Russian bomber, but also that it was years ahead of the best the Americans had or were likely to have in the near future. Avro was not unaware of the periodic warnings announced in the House of Commons in 1957 and 1958 regarding the government's ability to halt the programme. "On the other hand," a company official noted, "we had been told to press on with the utmost vigor with the development of the aircraft by the people that were overseeing us on the government's side, the R.C.A.F. and the Department of Defence Production."[19] It was not until early in 1959 that the action to be taken in case of cancellation was brought out into the open when government officials were present, but whether this went beyond the deputy minister level is open to question.[20]

The impact of cancellation on Avro's thousands of skilled workers and on the Canadian aircraft industry had not been overlooked by the government. In September, when the Prime Minister gave notice of possible cancellation, a determined effort was made to seek means of getting Canadian rights to manufacture aircraft, missiles, and other equipment, including naval and army weaponry, which could be given to Avro to help fill the gap in part should the Arrow be phased out.

At the same time, everything pointed to the need to cancel. Early in 1959 intelligence estimated that, two years after the Arrow became operational, the Russians would have about 750 ICBM's and SLBM's (Submarine Launched Ballistic Missiles) targeted on air defence control centres, retaliatory bases, and other key sites. Since there was no defence against missiles, Pearkes felt that any attack launched against the continent would use this weapon. Intelligence also estimated that Russian bombers might be reduced in quantity but that their quality was improving. The Arrow could match even this estimated quality by 1963, but could Canada stand the financial strain? Pearkes realized he was taking a chance. The bomber threat would nevertheless be a major concern until sufficient missiles were built and became operational. Bomarc surface-to-air missiles would help fill the gap when they became available, but more important to Pearkes was the assurance he had from the Americans that, in a crisis, they would sent their best fighter-interceptors north to help defend Canada.[21]

The decision, when it came, was the result of many painful hours of considering every aspect of the situation. The Chiefs of Staff were "pretty well unanimous" that the programme should be halted and expressed their opinion to the Prime Minister when he questioned them on it. Pearkes, who had wished the decision to cancel could have been avoided, had realized for some time that it was inevitable. As he said later:

> [To continue the Arrow programme] would have meant the cessation of any naval development which was going on, we could not have begun to have reequipped the Army with any . . . modern weapons and it would have meant very serious reductions in the strength of the army. It would have been all out of proportion . . . I could never have felt that I was justified in cutting the other services to the extent which would have been necessary to [buy] the Arrow. . . .
>
> Many RCAF officers would like to have seen the Arrow developed. On the other hand, there were others who felt as I did . . . that perhaps we should concentrate more on missiles. But the Chiefs of Staff as a whole considered this matter so carefully . . . and I took the col-

lective advice of the Chiefs of Staff. . . . At that time they felt that the balance of defence was necessary, and if more money wasn't available, then we would have to make some other arrangements . . . [these] being that there would be fighters from the American forces. . . .

I think it [the decision to cancel the Arrow] was the hardest decision I had to make while I was Minister of Defence, and I don't back down on the decision I did make. I think it was a wise decision. It was undoubtedly unpopular in certain quarters and it . . . hurt national pride. But we had to provide the best defence we could with the money which was available.[22]

The political as well as the economic impact of cancellation made it a cabinet decision which Diefenbaker announced in the House of Commons on Friday, 20 February, 1959. The decision, when it came, pleased Pearkes only in that it had finally been made and the drain of millions of dollars from his defence budget had been stopped.[23]

Diefenbaker spoke first, announcing the government's decision to terminate the contract. It was made, he said, "in the light of all the information available concerning the probable nature of the threats to North America in future years, the alternative means of defence against such threats, and the estimated costs thereof."[24] He felt that "the bomber threat against which the CF-105 was intended to provide defence "has diminished and that potential aggressors now seem more likely to put their effort into missile development than into increasing their bomber force." The long-range bomber would remain a threat even in the 1960's, but it would probably be "relegated to supplementing the major attack by these missiles."

It was not until after the weekend recess that Pearkes spoke on the Arrow. After sketching the history of its development, he described the rising costs, the delays, the unexpected competition initiated by the United States, and the changing strategic posture as better missiles came into production. He stressed, as had Diefenbaker, that "all the information . . . from all the sources which are available to the government indicates that the threat of the manned bomber against this country is diminishing."[25] Pearkes told of the attempts made to interest other NATO allies in buying the Arrow. He informed the House that the new destroyer escorts then being built would cost about $350 million, that the Argus aircraft being developed would cost another $237 million, that another $140 million would be required to provide air transport for the army's brigades, and that these sums by no means covered all the equipment, weaponry, and other needs of the armed forces. He ended his speech by stressing, as he had in 1957 and in 1958, the indivisibility of continental air defence. He felt that while

Canada was and should be providing as much as she could with respect to radar lines, bases, and so forth for air defence, the United States would provide the greater portion of the air defence of North America.

As might be expected, there was a storm of criticism of the government's action, which was given greater force by the immediate layoff of thousands of men by the A. V. Roe Company. Diefenbaker and Pearkes received hundreds of letters and telegrams.[26] In the House of Commons, the C.C.F. and especially the Liberals went after the government. Hazen Argue of the C.C.F., for example, wanted to know what was to happen to the workers who were out of work and whether the government had found alternatives to the Arrow for the aircraft industry. "What happens," he asked, "to Canadian sovereignty in the very unbalanced partnership that the government has agreed to on behalf of this country?"[27] On the Liberal benches, Lester Pearson and Paul Hellyer led the attack. The latter first criticized the manner in which the cancellation was done, especially as there was no alternative project to take its place. He said the Russians still had between one and two thousand bombers capable of threatening Canada, that they could fly under the Bomarc missile defence, and that the Bomarc missiles themselves had not yet been proven satisfactory. He wondered if Canadian salesmen trying to sell the Arrow abroad had been persuasive enough and questioned whether the CF-100's could handle Russian jet bombers. Hellyer questioned the costs of the Arrow programme.[28] Lester Pearson, whose riding, unlike Hellyer's, was some distance from Toronto where the impact of cancellation would hit hardest, spent more time on a critical analysis of the defence situation. He questioned whether Canada was not only accepting aid from the Americans for the first time, but also tying itself more closely to American military production. He called for collective production in collective defence (which Pearkes was already stressing in his talks with American defence officials in Washington, Camp David and elsewhere) and, like other opposition speakers, expressed his regret that the Canadian aircraft and associated industries, having gathered together such a pool of talent and having created such an excellent interceptor, should now be forced to retrench.

The criticisms and defence of the Conservatives' action with respect to the Arrow continued into March and reappeared periodically during the summer of 1959. Pearkes never doubted his decision. However, his entire career made him think in a pragmatic rather than a political way, and this was not the way John Diefenbaker thought. To Diefenbaker the Arrow had a political rather than a military effect, and he did not like the buffetting he received. His majority in the House, if anything, tended to make him more cautious and indecisive, not only because he wished to avoid the label of being arrogant, but also because he was determined to show the country that his party deserved the overwhelming confidence placed in it by the public.

The Prime Minister's relations with the top military advisers whom he met in the cabinet defence committee ranged from cool to correct. They were, for the most part, appointees of the Liberal government, and he admitted to the Chairman of the Chiefs of Staff that he did not like generals or the way they thought.[29] Diefenbaker's "whole personality and character," one of his cabinet ministers reflected later, "is the antithesis of what is regarded as the military personality and character. . . . [they] are opposites. They have no empathy."[30] Diefenbaker's experience with the Arrow thus tended to increase his dislike and distrust of military advisers because, as a colleague put it, "[he] always felt that we had been jockeyed into the position of cancelling the Avro Arrow by the military . . . and some other senior advisers of the government."[31] There were others in the cabinet who felt the senior military commanders were unaware of political realities, and it is probably true also that these senior people felt that the government was not facing up to the realities of defence. The time factor in a future war had moved from weeks to days and was in the process of moving to hours if not minutes.

How long and how serious the threat of bombers against North America would remain was a matter of conjecture by military strategists, most of whom at the time placed more emphasis on the great strides Russia apparently had made in missilery. But even as the rivals worked feverishly to increase their arsenals of ICBM's, there remained in operational readiness dozens of squadrons of bomber aircraft which, with their atomic payloads, could pulverize military and civilian targets. With the cancellation of the Arrow, Pearkes had to and did assume certain risks—primarily that Russia would not risk an all-out attack until her ICBM arsenal was sufficiently full. As well as arranging to have American fighter-interceptors operate from northern Canadian bases should a crisis arise, he took advantage of the American offer to locate two Bomarc surface-to-air missile bases north of the border to help guard Canadian bases and cities while, at the same time, offering a defence in depth to eastern American cities.

In the mid-1950's, the United States Air Force plan for providing air defence included a chain of Bomarc installations situated just south of the Canadian border and part-way down each coast. Information regarding the American plans became available to Canada even before the NORAD agreement. The reconnaissance team which was siting the missile locations south of the Great Lakes suggested to the R.C.A.F. that if Bomarc missile sites were located in northern Ontario and Quebec instead of Michigan and New York, better coverage would be provided not only for Canadians but for Americans as well. Moreover, any nuclear carriers shot down, or at least a greater proportion of them, would fall in the uninhabited rather than the populated areas of the continent.[32] Pushing continental air defence to the north was given further urgency as it was known that long-range strategic bombers were being equipped with bombs which could be launched accurately onto a target from several hundred miles away.

During the summer of 1958 Canadian officials were engaged in exploratory discussions with their American colleagues on all aspects of anti-bomber missile defence. The Nike-Hercules missile became operational in 1958 and had proved itself successful not only against high performance aircraft but also against short-range ballistic missiles. It could operate as part of a defence network or as an autonomous unit, and each battery was capable of detecting, tracking, and engaging aircraft. With almost four times the range of the Hercules, the Bomarc surface-to-air had the range necessary to intercept a bomber before its air-to-surface missile could be launched. Because of their operational differences, to protect the general area Montreal-Ottawa-Toronto-Hamilton-Chalk River-Sault Ste. Marie, one would need two Bomarc squadrons located in northern Ontario and Quebec. These would cost about $164 million with annual recurring costs estimated at $12 million. If the Nike-Hercules system was used, the total cost was estimated at $165 million with annual recurring costs almost triple the Bomarc installations. The Bomarc, therefore, was recommended to Pearkes by the R.C.A.F. as "the best and cheapest defence for an industrial complex covering a large area," and on 23 September 1958 the Prime Minister announced that Bomarc missiles should be introduced into the Canadian air defence system.[33] The Bomarc, the press release added, could be used with either a conventional high-explosive warhead or a nuclear warhead.

During November and December, at Pearkes's request, a more thorough comparison was made between the two systems as well as between the Bomarc-A and the Bomarc-B. "The Bomarc 'B'," as one senior officer described it, "is as different from the 'A', except in external appearance, that they might have well given it quite a different designation."[34] Of the three the Bomarc-B appeared to be the best for Canadian needs, even though it was not scheduled for operational service until 1961-62. Its cost was almost twice as much, but it would have a range about three times greater than the Nike-Hercules.

Two features about the Bomarc-B, however, were to cause a considerable amount of political controversy. First, the Bomarc-B was designed to carry only an atomic warhead. Second, it was still in its research and development stage and was dependent upon the construction of a semi-automatic ground environment (SAGE) then undergoing user trials. Thus, the reports given to Pearkes in the winter of 1958-59 were based on expert intelligence, but the weapon itself had not been proven. Millions of dollars had been poured into the weapon, and those charged with the completion of this highly sophisticated weapon were confident it would prove its planned capabilities. Moreover, exceptionally good terms had been arranged with the Americans, and as the outlook for the Arrow programme looked increasingly bleak, final arrangements were made to accept the Bomarc-B sites north of the border.

The formal announcement in the House of Commons that Bomarc-B missiles were to be acquired by Canada was made at the same time as the Prime Minister announced the cancellation of the Arrow.[35] With the Bomarc came the need to introduce the SAGE electronic control and computing equipment as well as to extend and strengthen the Pinetree radar control system. Canada, he announced, would pay one-third of the costs of these new projects, and, further, he said that agreements had been reached with the United States to engage in production sharing of defence equipment on a much larger scale than ever before. "The full potential of these defensive weapons," Diefenbaker noted, referring both to the R.C.A.F.'s Bomarc-B and the army's Lacrosse missile, "is achieved only when they are armed with nuclear warheads," and he continued to say that his government was examining the question of the latter with the United States, though he assured the House Canada would never attempt to produce such warheads herself.

Criticism of the Bomarc was interlaced with criticism of the Arrow's cancellation, but in the first instance the Arrow took priority. The Leader of the Opposition led off by suggesting that the Bomarc "might be out of date before it becomes operational in the R.C.A.F.," and, as might be expected, he not only had grave doubts about its effectiveness but also was fearful that the arrangements would likely tie Canada more closely to American production.[36] The Liberal's defence critic, Paul Hellyer, had more ammunition. He asked why the government had not pressed the United States to place all its proposed Bomarc sites along the border several hundred miles further north rather than only two. He then assailed the Conservatives for leaving the country at the mercy of the Americans for their defence, while suggesting strongly that the government had left the country without any defences whatever.[37] Harold Winch of the C.C.F. wondered why, if the Arrow was cancelled owing to the lessening bomber threat, the government should attempt to get any Bomarc missiles as they were useful only against bombers. Opposition members realized that the Canadian public was finding the increasing need to lean on American support for Canadian air defence hard to accept, despite the fact that the Liberals themselves admitted the indivisibility of the continent's air defence. The task of the Opposition is to oppose, however, and the Liberals were enjoying themselves as Pearkes and his advisers, caught in the whirl of rapidly changing weapons systems, attempted to assess the conflicting

intelligence coming in about Russian intentions and American technological advances.

The Bomarc-B missile, like any sophisticated weapon, ran into troubles
during the later stages of its development. The first eight firings of the
missile at the Elgin Air Force Base in Florida were scheduled to take place
between May and December 1959. Owing to delays, the sixth firing did not
occur until the end of January 1960. During the first five firings, faults in
the fuel regulating valve resulted in loss of power in the ram jet engine. By
the sixth firing, this fault had been corrected, but a malfunction in the
flight control system developed. Nevertheless, it was reported to Pearkes
that the missiles could be anticipated for the Canadian sites[38] then under
construction on the planned operational dates.

In the United States, however, where hundreds of millions of dollars
were being spent on a variety of missiles and where interservice and intercompany rivalry was intense, the sixth consecutive failure of the Bomarc
had worked up considerable criticism. Testimony made public by the
House Military Appropriations Committee showed the Bomarc had destroyed only one supersonic target in ten final shots. Early in March a
Bomarc-B had exploded at Cape Canaveral. The growing criticism in the
United States[39] did not go unheeded in Canada and was causing a considerable amount of embarrassment. Pearkes received reports after the
various tests assuring him that the defects were being overcome but, as he
said later, "had it worked from the very beginning, it would have been
easier!"[40] In the United States the controversy over the Bomarc was mixed
up with debates over the nature of American defence policy in general.
How wide was the missile gap? If the threat from manned bombers was
receding, how wise was it to continue pouring millions of dollars into such
programmes as SAGE and Bomarc? Would it not be better to build more
missile launching submarines? Should we harden our ICBM sites or are
Russian ICBM's already so accurate that hardening should be abandoned
in favour of random dispersal rail and road-mobile deployment?

Late in March, the New York *Times* reported that the U.S. Air Force
Chief of Staff, Gen. T. D. White, proposed cutting funds for the Bomarc
programme from about $420 million to $50 million in view of the "changing military requirements" brought about by Soviet shifts of emphasis
from manned bombers to ICBM's. Despite the $3 billion spent so far, it
was felt that technical difficulties had delayed the time when the Bomarcs
would be operational.[41] In April the United States House of Representatives eliminated all financing of the Bomarcs, including the funds it had
approved for 1960. During May, however, as a result of resubmitted
proposals by the U.S. Air Force, the U.S. Senate voted funds for ten (not
the original eighteen) Bomarc-B missile sites including the two proposed
in Canada at North Bay and LaMacaza and two additional sites on the

American West Coast. Later, compromises between the House and Senate resulted in $224 million being set aside for the SAGE-Bomarc programme for a total of seven American and two Canadian sites.

For Pearkes it had been a grim period. Almost $.5 million of the $3 million contract for the North Bay site had been spent by the time the money had been restored to the programme by Congress. This was a tiny sum compared to what had been spent on the Arrow, but it represented the confidence he felt and continued to express in the Bomarc. If he put on a bold face, however, he was at times disheartened. "It was heart-breaking," he said later, "and I think that the strain was telling on me."[42]

While privately Canada voiced its complaints when cutbacks were made in a weapon system which she had been assured would play a key role in her air defence, the Opposition seized the opportunity presented by the confused situation in the United States.[43] One can only imagine the vast relief it must have been to Pearkes when, on 13 April 1960 he received a telegram from the Boeing Aircraft Co. stating in part: "Bomarc-B successfully launched today. . . . all objectives accomplished." In May two more successful tests were made in which the test objectives were exceeded at a range of about three hundred miles. The remarkable successes of the Bomarc-B, naturally, resulted in the change of heart by the U.S. Congress in restoring a great deal of the money it had withdrawn, and from that point on, the missile, the SAGE system it depended on, and the Bomarc-B bases went forward smoothly as originally planned.

The arguments in the House of Commons and in the press, however, did not enhance Pearkes's reputation. It was not so much that the Opposition derided the capabilities of the weapon, but rather there remained the somewhat distasteful fact that, with the Arrow cancelled, Canada now had to depend on United States weaponry to defend its skies, if only in part. One American commentator on Canadian defence policy summed up the situation in the summer of 1960 in these words:

> Canadians have been the victims of the sweeping and extraordinary rapid revolution in weapons systems, a change so extensive and of such headlong pace that no nation lacking an enormous industrial capacity, sizable reservoirs of technical skills, great wealth and technological and research facilities of impressive number can ever hope to contribute in a significant manner towards the requirements of strategic air or missile defence. . . . In weapon development, Canadians became subject not to the whims of the U.S. Defence Department but to the scope of the American effort. . . . No one could ever deride the *quality* of Canadian research and weapons development, but the *scale* on which these programmes must be conducted precludes most

nations, including Canada, from participating meaningfully in the race.[44]

It was perhaps fortunate for Pearkes and his successor that in 1959 and 1960 intelligence estimates about the "missile gap" began to moderate. Consequently, it was realized that the manned bomber would indeed continue to be both the main threat and deterrent (depending on which side of the Arctic one stood) for some time. To claims that the government was too dependent on allies, especially the United States, Pearkes responded in the House that "we are in a partnership, and that our partners fully appreciate our position, our sovereign rights and the efforts we are making."[45] It was not a particularly popular line to take when there was a certain anti-American element not only in the cabinet but among Canadians as well. Pearkes, however, always had uppermost in his mind his duty as the minister responsible for defending the country, and if the Bomarc-B had been offered to Canada by the British, the French, or any other ally, he would have accepted it. As one former senior officer reflected: "I would think he was trying to do the best military job he could. . . . He was first of all a soldier and secondly a politician and at his age I don't think you switch very rapidly."[46] From the point of view of military efficiency, which was Pearkes's primary concern, to achieve its maximum effect, the Bomarc-B should be equipped with a nuclear warhead. This question was coming more and more before the public at this time and ultimately was to lead to a crisis in the Conservative leadership.

The Bomarc-B was, as one senior officer described it, "the cheapest and most cost-effective weapon system that the Royal Canadian Air Force ever had, right up to the end when it was actually taken out."[47] It had a response measured in seconds, and, unlike a fighter-interceptor, it travelled supersonically all the way to its target. Its range was well beyond four hundred miles, and it was capable not only of striking a supersonic bomber but of knocking out an air-to-surface missile it might launch. The Bomarc's ability to search out and home in on a target was very good. Its "look-down-shoot-down" capability was far in advance of any manned fighter, and at the same time it had built into it numerous safeguards which, among other things, would prevent its warhead detonating, for example, at low levels, over Canadian cities. It never had a flight accident, but the idea of something flying around without a man in it bothered some people including not a few R.C.A.F. pilots, some of whom tended to think that it was a substitute for, rather than a complement to, manned fighters. The annual cost of maintaining the Bomarc bases as compared to what it costs to maintain a squadron of fighter aircraft in northern Canada (if such a comparison can be made) was significant. If, as critics claimed, the Bomarc sites were static rather than mobile, to an extent the same can be said of the ordinary fighter aircraft bases. Unlike the latter, however, and, indeed, unlike its American counterpart, the Canadian SAGE control headquarters was hardened, and it would take more accurate ICBM's to knock them out than any potential enemy would have for some years after the sites became operational.

The Bomarc-B had its limitations, but it did help protect a large portion of Canada which otherwise would have had to depend on too few fighters operating from airfields too close to the area to be defended. Pearkes had taken a risk when he accepted an unproven but promising weapon. As events turned out, it was a very sound decision. Moreover, he could claim, quite truthfully, that while the United States provided the missiles and much of the complicated electronic equipment for the Bomarc-SAGE bases, he was steadily replacing American servicemen in Canada with Canadian personnel.

The Arrow and the Bomarc were of particular Canadian and North American concern, but in defence as in other matters, what occurs in one area affects, or is affected by, events in another. Canada was also committed to the support of the North Atlantic Treaty Organization. When Pearkes became minister in 1957, he was briefed on the problems facing NATO, especially those which delayed the full implementation of NATO's planned strength. Rising costs owing to increasingly expensive and quickly obsolescent weaponry was one of them. To meet the commitments desired by the professional military planners, it was felt necessary that all members of NATO would have to increase their defence budgets by 4 to 8 per cent each year, an overall increase of about 20 per cent by 1963. The replacement of parts for conventional weapons becoming outdated was a problem, as was the difficulty in procuring land for airfields, depots, missile sites, headquarters, and other needs overseas. The need to maintain economic superiority over the Warsaw Pact countries as well as to maintain their defensive capabilities was a continuing strain, especially in view of the European manpower shortage.

In Opposition Pearkes criticized the government for maintaining the large number of army personnel in Europe, but when be became minister, he found it advisable to continue Liberal policies. When he was queried about this apparent change, he replied:

> when the forces of West Germany are reorganized and their training has been completed, and they have in existence the number of troops contemplated, there may then be an opportunity of reducing our commitment in Europe. . . . Until it is agreed by our allies that our forces

should be withdrawn, I do not see how we can make any material reduction in those forces.[48]

The cost of maintaining the army brigade and air division in Europe came to approximately $120 million and each year costs were increasing, but once Pearkes had full access to Canada's commitments to NATO and the problems that organization faced, he became completely committed to its support. He was, for example, all in favour of West German rearmament, not only because of the additional strength it offered, but also he felt it was safer both for West Germany and Russia that she should be in NATO since this would permit NATO some knowledge of and control over German forces at a time when the peace and security of Europe might easily be placed in jeopardy owing to the strong movement for German unification. Thus, although Canada's contribution to NATO was modest, from the standpoint of the unity and strength of the alliance, as well as the prestige and position of influence within NATO[49] which Canada had built up over the years, there were both political as well as military reasons for a Canadian presence.

Pearkes did bring about some changes. He increased the amount of armour available to the brigade to make it a more balanced force, changed the rotation process so that one battalion was rotated once every year instead of rotating the entire brigade once every three years, and increased the number of transport aircraft in the R.C.A.F. There never were as many transport aircraft available as Pearkes and his senior officers would have wished. To purchase and maintain sufficient cargo- and troop-carrying aircraft to move all three brigades designated for NATO was a task far beyond Canada's capabilities. Pearkes noted that it would require 120 "CC-106" and 336 "C-130B" type of aircraft. This would mean a capital outlay of about $2 billion and recurring costs of some $994 million. It would need an R.C.A.F. strength of about seventy-eight thousand officers and men in Canada and Europe, and, if the budget remained fixed, the other two services would be reduced to unacceptable levels.

The need to keep the Canadian brigade group in Europe organized on the basis of a streamlined, self-contained force increased with the development of both strategic and tactical nuclear weapons. In the early 1950's, it was planned that the brigades in Canada would be rushed to Europe in the early stages of the outbreak of war. By the late 1950's, however, it was felt that the chances of reinforcing the brigade group in the first few weeks of the conflict would be remote. With the weapons then either available or coming into production, many strategists believed that the first phase of a European war would see a period of violent, large-scale, organized fighting, made brutal by the intensity of nuclear exchange. As Pearkes observed in the House:

> The nuclear concept of war postulates the possibility that our major ports and lines of communication could be severely damaged in the initial enemy attack. Hence there is some doubt as to whether or not formations on this continent could reach Europe during the early and critical phase of the war. Canada, however, remains committed to furnishing the balance of an infantry division to NATO in the event of hostilities, but the portion of these forces stationed in Canada is now regarded as a strategic reserve.[50]

It was thought most improbable that a nuclear exchange would be limited to Europe, and thus the need to have the brigades in Canada well versed in survival training for possible use in their own country made a great deal of sense under the circumstances.

Pearkes "felt that the Canadian troops . . . should be given the very best equipment you could get for them."[51] Thus, for example, when Lt.-Gen. S. F. Clark, the Chief of the General Staff, proposed the acquisition of the "Honest John" surface-to-surface missile for the NATO brigade—a missile which could use either an atomic or high explosive warhead—Pearkes favoured it. As the "Honest John" would be more efficient with the nuclear warhead, it can be assumed that both Clark and Pearkes considered that negotiations with the United States would result in the provision of these warheads under the usual safeguards for their storage and control.

Canada's naval contribution to NATO, and indeed Pearkes's policy with respect to the Royal Canadian Navy, did not change markedly from that of the previous government. Among the nations in NATO, Canada stood fourth after the United States, France, and Great Britain in the percentage of the gross national product spent on defence. In the fiscal year 1958-59, this represented well over $1.5 billion, and of this the R.C.N. received approximately $280 million. In wartime, most of Canada's wartime naval forces would be committed to NATO, so that should hostilities occur, one aircraft carrier, eighteen destroyer escorts, and eleven frigates would be made available. Pearkes agreed with the anti-submarine role of the R.C.N., but with the navy as with the other forces, the changing technology, especially the prospect of nuclear-powered submarines carrying missiles with atomic weapons, was posing a future problem. Pearkes was content to carry on the programme of naval construction started by his predecessors. There were, of course, the usual problems to be faced as construction tapered off in the late 1950's. Shipbuilding and repair companies in the

East and West both clamoured for more naval work to keep their yards busy and their men employed and so keep their skilled and technical staffs together. However, there were more shipyards than there were ships to be built. All that could be done was to strike a balance between production costs and the desire to maintain shipyard facilities on both coasts by parcelling out contracts in a vain attempt to satisfy both East and West.

Pearkes gave special attention to submarines. For some time he seriously considered constructing them rather than buying or renting them from the British or Americans. The submarines were needed for training in connection with the R.C.N.'s anti-submarine warfare role, but it was decided ultimately to make use of those produced by both British and American yards. Nuclear submarines were coming into use, and Pearkes felt that if Canadian shipyards attempted to build a conventional submarine the defence department would be criticized. The pros and cons of building versus buying and of the merits of American versus British submarines carried over into the period of Pearkes's successor. The first of three submarines to be commissioned into the R.C.N. in the postwar period, H.M.C.S. *Grilse*, became operational in the spring of 1961. The training of the crew, together with the groundwork for their acquisition, took place while Pearkes was still in office.

Canada's No. 1 Air Division in Europe at this time had twelve squadrons of fighter aircraft, eight of them with F-86 Mk VI's and four equipped with CF-100's. The Air Division, which formed part of the 4th Allied Tactical Air Force under NATO command, was looked upon as one of the finest professional forces of its kind available to NATO. By the mid-1950's, even though the Air Division had fighters capable of matching the best any potential enemy might send against them, staff planners were beginning to question the basic concepts that there would be a battle for air superiority in view of the limited air space available in Europe. Since fighter aircraft seek height, would pilots flying at, perhaps, forty-five thousand feet be able to see and to strike a squadron flying in low, even below radar coverage? "We began to have some doubts about our role," a former wing commander in the division recalled, "and yet we were committed to some sort of an independent role because of the desire to retain Canadian command of the force."[52]

To maintain Canadian control meant that the role for the Air Division should be such that it would call for the force to be tasked not below the Allied Tactical Air Force level or higher. Among those suggested was the tactical bomber role using light, high-speed jet bombers which, should the need arise, could strike at enemy armed forces massed for an attack or at troop or other concentrations of armed power assembled to carry forward an attack which had already started. In December 1957 when Diefenbaker, Pearkes, and the new Secretary of State for External Affairs, Sidney

Smith, attended the Heads of State NATO meeting in Paris, the Canadian delegation agreed without reservation to the principle of accepting tactical nuclear warheads by NATO forces in Europe. This, of course, included the Air Division as well as the other two services, and as a result the possibility of having all or part of the Canadian squadrons equipped with aircraft designed to carry a tactical nuclear bomb was given serious consideration.

Pearkes was briefed on the problem of a possible new role for the Air Division when he assumed office. Four months later he met and had a long talk with Gen. Lauris Norstad, the Supreme Allied Commander, Europe, when the topic was also discussed. In 1958, Gen. Norstad completed a study of the minimum force requirements to implement the deterrent strategy approved by the NATO council, and in the spring of 1959, he came to Ottawa to brief the cabinet on the need to re-equip the Air Division. By the time Norstad arrived, an immense amount of work had been done by R.C.A.F. and Defence Production investigation committees. Their findings had been critically examined by the Chiefs of Staff Committee and the defence committee of the cabinet. Over twenty types of aircraft were examined, the criteria being their suitability for the new role, their serviceability and availability, their cost, and the amount of work which Canada might share directly or indirectly in their production. The aircraft selected was the CF-104, and the new role, announced by Pearkes in the House of Commons in July, was termed "strike reconnaissance."[53]

The fact that the Canadian pilots would be able to make a comparatively fast change from one type of aircraft to another without being pulled out of the line for a long period of training was one factor as was the timing of the change itself. Further, aside from simplifying command control arrangements, the Canadian squadrons would make a direct contribution to the deterrent forces of the NATO shield, and it provided them with greater flexibility and the possibility of redeployment.

The term used to describe the new role, i.e., "strike reconnaissance," was not the easiest one, Pearkes found, to explain to his colleagues. It sounded too much like "shoot first and enquire later" rather than the other way around, especially at a time when there was growing resistance to the idea of Canada having anything to do with nuclear weapons. The aircraft chosen, the Lockheed F-104 "Starfighter," held the world's speed record at the time of about 1400 miles per hour. It could climb under test conditions to 82,000 feet in under half a minute, it was capable of deeply penetrating enemy held territory under all weather conditions, carried a variety of weapons including air-to-air missiles, had excellent navigation and finder equipment, and was expected to be operational in 1961. They were proven aircraft, but they did need considerable modification to be used in the strike-reconnaissance role. Some have questioned whether or not Pearkes realized that it could not readily be used for an alternative role. Pearkes was well aware not only of its capabilities but also of its limitations, and in so far as committing the Canadian squadrons to a nuclear role, he appreciated that as well. The role of the Air Division was to deter and defend. Since Canada had accepted the principle of the use of nuclear weapons in December 1957 and since the cabinet had accepted the new role, which, incidentally, had been examined previously and approved by the Chief of the Air Staff and his advisers, Pearkes felt it his duty to provide the best means available to carry out the task.

It would not be correct to believe that Pearkes alone determined and directed Canadian defence policy during the years he was in office. Indeed this probably can be said of any Canadian Minister of Defence. Aside from such fundamental matters as geography, industrial capacity, inherited alliances, popular support for the government in power, to mention only a few considerations, there are other factors which constantly exert pressure on the minister in performing his task. Of these, one of the most fundamental is the budget he must work for every year, which in turn depends upon the support he receives in cabinet, the state of the nation's economy, and the competing demands from other ministries. Another factor, of course, is the danger which appears to be threatening the country, together with the decision by the government whether it is best to pile up armaments against a potential aggressor, or to work mightily to reduce the danger of conflict by lowering the nation's sword and shield as a token of peaceful intent and possible later disarmament. Another consideration is the relationship of the minister with the Prime Minister and his cabinet colleagues, a relationship which should never be considered as static. Added to this is the information and advice the minister receives on which he bases his decisions and, to no small degree, the approval or otherwise by the public of the way in which the minister seems to be handling his job.

Most of the major problems facing Pearkes as minister have been described, but there is one more which must be dealt with, which, like a magnifying glass, seemed to focus all the contending pressures to which he was subject. This was the use, control, and storage of atomic warheads by Canadian forces both in Canada and Europe. The official files are still not open for examination, but a sufficient amount of information is available to describe the problem which, probably more than any other, led to such massive frustration that he was not altogether unhappy to retire.

Canada does not manufacture atomic warheads nor, at any time, has she "owned" any. Gen. Charles Foulkes put it succinctly:

These weapons are manufactured and paid for by the United States and are not bought by Canada; they remain the property of the United States. They are provided solely for joint use or multilateral defence of the NATO area which includes Canada. The United States' law restricts the release of nuclear components to the President. This is a safeguard to ensure that they are not used for any other purpose. This release is not an order to use them; it is only a release to the country concerned. The decision to use the weapons, like the decision to go to war, is a national government decision.[54]

During the course of his career, there was probably no other matter on which Pearkes received more letters from citizens and organizations across Canada.[55] These, in general, either complained or enquired about the possible storage of nuclear weapons by Americans on Canadian soil or the use of Canadian air space by bombers of the U.S. Strategic Air Command carrying nuclear weapons. It was sometimes difficult, for security reasons, to reply to the enquiries, especially in cases where sites were constructed for the storage of the warheads (for example the Bomarc si.es) but no warheads were in them. To say there were no nuclear weapons in a site would help a potential enemy; he also would be helped if he knew there were. Mixed with these letters were those demanding that nuclear tests be banned and others seeking the abolition of any possibility of nuclear warfare.

Generally speaking, public opinion, as expressed in letters and in newspapers and journals as well, was divided into a very vocal though small "anti-nuclear" group and a much quieter "pro-nuclear" group. Of the former some said that it would be an immoral act for Canada to acquire nuclear weapons. These people tended to feel that defence money would be better spent on social advancement and that Russia was armed to the teeth only through fear of the Western powers. Others felt that the acceptance of nuclear arms would only increase Canadian dependency on the United States. Some believed that enlightened American self-interest dictated the protection of Canada without Canadian participation. There were those, too, who felt that any contribution Canada could make would be insignificant should a nuclear exchange take place, and indeed many in this group believed there would never be a nuclear war.

The "pro-nuclear" group tended to look upon the atomic weapon in terms of a balance of terror. Canadian NATO troops were located in the "bowling alley of Europe" where the brunt of an invasion would likely fall, and as such they deserved the best support available. It was felt that the NATO alliance would never be the aggressor, and thus atomic weaponry would only be used as a last resort in the defence. If Canada accepted weapons systems which called for an atomic warhead to be efficient, the only rational, logical thing to do was to acquire them. They were, some wrote, merely a new type of weapon in a business which is and always has been dirty and nasty.

Among this group were many military men, and certainly the Chiefs of Staff, as Pearkes said later, "were all for it—one hundred percent."[56] Obviously Pearkes himself favoured the use of nuclear weapons for defensive purposes. He never imagined, when he supported their acquisition for Canadian forces, that there would be such a controversy over the matter. "It seemed so practical to me," he related, "that you were going to give the people who are defending Canada the best possible weapons. . . . If the enemy was over our land, you should use the best weapons you could against them. I think that is the role of the Defence Minister."[57] Pearkes felt that the chances of a major European war being fought without using nuclear weapons were extremely remote. "The moment one side begins to get the advantage over the other, the other is going to escalate and come back. And facing defeat, the country is going to use every weapon that it has. I think we have to face up to it."[58] Others in the cabinet were more reluctant to face up to it.

When the Conservatives came to power, it was understood that American overflights would be cleared through regular diplomatic and military channels and that in every case Canadian permission would be received. It was not until after the NORAD treaty had been announced that the United States proposed to Canada the possibility of introducing atomic capabilities for continental defence north of the border. The development of air-to-air atomic weapons, for example, and the value of the ability of American aricraft to disperse to Canadian airfields made the idea of storing such weapons in Goose Bay or elsewhere a logical and important step in planning the defence of North America. Another consideration, of course, was the storage and control of atomic warheads for the Bomarc missiles which, although still in the development stage, merited early consideration. Shortly after these proposals had been made, Canada, along with the other NATO members, had unreservedly concurred with the agreement in principle to establish nuclear warhead stockpiles in Europe. Pearkes, one of the Canadian delegates to the December 1957 NATO meeting, fully concurred with the principle, and Sidney Smith of External Affairs offered no objection. Diefenbaker, attending his first major conference of this type, agreed with the other Heads of State although Pearkes, in the light of later experience, was to confess that he doubted very much if the Prime Minister realized the full implications of agreeing to the use of tactical nuclear weapons.[59]

In the month following their return from the NATO meeting, approval was given to further American-Canadian discussions among officials dealing with the question of the storage of nuclear arms. By April 1958 the cabinet defence committee had considered some proposals placed before them, but a decision was deferred. There were many ramifications of the problem to be considered, especially over what constituted control. Storage was a lesser problem, but even this could be troublesome. If atomic warheads for torpedoes or mines were carried in an American warship anchored in a Canadian harbour, for example, did this constitute "storage" in the same sense as atomic warheads buried deep underground near a Canadian airfield? And what rules should govern the deposit or movement of atomic warheads from such places of storage? It was one thing for an American aircraft to fly from an American base with an atomic bomb through Canadian skies and back to an American base, but the implication of the weapons being on Canadian soil and under joint control was something else.

Although the Arrow was designed to be capable of carrying an air-to-air missile armed with an atomic warhead, it was not until 20 February 1959, when the Prime Minister announced the cancellation of the Arrow programme and the decision to acquire the Bomarc missile, that he announced in the House of Commons some idea of the government's thinking on atomic weapons. "Careful thought is being given to the principles that in our opinion are applicable to the acquisition and control of nuclear weapons," he said. When he added: "The full potential of these defensive weapons [Bomarc and Lacrosse missiles] is achieved only when they are armed with nuclear weapons," it was generally assumed, and quite rightly, by Canadians and Americans alike that the government would not acquire the weapons if they were not to be given their full potential. The Prime Minister stated that discussions with the United States were underway, but he added immediately that Canada believed in the importance of limiting the spread of nuclear weapons at the independent disposal of national governments. He stressed the need for disarmament and indicated that it was with reluctance that, in the present circumstances, Canada had need of atomic weapons of a defensive character.

The duality of sentiment expressed in his speech reflected, in no small degree, the divergent opinions in the cabinet, especially as represented by Pearkes and Howard Green. Green had replaced Sidney Smith as Secretary of State for External Affairs following the latter's untimely death in 1959. Green had served both as a member of Parliament and as a cabinet minister for over twenty years. For years he had been the Conservative party leader's representative in British Columbia, and it was Green who had urged Pearkes to run as a candidate in 1945. His loyalty and seniority were something which the Prime Minister did not and could not ignore. As a senior cabinet minister he frequently represented the Prime Minister, and usually, in Diefenbaker's absence, he chaired cabinet meetings. Veterans of the Great War, and proponents of conscription in 1944, Pearkes and Green had much in common aside from being M.P.'s from British Columbia. One thing they did not share, however, was a similar view of Canadian defence policy.

Prior to Green's assuming control of External Affairs in June 1959, however, certain steps had been taken related to the possible acquisition of nuclear weapons. The government had concurred in the establishment of stocks of nuclear weapons in Europe. When Canada had signed the NORAD Agreement, U.S. forces assigned to NORAD were equipped to employ nuclear weapons. In June 1958 an agreement was extended which allowed the deployment of U.S. nuclear armed interceptors over Canada with Canadian concurrence during a state of air defence readiness. In September 1958 Diefenbaker announced Canada would obtain the Bomarc missile which would achieve full potential only when armed with nuclear weapons. The decision to equip the Air Division in Europe with the CF-104 and the army with the "Honest John" missile—both of which required atomic weapons to reach maximum effectiveness—were further steps which were designed to give to the Canadian forces a capability Pearkes would have desired.

Green did not approve what he considered to be Canada's march towards becoming an atomic power. He felt that a nuclear war would destroy civilization. To avoid such a holocaust, Green believed that Canada should bend her efforts to achieve as great a measure of disarmament as possible, both nuclear and non-nuclear, and at the same time he, and many others, feared that if additional nations gained nuclear capability and thus increased the number in the "nuclear club," the chances of a nuclear conflict, by design or accident, would increase.

From the outset Howard Green was determined to achieve what he could to reduce nuclear testing, nuclear proliferation, and the likelihood of nuclear—or indeed any—war. It was a laudable aim, supported by the public in Canada and elsewhere, and a goal which Diefenbaker and the rest of the cabinet agreed upon. The U.S. and the U.S.S.R. were polluting the atmosphere with their nuclear tests, and at the United Nations Canada, Japan, India, the Scandinavian countries, and others were working hard to bring the tests to a halt. Canada was also among the leading countries at the U.N. attempting to halt the spread of nuclear weapons beyond the three powers already possessing them—the U.S., the U.S.S.R., and Great Britain. Green felt that Canada would place herself in an impossible role if, on the one hand, she brought nuclear weapons onto her soil while, on the other, she pleaded with other nations to refrain from "going nuclear." His position, therefore, was very different from Pearkes's. This is not to say that one was a "hawk" and the other a "dove." Both wished to avoid war. But if war did break out, Green could have the satisfaction of knowing he had done his utmost to prevent it. Pearkes, on the other hand, would be faced with the stark reality of defence. Canada's contribution to continental defence might be marginal, but to the extent that it helped to assist the capability and therefore the credibility of the American deterrent it had great value. Pearkes felt that every effort should be made towards disarmament, but his experience and his background convinced him that the shield should not be lowered and the sword, if sheathed, should be kept sharp. Believing firmly that Canada could not be neutral if the U.S.A. was attacked by Russia and convinced that the defence of the continent was indivisible, Pearkes opted for nuclear weapons.[60]

Pearkes and Green, therefore, found themselves poles apart on defence policy, and since Green was a senior cabinet minister, a member of the cabinet defence committee, and sat on the joint Canadian-American ministerial meetings, Pearkes found it increasingly difficult to reach an agreement with the United States. Added to his problem was Green's suspicion of the Pentagon and the influence he felt it wielded to influence American politicians and allies. Green was not an isolationist or a neutralist, and indeed on his first official visit to Europe in October 1959, he gave NATO his warm support. However, it is difficult, if not impossible, to separate disarmament planning from strategic planning, and as there appeared to be some possibility for a détente with the U.S.S.R., Green stressed the need for NATO policies to be made by NATO politicians. At the meetings at Camp David, Maryland, and the Seigneury Club at Montebello, Quebec, when the Ministers of Defence, Finance, and External Affairs met informally with their opposite numbers from Washington, Green was almost a silent partner. Obviously he was not impressed with the arguments he heard. He was in a position to slow up the negotiations with the United States for the acquisition and storage of nuclear weapons for Canadian forces, and this he did.

A clash of policy such as this normally might be settled by the Prime Minister or perhaps decided in the cabinet or cabinet defence committee. There were fewer meetings of the latter under Pearkes than his predecessors. Commenting later on this Pearkes said:

> I don't think, really, that I am altogether to be blamed for not having more defence committee meetings, although I must be honest, I wasn't too enthusiastic about them because I didn't think they knew a damn thing about [the problems]. . . . Fleming was always helpful . . .; he was always realistic but some of the others who attended occasionally [were not]. And it always meant arguments with Howard Green. Diefenbaker didn't want these committee meetings; there is no question about that. He didn't want to discuss in front of the Chiefs of Staff all

the various problems. He hated talking in front of generals and he had never been a strong committee man.[61]

Pearkes was always willing to meet with cabinet ministers to explain defence matters, but "they were just so busy with their own departments that they didn't want to be mixed up with defence." "It was hard," he added, "desperately hard, to get time at a cabinet meeting to discuss these various things. Papers were submitted but all too frequently were passed over very quickly."[62]

The Prime Minister liked cabinet meetings and had them very frequently. If, especially in the latter part of 1959 and in 1960, Pearkes had felt he was making progress in swinging more support behind his policy to acquire nuclear warheads, he would have been much less concerned about the time they were taking, but such was not the case. "There was more argument in the Cabinet about everything," he said later. "I don't know whether Cabinet was losing confidence in me in connection with the Bomarc or not. But there was a continual lack of confidence shown by Diefenbaker in the Chiefs of Staff."[63] The continual wrangling, coupled with the anti-Americanism of some of the ministers, was quite contrary to Pearkes's way of thinking. "I have been a man of action all my life," he reflected, "and this idea of having to go and postpone [a military decision] so a lot of people can talk about it infuriated me."[64]

Unlike his Chairman of the Chiefs of Staff, Pearkes did not find the Prime Minister extremely difficult to deal with, but rather a man whose interest was not directed towards military affairs and who was unwilling to devote the time to study the complexities involved. Diefenbaker did acquiesce in the principle of using nuclear warheads for NATO forces, but later Pearkes was to admit that he doubted very much if Diefenbaker "realized the full implications of agreeing to [their use]."[65] When Pearkes would visit him in his office to explain some matter, he often found that the Prime Minister wanted to do the talking not the listening. If Pearkes reinforced his argument for a course of action which Diefenbaker found politically inadvisable to pursue by saying that his Chiefs of Staff were in favour of it, the Prime Minister claimed that he should not pay too much attention to these senior "Liberal" military advisers. Pearkes, and others, tried to get Diefenbaker to visit NORAD headquarters, but he would never come. When Pearkes would return from a NATO meeting, the Prime Minister rarely if ever enquired about the results of his visit. Try as he might to explain the "twin key" concept involved in the proposed joint security measures for atomic weapons if they were stored in Canada, Diefenbaker did not seem to grasp it. After Green began to exert his pressure on the Prime Minister, it almost appeared that Diefenbaker became increasingly reluctant to commit himself to a defence policy which made obvious Canada's close relationship to the American deterrent.

There seems also to be little doubt that the Prime Minister was not pleased with the criticism the government had to endure as a result of a rapidly changing military and scientific technology. The Arrow cancellation was politically embarrassing. For months the Bomarc tests were unfavourable. Moreover, Diefenbaker was sensitive to the cry of the small minority which claimed that Canada's sovereignty was being eroded.

Diefenbaker probably wished the problem would go away, especially as the conflict involved two of his most senior and most respected political and cabinet colleagues. Green possibly might have resigned if the government brought in atomic weapons. Pearkes was older, and he had told the Prime Minister that he did not intend to run again. Pearkes felt that there was little chance he could change Howard Green's stand on nuclear weapons or win over the Prime Minister to make a firm pro-nuclear decision. He did not want a seat in the Senate, and he felt if he took a different cabinet portfolio it might be unfair to the new Minister of National Defence. To resign as minister and remain in the House of Commons as an ordinary member of Parliament was something which neither he nor the Prime Minister wanted.[66]

A happy solution was the suggestion that Pearkes should accept the lieutenant-governorship of British Columbia. Although honoured, Pearkes was hesitant, for traditionally the incumbents of Government House could afford to subsidize the expenses which went with the office. His doubts were mingled with his desire to continue to serve, and assured of some financial assistance until the provincial and federal governments raised their allowances, Pearkes decided to accept. He had done all he could for the defence of his country as a soldier and a politician. As the Queen's Representative in British Columbia, new duties called and a new challenge was accepted.

17

Lieutenant-Governor of British Columbia

Speculation regarding the successor of the Honourable Frank Ross, the Lieutenant-Governor of British Columbia, had been rife for some time. As early as July 1960 a newspaperman writing in one of Victoria's newspapers claimed:

> It has been an open subject of gossip in government circles for months that General Pearkes would crown his political career by becoming The Queen's Representative. However, it is well known that the position imposes a heavy financial burden on its occupant and General Pearkes is not classed as a wealthy man.[1]

Aside from some modest investments Pearkes depended almost entirely on his salary, and when he retired his income consisted primarily of his army pension. The salary of the lieutenant-governor at this time was $9,000 together with an additional $12,000 to cover travelling and entertainment. The provincial government paid for the maintenance of Government House and the staff other than the domestics to maintain it. Extra entertainment and other costs, however, came out of the lieutenant-governor's pocket.

In any event, it was a well-kept secret. Public announcement of the appointment was made on 11 October when the Prime Minister gave the news of the reshuffling of his cabinet. On 13 October when the Pearkeses left Ottawa's Uplands Airport, the cabinet and some seventy-five military and civilian members of his "military family" were on hand, and as they stepped into their Comet jet, the R.C.A.F. Pipes and Drums started to play "Over the Seas to Skye." It was an especially significant parting in a capital not noted for its farewells to retired cabinet ministers.

In Victoria Pearkes was greeted by a fifty-man guard of honour from the 1st Battalion, Princess Patricia's Canadian Light Infantry, a personal tribute by the regiment to one of their former officers. At the Patricia Bay airport also were the Acting Premier, Eric Martin, the Provincial Secretary, Wesley Black, the Deputy Provincial Secretary, L. J. Wallace, the Secretary at Government House, Cmdr. Gar Dixon, and a number of other civilian as well as senior military officials. That evening in Government House, to the sound of a fifteen-gun salute, Pearkes was sworn into office by Chief Justice A. C. Des Brisey.[2]

In the years that followed George and Blytha Pearkes emphasized the duties of the office while accepting the privileges with grace and dignity. One of the first things Pearkes had to consider was a suitable uniform. Fortunately a friend in Victoria had a complete outfit, including the sword and cocked hat, which had belonged to a close relative who had been a lieutenant-governor in one of the prairie provinces. With some small alterations, he was able to appear in his "new" Civil Uniform Class II at very little expense.

Pearkes also found that his new office carried certain privileges with it. He became the official "Visitor" to the universities in the province and did his best to attend their convocation ceremonies. Several senior men's clubs in Victoria and Vancouver offered him honorary memberships. He received a free pass on the provincial ferries, and the Canadian National and Pacific Great Eastern Railways provided him with passes as well. Frequently, when visiting a town or city in his official capacity, he was presented with gifts. Some were for Government House, some were personal, and at times it was difficult to know which was which. If in doubt, his "rule of thumb" was that if it was inscribed to him or had his name on it, the gift was personal, otherwise it was registered as being received for Government House itself.

As the Queen's Representative, Pearkes received a small but steady stream of petitions as well as requests for patronage. The former might range from one with several hundred signatures requesting that an act or ruling of the provincial government be reversed to a one-name petition seeking a righting of a real or imagined wrong. Most could be referred to government departments for action or information, but there were always some which called for consultation with a minister or deputy minister before a decision could be made. Requests for the lieutenant-governor to give his patronage to some affair came from a great variety of sources. Some from well-known associations such as the Red Cross or Boy Scouts almost automatically received vice-regal patronage. Other requests meant soliciting enquiries about the associations and although most were granted, there were times when Pearkes "felt that they didn't have quite the backing and the community standing which would deserve having patronage from the Queen's representative."[3]

Invitations to Government House were also sought after. Pearkes opened up his official residence to more associations and societies than any of his predecessors. Aside from the traditional functions such as the New Year's Day Levee or the summer Garden Party when between one and three thousand people came to pay their respects, there were numerous occasions when an association was having its annual meeting in Victoria and would request the lieutenant-governor to invite the members or their wives to tea. Pearkes took a very liberal attitude to such requests, especially if the association had a wide representation. "I felt," he said,

> that these are people who are tax-payers in the province and that they have a desire to see Government House and there is no reason why they shouldn't. The expense of giving them tea and biscuits is not great, and it satisfies a group of people who have come in from all over the province [or from further afield]. . . . If it's a provincial, national or international organization, I try to make arrangements for them to come. I'm more reserved about the purely local ones.[4]

During his years of office, well over a hundred different groups were invited to Government House, usually on more than one occasion. Members of The Canadian Legion, business associations, hospital auxiliaries, Boy Scouts, C.G.I.T., United Appeal executives, Rotary, Royal Commonwealth Society, societies for the blind, crippled, and orphans, university alumni associations, and many others shared in the hospitality at Government House.

A great variety of people were invited to dine at the vice-regal residence and not infrequently to stay there for several days as well. Among the first were Pearkes's son and his family,[5] and his mother and sister also came frequently. Cabinet ministers visiting Victoria were usually invited to spend a night, providing there was no election in progress. Often they preferred to stay at the Empress Hotel, but usually they would come for lunch or dinner when Pearkes would arrange to have a group to meet them. The same generally held true for visiting ambassadors, senior military officers from Eastern Canada, Great Britain, and, at times, the United States. Pearkes, with Dixon's help, was able to vary the list of guests so that as wide a variety of people as possible were able to dine at Government House.

At times functions at Government House were very much "family" affairs. At Hallowe'en, for example, the Pearkeses made ready for "trick-or-treating" as they would if they were at their own home only on a larger scale. In 1966, to select only one year, some 350 children from the neighbourhood came to the door and were ushered into the red-carpeted entrance hall. There, by the fireplace, the Pearkeses, Mrs. Abelson, the housekeeper, and several of the domestic staff handed out bags of candy and apples. George and Blytha entered fully into the spirit of the occasion, and their informality and banter quickly dispelled any shyness among their costumed visitors. Invariably the Pearkeses had as much fun as the "ghosts and goblins" who visited them.

Another group of children who looked forward to their annual visit to Government House were the orphans who came each year for a Christmas party. Preparations for Christmas started two weeks ahead of the holiday with the erection and decoration of two huge trees in the entrance hall, a tableau placed over the fireplace, and hundreds of greeting cards, stapled to long, red streamers, hung from nearby pillars.[6] In the two weeks before Christmas, children from the Protestant Orphanage came to the lower lounge where the tables were loaded with pastries, turkey sandwiches, ice cream, and cakes, after which they would go to the main ball room to meet a Santa Claus.

In this period, too, a Christmas party would be held for the gardeners and for the aide-de-camps and their children. The staff had a formal dinner, and to make it as relaxed and intimate as possible, the Pearkeses, after joining them briefly for a pre-dinner drink, usually arranged to be elsewhere that evening. About one hundred persons from the area around Government House were invited for an evening of songs and carols, accompanied by the Salvation Army band. No matter how large or small the party might be, there was always a warm, homely atmosphere when the Pearkeses entertained. "I wouldn't say there is no formality," their house supervisor remarked at the time, "but there is no more formality than is absolutely necessary for the proper running of the place."[7] The more formal social functions—the State Dinner and the State Ball—took place in January or February of the new year, and, of course, when members of the Royal Family or visiting heads of state came to visit, formality, protocol, and security all had to be taken into consideration as well as arrangements for the sometimes large staff which accompanied such distinguished visitors. The vice-regal residence, with its ninety-seven rooms and fifteen fireplaces, its maids, gardeners, cooks, handymen, and other staff members was to have a great variety of people pass through its portals each year, and few if any were to leave without remarking on the friendliness and warmth they encountered from their hosts.

Blytha Pearkes felt the new position would give her husband more leisure than he had had as cabinet minister. By its very nature the person who held the office could expand or limit the amount of time he wished to spend on the non-constitutional aspects of it. Pearkes followed two wealthy predecessors, both of whom were still active in business. He did not have their financial resources, but at the same time he did not need to spend time looking after business affairs. Thus, although he could not afford $50,000 or more annually from his own pocket on entertainment[8] as some of his predecessors had done, he could spend more of his own time enabling more British Columbians to meet their lieutenant-governor. Added to his sense of duty was his genuine interest in meeting other British Columbians. "The people of the province," as his private secretary put it, "were 'his' people, no matter what rank or in what place or what climate."[9] Reflecting on some of these visits he added:

He went in a dugout canoe [to some of the Indian villages]. He was in seaplanes, up and down rivers by riverboat. He visited the Babine Lake and the Indians at its northern end via an old flat-bottomed riverboat. He came down to Mackenzie by river barge. General Pearkes visited more Indian villages. He had an affinity with Indians, I don't know why, and [with] school children. He could talk extemporaneously to a group of elementary school kids sitting on the floor, to Indians gathered out in a field, or to high school students or to a national resources conference. [I don't know] whether he mulled this over in his mind ahead of time, but it appeared to be spontaneous, and he seemed to reach their level.

He was interested in farming, the same as Mr. Ross was. He got particular joy out of going to horse shows, not the fancy, international horse show they have in Vancouver, although he appreciated that, but to the . . . International Exhibition at Armstrong or the November [Cattleman's Association] show in Kamloops. . . .

Mrs. Pearkes accompanied him everywhere except, of course, if it was a service or stag [affair]. . . . He relied on her; she has a tremendous memory and could remember people's names and little incidents.[10]

It soon became apparent that the new lieutenant-governor was available to officiate at more public affairs than ever before, and during his years in office Pearkes kept his promise to travel widely. There were, of course, a large number of functions he attended in the larger centres of the Lower Mainland. A sample of some of these were: opening the newly reconstructed city hall in Victoria, attending the opening concert of the Vancouver Symphony, attending the fiftieth anniversary of the Red Chevron

Association of Vancouver Island, receiving leaders of the Provincial Conference of the C.G.I.T. Movement, presenting certificates to blood donors to the Red Cross, lunching with the Pacific Northwest District Board Meeting of the Kiwanis International, opening the YMCA building in Vancouver, attending dedication services for a cemetery for servicemen near White Rock. He took the salute at one or more parades on Remembrance Day, attended mess dinners at almost every naval, army, and air unit in the province, and at one time or another inspected almost every military or civilian association in uniform from the regular armed forces to the newest boy scout troop. He planted trees, dug the "first shovel-full of earth," laid cornerstones, cut ribbons, fired starting guns, received debutantes, presented prizes, beamed at beauty queens, and did all the other duties expected of him in an ever-increasing volume.

Mrs. Pearkes opened bazaars and auctions for women's auxiliaries to hospitals and orphanages, presided at arts and crafts sales and other money-making functions put on by women for their favourite charities, attended teas for a variety of women's organizations, opened fashion shows, welcomed literally thousands of wives of delegates attending functions in Victoria, and was called upon either to patronize or preside over a seemingly endless number of similar affairs involving women's work or interests. It was an exhausting pace, especially in the centennial years, but both felt that it was well worth the effort.[11]

The Lower Mainland cities and towns may have seen more of the lieutenant-governor and his wife owing to their greater density of population, but throughout his tenure of office Pearkes made a special effort to visit the interior of the province and some of the more remote areas in the north and along the coast. To reach the latter, each summer he took advantage of the naval ships travelling north from Victoria to engage in manoeuvres or "showing the flag." His activities on one of these visits was described in "The Globe Magazine" in the summer of 1961 as follows:

> The most notable thing General Pearkes does on these trips is give the impression he is not just performing a duty. Whether throwing the first stone in the curling championship in Prince George, receiving debutantes in Vancouver, watching an amateur group perform in Duncan, or opening a winter carnival in Vernon, he always seems to be enjoying himself.
>
> His visit to Friendly Cove was only one stop in a remarkable tour which took him to seven isolated settlements on the ruggedly beautiful coast of Vancouver Island and one distant part of the British Columbia mainland. He shook hands and chatted with hundreds of Indians

and with others who had never seen a lieutenant-governor and who rarely have a visitor.

None of the settlements has road connections to the outside world, and the only practical way of reaching them is by ship or seaplane. . . . Starting from Esquimalt Harbour [and accompanied by his private secretary, Commander Dixon], he called at Bamfield, a mixed Indian and white community of about 300 persons; Opitshat, an Indian reserve of about 250 near Clayoquot; Friendly Cove where Chief Maquinna heads a band of about 200 Indians; Quateesh, an Indian village of about 80 near Quatsino; Bella Coola . . . harbouring about 1,700 Indians and whites; Sointula, a closely-knit community of about 650 . . . and Port McNeil, a logging community of about 250 whites. . . .

The tour was marked by General Pearkes' friendly informality. In Bamfield, presented with a hand-carved walking stick by Louis Nookamis, 81, hereditary chief of the Ohiat Indian band, General Pearkes put an arm around the chief's shoulder and said "I hope you live to be 100." Replied Louis: "I hope you do too." To Mrs. Georgia Johnson, 61, who performed an energetic Indian dance wearing a ceremonial Indian costume he said: "You dance like a girl of 18."

In Friendly Cove, confronted by a beseeching group of Indian children as he prepared to leave, the lieutenant-governor squatted on the ground and autographed half a dozen small paper flags. In Sointula, as he stepped into a small boat to rejoin the R.C.N. squadron, a group of youngsters asked if he would fire a naval gun for them. [He] did not forget. Just after he boarded the ship a dummy mortar shell arched into the blue sky.

In Alert Bay, where his visit coincided with the opening of an Annual Indian Sports festival, he dashed away from his official party to shake hands with members of the two soccer teams. "I wish I was a little younger," he said to them. "I'd play with you." Later . . . he delighted Indians in a salmon barbecue by eating with his fingers, smacking his lips . . . and eagerly asking for more.

The tour officially ended in Alert Bay with a dusty General Pearkes drinking beer at the Legion Hall which has the only bar in any of the communities visited. Drinks for all visitors that day were on the house.[12]

That five-day tour, the first of many, took Pearkes over seven hundred miles, but this was only a small part of the thirty thousand or so miles he travelled each year. His genuine interest in the Indians and his efforts on their behalf were appreciated by them, and during his lieutenant-governorship he was made honorary chief of the Cowichans, the Clayoquot band of the Opitshat, and the Nanaimo Indians, and an hereditary chief of the Nishgas.

Other groups honoured him during the period he was in office also, but by no means merely because of the position he held. In 1965 and in 1967 respectively he received honorary Doctor of Laws and Doctor of Philosophy degrees from the University of Victoria, Simon Fraser University, and the University of Notre Dame, bringing the total he received to five.[13] In 1962 he was especially pleased to accept the appointment of Honorary Colonel of the British Columbia Dragoons. This regiment perpetuated the former 2nd Canadian Mounted Rifles, the unit he joined as a trooper. When he visited the Dragoons in the Okanagan, periodically he would camp out in the field under canvas with them if they were on manoeuvres, a most unusual but most appreciated gesture by any honorary colonel of any regiment.

The Okanagan, the East and West Kootenays, Atlin, the Cariboo, the Peace River country—there were few if any places in British Columbia the Pearkeses did not visit. In some areas it had been fifty to one hundred years since some of the towns had seen the Queen's Representative, and in a few cases the last recorded time had been in colonial days. Wherever they went, they won the hearts of community. Quite typical is the following newspaper account of a visit to Nelson:

> Lieutenant-Governor . . . Pearkes won the friendship of Nelson with his kindness, warmth and good humour when he visited here on Saturday. [He] was spending the third day of his West Kootenay visit carrying out a wide variety of functions. He vigorously shovelled earth in a tree planting ceremony, rode a big caterpillar tractor, presented scrolls to three new freemen of the city and showed an avid interest in everything he saw. . . .
>
> It was the distinguished visitor's indomitability which had so endeared Nelson folk to him. In twelve hours the 76-year-old veteran soldier of both wars never showed any signs of fatigue or disinterest. And he spared his smiles and brisk handshakes for no one he saw during his visit.[14]

Many stories could be told about the Pearkeses and their visits to the distant parts of British Columbia. Newspaper accounts of the various events and ceremonies in which they were involved are legion. The impression they made wherever they went could not have been better, and when, in 1965, Pearkes wrote to the Prime Minister suggesting he should step down, Lester Pearson put off a definite answer as he was planning to visit Victoria in August. There was no doubt of the high esteem in which he was held by the people. Premier Bennett, when extending congratulations to him in the Legislature on his seventy-sixth birthday said that "no lieutenant-governor has ever excelled the qualifications of the present lieutenant-governor." The Leader of the Opposition, Robert Strachan, called him "outstanding," while the leader of the provincial Liberal party had equally warm praise for Pearkes.[15] Pearson, when he stayed at Government House late in the summer, asked Pearkes to remain in office at least until the conclusion of the centennial year, 1966. Pearkes agreed to do so, even though it meant another year of continual work and loss of pay when, at his age, most men had been retired for over a decade.[16]

The renewal of his term was for no definite time, and after an exhausting year of centennial duties as well as the additional calls made on him by the 1967 centennial events,[17] Pearkes wrote the Prime Minister in May 1967 suggesting that he should resign in October the same year. The Prime Minister replied in part:

I do not like to take advantage of your "devotion to duty" further, but I am wondering whether you would not be able to see us through centennial year and perhaps until next spring. I am bold enough to make this suggestion first because your health is so much better after the difficult time you had a year ago and, secondly, because all reports from British Columbia show that Blytha and you have been so wonderful during the extra pressure and obligations of centennial year that it would seem a shame to make a change before the end of that year or, if you are agreeable, until, say, May 1968.

I do not wish to embarrass you by making anything more than a tentative suggestion to this effect but, if it appeals to you, I would certainly be delighted, and I know it would be very well received in your province.[18]

The Prime Minister could not have made a better appeal to Pearkes than to his "devotion to duty," and Pearkes agreed to the precedent-making second renewal of his term of office. The centennial year, 1967, brought to Government House a large number of very distinguished people, among whom were the Emperor Haile Selassie of Ethiopia, Princess Alexandria of Great Britain and her husband, Queen Juliana of the Netherlands, Prince Ranier and Princess Grace of Monaco, the Bavarian Prime Minister, Their Imperial Highnesses Prince and Princess Takarnatsu of Japan, Prince Harrald of Norway, Princess Margrethe of Denmark,

Prime Minister Micko Spiljak of Jugoslavia, and a variety of others. The Queen Mother, as well as Queen Elizabeth and Prince Philip, had been guests of the Pearkeses as had the Princess Royal and other members of the Royal Family.

The remarkable thing about Pearkes during his lieutenant-governorship was his ability to be as at ease among visiting royalty as he was among the loggers, farmers, and fishermen in the remoter parts of the province. The esteem in which he was held is reflected by some of the honours bestowed on him, only some of which can be mentioned here. He was the first to be named freeman of Alberni, Burnaby, and Saanich, the highest honour any civil government can bestow.[19] He was also made a freeman by Victoria, Vancouver, Vernon, Kelowna, Penticton, and Nelson. He was named citizen of the year (1966) by the Victoria Kiwanis Club and presented with the Governorship Award for outstanding service to Canada by the city's Junior Chamber of Commerce. He was elected Grand President of the Royal Canadian Legion in 1966, a tribute from the veterans of both wars which he prized very highly indeed. He was given honorary membership in No. 800 Wing, R.C.A.F. Association, the 4-H Honour Club, the Canadian Red Cross Society, and other associations. He was named British Columbian of the Year by the Newsmen's Club of British Columbia (1968) and a few months later was presented with the province's "Order of the Dogwood" by Premier W. A. C. Bennett. Pearkes's interest in sports was taken into consideration when Esquimalt named its ice arena after him, and his support for retarded and handicapped children won him the Heart and Humanitarian Award from the Variety Club as well as the naming of the local handicapped children's clinic after him. Of all the awards and honours he received in his last year of office, none illustrated greater national appreciation for his long career in the service of Canada than his being made a Companion of the Order of Canada.

In the early summer of 1968, as the Pearkeses approached the final weeks of their residence in Government House, tributes to both of them poured in from all sides. At the end of June 1968, well into his eightieth year but as vigorous as he had been thirty years earlier, George Pearkes spent his last day as lieutenant-governor in typical fashion—working. On 1 July he went into retirement. Although there are no "official" duties to perform, George and Blytha are still very much in demand to carry out numerous duties in Victoria and throughout the province.

Notes

NOTES TO CHAPTER TWO

1. "Correspondence to the Editor," *The Berkhamstedian* 25, no. 156 (December 1905): 146–48.
2. Interview with Major-General George R. Pearkes, 21 July 1969, p. 7, Pearkes Papers, University of Victoria Library.

3. Ibid., 13 August 1965, p. 1.
4. Ibid., 21 July 1969, p. 10.
5. Ibid., p. 13.
6. Ibid., 30 July 1965.

NOTES TO CHAPTER THREE

1. Interview with Maj.-Gen. Pearkes, 30 July 1965, p. 14. A recruit signed up for a term of five years and was able to purchase his discharge under normal circumstances at the end of three.
2. Ibid., p. 23.
3. He was commended by Supt. J.D. Moodie for his "excellent work" in the "Report of the R.N.W.M.P." (Canada, Parliament, *Sessional Papers*, 1915, vol. 50, no. 23, p. 225).
4. Letter, Mrs. Samuel S. Steinhauser to author, 21 July 1969.
5. Guy Lawrence, *40 Years on the Yukon Telegraph* (Vancouver: Mitchell Press, 1965), p. 33.

6. Photostat letter, No. 5529, Constable G.R. Pearkes to the Officer Commanding, R.N.W.M. Police, Whitehorse Sub-District, 26 December 1914, letter in possession of the author. Pearkes sold his homestead six years later to his neighbour, Mr. Ralph Sinclair.
7. Pearkes had paid fifty dollars to secure his release. Later, when the war was over, he applied for and received a remission of the purchase money which was refunded to constables leaving the force to join the Canadian Expeditionary Force.

NOTES TO CHAPTER FOUR

1. R.H. Roy, *Sinews of Steel* (Toronto: Charters Publishing Co., 1965), pp. 39ff.
2. The change from leather to web equipment did not occur until the unit reached Great Britain.
3. Victoria *Daily Colonist*, 9 May 1915, p. 7.
4. The 48th Battalion, C.E.F., were also camped at Willows.
5. Interview with Maj.-Gen. Pearkes, 1 August 1965, p. 21.

6. In the 1911 census, 10.4 per cent of Canada's population of 7,206,643 was foreign born, i.e., not born in Canada or Great Britain. Almost one-half of that number (303,680) were born in the U.S.A., and of the Americans residing in Canada, 136,720 were of British origin (Canada, Department of Trade and Commerce, *The Canada Year Book, 1915* [Ottawa: King's Printer, 1916], pp. 82–84).

7. The infantrymen rolled their puttees from their boots to their knees; cavalrymen started from below the knees and rolled the puttees to the boot, tying them at the ankle.

8. M.V. McGuire et al., *The 2nd Canadian Mounted Rifles (B.C. Horse) in France and Flanders* (Vernon: Vernon News Publishing Co., 1932), p. 9.

9. Interview with Maj.-Gen. Pearkes, 13 August 1965, pp. 9–10.

10. At this time, with the arrival of the 2nd Canadian Infantry Division, the Canadian Corps was formed. Initially the 2nd C.M.R., together with other dismounted cavalry units and infantry battalions, formed part of the Corps Troops under Maj.-Gen. M.S. Mercer. In 1916 the 2nd C.M.R. became part of the 8th Brigade of the 3rd Canadian Infantry Division.

11. Interview with Maj.-Gen. Pearkes, 13 August 1965, pp. 18–20.

12. McGuire, *The 2nd Canadian Mounted Rifles,* p. 12.

13. Interview with Maj.-Gen. Pearkes, 13 August 1965, pp. 27–31.

14. "My luck is out for I have been left behind as an instructor at the school. Do you know, I just hate the idea of the boys being in the front line and my not being with them" (letter, Pearkes to his mother, 25 November 1915).

15. "I know you will feel pleased," Pearkes wrote his mother, "as it is really an honour to win a commission in the field. As a matter of fact I know I do not deserve it one bit more than hundreds of others" (letter, Pearkes to his mother, 14 May 1916).

16. Letter, Pearkes to his mother, 31 July 1916.

17. A term referring to a wound sufficiently severe to require hospitalization in England.

18. Interview with Maj.-Gen. Pearkes, 23 September 1965, p. 10.

19. G.C. Johnson, in McGuire, *The 2nd Canadian Mounted Rifles,* p. 28. Pearkes was mentioned in despatches however.

20. Interview with Maj.-Gen. Pearkes and Mr. G.W. Pearson, 4 November 1969.

NOTES TO CHAPTER FIVE

1. Public Archives of Canada, War Diary, Headquarters, 8th Canadian Infantry Brigade, September 1916, "Summary of Operations from 11th to 17th September."

2. P.A.C., War Diary, 5th Canadian Mounted Rifles, 15 September 1916.

3. The method would depend on the extent to which the barbed wire was cut.

4. The slight rise of ground prevented the artillerymen from observing their fire.

5. W.D., 5th C.M.R., 1 October 1916, "Report by Lt. G.R. Pearkes."

6. He was awarded the Military Cross for the part he played in this action. In his report of the fight in the battalion war diary, he never mentioned that he was wounded and, with typical modesty, gave little indication of his own role in the action. To his mother he wrote: "I was in charge of the Company during an attack at the Somme in which, thanks to the courage of my men, we were successful, and as to remaining on duty though wounded, well the wounds were so slight that it would hardly have been

playing the game to have left at that stage" (letter, Pearkes to his mother, 17 January 1917).

7. "Report by Lt. G.R. Pearkes."

8. Pearkes was promoted to acting captain on 16 October, and two days later he became acting major "while commanding a company."

9. Pearkes stated later: "The flower of British manhood went on the Somme, in my opinion. The casualties during the July fighting. . .were so appalling that I don't think that the British Army was ever quite the same" (interview with Maj.-Gen. Pearkes, 12 October 1965, p. 35).

10. Letter, Mr. A. Sayer to author, 7 November 1965.

11. G.W.L. Nicholson, *Canadian Expeditionary Force, 1914–1919* (Ottawa: Queen's Printer, 1962), p. 245.

12. W.D., 5th C.M.R., 8 April 1917.

13. Interview with Maj.-Gen. Pearkes, 12 October 1965, p. 11.

14. W.D., 5th C.M.R., 9 April 1917.

15. The 5th C.M.R. had ninety-one

casualties.
16. Letter, Pearkes to his mother, 7 June 1917.
17. By this time, his brother Ted, who had come overseas in 1916, had come to the 2nd C.M.R. to be with his brother. George, of course, had transferred to the 5th C.M.R. Ted, an N.C.O. at this time, was dependent on his army pay also.
18. Interview with Maj.-Gen. Pearkes, 26 October 1965, p. 1.
19. Ibid., pp. 10–11.
20. Ibid., p. 13.
21. W.D., 5th C.M.R., October 1917, Appendix "G", "5th C.M.R. Battalion, Summary of Operations, October 30th–31st, 1917," p. 4.
22. Much of the information about the situation at the front was received at advance battalion headquarters from the walking wounded.
23. The battalion of Artists Rifles, flanking the Canadians, were hit by machine-gun and artillery fire immediately the attack began. "The ground to be traversed was simply mud and swamp. . . as compared with the Canadians on the right, who, being on higher and drier ground, got on further" (H. A. R. May, *Memories of the Artists Rifles* [London: Howlett and Son, 1929], p. 182). This regimental historian continues: "Many Artists got over the Paddebeeke stream, but the Battalion, after suffering 350 casualties (170 killed) had to consolidate on the near side" (ibid.).
24. Letter, Capt. C.S. Rutherford, V.C., M.C., M.M., to author, 27 October

1965.
25. Interview with Mr. A. Molyneux, 11 December 1965, p. 6. Molyneux had been selected by Pearkes as a batman because he was the best runner in the 5th C.M.R. Both used to run when in rest, and had Pearkes not been in excellent physical shape, he could not have carried on as long as he did.
26. Interview with Maj.-Gen Pearkes, 26 October 1965, p. 21. Pearkes also gives credit to the assistance given by the machine-gun barrage fired by heavy machine-guns. These weapons were back at the start-line, but something of the action could be seen from that point.
27. "5th C.M.R. Bn., Summary of Operations," p. 8.
28. Interview with Maj.-Gen. Pearkes, 26 October 1965, p. 23.
29. When Mavor was sent back he carried a message from Pearkes which said in part: "Reinforcements might get through after dark. They are most urgently needed, also S.A.A. [small arms ammunition]. Men of 5th C.M.R. Bn. all in. Do not think I can hold out until morning" ("5th C.M.R. Bn., Summary of Operations," p. 9).
30. Interview with Maj.-Gen. Pearkes, 26 October 1965, p. 28.
31. London *Gazette,* no. 30471, 11 January 1918.
32. Letter, Pearkes to his mother, 11 November 1917.
33. Letter, Mr. A.C. Philps to author, 6 July 1969.

NOTES TO CHAPTER SIX

1. Letter, Pearkes to his mother, 30 April 1918.
2. E.P.S. Allen, *The 116th Battalion in France* (Toronto: Hunter Rose, 1921).
3. The 9th Canadian Infantry Brigade was composed of the 43rd, 52nd, 60th, and 116th Battalions.
4. Allen, *The 116th Battalion,* p. 28.
5. He became temporary lieutenant-colonel on 27 March and retained the brevet rank of lieutenant-colonel after the war. Lt.-Col. Sharpe did not return to the battalion. Re-elected in 1917, he returned to Canada and met with a fatal

accident in May 1918.
6. Letter, Mr. A.G. Elford to author, 3 June 1969.
7. Letter, Mr. L.H. Harron to author, 17 January 1966.
8. Letter, Mr. E. Pearson to author, 15 December 1965.
9. Letter, Mr. J. Hughes to author, 14 May 1969.
10. Letter, Dr. R.S. Blackstock to author, 18 August 1969.
11. P.A.C., War Diary, 116th Canadian Infantry Battalion, 27 March 1918.
12. Ibid., 1 April 1918.

13. Letter, Pearkes to his mother, 23 May 1918.
14. Letters, Pearkes to his mother, 7 April and 23 May 1918. Edward had asked for the transfer when Pearkes was still with the 2nd C.M.R. Shortly afterwards Edward was wounded and was in hospital in England when the war ended.
15. Letter, Mr. L.W. Harron to author, 17 January 1966.
16. Ibid.
17. W.D., 116th Battalion, 1–5 August 1918.
18. Allen, *The 116th Battalion,* p. 63.
19. W.D., 116th Battalion, August 1918, Appendix 1, "Narrative of 116th Battalion in the Third Battle of the Somme."
20. Letter, Tennant to author, 16 January 1966.
21. The tanks were especially handicapped and lost direction. They operated mostly on the flank, between the 116th Battalion and the 43rd Battalion, but two rejoined the 116th when the fog cleared.
22. "Narrative of the 116th Battalion... Battle of the Somme."
23. Interview with Maj.-Gen. Pearkes, 30 April 1970.
24. "Narrative of the 116th Battalion... Battle of the Somme."
25. Interview with Maj.-Gen. Pearkes, 9 November 1965, p. 11.
26. A few days before this award was published in the *Gazette,* Pearkes was also awarded the French Croix de Guerre.
27. Commanded by Lt.-Col. W.W. Foster, whom Pearkes knew from the days when he was with the 2nd C.M.R.'s. At this time Pearkes was sharing his headquarters with Lt.-Col. H.M. Urquhart of

the 43rd Battalion. Urquhart was severely wounded during the attack.
28. W.D., 116th Battalion, August 1918, Appendix No. 3, "Narrative of the 116th (Ontario County). . .Battalion During the Operations from 26th to 29th August 1918."
29. Letter, Mr. W. Carmichael to author, 2 January 1968.
30. Allen, *The 116th Battalion,* p. 79.
31. "Mr. Pearkes Sr. was what I call a fine old English gentleman. He was so very nice, thanking me for donating my blood to his son" (letter, Carmichael to author, 2 January 1968).
32. "The whole Canadian Corps was enquiring about him," Ormond stated later, "He was a V.C. who rose from private to battalion commander and was well known" (interview with Maj.-Gen. D.M. Ormond, 15 May 1970).
33. Quoted in the *Victoria Daily Times,* 9 November 1918.
34. Interview with Maj.-Gen. Pearkes, 23 November 1965, p. 21. A regular uniform with a blue band on the sleeve also denoted the wearer had been wounded and was convalescing.
35. Two stone and bronze memorials have been erected at this spot. One was placed by the 4th Dragoon Guards, the British regiment which first encountered the Germans; the other was unveiled by Pearkes in July 1956 and erected by veterans of the 116th Battalion.
36. Letter, Pearkes to his mother, 16 December 1918.
37. Maj.-Gen. Lipsett, the former commander, was killed a few days after Pearkes was wounded.

NOTES TO CHAPTER SEVEN

1. The 116th Battalion is perpetuated by the Ontario Regiment. This unit became a tank battalion as a result of the reorganization of the Canadian militia in 1936.
2. There were five holders of the Victoria Cross among the students and one on the instructional staff.
3. For example, when Pearkes was Director of Military Training in Canada, Gort held the same position in India. They exchanged views and information

which, under routine procedure, would not be available to either.
4. Interview with Maj.-Gen. Pearkes, 30 November 1965, p. 10.
5. B.H. Liddell Hart, *Memoirs* (London: Cassell, 1965), 1:94
6. Interview with Maj.-Gen. Pearkes, 30 November 1965.
7. He retained his brevet rank of lieutenant-colonel, but all wartime commissions were temporary. On appointment to the P.P.C.L.I. he was

appointed a major in the permanent force (Canada *Gazette,* 20, 22 November 1919).

8. Interview with Maj.-Gen. Pearkes, 30 November 1965, p. 20.
9. Ibid., p. 9.
10. Interview with Mr. Fred Auger, 10 May 1966.
11. Letter, Dr. D.G. MacLeod to author, 5 June 1969. Dr. MacLeod was one of the scouts in No. 14 Troop.
12. See *The Boys' Own Herald,* 18 August 1923, p.1.
13. The Calgary *Albertan,* 15 March 1954.
14. Ibid.
15. Ibid.
16. Interview with Mr. Fred Auger, p. 7.
17. Directorate of History, Personal File, Maj.-Gen. G.R. Pearkes, letter, MacBrien to deputy minister, 16 March 1923.

18. Interview with Maj.-Gen. Pearkes, 30 November 1965, p. 24.
19. Ibid.
20. Interview with Maj.-Gen. Pearkes, 14 November 1965, p. 1.
21. Ibid, p. 4.
22. Every militia officer was required to take an equitation course before he came. Pearkes, an excellent horseman himself, said later; "I think some of the horses would have been a little surprised at the [equitation] certificates which had been issued."
23. Letter, Pearkes to William Carmichael, 21 October 1925. Carmichael was the veteran who had given Pearkes his blood when he had been severely wounded in 1918.
24. Interview with Mrs. G.R. Pearkes, 22 February 1965, p. 15.
25. It never did.

NOTES TO CHAPTER EIGHT

1. Letter, Pearkes to William Carmichael, 21 October 1925.
2. Interview with Maj.-Gen. Pearkes, 14 December 1965.
3. R.H. Roy, *Ready for the Fray* (Vancouver: Evergreen Press, 1957), p. 37.
4. Interview with Maj.-Gen. Pearkes, 29 December 1965, p. 4.
5. D. Hist., Personal File, Maj.-Gen. G.R. Pearkes, "Annual Confidential Reports," 1 May 1928-31 December 1928.
6. Ibid.
7. Stuart was to become Chief of the General Staff.
8. R.H. Roy, *The Seaforth Highlanders of Canada, 1919-1965* (Vancouver: Evergreen Press, 1969), p. 27.
9. *The Times,* 11 November 1929.
10. Sir John Smyth, *The Story of the Victoria Cross, 1856-1963* (London: Frederick Muller, 1963), pp. 327-39.
11. Named after Commodore R. Barrie, R.N., who was in charge of the Navy Yard at Kingston from 1819 to 1834. The house was built in the 1820's and occupied for a short time by the naval store keeper and later by others associated with the early military and political life of Kingston. It was sold to

the federal government during the Great War.
12. *Royal Military College Review* 13 (December 1932): 48.
13. Keller was to be Pearkes's brigade major when war broke out and later his G.S.O.I. when Pearkes was given command of a division. In 1944 Maj.-Gen. Keller commanded a division in the D-Day assault on Normandy.
14. At the time Pearkes took over, new Field Service Regulations were adopted by the British and, thus, the Canadian forces. These incorporated the latest thinking on military matters and consequently all the earlier précis had to be revised, a major task in itself.
15. Letter, Brig. G. Roupell to author, 5 September 1969.
16. Letter, Maj.-Gen. C.A.P. Murison to author, 29 May 1969.
17. Interview with Maj.-Gen. Pearkes, 6 January 1966, p. 18.
18. See, for example, E.L.M. Burns, "A Step towards Mechanization," *The Canadian Defence Quarterly* (1935): 298-305.
19. Interview with A/V/M G.R. Howsam, 11 May 1966.
20. Letter, Mr. T.L. Brock to author, 2

November 1970.

21. "Observations Upon National Defence in Canada: Confidential," a précis written on 30 June 1930 by G.R. Pearkes. The original copy is in the possession of A/V/M George Howsam.

22. It read, in part: "An outstanding officer in all respects. A strong and determined character with a cheerful and pleasing personality."

NOTES TO CHAPTER NINE

1. Pearkes was appointed to the position on 1 January 1935.
2. The Director of Organization and Director General of Medical Services respectively.
3. Burns had a small hut at the Rockcliffe Air Station where he developed his air mapping programme. He followed principles which had been used by E.O. Wheeler while mapping the British Columbia-Alberta boundary, getting triangulations from mountain tops. Pearkes used to visit Burns on numerous occasions. Wheeler lived in Sidney, B.C., and was a close friend of the Copemans and had loaned his cottage at Banff to George and Blytha for their honeymoon.
4. See John Swettenham, *McNaughton. Volume I. 1887-1939* (Toronto: Ryerson, 1969), pp. 270 ff.
5. Interview with Maj.-Gen. Pearkes, 1 February 1966.
6. Ibid., p. 11.
7. Quoted in James Eayrs, *In Defence of Canada, From the Great War to the Great Depression* (Toronto: University of Toronto Press, 1964), p. 301.
8. C.P. Stacey, *Official History of the Canadian Army in the Second World War. Volume I. Six Years of War* (Ottawa: Queen's Printer, 1955), p. 6.
9. Interview with Maj.-Gen. Pearkes, 1 March 1966, p. 7.
10. Vincent Massey, *What's Past is Prologue* (Toronto: Macmillan, 1963), p. 240.
11. Ibid., p. 231.
12. Ibid., p. 232. Of course, Canada was not alone in its timidity in the international arena.
13. Interview with Maj.-Gen. Pearkes, 1 March 1966, p. 3.
14. It should be remembered the scheme was revised constantly up to the beginning of the war.
15. Interview with Maj.-Gen. D.C. Spry, 15 June 1967, pp. 5-7.
16. Interview with Lt.-Gen. H.D. Graham, 24 September 1970, p. 2.
17. Ibid., p. 3.
18. Interview with Maj.-Gen. Pearkes, 28 April 1967, p. 25.
19. Ibid., 1 February 1966, p. 8.
20. Their son John accompanied them, but their young daughter Priscilla had died during the Easter weekend in 1935 of splenitis.
21. Accompanying Pearkes from Canada was W/Cdr. G.O. Johnson of the R.C.A.F.
22. Interview with Maj.-Gen. Pearkes, 1 March 1966, p. 15.
23. Broad was in charge of Administration, Aldershot Command, at this time. He was to be G.O.C., Aldershot Command, at the time the 1st Canadian Infantry Division arrived there in 1939.
24. Interview with Maj.-Gen. Pearkes, 8 March 1966, p. 13. Pearkes was careful to draw a distinction between the thrill he felt in taking part in modern military manoeuvres and liking warfare. Army life appealed to him. As a professional soldier he was keenly interested in the improvements he saw and thoroughly enjoyed the new experience and freedom of movement of a modern division. To be interested in this way, however, "doesn't mean that one loves war."
25. Ibid., Appendix "A".
26. Defence expenditures increased, in round figures, from $23 million in 1936-37 to $33 million in 1937-38. An additional $2 million was granted for 1938-39. The R.C.A.F. was the chief beneficiary.
27. Interview with Maj.-Gen. Pearkes, 8 March 1966.
28. Ibid., pp. 18-19.
29. Ibid., pp. 19-20.

NOTES TO CHAPTER TEN

1. Calgary *Herald*, 1 September 1939, p. 11.
2. Interview with Maj.-Gen. Pearkes, 8 March 1966; Calgary *Herald*, 1 September 1939, p. 11. Construction of the huts at Mewata Park, Calgary, to house two thousand troops began on 5 September.
3. Calgary *Herald,* 13 October 1939, p. 21.
4. The letter was sent on 23 October. C.A.S.F. Routine Order No. 246 of 6 January 1940 authorized Pearkes to vacate his appointment as District Officer Commanding M.D. XIII on 16 October. Actually he continued to function in both capacities until 4 December 1939. The public announcement of his appointment on 1 November met with wide editorial approval.
5. The N.C.O.'s were chosen from the Princess Patricias, the other ranks from the other units in the brigade.
6. P.A.C., War Diary, Headquarters, 2nd Canadian Infantry Brigade, 17 December 1939.
7. Interview with Maj.-Gen. Pearkes, 17 March 1966, p. 18.
8. Roy, *The Seaforth Highlanders* pp. 71–72.
9. Interview with Maj.-Gen. Pearkes, 17 March 1966, pp. 21–22. In France he met Maj.-Gen. (later Field Marshal) H.R.L.G. Alexander for the first time. He also renewed his acquaintance with Gen. Lord Gort, who commanded the British forces in France.
10. G.R. Stevens, *A City Goes to War, History of the Loyal Edmonton Regiment* (Brampton: Charters Publishing, 1964), p. 189.
11. W.D., H.Q., 2nd Cdn. Inf. Bde., 8 February 1940.
12. Ibid., 20 February 1940.
13. Roy, *The Seaforth Highlanders,* p. 76.
14. Interview with Maj.-Gen. Pearkes, 17 March 1966, p. 20.
15. Ibid., p. 15. See also W.D., H.Q., 2nd Cdn. Inf. Bde., 24 February 1940.
16. Later he met two cadets at the hospital who were convalescing from the same disease, so apparently he caught it at Sandhurst.
17. Interview with Maj.-Gen. Pearkes, 17 March 1966, p. 19.
18. W.D., H.Q., 2nd Cdn. Inf. Bde., 15 March and 6 May, 1940.
19. Stacey, *Six Years of War*, p. 259. At that the units involved had to borrow 3-inch mortar stores from the 1st Brigade to complete their war establishment.
20. John Swettenham, *McNaughton. Volume II. 1939–1943* (Toronto: Ryerson, 1969), pp. 69–90.
21. Maj.-Gen. G.R. Pearkes, File: "Notes and Comments."
22. Ibid.
23. The brigade's transport and drivers arrived in Brest on 12 and 13 June. The main body of the brigade landed on the 14th.
24. Stacey, *Six Years of War*, p. 287.
25. Interview with Maj.-Gen. Pearkes, 17 March 1966, pp. 16–17.
26. Interview with Maj.-Gen. Pearkes, 2 May 1966.
27. Ibid., pp. 3–4.
28. Ibid., p. 15.
29. Farley Mowat, *The Regiment* (Toronto: McClelland and Stewart, 1955), p. 37.
30. Kim Beattie, *Dileas: The 48th Highlanders of Canada* (Toronto, 1957), p. 136.
31. Roy, *The Seaforth Highlanders,* pp. 99–100.
32. See P.A.C., War Diary, Headquarters, 1st Canadian Infantry Division, August-September, 1940.
33. Originally, Hitler was to decide on 10 September if the invasion would take place. It was not until 17 September that Operation "Sea Lion" was postponed.
34. W.D., H.Q., 1st Cdn. Inf. Div., 13 September 1940.
35. Ibid., 17 September 1940.
36. G.R. Stevens, *Princess Patricia's Canadian Light Infantry. Volume III. 1919-1957* (Griesbach, Alta., published by the regiment, 1958), p. 204.
37. Roy, *The Seaforth Highlanders,* pp. 103–4.
38. Interview with Maj.-Gen. Pearkes, 21 April 1966, p. 17.
39. Ibid., p. 7.
40. Stevens, *Princess Patricia's,* p. 44.
41. Interview with Maj.-Gen. Pearkes, 21 April 1966, p. 44. In far too many cases officers who were unable to do their job

in the field were "kicked upstairs" to command training camps and so forth, in both Britain and Canada. Pearkes, it is claimed, tended to be too easy in this respect, retaining officers who should have been released to civilian life, thus blocking promotion for more efficient and more vigorous officers in the training depots.

42. "There was a feeling abroad at that time," Pearkes said later, "that the life of the average permanent force officer had been too narrow and too restricted for him to blossom out and be able to assume executive responsibilities far greater than anything he had been accustomed to. Thus possibly a business executive who was capable of handling large numbers of men and a complicated organization would make a more successful commander than a regular officer who hadn't had the broadening experience of commerce" (interview with Maj.-Gen. Pearkes, 26 May 1966, pp. 13–14).

43. Simonds left divisional headquarters shortly after Pearkes arrived and took command of the 1st Field Regiment, R.C.A. Later he was to command the division and, ultimately, the 2nd Canadian Corps.

44. On 25 December the 7th Corps was dissolved, and the 1st Canadian Corps came into being, composed of the 1st and 2nd Canadian Infantry Divisions.

45. Interview with Maj.-Gen. Pearkes, 26 May 1966, pp. 21–22.

46. The 3rd Canadian Infantry and 5th Canadian Armoured Divisions arrived in 1941. The former was commanded by Maj.-Gen. C.B. Price, formerly commanding the 3rd Brigade in the 1st Division.

47. Interview with Maj.-Gen. Pearkes, 26 May 1966, p. 9.

48. Ibid., 21 April 1966, p. 7.

49. Stacey, *Six Years of War*, p. 238.

50. Pearkes, "Notes and Comments."

51. Interview with the Honourable Douglas Harkness, 22 June 1966. At this time Harkness commanded a battery of anti-tank guns attached to divisional headquarters.

52. Interview with Maj.-Gen. Pearkes, 15 July 1966, p. 6.

53. Stacey, *Six Years of War*, p. 238.

54. Interview with Maj.-Gen. Pearkes, 15 July 1966, p. 6.

55. Interview with Maj.-Gen. C.B. Price.

56. Interview with Maj.-Gen. D.C. Spry, 15 June 1967, pp. 11, 13.

57. See W.D., H.Q., 1st Cdn. Inf. Div., 2, 3, 5, 8 July 1941.

58. Stacey, *Six Years of War*, p. 239.

59. Interview with Maj.-Gen. C.B. Price, p. 10.

60. Interview with Maj.-Gen. Pearkes, 15 July 1966, p. 12.

61. Ibid., pp. 15–16.

62. Interview with Maj.-Gen. Pearkes, 25 July 1966, pp. 8–9.

63. Ibid., p. 10.

64. In other words, a day during which the company commanders were given complete discretion as to where their men would train as well as the manner of training. This usually led them beyond the battalion's immediate area and permitted the company commander complete freedom as to the area he chose provided he returned within an allotted time.

65. Interview with Maj.-Gen. Pearkes, 25 July 1966, p. 11.

66. Ibid., pp. 11–12.

67. Ibid., p. 14. It might be noted here that McNaughton was in Canada during February-March 1942. A week after he returned Headquarters, First Canadian Army was formed, commanded by McNaughton. The 2nd Canadian Corps was not formed until January 1943.

68. Interview with Gen. Charles Foulkes, 5 June 1967, p. 26.

69. Ibid., p. 27.

70. Stacey, *Six Years of War*, p. 244.

71. W.D., H.Q., 1st Cdn. Inf. Div., 29 May 1942.

72. Ibid., 30 May 1942. Crerar made some very complimentary remarks on the division's performance during the exercise. The corps commander may have been a "new boy" with respect to field manoeuvres, but he did inherit a first-rate staff, well trained in their duties.

73. Interview with Maj.-Gen. Pearkes, 25 July 1966, pp. 3–4, Gen. E.L.M. Burns, who later commanded the 2nd Canadian Infantry Division, held the same opinion as Pearkes and expressed himself in very similar words in his book *General Mud, Memoirs of Two World Wars* (Toronto: Clarke, Irwin, 1970), p. 115.

74. Ibid., pp. 14–15.

75. Paget, an old friend of Pearkes, was at this time commanding at G.H.Q. Home Forces and knew all about the raid.

76. Interview with Maj.-Gen. Pearkes, 2 August 1966, pp. 22–23.

NOTES TO CHAPTER ELEVEN

1. D. Hist., Personal File, Maj.-Gen. G.R. Pearkes, volume 3, confidential memorandum, Stuart to Ralston, 18 August 1942.
2. Ibid.
3. D. Hist., Personal File, Maj.-Gen. G.R. Pearkes, telegram, Letson to Stuart, 20 August 1942.
4. Stacey, *Six Years of War*, p. 171. It is rather interesting to note that in August 1940 Crerar, then Chief of the General Staff, stated to the Minister of National Defence, "that our sources of military intelligence from abroad state that it is most improbable that Japan will commit any warlike act likely to involve her in war with Great Britain or the United States so long as the British navy remains supreme in the North Atlantic waters and the United States navy remains concentrated in the Pacific" (P.A.C., Colonel J.L. Ralston Papers, volume 48, box 33, memorandum, Crerar to minister, 15 August 1940).
5. F.E. LaViolette, *The Canadian Japanese and World War II* (Toronto: University of Toronto Press, 1948), p. 27.
6. Stacey, *Six Years of War*, p. 171.
7. Canada, Parliament, House of Commons, *Debates,* 29 June 1942, p. 152.
8. Newspapers in both Victoria and Vancouver assumed Pearkes would be promoted to lieutenant-general.
9. P.A.C., War Diary, General Staff, Headquarters, Pacific Command, October 1942; Appendix 2–20, letter, Pearkes to secretary, Department of National Defence, 20 October 1942. See also Marion I. Angus, "The Rangers," *The National Home Monthly,* July 1943, pp. 6–7, 28. By the end of 1942 the P.C.M.R. had a strength of 507 officers and 11,941 other ranks. Late in 1943, after reaching their peak strength, the organization was reduced to approximately 10,000 all ranks.

10. It is interesting to note that the G.O.C.-in-C., Atlantic Command, Maj.-Gen. L.F. Page, had farmed close to Pearkes near Red Deer before the Great War.
11. P.A.C., War Diary, Headquarters, 13th Canadian Infantry Brigade, June 1943, Appendix 9.
12. D. Hist., "Instructions for the Guidance of General Officers Commanding-in-Chief, Atlantic and Pacific Commands, September 4th, 1942."
13. W.D., G.S., H.Q., Pacific Command, September 1942, Appendix 2, Minutes of the Joint Services Committee, 8 September 1942. The idea of the joint **headquarters were separate (letter,** Stevenson in December 1941. Eventually there was a joint operations room at Jericho Beach, but the administrative headquarters were separate (letter, A/V/M L.F. Stevenson to author, 7 July 1971).
14. W.D., G.S., H.Q., Pacific Command, 28 September 1942.
15. Ibid., 6 and 18 October 1942.
16. Ibid., 2 November 1942.
17. Ibid., September 1943, Appendix 6-27, letter, Pearkes to W.C. Mainwaring, Chairman, Provincial Civilian Protection Committee.
18. Ibid., November 1942, Appendix 4, "Pacific Command Operation Instruction No. 53" and August 1943, Appendix 4-11, letter, Pearkes to secretary, Department of National Defence, 11 August 1943.
19. Ibid., November 1942, Appendix 1-11, Minutes of Meeting, Joint Services Committee, Pacific Coast, 30 October 1942.
20. D. Hist., 322.009(D9), Mountain Training, Correspondence. . . , "Report on Mountaineering Course, 19 July–1 August," dated 13 August 1942, by Mr. E.C. Brooks.
21. Ibid., letter, Ralston to Brooks, 25

August 1942. Pearkes's comments on his meeting with Brooks are handwritten on his copy of this letter.

22. H.J. Graves, "Little Yoho Valley Military Camp," *Canadian Alpine Journal* 28, no. 2, pp. 237-38.

23. For an account of the joint planning between the two countries especially as it related to the Pacific Coast, see S. W. Dziuban, *United States Military Collaboration with Canada in World War II* (Washington, D.C.: Officer of the Chief of Military History, 1954).

24. Interview with Maj.-Gen. Pearkes, 12 August 1966, pp. 9-10.

25. P.A.C., R.G. 24, vol. 2921, file HQS 9055-1, vol. 5, letter, Pearkes to Stuart, 24 July 1943.

26. Stacey, *Six Years of War*, p. 497. See also Dziuban, *United States Military Collaboration with Canada*, p. 540.

27. See J.W. Pickersgill, *The Mackenzie King Record* (Toronto: University of Toronto Press, 1960), 1: 494.

28. M.A. Pope, *Soldiers and Politicians* (Toronto: University of Toronto Press, 1962), pp. 214-16. Pope at this time was Chairman of the Canadian Joint Staff Mission in Washington.

29. Pickersgill, *The Mackenzie King Record,* 1: 516-17.

30. Pearkes to Stuart, 24 July 1943, "Report on Operation 'Greenlight.'"

31. Both had been selected originally for the Amchitka force.

32. Pearkes to Stuart, 24 July 1943; W.D., H.Q., 13th Cdn. Inf. Bde., July 1943, Appendix 15, "Memorandum of meeting held. . .at 1100 hours, July 4th 1943, H.Q., Pacific Command."

33. Interview with Maj.-Gen. Pearkes, 12 August 1966, p. 20.

34. Adm. T.C. Kinkaid was in overall charge of the operation. It was he who ordered DeWitt to advance the date of the assault owing partly to the need to release some of his naval force for other operations in the Pacific by a specific date and partly to his desire to take even greater advantage of weather conditions in the Aleutians.

35. Interview with Maj.-Gen. Pearkes, 9 September 1966, p. 7.

36. W.D., H.Q., 13th Cdn. Inf. Bde., 7 July 1943. DeWitt arranged to provide four hundred .30 calibre carbines for the use of officers and stretcher bearers in the brigade.

37. W.D., H.Q., 13th Cdn. Inf. Bde. 20 July 1943.

38. Ibid., 8 August 1943.

39. Ralston Papers, vol. 42, box 31, memorandum, G.S. Currie, Deputy Minister (Army) of National Defence to J.L. Ralston, 19 July 1943.

40. The brigade war diarist wrote on August 9th: "Captain Bagley reports that almost all activity on Kiska had ceased; their radio to Japan is out and their radar no longer functions. Three guesses are made—one, they have evacuated; two, mutiny; three, they have abandoned their main camp and gone into the hills. If the latter is true then ours may well be the long hard job of digging them out."

41. Interview with Maj.-Gen. Pearkes, 9 September 1966, p. 13.

42. Memorandum, Gus Sivertz to author, September 1966.

43. Stacey, *Six Years of War*, p. 499.

44. Prior to leaving, Murchie cautioned Pearkes that he must not permit the troops to leave without confirmation from Ottawa.

45. Interview with Maj.-Gen. Pearkes, 9 September 1966, pp. 15-16. On 12 August Pearkes had written an official letter to Foster taking upon himself the authority to order Foster "to proceed under the command of General Charles H. Corlett for the occupation of the Island of Kiska and the destruction of the enemy forces thereon" (see D. Hist., 322.009(D482): "Progress Reports— Operation 'Greenlight.'").

46. See Stacey, *Six Years of War*, pp. 500ff.

47. W.D., H.Q., 13th Cdn. Inf. Bde., 17 August 1943.

48. Among others he met Maj. Sivertz who had landed with the first wave of the Canadians and took photos of the assault from the beaches. At Sivertz's request, Pearkes took with him a fat envelope containing the despatches from AP, UPI, *Life* and *Time* correspondents for delivery to Lt.-Cmdr. Neuberger at Adak. He was the first to bring out the stories of the Kiska affair which were published several days later.

49. Pearkes visited Kiska again in November. At Anchorage, Alaska, he was awarded the Legion of Merit (Degree of Commander) for the part he played in co-ordinating the joint action between the American and Canadian forces as well as for his promoting

greater understanding and co-operation between the two Commands from the time he became G.O.C.-in-C.

50. P.A.C., R.G. 24, vol. 2921, file HQS 9055-1, vol. 4, letter, Pearkes to Stuart, 16 November 1943.

51. Ralston Papers, vol. 42, box 31, memorandum, Currie to Ralston, 19 July 1943.

52. D. Hist., 322.009(D482): "Progress Reports—Operation 'Greenlight,'" letter, Pearkes to Bostock, 9 August 1943.

53. In an Associated Press despatch from Adak, Adm. Kincaid was quoted as saying: "The northern route—the shortest route to Japan—now is cleared, and from Attu we are only 630 miles from Paramushiro, Japan's northernmost naval, air and army base" (Vancouver *Daily Province*, 23 August 1943, p. 6).

54. See P.A.C., R.G. 24, vol. 2921, file HQS 9131, vol. 1, memorandum, Murchie to

Minister of National Defence, 19 October 1944.

55. W.D., G.S., H.Q., Pacific Command, May 1943, Appendix 1-17, letter, Pearkes to Stuart, 17 May 1943.

56. Ibid., May 1944, Appendix 26-2, "Second Report, May, 1944, Pacific Command Japanese Language School."

57. Interview with Maj. Roger Cheng, 22 February 1971.

58. Interview with F.W. Kendall, 16 July 1968, pp. 11-12.

59. D. Hist., 322.009(D478): "Report of Proceedings of Committee Formed to Study the Disposal of Men of Chinese Racial Origin Called up For Service Under N.R.M.A., 2nd September 1944."

60. W.D., G.S., H.Q., Pacific Command, September 1944, Appendix 5-2, letter, Pearkes to secretary, Department of National Defence, 4 September 1944.

NOTES TO CHAPTER TWELVE

1. W.D., H.Q., 13th Cdn. Inf. Bde, 3 January 1944.
2. Stacey, *Six Years of War*, p. 184.
3. Although all were volunteers, many would never be selected for overseas for reasons such as health or age.
4. Divisional headquarters was moved from Esquimalt to Prince George. Maj.-Gen. A.E. Potts was succeeded by Maj.-Gen. H.N. Ganong as G.O.C. in October 1943.
5. Stacey, *Six Years of War*, p. 185.
6. Interview with Maj.-Gen. Pearkes, 21 September 1966, pp. 8-9.
7. W.D., G.S., H.Q., Pacific Command, 24 July and 4 August 1944.
8. Ibid., 14 September 1944.
9. D. Hist., 322.009 (D67): "Report on 6th Cdn. Div. Mountain and Jungle Warfare School, Terrace, B.C.-15 September, 1944."
10. G.N. Tucker, *The Naval Service of Canada. Volume II. Activities on Shore During the Second World War* (Ottawa: King's Printer, 1952), pp. 231-32.
11. D. Hist., P.C.S. 504-7-BG-1, Chief of the General Staff to Pearkes, 29 January 1944.
12. W.D., G.S., H.Q., Pacific Command, 9 December 1943.

13. D. Hist., 112.21009 (D185): Letter, Brig. Sherwood Lett to Pearkes, 21 January 1944.
14. W.D., G.S., H.Q., Pacific Command, February 1944, Appendix 1-7: "Notes on Conference...5 February 1944."
15. Shortly after he arrived, Pearkes inaugurated a Pacific Command Study Week. His staff and senior officers were exercised in their commands, given staff problems to solve, and so forth. It gave them, too, a chance to meet with each other and discuss topics of common interest.
16. Stuart at this time was in London, holding the appointment of Chief of Staff, Canadian Military Headquarters, London. Presumably he would have heard Mackenzie King, speaking in London on 11 May, say: "Today our army awaits the word of command to join with their comrades in the liberation of Europe. The morrow will witness Canadian forces taking part in a final assault upon Japan." The speech brought cheers, but the words were too vague for serious planning (*The Times*, 12 May 1944, p. 8).
17. See C.P. Stacey, *Arms, Men and Governments, The War Policies of*

Canada, 1939–1945 (Ottawa: Queen's Printer, 1970), pp. 54–62.

18. Ibid., p. 58. King felt sure that if Canadians were used to help Britain reconquer her colonial possessions it "would help hand over the government to the C.C.F." (p. 60).

19. W.D., G.S., H.Q., Pacific Command, 7 February 1944.

20. Brig. W.H.S. Macklin assumed command on 9 February 1944. Foster returned overseas where he later commanded the 1st Canadian Infantry Division.

21. D. Hist., "Mobilization of 13 Bde. On An Active Basis," Report by Brig. W.H.S. Macklin, 2 May 1944.

22. Canadian Army Routine Order No. 3456, 27 July 1943.

23. Montreal *Gazette,* 24 April 1944.

24. Ibid.

25. Victoria *Times,* 6 April 1944, p. 13.

26. Toronto *Globe and Mail,* 27 April 1944, p. 21.

27. Montreal *Gazette,* 24 April 1944. This brought forth a query from the member of Parliament from Gaspé who enquired whether the Minister of Defence "endorses and supports the language or talks of Major-General Pearkes which he used speaking to the draftees last Friday at Vernon and Saturday at Victoria" (P.A.C., Ralston Papers, vol. 81, box 45, "Orders of the Day").

28. Macklin Report, pp. 9–10. The greater part of this report is printed as Appendix "S" to Stacey's *Arms, Men and Governments.* The report, Pearkes stated later, "expressed our combined views" (interview with Maj.-Gen. Pearkes, 21 September 1966, p. 26).

29. P.A.C., Ralston Papers, vol. 81, box 45, telegram, Ralston to Pearkes, 2 May 1944. It was Pearkes who had suggested to the Adjutant General that, if the volunteers were sent over as complete units, the conversion of soldiers from N.R.M.A. to G.S. status would be easier.

30. Macklin Report, pp. 12–13.

31. D. Hist., letter, Pearkes to Macklin, personal and secret, 13 May 1944.

32. D. Hist., letter, Pearkes to all commanding officers, 23 April 1944.

33. Ibid.

34. Interview with Maj.-Gen. Pearkes, 29 September 1966, pp. 14–15.

35. W.D., G.S., H.Q., Pacific Command, 15 May and 19 June 1944.

36. Such as graduates from the Japanese Language School and officers with experience in jungle warfare.

37. W.D., G.S., H.Q., Pacific Command, June 1944, Appendix 1–2, "Intensified Recruiting Activities, Pacific Command, May 29th, 1944."

38. Named after the green, diamond-shaped patch worn on the sleeves of all members of Pacific Command.

39. An excellent account is given in Stacey's *Arms, Men and Governments,* chapter 7, "Manpower and Conscription." The statistics quoted are from the same source, Appendix "T", Canadian Army Enlistment Statistics.

40. Quoted in Stacey, *Arms, Men and Governments,* p. 443.

41. Ibid., pp. 446–47.

42. P.A.C., Ralston Papers, volume 43, box 31, looseleaf notebook.

43. The Honourable A.L. Macdonald was Minister of Defence for Naval Services. He was a good friend of Ralston and a fellow "conscriptionist."

44. Ralston Papers. It should be noted that Pearkes thought in terms of a conscription order which would affect *all* N.R.M.A. men, not a portion of them.

45. Interview with Maj.-Gen. Pearkes, 21 October 1966, p. 19.

46. Vancouver *Sun,* 2 November 1944, p. 1.

47. The Chief of the General Staff (Murchie), the Adjutant General (Walford), the Quartermaster General (H.A. Young), the Master General of the Ordinance (J.V. Young) and the Vice Chief of the General Staff (Gibson). Murchie acted as chairman.

48. D. Hist., HQS 20-6, vol. 81: "Minutes of a Conference. . . , 14 Nov. 44."

49. Interview with Maj.-Gen. A.E. Potts, 15 October 1971, p. 14.

50. Interview with Maj.-Gen. Pearkes, 21 September 1966, p. 27.

51. One of the most outspoken was Maj.-Gen. H.N. ("Hardy") Ganong. He asked McNaughton: " 'Sir, do you want us to let our hair down and tell you what we really think?' I remember McNaughton said, 'Yes, Hardy, certainly I do.' Then Hardy swore and said 'We have done everything and we have tried everything.' In other words he spoke as

Pearkes had, except in rather a less courtly language" (interview with Lt.-Gen. H.D. Graham, 24 September 1970, p. 16. Graham was an observer at the meeting, not a participant).

52. W.D., G.S., H.Q., Pacific Command, 14 November 1944.

53. General McNaughton explained to Mackenzie King "That his confidence lay in the fact that while they [the District Officers' Commanding] had spoken frankly of their doubts, they had nevertheless given the assurance they would make another try and that he, himself, felt with that attitude and all the forces that were at work. . .for example, the individual efforts from the men's families, the Parliamentary meeting, public opinion shaping up, etc., etc., that everything would come through all right" (King Diary, entry for 19 November 1944, P.A.C., King papers, MG 26, J13, vol. 92, p. 1201).

54. The District Officer Commanding in Winnipeg was so furious that he resigned. Pearkes and Maj.-Gen. Potts tried to get him to remain in office or at least defer his resignation until later but without success. Pearkes thought it unwise for him or anyone to resign at a time when McNaughton's policy had not been given a chance. In Ottawa Mc-Naughton told King "That he had to handle these men very carefully. That if they began to oppose him he might have a revolt on his hands and a situation which would be very difficult to manage. The one thing to do was to avoid any quarrel" (King Diary, ibid).

55. Pearkes Papers in possession of the author, File: "Notes for Biography of Major-General George R. Pearkes."

56. Swettenham, *McNaughton. Volume III. 1944-1946* (Toronto: Ryerson, 1969), pp. 55-56.

57. King Diary, 20 November 1944.

58. Stuart's resignation was in the mail as soon as he heard of McNaughton's appointment as minister owing to strong differences between the two over policy matters.

59. Stacey, *Arms, Men and Governments,* p. 470.

60. King Diary, 22-23 November, pp. 1216-33.

61. For a detailed description of what occurred in the 15th Brigade in Terrace,

see R.H. Roy, "Mutiny in the Mountains-the Terrace Incident," *The Canadian Defence Quarterly* (Autumn 1976): 42-55.

62. As soon as Lt.-Gen. Sansom left on 26 November for Ottawa, Pearkes himself left for Terrace and was there by the twenty-ninth.

63. All during 1944, and especially since the recruiting drive began in April, Pearkes had warned his superiors in Ottawa about the effect withdrawal of General Service N.C.O.'s was having on the efficiency of units in the 6th Division.

64. W.D., G.S., H.Q., Pacific Command, December 1944, Appendix 5-1: "Report, G.O.C.-in-C. Pacific Command to the Secretary, Department of National Defence, 5 Dec. 44."

65. D. Hist., "Memorandum, Walford to the Minister, 5 Dec. 44."

66. Ibid. McNaughton was keeping a keen eye on public opinion as expressed in Canadian newspapers. See, for example, the thirty-nine folders of newspaper clippings in the A.G.L. McNaughton Papers, P.A.C. (MG30, G12, vol. 277, folders 32-71).

67. Vancouver *News Herald.*

68. Citation for the Award of Companion of the Order of the Bath to Major-General G.R. Pearkes. In October 1944 he received his first honorary degree – an LL.D. from the University of British Columbia. He was to be further honoured a few months later while still G.O.C.-in-C., Pacific Command, by having a mountain named after him. Mount Pearkes lies back of Princess Royal Reach.

69. To quote the Adjutant General: "It is essential to maintain supplementary records both in Ottawa and London for NRMA personnel dispatched overseas. Obviously the smaller the number remaining NRMA the less the burden of the duplicated records."

70. W.D., G.S., H.Q., Pacific Command, January 1945, Appendix: "Letter, Pearkes to the Secretary, Department of National Defence, 23 January 1945." By January 1945 there were well over six thousand absentees or deserters in Canada.

71. McNaughton had referred Pearkes's letter as well as several previous communications to the Judge Advocate

General again to see if he had exposed himself to disciplinary action. The J.A.G. replied that it was most unlikely a case could be made against Pearkes for expressing his opinions frankly and

forcibly as he had.
72. P.A.C., Ralston Papers, vol. 26, box 18, File "Miscellaneous—P, Letter, Ralston to Pearkes, 5 March 1946."

NOTES TO CHAPTER THIRTEEN

1. Vancouver *Sun*, 17 February 1945, p. 1.
2. Winnipeg *Tribune*, 19 February 1945, p. 6.
3. Interview with the Honourable Howard C. Green, 16 December 1971, p. 4. Green's son had been wounded a few days earlier.
4. Ibid., p. 6. Pearkes was also asked by Mr. George Black to contest a riding in the Yukon (interview with Maj.-Gen. Pearkes, 13 December 1971, p. 1).
5. His brother Ted was living in California at this time and was to remain there until his death in 1969.
6. He did request the privilege of being nominated, but this was a formality, and he turned the nomination down in Pearkes's favour.
7. Interview with Maj.-Gen. Pearkes, 1 November 1966, p. 16.
8. Interview with Mr. C.H. Rennie, June 1966, p. 6.
9. Victoria *Times*, 28 May 1945, p. 2.
10. Interview with Maj.-Gen. Pearkes, 1 November 1966, pp. 17–18.
11. Interview with Howard Green, 16 December 1971, p. 15.
12. Vancouver *Sun*, 12 May 1945. He suggested a training period of from eighteen to twenty-four months for young Canadians.
13. Interview with Maj.-Gen. Pearkes, 13 December 1971, p. 13.
14. Interview with Maj.-Gen. Pearkes, 9 February 1967, pp. 7–8.
15. Interview with Douglas Harkness, 22 June 1966, pp. 23–24.
16. Interview with Maj.-Gen. Pearkes, 7 December 1967, pp. 4–5.
17. Victoria *Daily Colonist*, 15 September 1946, p. 9.
18. Victoria *Daily Colonist*, 27 June 1946, p. 1. Pearkes made this claim in the House while speaking on a bill to reduce from 5 per cent to 3 ½ per cent the interest rate to soldier settlers under the Soldier

Settlement Act. Canada, Parliament, House of Commons, *Debates*, 16 May 1950, p. 2558.
19. Canada, Parliament, House of Commons, *Debates*, 27 March 1953, pp. 3379–81.
20. Ibid., 28 May 1948, p. 4532.
21. Ibid., 23 June 1948, pp. 5761–62.
22. Ibid., 2 May 1947, p. 2716.
23. Ibid., 11 September 1945, p. 78.
24. Ibid., 9 April 1946, pp. 703–4.
25. His secretary during the latter part of his presidency was a young veteran named Robert Bonner, who later became attorney-general of B.C.
26. Interview with Maj.-Gen. Pearkes, 15 December 1966, pp. 10–11.
27. Unpublished MS, "Summary of the Position of the British Columbia Co-Ordinating Council and of the Kamloops Federal Conservative Association in Soliciting Membership," 23 May 1955, by E. Davie Fulton (copy in possession of Mr. Leon Ladner, Vancouver, B.C.)
28. Pearkes was asked to assume Anscomb's position as provincial leader but he declined.
29. Interview with the Honourable E. Davie Fulton, 10 May 1972.
30. Interview with Maj.-Gen. Pearkes, 20 January 1967, p. 5.
31. According to the Ottawa *Journal* (2 October 1948) "Pearkes...perhaps stole the show. An old soldier, up to then lacking any reputation as an orator, he emerged suddenly and unexpectedly as the speaker of the night."
32. Shortly after Drew's resignation, the Canadian Institute of Public Opinion took a poll of the public's reaction to a nominee to succeed him. Fifty-five per cent of P.C. voters favoured Diefenbaker ("Information for Delegates from the Committee for John Diefenbaker." This brochure and similar Progressive

Conservative party material relating to the 1945–60 era has been loaned to me by Mr. Leon Ladner of Vancouver, B.C.).

33. See Pierre Sevigny, *This Game of Politics* (Toronto: McClelland and Stewart, 1965), pp. 36–40.

34. Interview with Maj.-Gen. Pearkes, 12 July 1967, pp. 6–7. See also John Meisel, *The Canadian General Election of 1957* (Toronto: University of Toronto Press, 1962), pp. 31–32.

NOTES TO CHAPTER FOURTEEN

1. Vancouver *Sun*, 12 May 1945, p. 9.
2. Victoria *Daily Colonist*, 30 November 1945, p. 1.
3. Canada, Parliament, House of Commons, *Debates*, 9 July 1947, p. 5270.
4. Ibid., 4 October 1945, p. 783.
5. Ibid., p. 786.
6. Interview with Maj.-Gen. Pearkes, 7 December 1967, pp. 22–23.
7. Ibid., 20 January 1967, p. 16.
8. Interview with E.Davie Fulton, 10 May 1972, pp. 6–7.
9. Canada, Parliament, House of Commons, *Debates*, 29 April 1948, p. 3449.
10. Ibid., 24 June 1948, p. 5790.
11. Ibid., p. 5787.
12. At one point Claxton mentioned privately to Pearkes, "Your speeches are helping," referring to Claxton's desire to get cabinet support for many of the improvements he was trying to bring about (interview with Maj.-Gen. Pearkes, 11 January 1967, p. 6).
13. Canada, Parliament, House of Commons, *Debates*, 18 November 1949, pp. 1957–61.
14. Eric Harrison, "Strategy and Policy in the Defence of Canada," *International Journal* 4 (Summer 1949): 226–27.
15. H.D.G. Crerar, "The Case for Conscription," *Queen's Quarterly* 58 (Spring 1951): 1–13.
16. Wallace Goforth, "We Didn't Plan for This Kind of War," *Saturday Night*, 15 August 1950, pp. 9, 12.
17. Canada, Parliament, House of Commons, *Debates*, 1 September 1950, pp. 130–34.
18. Ibid.
19. Ibid., 5 February 1951, p. 98.
20. Pearkes also advocated securing a second aircraft carrier for Pacific Coast defence with the idea of using it as an advanced anti-bomber base, among other uses (interview with Maj.-Gen.

Pearkes, 11 January 1967, p. 8).
21. Canada, Parliament, House of Commons, *Debates*, 3 April 1952. For Pearkes's initial reaction to the problem of Canada's contribution to NATO after his trip to Europe, see pp. 1089–95.
22. Ibid., 17 June 1952, p. 3330. Germany became a member of NATO in 1955.
23. Ibid., 20 January 1955, pp. 389–93.
24. Ibid., 21 March 1952, p. 704.
25. Ibid., 2 February 1952, pp. 1536–37.
26. Ibid., 30 November 1953, p. 455.
27. By this time Claxton had been replaced by the Honourable Ralph Campney, who represented Vancouver Centre and had been Claxton's associate minister.
28. Canada, Parliament, House of Commons, *Debates*, 16 June 1955, p. 4868.
29. Ibid., p. 4869.
30. Pearkes said later: "I was stressing it to the Conservative Party as much as to anyone else that we had to surrender something of our sovereignty in allowing. . .American troops to come in" (interview with Maj.-Gen. Pearkes, 14 February 1967, p. 16).
31. Canada, Parliament, House of Commons, *Debates*, 21 June 1954, p. 6393.
32. Ibid., 18 November 1949, p. 1961; 10 March 1950, p. 663.
33. Ibid., 16 June 1955, p. 4871.
34. Ibid., pp. 4872–73.
35. A few months later Canada was to contribute troops to the United Nations' peacekeeping forces in Egypt.
36. Ibid., 30 March 1957, p. 2904.
37. Ibid., 1 April 1957, pp. 2912–14. Montgomery was Deputy Supreme Allied Commander, Europe.
38. Almost all the British Columbia newspapers predicted that he would be selected for the post. Davie Fulton and Howard Green were also mooted by the press for cabinet posts.

NOTES TO CHAPTER FIFTEEN

1. These were Gen. Charles Foulkes, Chairman, Vice Adm. H.D. DeWolf, Chief of the Naval Staff, Lt.-Gen. H.D. Graham, Chief of the General Staff and A/M Hugh L. Campbell, Chief of the Air Staff. Miller, the Deputy Minister, had been an air vice-marshal.

2. On the evening of 26 June the delegates to the prime ministers' meeting and their wives were invited to a state dinner by Her Majesty and H.R.H. Prince Philip at Windsor Castle. Dining from gold plates in the Waterloo Room was a far cry from eating bannock when Pearkes was homesteading in Alberta! It was on this occasion that Queen Elizabeth said to him: "You are the only V.C. cabinet minister I have."

3. Estimated at an annual cost of $16.5 million.

4. Information supplied by Command History Division, Headquarters, North American Air Defence Command.

5. Interview with Gen. Charles Foulkes, 9 March 1967, pp. 3–5. Campney was the then Minister of National Defence. Foulkes would have been more precise if he said that representatives from the Privy Council and External Affairs attended the Chiefs of Staff Committee when matters involving External Affairs and the Privy Council were on the agenda.

6. At this time Chairman of the U.S. Joint Chiefs of Staff.

7. Interview with Gen. Charles Foulkes, 9 March 1967, pp. 6–7.

8. Ibid.

9. Interview with Maj.-Gen. Pearkes, 9 March 1967, pp. 22–23.

10. Ibid., 13 April 1967, p. 11.

11. Ibid. Among other tasks, in the first eight months of office Pearkes travelled 44,968 miles, visited sixty-two separate places and made ninety-one speeches, all in connection with departmental business (Pearkes Miscellaneous Papers, "memorandum undated").

12. Interview with Maj.-Gen. Pearkes, 14 February 1967, p. 16.

13. As Secretary of State for External Affairs, Mr. Sidney Smith, did not assume office until 13 September, only four weeks before the new Parliament met. He had been the president of the University of Toronto and had no previous experience in the House of Commons.

14. Letter, Mr. John W. Holmes to author, 5 December 1972. McCardle was Secretary, Canadian Section, Permanent Joint Board on Defence.

15. Letter, Pearkes to Diefenbaker, 8 June 1965, Pearkes Papers, copy in the author's possession.

16. Gen. Charles Foulkes, "Canadian Defence Policy in a Nuclear Age," *Behind the Headlines* 21 (May 1961): 11.

17. Canada, Parliament, House of Commons, *Debates*, 4 November 1957, p. 702. The formal Exchange of Notes establishing NORAD did not take place until 12 May 1958.

18. See ibid., 4 January 1958, pp. 2862-64.

19. Ibid., 7 November 1957, p. 850. For a brief description of how consultation and control might be expected to work in times of an emergency, see Charles Foulkes, "The Complications of Continental Defence" in *Neighbors Taken For Granted: Canada and the United States,* ed. Livingston T. Merchant (New York: Praeger, 1966), pp. 101–33.

20. Canada, Parliament, House of Commons, *Debates,* 19 May 1958, pp. 191–92.

21. Ibid., 10 June 1958, p. 998.

22. Reported in the Guelph *Mercury,* 24 November 1959.

23. Letter, Pearkes to Foulkes, 15 October 1962, Pearkes Papers, Lieutenant-Governor's Personal Correspondence.

24. Interview with Maj.-Gen. Pearkes, 23 March 1967, p. 17.

25. Ibid., 30 January 1967, pp. 2–3. When the Conservatives came to power there were about fifteen thousand American servicemen stationed in Canada, most of them in Newfoundland and Labrador.

26. Canada, Parliament, House of Commons, *Debates,* 16 June 1955, p. 4872.

27. Ibid., 16 October 1957, p. 37. It should be noted that the training directive resulted from a decision taken when the Liberals were in power. In 1956 Campney had announced that special training in civil defence would be taken by both the regular and reserve forces.

The impact of the new emphasis was not felt until the Conservatives assumed power. For a detailed account, see the chapter by G.W.L. Nicholson in *Policy by Other Means*, eds. Michael Cross and Robert Bothwell (Toronto: Clarke, Irwin, 1973).

28. P.A.C., Harkness Papers, file no. 87-0, letter, Pearkes to the Hon. J.W. Monteith, 14 November 1957.

29. Ibid., letter, R.H.N. Roberts to Brig. A. McB. Bell-Irving, 19 November 1957.

30. Toronto *Globe and Mail*, 7 January 1958. Mr. Monteith used this editorial as a lever to convince the cabinet that there should be a special study undertaken by Graham (letter, the Honourable J. Waldo Monteith to author, 23 July 1973).

31. Interview with Lt.-Gen. S.F. Clark, June 1967, pp. 16–17.

32. Ibid., 18 February 1971, pp. 12–13.

33. Saskatoon *Star-Phoenix*, 4 May 1959.

34. Toronto *Star*, 20 May 1959.

35. Windsor *Star*, 16 June 1959.

36. Peterborough *Examiner*, 27 July 1959.

37. Ottawa *Citizen*, 3 October 1959.

38. Ibid., 1 October 1959.

39. Toronto *Globe and Mail*, 5 October 1959.

40. Toronto *Star*, 8 October 1959.

41. Memorandum, Lt.-Gen. S.F. Clark to Pearkes, 23 November 1959, Harkness Papers, file no. 87-0. Pearkes agreed, and the result was the compilation of the "Booklet for Survival."

42. "Canadian Institute of Public Opinion Release," 22 June 1960, Harkness Papers, file no. 87-0, vol. II. For an example of the pros and cons of civil defence in the U.S., see "Civil Defence is Possible" in *Fortune*, December 1958, pp. 98–101.

43. Canada, Parliament, House of Commons, *Debates*, 4 August 1960, p. 7571. Hellyer was the Liberals' chief military critic at this time.

44. These figures are taken from Canada, Parliament, House of Commons, "Special Committee on Defence Expenditures. Minutes of Proceedings and Evidence, No. 8, 1 June 1960," pp. 200–211.

45. At the time there were about three servicemen for every civilian in D.N.D.

46. Between 1 April 1958 and 1 August 1960, for example, a dozen R.C.A.F. head-quarters, depots, schools, and stations were disbanded (memorandum, A/M Hugh Campbell to Pearkes, 23 September 1960, Harkness Papers, file no. 61-104).

47. Letter, Fleming to Pearkes, 16 March 1969, Harkness Papers, file no. 601-12.

48. Letter, Pearkes to Fleming, 22 July 1969, Harkness Papers.

49. Foulkes had suggested to Campney that it should be disbanded but the Liberal minister delayed his decision up to 1957. Lt.-Gen. Graham, according to Foulkes, did not want to disband it, and Pearkes felt it had a role in survival operations (interview with Gen. Charles Foulkes, 5 June 1967, pp. 4–5).

50. Letter, Pearkes to Fleming, 7 September 1960, Harkness Papers, file no. 101-12, vol. I.

51. Letter, Clark to Pearkes, 11 July 1960, Harkness Papers, file no. 61-108.

52. Interview with Lt.-Gen. S.F. Clark, 7 July 1971, pp. 12–13.

53. There were 9 in Kashmir, 10 in Palestine, about 130 in Vietnam, Laos, and Cambodia, 951 in Suez, with about 300 R.C.A.F. personnel in a supporting air transport unit based in Naples, and some 30 in a medical unit still in Korea. Several hundred additional servicemen were to be stationed in the U.S.A. following the NORAD agreement.

54. See V.J. Kronenberg, "All Together Now: Canadian Defence Organization" (Master of Arts thesis, Carleton University, 1971).

55. Canada, Parliament, House of Commons, *Debates*, 3 January 1958, p. 2826.

56. Favoured by Gen. Foulkes.

57. Interview with Maj.-Gen. Pearkes, 2 June 1967, pp. 2–3.

58. Ibid., 31 October 1968, p. 8.

59. Interview with Gen. Charles Foulkes, 5 January 1967, p. 23.

NOTES TO CHAPTER SIXTEEN

1. Howe, then Minister of Transport, as quoted in Canada, Parliament, House of Commons, *Debates,* 28 June 1955, p. 5380.
2. Maj.-Gen. Pearkes, ibid., 23 February 1959, p. 1279.
3. Ibid.
4. Guy Simonds, "Where We've Gone Wrong on Defence," *Maclean's Magazine,* 23 June 1956, pp. 23, 26.
5. Quoted in the Toronto *Globe and Mail,* 5 October 1957, p. 5. The Arrow did not make its first flight until 25 March 1958 when it more than matched the hopes and expectations of its designers.
6. Canada, Parliament, House of Commons, *Debates,* 5 December 1957, p. 1929.
7. Ibid., 23 January 1958, p. 3674.
8. Earlier in the year the Canadian ambassador to the United States had approached informally James Douglas, Jr., the American air force secretary, about the CF-105 and was informed that there was no place for the Arrow in the United States Air Force.
9. *Time,* 18 August 1959, p. 7. Pearkes later flew on to Colorado Springs to visit NORAD headquarters, the first senior Canadian politician to do so. Despite his attempts, he was never able to get the Prime Minister to visit this headquarters.
10. Canada, Parliament, House of Commons, Votes and Proceedings of the House of Commons, 6 August 1958, p. 365. At the same time the committee suggested "that the Department [of Defence Production] encourage, assist and coordinate the growth of technical skills and knowledge in Canadian industry as a programme of industrial preparedness" (p. 369).
11. Canada, Parliament, House of Commons, *Debates,* 8 August 1958, p. 3237. This qualifying phrase was used time and again by Pearkes and others.
12. Interview with Maj.-Gen. Pearkes, 28 April 1967, p. 11.
13. For example, A/M C.R. Dunlop in his testimony before the Special Committee on Defence of the House of Commons on 16 July 1963.
14. Melvin Conant, "Canada's Role in Western Defence," *Foreign Affairs,* April 1962, p. 434.
15. Interview with Maj.-Gen. Pearkes, 5 April 1967, p. 9.
16. Reported by Canadian Press in the Vancouver *Sun* and elsewhere, 25 November 1958. Slemon was a strong advocate of the Arrow, but his speech had political repercussions as he contradicted the Prime Minister's statement. Consequently, Pearkes had to rap his knuckles.
17. John Gellner, "The Defence of Canada," *Canadian Commentator,* December 1958, p. 12. Pearkes, firmly believing in continental air defence, had no such apprehension.
18. Reported in the Toronto *Globe and Mail,* 3 November 1958.
19. Interview with A/V/M J.L. Plant, 18 December 1972, p. 20. Plant had retired from the R.C.A.F. and assumed the position of general manager of A.V. Roe Co. in 1956.
20. Ibid., pp. 20–21.
21. Interview with Maj.-Gen. Pearkes, 28 April 1967, p. 17, and 5 April 1967, p. 10.
22. Ibid., 25 May 1967, pp. 4–5. Pearkes added: "Not mentioning names, Liberals who have been in the Cabinet have told me that they were sorry for me, and that they would have done exactly the same thing. But when it came to being on the floor of the House, they played a different tune" (p. 5.) A former Chief of the General Staff claimed later: "I really honestly believe that the Liberals would have done it at the same time the Tories did, if the Liberals had been returned to power" (interview with Lt.-Gen. H.D. Graham, 24 September 1970, p. 24).
23. "Poor old George was almost going crazy because the continuation of this [Arrow programme] was costing a million odd dollars a day [*sic*] and ... he knew in his own mind that this wasn't possible. It wasn't a possible or practical thing to complete a programme that, every day it went on, was just another million odd dollars thrown down the drain. And he was having at the same time terrible difficulty trying to get a cabinet decision to take this step" (interview with Douglas Harkness, 22

June 1966, p. 33).
24. Canada, Parliament, House of Commons, *Debates,* 20 February 1959, p. 1221.
25. Ibid., 23 February 1959, p. 1280.
26. A good sampling of these letters may be found in the Harkness Papers, file 44-47, vols. I and II.
27. Canada, Parliament, House of Commons, *Debates,* 23 February 1959, p. 1284. For a list of companies—aircraft electronic, arms manufacturers and others—approached in search of alternative work for Avro see Pearkes's speech in Hansard, 2 March 1959, pp. 1515-16.
28. Ibid., 23 February 1959, pp. 1272-75.
29. Interview with Gen. Charles Foulkes, 9 March 1967, pp. 9-11.
30. Interview with E. Davie Fulton, 10 May 1972, p. 22.
31. Ibid.
32. Interview with Gen. Charles Foulkes, 9 March 1967, pp. 32-34.
33. This, of course, was part of the same press release which stated that "The number of supersonic aircraft required for the R.C.A.F. Air Defence Command will be substantially less than could have been foreseen a few years ago."
34. Interview with Lt.-Gen. M.E. Pollard, 24 April 1973.
35. Canada, Parliament, House of Commons, *Debates,* 20 February 1959, pp. 1221-24. Six months earlier Pearson had assumed Canada would be acquiring a missile such as the Bomarc which would, "of course, have nuclear warheads" (ibid., 8 August 1958, p. 3229).
36. Ibid., 23 February 1959, pp. 1292-93.
37. Ibid., 3 March 1959, pp. 1557-58.
38. By the time Pearkes stepped down from office, the Bomarc-B sites in Canada were 70 per cent complete.
39. New York *Times,* 30 January 1960, p. 7.
40. Interview with Maj.-Gen. Pearkes, 5 June 1967, p. 17.
41. New York *Times,* 25 March 1960, pp. 1-2.
42. Interview with Maj.-Gen. Pearkes, 5 June 1967, p. 18.
43. Canada, Parliament, House of Commons, *Debates,* 25 March 1960, pp. 2453-56.
44. Melvin Conant, "Canada and Continental Defence: An American View," *International Journal* 15 (Summer 1960): 226.
45. Canada, Parliament, House of Commons, *Debates,* 2 July 1959, p. 5357.
46. Interview with Lt.-Gen. S.F. Clark, June 1967, p. 28.
47. Interview with Lt.-Gen. M.E. Pollard, 15 May 1973, p. 19.
48. Canada, Parliament, House of Commons, *Debates,* 4 January 1958, p. 2850.
49. See R.S. Ritchie, "Problems of a Defence Policy for Canada," *International Journal* 14 (Summer 1959): 206-7.
50. Canada, Parliament, House of Commons, *Debates,* 8 August 1958, p. 3222.
51. Interview with Maj.-Gen. Pearkes, 5 April 1967, p. 4.
52. Interview with Lt.-Gen. M.E. Pollard, 24 April 1973, p. 8.
53. Canada, Parliament, House of Commons, *Debates,* 4 July 1959, pp. 5470-74.
54. General C. Foulkes, "Canadian Defence Policy in a Nuclear Age," *Behind the Headlines,* May 1961, p. 16.
55. There are fifteen folders on the topic in the Harkness Papers which cover the Pearkes-Harkness period.
56. "I don't blame them," he added, "They weren't responsible for thinking about public opinion. It was my job to sell the policy" (interview with Maj.-Gen. Pearkes, 13 April 1967, p. 5). The attitude of the senior officers this writer has interviewed was that the atomic weaponry, like ICBM's, was a fact of life and it could not be ignored. Like Pearkes, they had to "think about the unthinkable."
57. Ibid., pp. 4-5.
58. Ibid., p. 17.
59. Ibid., pp. 14-15.
60. See Canada, Parliament, House of Commons. "Special Committee on Defence Expenditures. Minutes of Proceedings and Evidence, No. 8, 1 June 1960" for an outline of Pearkes's ideas on defence policy. It is interesting to note that Lester Pearson, speaking in the House of Commons on 23 February 1959 (p. 1294), stated: "There is no way by which we in Canada can disassociate. . .ourselves from the United States in the defence of our country, and of the free world. It is obviously impossible, even if it were desirable, which it is not."

61. Interview with Maj.-Gen. Pearkes, 3 August 1967, p. 20.
62. Ibid., p. 21. Pearkes's personal assistant added: "Literally we would work hours and hours into the night doing things that should have been done during a normal working day, but he [the minister] hadn't been able to do them ...And he wanted to run his depart-

ment; he wanted to make changes" (interview with R.H.N. Roberts, 7 August 1968, p. 21).
63. Interview with Maj.-Gen. Pearkes, 2 June 1967, pp. 6–7.
64. Ibid., 3 August 1967, p. 17.
65. Ibid., 31 March 1967, p. 14.
66. Ibid., 26 July 1967, pp. 12–14.

NOTES TO CHAPTER SEVENTEEN

1. Lt.-Gov.'s Newspaper Scrapbook, vol. I. Three large scrapbooks, prepared by the staff of Government House, were filled during Pearkes's tenure of office and are presently in his possession.
2. The former lieutenant-governor, the Honourable Frank Ross, had left for Bermuda when his term was up. Des Brisey was administrator until Pearkes was sworn in. The Premier, the Honourable W.A.C. Bennett, was visiting New York at this time.
3. Interview with Maj.-Gen. Pearkes, 19 October 1967, p. 11.
4. Ibid., 31 October 1967, pp. 24–25.
5. John had graduated from law school at the University of British Columbia in 1956. He married Joyce Pope in 1958. Their first child, Anthony, was born in 1959. A second boy, Timothy, was born in 1961 when Pearkes was still in office.
6. The Pearkes sent, and received, about two thousand Christmas cards each year.
7. Interview with Mrs. M. Abelson.
8. Early in 1961 the provincial government provided an additional $25,000 for general expenses for Government House.
9. Interview with Cmdr. Gar Dixon, 9 February 1970, p. 5.
10. Ibid., pp. 5–7.
11. In 1962 the Pearkes entertained almost twelve thousand guests with receptions, teas, coffee parties, luncheons, and

official dinners (Lt.-Gov.'s Newspaper Scrapbook, vol. I, 17 January 1963).
12. The *Globe Magazine,* 5 August 1961, pp. 7–9.
13. In order of receiving them: University of British Columbia, Royal Military College, University of Victoria, Simon Fraser University, and University of Notre Dame. Mrs. Pearkes was given an honorary Doctor of Laws degree in 1968 by the University of Victoria.
14. Nelson *Daily News,* 22 August 1966.
15. Lt.-Gov.'s Newspaper Scrapbook, 27 February 1964.
16. Pearkes contributed his salary as lieutenant-governor as well as his pension from the army to the running of his office. While holding his position as the Queen's representative, he received no pension as a retired member of Parliament.
17. The year 1966 marked the 100th anniversary of the union of the colonies of Vancouver Island and British Columbia. The national centennial of 100 years of Confederation was celebrated in 1967.
18. Letter, L.B. Pearson to Pearkes, 25 September 1967, in Lt.-Gov.'s Correspondence File, "Extension of Term of Office" (This file is in the possession of Maj.-Gen. Pearkes).
19. Mrs. Pearkes shared the honour when Mayor Hugh Curtis of Saanich bestowed the honour on both of them.

Bibliographical Note

During the greater part of his life, Major-General Pearkes served the Crown. As a constable in the Royal North West Mounted Police, as a soldier and officer in the army, as a member of Parliament and cabinet minister, and finally as the lieutenant-governor of British Columbia, Pearkes worked for his adopted country for well over half a century. During this period he neither kept a diary nor made any effort to retain any correspondence. When he left his various offices or appointments, he walked out carrying with him nothing more than a lightly filled briefcase.

For any biographer this was a rather disastrous revelation. Evidently his mother kept a number of his letters written to her from France and, possibly, when he was in Alberta or the Yukon. She destroyed all but a dozen of these when she was well advanced in age. As a result, it was not until Pearkes became Minister of National Defence that his correspondence over a period of years becomes available for the researcher. When he left office, his ministerial files were turned over to the Honourable Douglas Harkness who, in many cases, continued to use the same files and built them up into one or more volumes. When Harkness left office, he turned eighty-five cartons of correspondence, reports, and similar material over to the Public Archives. These "Harkness Papers," to which I was given access, are really a record of both Pearkes and Harkness during the period when they were Ministers of National Defence. I was also given access to the Ralston Papers and the McNaughton Papers in the Public Archives, and through the courtesy of the Historical Division of the Department of External Affairs, I was permitted to read a number of files relating to defence matters during the period Pearkes held office.

During the years I was preparing the biography I accumulated a considerable amount of material which has been deposited in the library of the University of Victoria under the title "The Pearkes Papers." Aside from transcripts of tapes, newspaper clippings, photographs, copies of speeches from Hansard during the time Pearkes was a member of Parliament, xerox copies of articles in periodicals in the same period, and similar items, there is the correspondence I have had with people who have known Pearkes ever since he was a mountie in the Yukon. In his own possession Pearkes still retains the correspondence, almost all of it official, which he had when he was lieutenant-governor. He and Mrs. Pearkes also retain the original notebooks they sometimes kept on trips, as well as newspaper scrapbooks, photograph albums, and other similar items.

I was not able to gain access to all the "papers" I would have liked to examine. The Crerar Papers are a case in point, to say nothing of the Diefenbaker Papers. Other material, most of it classified, in the Department of National Defence has not been made available to the public. However, as mentioned elsewhere, I considered my main task was to concentrate on the man rather than the party he belonged to or the details of the policy he promoted.

The Directorate of History at National Defence Headquarters is a gold mine of information for any student of Canadian military history, and I owe both directors and staff a great deal for the help they have given me. Great War trench maps, citations for awards, war diaries at various levels, reports on operations, progress reports, confidential reports, minutes of meetings, instructions, letters, telegrams, statistics—the list of official and semi-official material I was able to see and copy is almost endless. The military files, diaries, photographs, and so forth, both at the Directorate and in the Public Archives of Canada, were invaluable to the preparation of this volume. A great many files examined from this source are not necessarily footnoted, but something of the variety seen and perused are cited and give, I believe, some indication of the hundreds of files examined over the course of the last six years.

A major source of information for this book has been the large number of tape-recorded interviews I have had with Major-General Pearkes and those who knew him throughout his career. The latter have ranged from soldiers who served with him in the trenches to colleagues who were with him in cabinet from 1957 to 1960. These tapes, transcribed and with his additional notes on them, are deposited with the Pearkes Papers. In addition I have written to dozens of people who knew him well at various stages of his career and almost invariably I have had my enquiries answered. The replies have varied from one to several typed pages and have been a rich source of information when trying to piece together Pearkes's life and the reasons for certain actions he had taken. This correspondence will also be found in Pearkes Papers which, incidentally, will be closed to the public except by permission until 1985.

The printed material on Pearkes or dealing with him and Canadian military affairs in general runs all the way from Hansard, the debates in the House of Commons, to "The Berkhamstedian," the school annual published when he was attending Berkhamsted. Newspaper accounts about Pearkes started during the Great War and have continued on and off up to the present day. Histories of the regiments with which he served have been helpful as have biographies of some of the people who were an influence on his life—for example, McNaughton and Mackenzie King. The official histories of the Great War and the Second World War—Canadian, British, and American—have been extremely helpful and so too have been a number of books written in recent years about Canadian defence policy. A considerable amount has been written about the defence policy of the Progressive Conservatives in the Diefenbaker years, much of it critical. This is especially true if one examines the articles in periodicals written in the past fifteen years and particularly those written at a time when missiles were growing in size and range, when the role of the fighter-interceptor aircraft was being questioned and when Canada was undergoing a change of policy which was bringing her increasingly into the American sphere and away from her traditional British sphere of influence in military affairs. These articles have been too numerous to mention, and although many have an emotional or political prejudice, their impact on the public cannot be disregarded. I have had this critical comment in mind when dealing with Pearkes as minister and have tried to summarize the criticism of some of his policies without going into vast detail on my sources.

I am indebted to many people who supplied me with information and background material for this book, both directly and indirectly. It would be invidious to mention some and not others. The ultimate selection of the information has been mine, as has the interpretation of the information provided. There is more to be written and I, for one, shall look forward to other historians' comments on the era as they uncover or are given access to material presently beyond my reach.

Index

(Military ranks given are those held at time of first mention.)